Pieces of Portland

Come
on
in

i

Pieces of Portland

An Inside Look at America's Weirdest City

Marie Deatherage
narrative, design, layout

Joyce Brekke
photography

ISBN: 978-0-9963862-0-3

Please direct inquiries to:
  Quiltlandia
  PO Box 14822
  Portland OR 97293

  piecesofportland.com

Printed in USA by Versa Press

Photo credits: All photos by Joyce Brekke except: page 50, Urban Scout photo by Tony Deis; page 71, Sunnyside Circle painting party provided by City Repair Project; page 72, Rick Turoczy photo by Reid Beels; page 75, People's Food Co-op staff by Bryn Harding; page 98, 2014 World Naked Bike Ride photo by Jonathan Maus, bikeportland.org; page 100, lower photo of Wakefield/Grossnickle garden by Bruce Wakefield; page 102-03, plant photos by Marie Deatherage; page 152, athletic granddaughters photo by Marie Deatherage; page 162, house moving photo by Ric Seaberg; page 165, Cinderella Story quilt photo by Marie Deatherage; page 172, poster pole photo by Marie Deatherage; page 175, lost dog photo by Marie Deatherage; page 177, sheet metalist sign photo by Marie Deatherage; page 180, original Art Fills the Void photo by Frank DeSantis; page 202, Street Library photo by Jan Darby; page 217, keep pretending portland by Ric Seaberg; page 228, quilt wall by Ric Seaberg; page 231, abandoned gas station photo provided by June Key Delta Center; page 232, lower photo of trackers earth participant by Tony Deis; page 247, photo of Blaine Deatherage-Newsom by Willie Koo; page 249, The Decemberists quilt photo by Caroline Smith; page 250, Joyce Brekke portrait by Tom Chin.
  Public domain photos: Mt. St. Helens eruption (USGS photo), Celilo Falls fishing (wikimedia commons, Corps of Engineers archives), Chinook head flattening (wikimedia commons, Paul Kane painting), Portland's Hooverville (wikimedia commons, US government), cat herd (wikimedia commons, Cats by Boksi), Vanport (wikimedia commons, City of Portland archives), Map of Eliot neighborhood (City of Portland archives).

Fonts :
  Title page: Bell Gothic Std
  Headings: Avenir Next Condensed
  Text: Garamond Premier Pro
  Captions: Helvetica
  Cover: Bell Gothic Std, SignPainter

Pieces
of
Portland

For Blaine

Pieces
of
Portland

Table of Contents

Pieces
of
Portland

Pieces
of
Portland

Acknowledgements

Where to begin to thank all the people? So many pieces of Portland came together to make this book happen.

Let's begin with deep gratitude to all the people who agreed to appear in the book, because without them it would just be mostly about dogs and goats and plants. With a few bridges over troubled waters thrown in to round it out.

So we offer profound thanks to all the people in the pictures and profiles: Terry Currier of **Music Millennium**; **Unipiper** Brian Kidd; Ric Seaberg; Elizabeth Woody; Mike Houck of **Urban Greenspaces Institute**; Peter Bauer and Urban Scout of **Rewild Portland**; Mayor Bud Clark; Elliot Shuford and Tyrone Reitman of **Healthy Democracy**; Sam Adams of **Portland City Club**; Rick Turoczy of **Portland Incubator Experiment**; Stephen Couche of **Southeast Portland Tool Library**; Ann Pernick and Laurie Sugahbeare at SE Tool Library Repair Cafe; Shawn Furst of **People's Food Co-op**; Richard Seymour and Blaine Deatherage-Newsom of **Free Geek**; Justin Yuen and the rest of the gang at **FMYI**; Marshall and Mikalina Kirkpatrick of **Little Bird**; Ward Cunningham; A. Rose McCoy; Michelle Lezniak; Kelley Roy of **ADX**; Tom Chin; the Sprockettes; the Shifties; CHUNK 666ers; Rev Phil Sano; Bruce Wakefield and Jerry Grossnickle; Albert Kaufman of **Farm My Yard**; Ian Winters of **Winters Farm**; Javier Hurtado of **Cha!Cha!Cha!**; Christopher Frankonis of the **Belmont Goats**; Steve Smith of **Steven Smith Teamaker**; Jim and Patty Roberts of **Jim and Patty's Coffee**; Oblique Coffee; Ryan Saari at **Oregon Public House**; Luba Gonina of **Lutheran Community Services** and all the members of the Karen Weaving Together group; Aviva Zelkind; Elizabeth and Nataliya Chumak; Lord Peter and all the **Mondo Croquet World Championship Tournament** participants; Marilyn Sewell; Caitlyn Stoutt, Calla and Ellery Norton; Sarah Mirk of **Bitch Media**; Carolyn Lee; Kol Peterson and Deb Dolman of **Caravan, the Tiny House Hotel**; Ibrahim Mubarak of **Right2DreamToo**; Beth Bonness and Jeffrey McCaffrey; Howard Barney; Haidee Vangen; Frank DeSantis; Rowan DeSantis; Karissa Lowe; Barron of the **Deluxe Mystery Hole**; all the **Animal Eyes** (Sam, Tyler, Colin, Figley and Haven); street musicians; Miriam Sontz of **Powell's Books**; Laura Moulton of **Street Books**; Lori Lematta and Israel Bayer of **Street Roots**; **Independent Publishing Resource Center**; Jean Loomis of **June Key Delta Center**; Terra Fleischer, Tony and Robin Deis of **TrackersEarth**; Amy Sample Ward and Max Ward; Tim and Barbara Sample; Sage Wolffeather; Kay Reid and Susi Steinmann of **Portland Meet Portland**; Sam Smith of **Community Supported Everything** and Skye Blue of **Skye Blue Can Sew**.

Special thanks to **Raymond Kaskey** and **Travel Portland** for giving us permission to photograph their wonderful sculptures and use them in the book. Thanks as well to people and organizations providing photos, including Ridhi D'Cruz and Chrissy of City Repair; Rick Turoczy of Portland Incubator Experiment; Laura Moulton of Street Books, Shawn Furst of People's Food Co-op, Jonathan Maus of bikeportland.org and Skye Blue of SkyBlueCanSew. Thanks to others who helped in a variety of ways, including Cameron Whitten, Sara Heise at Voodoo Doughnut, Keith Lachowicz at RACC, Michael Anderson, Teresa Boze, Christen McCurdy, Molly Deis, Sarah Altman, Meredith Baker. Special thanks to Sally Yee and Phoebe O'Leary for being my very first quilt patrons, and for being wonderful friends. Many thanks to Olivia Keenan and Paden McDonough for walking by Sunnyside Circle right when we needed help holding up a quilt. Thank you, Amy Jo Rist, for allowing us to use a photo of your handsome son!

Huge thanks to all my family and friends who haven't seen or heard from me in a long time, I hope they still remember who I am. Special thanks to my Granny Ora Maude Grogan Deatherage at whose knee I first saw quilting happen, my mother Ethel Deatherage, who took up quilting in a serious way when she retired and has been an inspiration to me as she's continued it over the years. I have so loved the time we've been able to quilt together. Profound thanks to Annamaria Clayville, Pat Arnold and Francesca Ervin for providing loving care and help to Blaine over the past few years, I wouldn't have even been able to think about this project without your support.

I will always be especially grateful for emotional support during the darkest hours and days of the last year from Joyce Brekke, Tom Chin, Lynne Cartright, Dave, Sarah and Jeff Koss, Richard Seymour, Marilyn Sewell and Grant Kruger. xoxo

Of course I thank my son, Blaine, who has been my soulmate all his life, for just being and doing things together. In so many ways he made me who I am today and was actively and enthusiastically involved in this book.

My dear friend and typography goddess Denise Brem gave me invaluable help getting this ready to send to the printer. I really think she saved the day. I seriously owe you, Denise. And thanks to Rev Phil Sano for arriving on his trusty steed just in time to provide a big hand at the very end. Thanks to Amy Sample Ward for help and encouragement right when I needed it! And so many thanks to Joyce, for going through every step with me on this book and being friends for the last 48 years!

I've kept the biggest thanks for last. It's for my wonderful husband Ric Seaberg, who pretty much took over the household chores for the last few months so I could finish this. His love and support are what made the words flow. Now I know what it means to have deep support from a partner, I had no idea this actually existed. When you feel that kind of support, you start to believe you can do anything. So you just start doing it! Love forevermore, Ric. You're the best.—MD

§

Special thanks to Mark Fitzgerald for post-processing help with many of the photos in this book, to Eileen and Doug Leunig for commenting on parts of this book as we were working on it, for Photoshop help over the years, and for being the best sister- and brother-in-law on the planet. Most of all, thanks to my partner Tom, who has been a loving companion in work, home, travel and life for nearly thirty-five years. And thanks too, Tom, for doing even more cooking than usual as Marie and I took more and more time on this project.—JB

INTRODUCTION

So yeah, I get that this is the greatest book ever about Portland, but what's with the quilts?

This was going to be a quilt book. Its origin can be traced back to a quilt show I did at the BedMart on NW Glisan Street for First Thursday in October 2011. To help explain the quilts and their meaning, my dear friend Joyce Brekke and I had traveled around the city photographing my quilts in iconic Portland places.

For example, the Plate Tectonics quilt was draped over the fence in front of the exposed part of the volcano that is Mt. Tabor. I wrote a bit about each quilt to go with the photos, which were displayed alongside them. At the time I thought, "Hey, if I did a bunch more of these, it would make a cool book." Then Rose McCoy told me that I should make a coffee table book of my quilts. You know how you don't think much of your own ideas until someone else says them out loud? I decided to hold that thought until after I retired from a job that took so much of my time and brain waves.

In mid-2014, we started to work on it in earnest. Joyce and I roamed the city, visiting interesting places and people and events for her to photograph. I started writing and the words just kept coming and coming and coming.

Like Nike says, there is no finish line. But there is a stopping point, and today we reached it. This is our story about Portland.

It's not a traditional guidebook. That's not our aim…good thing, because there's so much happening here it would be out of date the moment it left the printing press. In just the last few weeks, several decades-old restaurants I thought would last forever have closed. New ones are opening hourly, it seems. Print can't keep up, that's the purview of the web now.

Neither is this a comprehensive survey or scholarly analysis of Portland. I drew on knowledge I acquired teaching *The Environment of Portland* at Portland State University and then met amazing people doing amazing things while working at Meyer Memorial Trust. And what I absorbed living here so long.

I come at this with an unabashed love of Portland. It's been my home for more than 40 years and I rather imagine I'll die here. I find it an incredible place with truly amazing people. Sometimes I think about why it became a place that attracts me so much. And exactly what it is about Portland that makes me feel so much at home here.

Just because you love something with all your heart doesn't mean you can't be critical or at least honest about its weaknesses or problems. We've got them, that's for sure. And we're not afraid to get into some of that.

You might say this book represents a patchwork of Portland. Like pieces in a quilt. Like a quilt. A quilt of Portland. Portlandia's quilt. Quiltlandia. That's what we were going to call the book at first, when it was just going to be mostly beautiful photos of Portland places with our quilts showing.

But adding stories took us to many wonderful and interesting places. We met a lot of people and had a lot of fun. As it turns out, there's a lot of serious content inside these pages. Maybe some things you didn't know. Much to ponder. Perhaps you'll be moved to action about some.

It's been many many years since I was able to fully use my own voice; I lost it for a while. So once the genie left the bottle, there was no getting her back inside. I feel a little vulnerable putting my heart and soul on display for all to see, but in the end, there was no other way. I hope you can take it.

And you still get to see our quilts! And yes, I admit, this makes the book a little unusual. Weird even.

As you have every right to expect.

Opposite Page: A windy day in spring scattered a carpet of pink blossoms from the cherry trees in Portland's Japanese American Historical Plaza, a memorial created in 1990 to honor Japanese Americans interned in prison camps during World War II. The Japanese Grain Importers Association gave the beautiful trees to the City as a gift of friendship.
■ Quilt information on page 12..

Pieces
of
Portland

What Is This Portland You Speak of Today?

Portland is the largest city in Oregon and in the basin of the mighty Columbia River. It ranks 29th in population among cities in the United States, with an estimated 609,500 in 2013. It's located about 100 river miles up the Columbia River from the Pacific Ocean, and is the fifth largest port on the U. S. west coast. Its largest export is wheat grown from the Columbia Basin, especially eastern Oregon and Washington.

Hold on, this is beginning to sound like a textbook. That's not what we're doing here, nor why you picked up this book. And it's not really what one has in mind when asking "What is this Portland you speak of today?"

One of the most popular perceptions about Portland now is reflected in Karissa Lowe's Facebook status update from August 2014, shown on this page. Yes, these things really happen in parts of Portland and they're not even rare. And we appreciate and even love them!

Karissa Lowe
August 8

On my commute home I passed the Unipiper on the Burnside bridge (apparently he has a Segway now?), then drove past a pretty girl in a sweatsuit and juggalo makeup who appeared to be having an argument with herself (or maybe she was on a bluetooth headset thingy?), then waited for a light to change as a woman covered in glorious tattoos (including her hands and face) crossed the street with her cute mutt and a stroller. Oh Portland, I heart you!

There was a time not so long ago that nobody knew us. We always had to clarify that we were from the Portland in Oregon, not Maine. Very few radars picked up our signal, which was not powerful. But beginning in 1974, when it was named "America's Most Livable City," Portland slowly started building a national reputation. A couple of decades ago, we began achieving something like national fame. Now we're at or near the top on a lot of "Top Ten" and "Best Of" lists. Lately, Portland seems to have become known to the universe and viewed as something of a celebrity.

How many cities have an acclaimed television show devoted to making fun of their odd charm, like we have in *Portlandia*?

I spend time now and then surfing the web to see what's being said about us. First, it's obvious that we're getting a lot of attention and we're on a lot of minds. For example, in early 2015, *Monocle Magazine* named the "Top 25 Most Livable Cities in the World." Portland is the only U. S. city that made the cut. It's a very exclusive list, the brow above the monocle is very high indeed.

Keeping in the international zone for a moment more, Parisians appear to regularly hold *Keep Portland Weird* festivals?!

Opposite page: When it's not traveling around showcasing many Portland attractions, Travel Portland's 24-foot-tall cuckoo clock carved from a single maple tree is displayed at PDX. A rooster representing urban farming and farm-to-table food crows the hour. Also represented are Sasquatch, bikes (and naked riders), craft beer, coffee, donuts, Portlandia and more. Sometimes the Unipiper pops out the door, where we added a quilt for this photo (it's not part of the exhibit).
■ Quilt information on page 12.

We're also judged to be Number One in best place to live, best beer, most fit, most courteous driving, highest voter turnout, best sports city in North America, best live music in the country, most movie lovers, most dog-friendly and most kinky. We came in second in nerdiness and in attracting and retaining college-age people, and fourth in most steampunk, most food lovers and best biking in 2014 (which has caused us much consternation as we used to be first). Clearly some of these categories require further investigation.

It's been noted that Portland is very big on a wide range of things, including breastfeeding, consignment/vintage clothing shops, riding bikes while naked, opposing adding fluoride to drinking water, sustainable everything, green technology and preschools that teach homesteading skills.

I am stunned by the number of tourists I encounter these days. It wasn't that long ago that Portland was considered a great place to live, but not a very exciting vacation destination.

Sure, organized groups came to study our city planning, sustainability and green ways of being. They were impressed by our Urban Growth Boundary (UGB) and the fact that it has expanded by only 12% while our population grew by 60% in the nearly 40 years it's been in effect. The UGB has not only protected nearby farmland, but land in agricultural production in the metropolitan area actually grew from 375,000 acres in 1978 to 670,000 in 2014. Visitors still come to see the effects of our urban planning and sustainability initiatives, but now they also come to experience our food, beer, spirits, wine, coffee, tea, designers, makers, tiny houses, village building, place making, music, art, crafts, bicycles and entrepreneurs. And the list just keeps on going.

They also want to see the Portland described in Karissa's Facebook post, visit *Portlandia* locations and watch the Unipiper, for instance. They will ask you where the *Keep Portland Weird* sign downtown is so they can photograph it.

A guidebook to Portland has been written and published in Japan, with charming descriptions of the wonders that await visitors, like this one in *Popeye Magazine for City Boys* in June 2014:

Why not go to Portland this summer? It's a cozy place. You can even ride a bike from one end of the city to another in a course of one day and explore so much about it. It's a happening city. People are lively and active. There are ateliers in every corner of the city for leather craftsmanship, pottery, glassblower, letterpress, hut building, that Portland is proud to present. Everything is very well made and you cannot resist but to buy them all. I bet your suitcase will be filled with gifts to bring back. Portland city boys spend everyday chilling out in a cafe with mates, hanging out at boutique stores and food cars, records stores and zine bookstores and all those places can be found on this edition of "Portland City Guide". It reminds us of San Francisco of some years ago when the city was filled with the liberal feel and mood. Portland is not the city of gloomy rain. Instead you will witness the moment when the city is being built up."

Yes, we hang out and have fun, but Portland also has a strong work ethic. A 2014 study found that the Portland area has the second-highest average revenue among small businesses (those with fewer than 250 employees or under $10 million in revenue) in the U.S. Portlanders are 50% more likely to start their own businesses, and the city is full of people who are rethinking and redefining what career and work mean.

A lot of the most interesting things about Portland aren't on a list somewhere. You pretty much have to live here to discover them. And since I live here, I thought I would try to help. I'll even try to make sense of it all. And introduce you to people and places and things that truly make Portland Portland.

But let's get one thing straight. Portland has a lot of pieces. A plethora of pieces and places. Living in my Hawthorne neighborhood (Buckman to be precise) is a whole lot different than living in Alameda, which is a whole lot different than living in St. Johns. Which is light years from living in Dunthorpe. Which can feel at least a universe away from living in Powellhurst Gilbert.

In Portland, geography matters. It's location, location, location. There's reputation, then there's reality.

Except for a short stint in an old, cheap, rather dismal apartment downtown near Portland State University, I've lived the past four decades on the east side of the Willamette River. But it didn't take long after arriving here for me to learn that there were Westsiders and Eastsiders. Back then, westsiders sometimes openly admitted they never crossed the Willamette River because there was no reason to do so.

But many—if not most—of the things that brought Portland national exposure over the past two decades have happened on the east side, and many people now find those neighborhoods to be most vibrant. The Willamette is no longer a big divide.

When I began working in a downtown office for a private foundation in 1996, I was the only one among 13 staff members who lived on the east side. When the lease was coming up for renewal and the organization was looking to relocate in 2003, I overheard a staff member say if we moved to the east side, she would quit. We ended up in a brand new building in the Pearl District, where a very rapid transition was underway from industrial and warehouse spaces to trendy, luxury (by Portland standards) apartments, boutiques and chic loft-style offices. Some of us worried that many of the organizations the foundation served would not feel comfortable coming to the high-income neighborhood and its artsy designscape, but those fears could not overcome the resistance to crossing a bridge, as three-fourths of the staff still lived on the west side.

By the time I retired in 2014, the majority of the staff of 24 lived on the east side. And I bet the next time the office moves, it will have an east side address.

Many in Portland consider 82nd Avenue to be the eastern edge of the city. When Interstate-205 (a north-south, six-lane freeway that allows one to avoid downtown Portland) opened in 1983, it formed a kind of an outer ring road at approximately 92nd Avenue.

And to be honest, if it weren't for Fabric Depot on 122nd Avenue, I might not get out there much myself.

I think it would be fair to say that outer east Portland does not see itself reflected in *Portlandia*, and maybe not even feel part of Portland. Some people say Portland is actually two very different cities and some on the far east side say they wish Portland had never annexed them in the 1980s and 1990s.

But from my point of view, it's far too simplistic to see two Portlands, the haves and the have nots, those east and west of a line. Because the closer you look, the more complex and nuanced the city becomes. Many in the close-in neighborhoods who do some of the most interesting and zaniest things subsist on very little income and live in shared housing.

A lot of the things people see as distinctly Portland take very little money and use very few resources. A kind of anti-greed ethic abounds, along with an appreciation for a little anarchy and a whole lot of freedom of expression. Much of the work I see being done by those within Portland's I-205 ring road is motivated by wanting to help those outside it, but they don't always know how to connect. The people you meet in the following pages are often working on a human-to-human, grassroots level that is another hallmark of Portland. Some are the ones working to fix the things that are broken. There are many ways Portland feels and shows we are all in this together.

A couple of years ago, the apartment complex next door was converted to vacation rentals, so we no longer have next door neighbors on that side. But we see lots of visitors coming through, and sometimes, when they are sitting outside next to our driveway, it feels like they are watching us, examining our ways. Sometimes I think they regard us with curiosity and a bit of longing. I wonder if they are about to ask us, "So is Portland really like *Portlandia*? Where can I find it, see it, taste it? What and where is the real Portland?"

I've thought about how I would answer. Maybe I would fall back on "It's hard to explain, but you'll know it when you see it." That feels a little lazy, though. Like any green-blooded Portlander, I want to be helpful and generous and open source my knowledge.

So I had that question in my mind as I wrote this book. What do we need to show and tell to help people understand Portland? To be sure, this book doesn't cover every possible thing about Portland. Guaranteed, everybody is going to think of things that could and should have been included, and we will agree. But we are operating under limits and have managed to pack a lot of really good ones in these 258 pages.

So, despite living and working here for more than 40 years, the work of writing this book—doing this research, talking with these people, visiting these places and attending these events—all helped me understand Portland better. And love it even more. And be more hopeful about its future than I expected to be.

I invite you to do the same as you explore a variety of pieces of the city's fabric that are joined together in sections like quilt blocks. In doing that, you'll help us connect the quilt that is Portland.

Opposite page: A MAX light rail train passes through downtown Portland's transit mall, beside the deer decked out in yarn-bombed so-called "ugly sweaters." The light rail was built with funds originally planned for a large freeway through the heart of SE Portland neighborhoods.

Keep Portland Weird!

The origin of *Keep Portland Weird* can be traced to one man. Naturally, it's a little weird because he actually lives across the river in Vancouver, Washington. He's probably done more to make a single word represent the city's reputation than any other person, but you'd never know it unless you ask this quiet, unassuming man just the right questions.

In the late 1990s, Terry Currier—owner of Portland's iconic record store Music Millennium, which appears later in this book—was thinking about ways to get a campaign going to support locally owned businesses in Portland. He had been talking with a guy at Waterloo Records in Austin, TX, where "a Borders store wanted to go in across the street from the record store run by the city's beloved son." A *Keep Austin Weird* movement had formed and "got lots of coverage in Austin's weekly and on the TV news. They did their research and came up with the figure that three-fourths of the money in chain stores leaves the state. They also found out that local businesses were paying more in taxes than chain stores, so they formed an independent business association, went to the City and got it to set aside a 'buy local' day. Now, there's a national independent business retail day, even publicized by American Express, on the day after Black Friday—Buy Local Saturday."

"That kind of clicked off in my head," Terry says, so he printed 500 *Keep Portland Weird* bumper stickers and 500 that read *Keep Portland Weird: Support Local Business*. He contacted 50 local retailers, told them he would sell to them wholesale. "I never had any grandiose idea. I didn't identify it with Music Millennium, I just let it grow organically."

Several times he bought ads in *Willamette Week*, but they didn't have his store's name on them. Before long, when the phrase *Keep Portland Weird* came up, he heard people say, "*Keep Portland Weird*, oh, that's that thing *Willamette Week* is doing."

"I kinda like the whole way that it's grown," he says now. "Things used to come and go, like all the 'I heart' stickers. But this sticker stuck."

"The great thing about this," he continues, "is it's open to interpretation about what weird means. There have been some detractors who say weird has negative connotations, like the local Fox News had a Portland State University professor on who said it referred to homeless people, drug dealers, all that kind of stuff."

"To me it was all about keeping Portland unique, staying away from turning Portland into strip malls with national chains that are in every other city USA."

He trademarked the phrase in Oregon, but couldn't get a federal trademark because it was deemed too close to the one in Austin. Others have tried to copy it, he's had to protect the trademark several times. "For the most part, the ones who copy it are motivated by greed. If you don't protect trademark, you lose it. All the sales proceeds are reinvested in promotion."

Terry has given many others permission to use *Keep Portland Weird (KPW)* for only $1, "like the downtown library had a *Keep Portland Weird* day, I licensed it to them for that, and to Dante's club downtown for the back wall of their building."

"It's embedded now. I hear from people who come here to make movies, commercials, I always license it to them," he says. "Now you couldn't drive a half a mile in this town without seeing *KPW* somewhere. Somebody brought in a *Keep Poland Weird* sticker the other day. I love it. The Portland Craft Beer Association has 'Keep Portland Beered.' Portland Electrical Association uses 'Keep Portland Wired.'"

In 2014, an Austin business evaluated the degree of weirdness in both cities to determine which was actually weirder. Portland came in first in nine of 12 categories, making it weirder by half, if that makes any sense. Portland topped Austin in Strangest People, Best for Hipsters, Best for Hippies, Most Tattooed, Most Bike Friendly, Best Beer, Craziest City, Most Pot Friendly, Top Green City and Top City for Dogs.

"I think it has done a lot of good for the city. A certain amount of people are aware of it, come to visit, next thing you know they move to town. Some people tell me it inspired *Portlandia*. That's Keeping Portland Weird to the extreme."

Not that there's anything wrong with that.

Opposite page: Terry Currier stands on the steps outside his Music Millennium office, holding the distinctive *Keep Portland Weird* stickers that are part of the movement he started to support local businesses in Portland. **This page:** A newspaper box that sits outside the store has one of the many other slogans *Keep Portland Weird* has inspired. Along with contributions from sticker nerds and graffiti artists. Or random taggers.
■ Quilt information on page 12.

"When the going gets weird, the weird turn pro."

—Hunter S. Thompson

When we explained our project—that we were quilters and wanted to explore what makes Portland tick, so it only seemed natural to go forth in the company of quilts—to the Unipiper, the man *Willamette Week* dubbed "Portland's mascot," he nodded affirmatively and said, "I get it. It's your own personal art project."

That kind of automatic acceptance is why there is a Unipiper and why he lives in Portland. Brian Kidd was learning to play the bagpipes when he found a discarded unicycle in a dumpster.

"It takes about a year before you can really play full bagpipes," he explained. "It takes a lot of discipline and muscle control. You have to keep the reservoir bag full while pushing air out of the pipes. Somehow I stuck with it." Which also gave him enough time to master the unicycle. Before long he combined the two, and the rest is history.

I remember when sightings of the Unipiper were remarkable, eliciting at least a tweet, Facebook post or a photo on Instagram. Something along the lines of "You're not going to believe this, but I just saw Darth Vader playing bagpipes that had flames coming out the back riding a unicycle!!" Nowadays his attendance is pretty much mandatory at any important and/or odd event in the city.

As he was learning the bagpipes and unicycle, Brian was studying marine biology at the University of Virginia, where he made friends with several students from Portland. "They were always talking about how awesome Portland is—how hip, fun and green it is and how it had such a great beer culture. They told me I would fit right in."

"So I moved here sight unseen. I found what they told me to be pretty much true, and now I can't see myself living anywhere else. In Portland you can be yourself."

Opposite page: Unipiper Brian Kidd rides alongside Portland's Saturday Market, one of his frequent performance venues and where he met the woman who became his wife. Here he appears in his Scottish Highland dress, but he has a wide array of costumes for practically any occasion. **This page:** It takes some strong pipes to play bagpipes. It took a year for Brian to feel he was accomplished enough to perform as a solo act. Now he plays with fire.

■ Quilt information on page 12.

During the day, the former deputy sheriff (he was deputized when he was a member of a Sheriff's Pipe Band in Virginia) works full time for Quantum Spatial, which calls itself "the go-to partner for organizations that want to map, model, and better manage their world." Fascinating side note: Quantum Spatial's aerial volcano mapping work recently caused the official height of Mt. Hood to be increased by eight feet! Please make a note of it.

Being the Unipiper is his full-time part-time job. He's applied some of his day-job skills to create live GPS-tracking of his gigs at whereistheunipiper.com. You can locate his impromptu performances on his live twitter stream (#seetheunipiper). And he hints that it's a good bet that you can see him crossing the Burnside Bridge around 8:30 a.m. and sometime between 5-7 p.m. on weekdays when the weather is nice as he makes his job commute.

Brian has achieved national as well as local acclaim, with appearances on Jimmy Kimmel live, the Today Show, the Tonight Show, Good Morning America and The Soup. You can keep up with his new appearances on Facebook.

He has played for just about every occasion, from birthdays to bar mitzvahs to weddings to funerals, street fairs, parades, sporting events, homecomings and too many others to mention. Recently he performed on top of a log at an Urban Forestry Festival in Portland's Pioneer Square.

The Unipiper comes in many guises: full Scottish highland dress, Darth Vader costume, Santa Claus getup, Gandalf, King Arthur, and more. He's even been spotted wearing a quilted cloak.

"You've got to keep people surprised," he said. "Fire was the obvious choice." He straps a propane tank to his back and has a trigger button he can push with his elbow as he plays his pipes. In summer 2014 he incorporated an electric unicycle, which promises to expand and enhance his reach.

"First and foremost, I have to entertain myself," he says. "And it's so great to see people smiling and laughing."

He admits he has "mild groupies." One person told him she came all the way from Wisconsin to see him. "I don't know how to feel about that," he admits.

The Unipiper met his wife one day when he performed at Saturday Market. She brought him an ice tea when the appearance ended. With her phone number written on the side.

"It was a good tip," he smiles.

Pieces
of
Portland

Index to Quilts

Pieces
of
Portland

SETTING

Pieces
of
Portland

Do We Deserve This?

I have seen a lot of scenery in my life, but I have seen nothing so tempting as a home for a man than this Oregon country. You have a basis here for civilization on its highest scale, and I am going to ask you a question which you may not like. Are you good enough to have this country in your possession? Have you got enough intelligence, imagination and cooperation among you to make the best use of these opportunities?

—Lewis Mumford address to Portland City Club, 1938

It is impossible to write something about Portland without acknowledging its magnificent setting. If you designed a city in Utoplandia, it would be challenging to start with a more idyllic landscape. Not only where the city is planted, but what it's near: on the west, an hour to what many consider the most scenic 300 miles of Pacific Ocean coastline; on the east, an hour to standing at timberline on the flanks of a magnificent volcano with glaciers; even closer to the east, the Columbia River Gorge, which is unlike any other place on earth; and close by to the south and west, the pastoral vistas of undulating hills of vineyards and farm fields among expansive oak savannah.

Naturally, many of the best views are from the city's priciest real estate. From Pittock Mansion, on a clear day, you can see most of Portland from north to south, both Willamette and Columbia rivers, out to the Columbia Gorge. On the clearest, from a high vantage, you can see five volcanos: Mountains Hood, St. Helens, Jefferson, Adams and Rainier. Yes, really. You simply cannot close your eyes to the natural beauty of our place.

Here's another remarkable thing. Stand in the city center, at a place where you can see the horizon, like on the city's bridges, and look in every direction. The horizon is ringed by trees and other natural features. I think that's a remarkable thing about our city and is something that should be protected. I still have not recovered from the travesty of the KOIN Center in 1984 blotting out the spectacular view of Mt. Hood that appeared when emerging from the Vista tunnel that connects the area west of the hills to downtown Portland. I daresay that building has done more to dampen the spirits of Portlanders than any eight months of rain, and I still want the top lopped off.

Living among this much scenery, there is an expectation that Portlanders will be inspired to protect it from ruination. It's only natural that there's a strong environmental movement here.

Portland adjusted to nature and accepted the consequences until technology and financial backing were available to pay for trying to gain control over it. The present-day Willamette bears little relation to the river that once flowed through Portland, as its form and course have been radically altered. Occasionally, natural features have been utilized by the city's structures: choice residential areas, for example, often are located on heights, as in the West Hills, Alameda Ridge and Mt. Tabor. The streambed of Sullivan's Gulch became the route for a railroad and Interstate-84. But more often, earth, water and vegetation have been moved to accommodate a growing city.

In fact, there are places in our city that became unlivable. For decades the Willamette River was used as an open sewer. Acres and acres of flora have been paved over, taking wildlife with it. Prime agricultural land underwent condominium conversion. Wetland wildlife habitat was replaced by shipyards. And so on.

Though Portland's landscape became littered with features that made it unattractive and unpleasant, clearly the tide was turned before the natural environment was lost entirely. In 1938, voters demanded through initiative petition that the Willamette River be restored to health, and now even salmon have returned. In the early 1970s, a new park along the west bank in downtown called attention back to the river, illustrated also by the construction of apartments at the very edge of the water next to the railway depot.

Portland was among the first cities in the nation to commit to urban renewal, often destroying affordable neighborhoods to make way for things most displaced people couldn't afford. At the same time, Portland has made an admirable effort to restore some buildings to their former grandeur in a popular historic preservation movement. Oregon has been a pioneer in establishing land-use laws to protect remaining agricultural land and open space. Portland's downtown transit mall limits automobile access, downtown pavement has been torn up and replanted with grass and trees, a riverfront highway was removed and turned into a park and a parking structure was torn down and replaced by a public square. Protection for a great blue heron nesting site was a requirement in a sand and gravel permit, and protection has been given to remaining wetlands.

There are a lot of mistakes to overcome, like the Superfund site in Portland harbor and brownfield areas with toxic industrial waste. Portland's policies and developments have not served all its inhabitants and neighborhoods equitably. Some have been outright destructive.

We have not appeared to prize social justice as highly as environmental protection, although people are now trying to connect both movements as we'll see later.

To be sure, Portlanders might well look back wistfully at the landscape that once was, the one that might have been. But we are an optimistic bunch, preferring instead to envision a Portland landscape, a Portland environment that still can be.

So what do you think? Have we been good enough to have this country in our possession?

Opposite page: As this view from Pittock Mansion illustrates, Portland's natural setting sets a high standard for the humans who live here. As Lewis Mumford asked, "Are we good enough to have this country in our possession?" It would be a good thing to ask ourselves every day, for every decision we make individually and collectively.
■ Quilt information on page 24.

Pieces of Portland

The Earth Is Not Finished Yet

In Portland, even the earth is young. There are no dinosaur skeletons waiting to be unearthed here, as this land was covered by warm seas until more than 40 million years after dinosaurs had disappeared.

Once this corner of the continent rose from the sea, nearly every kind of important landforming activity took place in or near Portland. And especially with the 1980 eruption of nearby Mt. St. Helens, Portland got to witness a spectacular testimonial that, in the Pacific Northwest at least, the earth is not yet finished. Not even close.

Let me walk you through how the land here came to be.

Beginning about 20 million years ago, the sea began to recede in the area that includes Portland, about the same time lava reached the area from the east. Then for several million years, beginning about 17 million years ago, Columbia River basalt flowed out of vents in eastern Oregon and Washington. These flows were massive, and include the longest known single lava flow on earth, reaching hundreds of miles from the interior to the Pacific Ocean. They left behind a 1,000-foot layer of basalt beneath Portland. A notable visible basalt landform in the area is Willamette Falls, where water drops 40 feet at the edge of a basalt shelf where one flow stopped.

Until these basalt flows pushed the Columbia River to its present course, the river flowed south of where Mt. Hood is now, depositing layer after layer after layer of sand and gravel known as the Troutdale Formation. In some places, the formation is as much as 1,000 feet thick.

Over the next several millions of years, fresh water lakes formed within ranges of folded hills and deposited silt and fine-grained sand across the area. Eruptions from composite volcanoes of the Cascade Range (like Mt. Hood) added ash layers to the land.

About two million years ago, a series of volcanic eruptions created cinder cones and lava flows at a number of points across Portland, including Mt. Tabor, where layer upon layer of cinders came to rest after they were blown into the air. Portlanders discovered it was a volcano when someone dug into the hillside. The exposed cinders were used as road-building material and in landscaping until the city made Mt. Tabor a park.

Then came the floods! About two and a half million years ago, the earth's climate began to cool and eventually glaciers covered the northern part of North America, including what is now Puget Sound. Although continental glaciers didn't reach as far south as Portland during the Ice Age, their effects certainly did. Glaciers in northern Idaho and western Montana had trapped large interior seas, and as they melted and collapsed, floods of unimaginable proportions poured over the land, heading to the Pacific Ocean. After carving out the Columbia Gorge, glacial meltwater backed up and formed a huge lake in the lower Columbia and Willamette river valleys. Gigantic boulders, rocks, gravel and coarse sand settled in Portland, creating things like the Alameda Ridge. The big boulders in the Tonquin area southwest of Portland came from those floods. Geologists estimate the glacial lake's catastrophic flooding

and reformation happened 40 or more times over a 2,000-year period between 15,000 and 13,000 years ago. That's almost like now in geologic time

Alpine glaciers on Mt. Hood were much larger during the Ice Age, carving out the huge U-shaped valley you see driving from Portland up to the mountain now.

Faults associated with earthquakes have been identified all across the city, and are especially notable along the eastern flank of the West Hills.

And of course by now we know that not far off Oregon's shore is the Cascadia Subduction Zone, where two tectonic plates are slamming together, getting hung up before the pressure builds enough to jerk past one another. A ginormous amount of energy will be released in that sudden massive movement. When it goes, we have been told to expect a 9.0 earthquake that might last five minutes. Yes, minutes! And, oh yeah, did I mention these megaquakes occur every 200-500 years or so on average? And the last one was in 1700. Let's do the math. 2015 minus 1700 is

315 years. We've been warned that all the bridges in Portland will collapse (except for the brand new ones that weren't ready when we went to press, although one should be open in September 2015), as well as all the old masonry buildings. I especially worry about structures and people who live on recent fill, next to rivers for example, because that soil will liquefy. There will be great loss of life. Some have warned it will be the worst natural disaster in the history of the United States. Did you get that? Worst. Ever.

Yes, I've paid a few thousand dollars to have my wood frame house megabolted to its foundation and for an automatic shutoff on the gas line. Will it make a difference in a worst case scenario? As the contractor who did the work said, it might be enough to give us time to get out alive.

In the meantime, Mt. St. Helens has been showing signs it might be heading for another explosive eruption. And the fire under Mt. Hood still burns. Sooner or later, we will again face an ash-covered city, as we did in 1980 when winds blew Mt. St. Helens ash in our direction and our street sweepers had to do ash removal. Many of us still have jars of ash we saved from that one, hoping it was a once-in-a-lifetime novelty.

What if the big quake and a massive volcanic eruption happened at the same time? What if they both happened during our worst ice storm of all time, and the polar vortex plunged us into a very deep freeze. Now that's an apocalyptic nightmare.

I actually think about these things. Living this close to the tectonic edge of imminent catastrophe does things to a person.

You'd be weird too!

> **Opposite page:** Every major landforming activity has been present in the Portland area, it's kind of a classroom for geomorphology. Our land is still active, seen in the multiple eruptions of Mt. St. Helens in 1980, shown in action on the far left. Many Portlanders like Ric Seaberg saved ash removal signs and jars of the glassy dust that fell on the city and covered it for weeks. **This page:** Part of a cinder cone on the side of Mt. Tabor was exposed when people started digging and using it for roads and paths.
> ■ Quilt information on page 24.

Someone Left the Quilt Out in the Rain

I don't think that I can take it. It took so long to make it,
And I'll never find that colorway again... oh no....
(with apologies to Jimmy Webb)

People grumble, gripe, bellyache and whine. Some can't take it and move away. But others just continuously and endlessly complain about the rain. I call them rainplainers.

So okay, I get it. It rains a lot here. Actually, not so many inches. Portland's annual precipitation is well below many other cities, like New York, Chicago and Miami, and half as much as New Orleans. But in the spirit of full disclosure, our official measurement station is at the Portland airport, which is just about the driest spot in the city. Rainfall amounts can vary by more than 15 inches within the city limits.

And let's face it, it's not really about how much, it's how often and for how long. More than the rain, maybe it's the overcastness of our winters that brings people down. In December and January, the average daytime sky in Portland is about 90% cloud-covered, with only about 20% of possible daily sunlight beaming through. Believe me when I say we have way more than 50 shades of grey. So why all the rain? Let's wade through the mud.

Tropical regions of the earth receive a lot more solar radiation than the poles. Sometimes there's more than a 200 degree difference in surface temperatures across our planet's surface, causing extreme differences in air temperatures. Air temperature differences create pressure differences, which form into zones. These patterns and the rotation of the earth sets all this in motion, with air masses moving across the surface in an attempt to create equilibrium, helped along by the jet stream.

The boundary where two kinds of air masses meet is a front. The warmest mass gets displaced upward and as it rises, its internal pressure drops, causing cooling. Moisture inside the air mass begins to condense, and when it becomes saturated, it falls as precipitation.

Portland's location is almost exactly halfway between the heat at the equator and the frigid North Pole. Warm and cold air masses from those places merge regularly in our vicinity during winter, and the jet stream and the storms to which it gives impetus often hit northwest Oregon broadside. These conditions last several months, creating extended periods of rain, showers and overcast skies in winter. Our eyes get so adjusted to the grey that when the sky clears, our traffic reports actually warn us about the most hazardous condition on the road: sunglare!

But here's the thing. When the front moves through, the rain is steady. But following its passing, there are intermittent showers, which means if you keep your eyes open, you'll notice that between the showers there are intermittent periods of clearing. So if you run outside real fast when they happen, you won't be so low on Vitamin D and perhaps avoid Seasonal Affective Disorder. (No extra charge for health tips!)

Temperature differences between air masses meeting here are generally not extreme, like they are so often in the Midwest and the South during tornado season, so the resulting uplift is relatively gentle, as is the rain it produces. Thus we give it soft names: showers, mist, drizzle, sprinkles, light rain. Occasionally the clouds do burst open. Portland's record 24-hour rainfall was 7.7 inches in December 1882. But mostly it's drizzle.

There's something else that affects precipitation in the Portland area. As the moisture-laden air moves from west to east, when it encounters ranges of hills or mountains, the air rises, pressure drops, the air becomes saturated and spills its moisture. That's what accounts for the significant difference in rainfall amounts within the city limits. The western slopes and high elevations of the West Hills get substantially more rain than the center of the city and the inner east side, which are located in the hills' rain shadow.

> **Believe me when I say we have way more than 50 shades of grey.**

Most of our winter precipitation falls as rain rather than snow because we enjoy the moderating effect of the Pacific Ocean. (Big bodies of water heat and cool more slowly than land.) It usually doesn't get cold enough to snow. Portland's mean January temperature is 39 degrees, compared with 14 degrees for Minneapolis, a city in the same latitude but in the continental interior.

Once in a while the jet stream shifts south allowing polar air to penetrate from the north, and significant snowfall can happen. If it does snow, there is a greater than 50 percent chance it will come in January, the most likely time for ice storms as well.

Portland is susceptible to freezing rain when rain from the Pacific is chilled by sub-freezing air from the interior that pours west through the Columbia Gorge. This opening to the interior of the continent is responsible for the rare truly harsh winter temperatures recorded locally. Frigid ground temperatures and extremely high pressure over the middle of North America cause air to seek outlets in the direction of lower pressure, like over the Pacific Ocean. Wicked east winds then whip through the Gorge, plunging Portland and its environs into an icy chill.

But no matter how rainy or snowy or chilly it gets in the grey months of the year, it's all worth it. Because Portland's summers.

Almost 90% of Portland's precipitation falls between October and May, leaving summers relatively, and often absolutely, dry. There were, for example, 71 consecutive days without rain in summer 1967. This trait actually makes Oregon unusual. Most places in the world receive most of their precipitation in summer months.

In summer, all things weather-wise move to the north, because the northern hemisphere is tilted toward the sun. The Pacific Ocean is relatively cooler than the continent, so high pressure forms and persists off Oregon's coast. Prevailing winds come from the north and northwest. Portland's typical July day has a high of 80 degrees, with a low of 57 at night. Because humidity is relatively low, even on days in the 90s, nighttime temperatures usually fall to the low 60s or

high 50s. We also enjoy late sunsets by summer's clock.

When heat builds up to the south of Oregon and then creeps our way, there is low pressure in western Oregon relative to the interior. When that happens, we get hot, dry east winds through the Gorge and some of our hottest summer temperatures.

But most of the time, Portland's summer days are the most perfect on earth. If this gets out, we are doomed.

Not that we aren't already doomed by global warming. I guess you could say we are fortunate in the Pacific Northwest because most of the worst effects won't be so visible here right away. Global weather patterns are predicted to still bring rain here, so we probably won't run out of water. At first, anyway. But even if climate change doesn't get us directly at first, we are in its cross hairs anyway. In fact, people are predicting we will become the home of many who are fleeing the effects of climate change elsewhere. When droughts go on and on and the ground water stops recharging, people will be on the move, many in our direction. We'll be adding "climate change refugees" to our vocabulary. And our neighborhoods. And our land.

Personally, I am astonished that somehow we've allowed climate change to become a political issue. And that we are not all scrambling as fast as we can to slow it down, that this has not

This page: The shell of the burned out Taylor Electric Building in southeast Portland created a great canvas for street artists whose art was reflected when the rainfall pooled on the concrete floors. But as you can see, sun always follows rain.
■ Quilt information on page 24.

compelled the entire planet to come together and focus on this issue this very moment just flat out disturbs me. It just makes no sense to me whatsoever, and we and the generations to come will all pay for our negligence and abuse.

Perhaps we need to pivot and take another approach. I always thought there was a lost opportunity decades ago when campaigns to get people to stop smoking focused on health consequences. I think almost everybody dismisses those warnings until they get a disease, because it's so much a part of human nature to think something bad won't happen to us. Denial may well be an evolutionary advantage at some level.

What do people care more about than their health? Their appearance. Not having wrinkles. Young looking skin. If the anti-smoking ads of yesteryear had aimed at vanity because your skin will get really creased and leathered and turkey-wattley, the tobacco plant may well have become extinct by now. Maybe I'm wrong, but I doubt it.

So here's my climate change idea: since we can't get humanity to take collective action to save the planet by warning about sea level rise or drought or famine or mass dying, let's see if hedonism might come to the earth's rescue. It turns out there are several deliciously awesome favorite things greatly threatened by global warming, and I am not joking. Let's do an ad campaign that shows us what it's like to live in a world without coffee, chocolate, seafood, cherries, wine, maple syrup and so forth. Won't somebody please steal my idea and jump on this?

Well, that was a tangent. Some days I feel I wasn't made for this world.

Pieces
of
Portland

A River Runs Through It

Where there is rain, there is water. And Portland has plenty of water. You could say that the river that runs right through it—the Willamette—is the biggest little river in the land. Lewis and Clark missed seeing the Willamette River on their first pass through the area, thinking it was a channel of the Columbia. When Capt. Clark found it on the return trip, its size convinced him it must be draining all the land west of the Rocky Mountains and south to the sources of the Colorado River and Rio Grande.

In fact, the Willamette drains an extraordinarily small area—less than 12% of the land of the state of Oregon—its basin extending only about 150 miles north to south and 75 miles east to west. But the volume of its flow is exceptional. No other river in North America carries so much water with that small a basin. For example, the Colorado River basin is more than 20 times larger than the Willamette, stretching over eight states, but the Willamette carries three times more water. It accounts for 15% of the average annual flow of the Columbia at its mouth.

Another remarkable feature is the exceptional vacillation of its flow from one season to another; the lowest ever recorded at Portland was less than 3,000 cubic feet per second to well over 600,000. The water year starts in October, when water levels start to rise with the onset of fall rain. The flow steadily increases in November, then drops noticeably in December or January, when precipitation turns to snow higher in the mountains, storing the water as ice until temperatures warm and the snow begins to melt. The river runs lowest in late summer, the driest time of the year in western Oregon.

A single-year hydrograph shows individual storm fronts moving through, as well as when water is held back or released from reservoirs according to the needs of flood control, irrigation, power generation, fish runs, recreation and navigation. Even the Rose Festival is detectable, if water is released from dams to allow large ships to travel further up the Willamette than usual.

Pacific Ocean tides reach 146 miles up the Columbia, and all the way up the Willamette past Portland to Willamette Falls in Oregon City. In central Portland, tides cause the level of the Willamette to rise and fall twice a day, sometimes by several feet. Because the bed of the Willamette in Portland is below sea level, with a downstream incline of less than an inch per mile, ebb tides cause the river to flow backward twice a day. Naturally, when there is a lot of water in the river, tidal effects are diminished. When the river runs at its lowest, it can take water nearly eight days to travel from the Sellwood Bridge to the

Multnomah Channel at the mouth of the Willamette, a distance of 13 miles. In fact, it sometimes takes the river as long to move the last 27 miles below the falls as it does to cover the first 160 miles. Under extreme conditions this last leg (14% of the length of the main stem) can take more than twice as long as the upper 86%.

You can imagine what can happen within this nearly stationary water sloshing back and forth: Garbage in, garbage stays in for a long time. There was a time when the Willamette was so polluted that dead fish lined the banks at Portland. In 1926, a water quality survey found it to be "an open sewer and nothing else." Measurements in the 1930s found no measurable oxygen in the water for several miles at Portland.

No wonder Portland turned its back on the river for so long. The seawall hid it on the west bank downtown and the east side was an unused, unsightly area next to Interstate 5 after construction was finished in 1966.

Opposite page: The Willamette River runs right through Portland, and downtown is visible from the entire length of the Eastbank Esplanade. This photo shows the Hawthorne Bridge and the downtown skyline just to the north. **This page:** People take to the river in all sorts of crafts each summer in The Big Float, after parading to the river near the Marquam Bridge and heading downstream. The event is a benefit for the Human Access Project, whose goal is to reclaim the river for generations to come.

■ Quilt information on page 24.

But this story has come to a happy place. After Oregon voters demanded action to clean the river in 1938, secondary sewage treatment was finally accomplished decades later by all towns and industries that discharged their waste into it by pipe. Now we are addressing nonpoint pollution (runoff from land and other areas) and riverine habitat restoration.

In the early 1970s, Portland removed Harbor Drive on the west side and replaced it with Tom McCall Waterfront Park. Now nearly all the city's celebrations take place beside the Willamette and there is direct access to the river. A new sandy beach area was added to the west bank under the Marquam Bridge in 2014, the first of several beaches that Human Access Project wants to create in the central city.

The east bank esplanade brought east side access to the water's edge when it was completed in 1994. A 1,200-foot section is the nation's longest floating walkway.

Now both salmon and people are back, and the Portland embraces its river. People fish the downtown section of the Willamette and I've seen a guy land a yard-long sturgeon along the seawall. Every summer Portlanders celebrate the river with the Big Float, where hundreds of Portlanders bring all manner of flotation devices and float/swim in the river between the Marquam and Hawthorne Bridges.

Oh snap, I forgot to tell you about the Superfund site. Hold on, it's coming.

Pieces
of
Portland

Before there were people on this land, much of it was covered in Pacific temperate rain forest, a landscape dominated by conifer trees. In fact, the old growth forest between latitudes 40 and 60 degrees N in the Pacific Northwest is the last best place on earth where conifers flourish, as they did before flowering plants out-competed them most everywhere else.

While native peoples had created an oak savannah grassland in much of the Willamette and Tualatin valleys by burning the vegetation every year, at the site where Portland began there were trees upon trees upon trees. In fact, if there hadn't been a small clearing in the dense forest, right beside the river, who knows where the largest city on the Willamette would have begun.

In northwestern Oregon forests, clearings were hard to come by. It's kind of awesome to know that old growth Pacific temperate forests have the largest biomass (volume of living and decaying material) of any ecosystem on the planet. That's really heavy, man. There are limited places where old growth forests remain. Within Portland, Forest Park comes closest to the original treescape hereabouts, but most of it was logged beginning soon after white settlement, so there is very little old growth left.

As soon as people started building a village in the clearing, they started felling the surrounding trees. Cutting a massive tree was such epic hard work that, in the early days, stumps were left standing. Hence the nickname Stumptown!

Much of the east side of Portland would have remained undeveloped longer but for a fire in 1846 that conveniently removed trees and undergrowth from what is now Mt. Scott north to the wetlands along the Columbia River. A 1854 cadastral map labels the area "Timber burnt and fallen."

Ironically, as soon as the native trees were cut, Portlanders planted trees from other places that reminded them from whence they came. Since many early Portlanders came from New England, they planted trees native to their homeland. That's why the Park Blocks downtown have such a wonderful stand of stately old American Elm trees. And since Dutch Elm disease has erased so many of the native elm elsewhere in the country, it's a very good thing we have the Park Blocks and Ladd's Addition, where the elms are treated to ward of the deadly disease.

The London Plane Trees along the downtown transit mall were planted in the manner of a European urban tradition. Portlanders are so protective of their trees that it's challenging to get a good solid look at the iconic Portlandia sculpture on the Michael Graves-designed Portland Building downtown. In Portland, trees often trump views, so the trees remain, making winter the best time to check her out.

If you want to piss off a Portlander, plan to cut down a giant old tree. We love trees. We hug them. A lot. In fact, for a brief time, we held the Guinness world record for tree hugging. Then Nepal went and beat us, and our last attempt fell short, with only 599 huggers. If they had counted our quilt, it would have been an even 600.

We also have our share of tree sitters, who occupy trees as an act of civil disobedience to keep trees from being cut. Even among professionals. On Earth Day 2014, 22 arborists climbed a large Paradox walnut tree in southeast Portland. Neighbors were fighting to save the tree from the chain saws of a developer who planned to build row houses there. Not only is the walnut rare in Portland (the state may have only two), an arborist called it the "bulkiest deciduous tree in Portland." Although the developer said he would save the tree, there were a few skeptics who weren't convinced.

I was on Portland's Urban Forestry Commission for a few years in a past life. Our meetings consisted mainly of hearing appeals from people who wanted to cut down trees in their parking strips. We were guardians of the street trees, but it

This page: It wasn't only people hugging trees when Portland attempted to regain its tree-hugging record in summer 2014. While we didn't break the record this time, we're pretty sure the first-place hugging fest in Nepal didn't include a hugging quilt, shown at left. Not that we're throwing shade. **Opposite page:** The Gingko forest in Chapman and Lownsdale Squares downtown shows how much beauty has been introduced to Portland when trees from other continents are planted. The squares were the site of Portland's Occupy camp in 2011.
■ Quilt information on page 24.

Pieces of Portland

could be a sad job when the petitioner was a widow on kidney dialysis who couldn't rake her leaves anymore. Chair Bill Naito, the very successful Portland business leader Naito Parkway is named after, resolved one such case by volunteering to go to her house to rake leaves for her. That's the kind of guy he was. And that's the kind of place Portland was. Still is? Hope so.

Portland has a pretty fine urban forest, with around 236,000 street trees (not counting the ones planted after 2013), 1.2 million trees in parks and gobs of still-uncounted trees on private property. And by the way, if data-walking is your thing, a street tree inventory is well underway, and the Urban Forestry Department is looking for more volunteers to count, identify and map Portland trees. While they're at it, volunteers look for street tree opportunities—places where there is room for more street trees to be added.

Many of the city's street trees planted since 1989 have been the work of Portland's Friends of Trees, with about half a million trees put in the ground by the group's more than 100,000 volunteers. From its modest beginning in Portland, Friends of Trees now works in 20 cities in Oregon and Washington.

Portland's Hoyt Arboretum was established in 1928 to "conserve endangered species and educate the community." Its nearly 200 acres is located in the West Hills as part of the Washington Park complex that also includes the World Foresty Center, Rose Garden and Oregon Zoo. The Arboretum has 6,000 trees of 1,400 species. Hoyt Arboretum has the largest collection of conifers in U.S., and its *Metasequoia* produced the first cones in the western hemisphere in 50 million years.

There are approximately 300 Heritage Trees throughout Portland. New trees are added each year, and anyone can nominate a Heritage Tree! Once designated, no Heritage Tree can be removed without the consent of the Urban Forestry Commission and the Portland City Council.

But many feel the city could do more to preserve its urban forest. A recent story caught my eye. The City of Portland cut down a 120-foot-tall Giant Sequoia tree in Pier Park in north Portland. Why? To build the North Portland Greenway. Yes, that is correct, they removed an 18-foot-circumference tree to make way for a pedestrian and bike greenway. The city said it looked for other options but decided removing the tree was the best alternative. Neighbors rallied, to no avail. But I suspect city officials secretly felt super guilty about it because they promised to plant seven Giant Sequoia trees in a nearby tree-deficient park and use the dead Sequoia lumber to build the first Nature Play area at Westmoreland Park.

Small businesses have formed in our area to ensure that trees removed in the city are put to good use—from becoming part of fine furniture to components for all kinds of tools and other projects to providing firewood to families for heating if there is no long-lasting purpose for it.

When you add composting to the mix, as you always must, nary a twig goes to waste.

Index to Quilts

Some of the quilts in this book are available for purchase from quiltlandia.com

Pieces of Portland

SETTLEMENT

During my lifetime, the estimated length of time humans have lived in North America has increased by many thousands of years. I first heard that people had migrated here from Asia when the sea level was low enough to create a land bridge across the Bering Strait. Sea levels rose and fell depending on how much of the Earth's water was in the form of ice. During the last Glacial Maximum (around 16,000 years ago), the sea level was about 400 feet lower than it is now. Then it gradually began rising, a process that continues today.

The climate was drier during the Glacial period. Huge grasslands in what is now eastern Russia supported large grazing animals. The land bridge migration story speculated that hunters followed animals east across Asia, then though Alaska, Canada, and across what is now the United States and then into Central and South America. By 12,000 years ago the land bridge no longer existed because the sea level had risen above it, and it's been submerged ever since.

Distinctive stone tools dating to around 11,500 years ago were found near Clovis, New Mexico, so the first inhabitants were called Clovis people. Similar tools were found in other parts of North America, leading scholars to assume there was but a single source for people in the New World.

More recently, new sites were discovered, analysis of archeological evidence grew more sophisticated and minds opened to alternative theories. We now know that humans were in the New World considerably earlier than Clovis dates, perhaps 50,000 or more years ago. Some researchers believe they have evidence of cultural exchanges in the New World between several different sources, and some would have had to come by sea (e.g., Polynesians sailing to and from Central and South America).

However, recent DNA analysis has found a single variant among descendants of Native Americans in North America, Greenland and the western Bering people. This suggests that they were "derived from a common founder population, which had been isolated from the rest of the Asian continent thousands of years prior to their migration to the Americas."

Oral histories of the first people living on the Oregon coast included tales of monsters arriving on the seashore that looked like whales with two trees on top and ropes hanging from the trees—a clear reference to a ship. The people had a word that meant "those who float ashore." Bear-like creatures (like themselves but covered in hair) emerged from the whales and stayed and lived among the people who greeted them. In one instance, an ethnologist in 1855 speculated that a ship from Japan brought people to the shore of the Pacific at some point, as some had a complexion "yellower than ordinary, and their eyes more oblique and elongated." Another who floated ashore had red hair

that subsequently appeared among the local people. Dozens of ships had floated ashore by the end of the 18th century.

People who lived along the Columbia River were called Chinook by the Euro Americans who wrote history. And even though there were considerable differences among them, the name came to be applied to all people living along and near the lower Columbia River from the Pacific Ocean shores north and south of the river's mouth to the giant falls (now drowned by The Dalles dam) nearly 200 miles upriver and up the Willamette River to what is now Willamette Falls. Both falls were break points in river transportation and where salmon filled the waters on their return to their headwaters.

The Chinook were not a single political tribe. Clusters of long-houses held extended families and relatives. They married outside their villages, extending their kin net-works, creating important social ties among them. There were linguistic differences among villages at different points along the river.

> **The Chinook had a thriving culture, with towns, houses, transportation, gardens and literature.**

When Europeans and Americans first visited the lower Columbia area, the culture they found was unlike others they had encountered elsewhere. Hunter-gatherers were assumed to be nomadic, living in small groups with very simple cultures. But the hunter-gatherers of the Pacific Northwest had a high population density, lived in permanent longhouses in villages (and seasonal camps for specific resources) that sometimes had more than a thousand people and had highly complex social and economic systems. The 2013 book *Chinookan Peoples of the Lower Columbia* described the area as "a thriving culture, with towns, houses, transportation, gardens, and literatures."

In 1966, an anthropologist called his study of the Chinook *Coping with Abundance*. While there are a few reports of running short of food in winter, this may well have been the most productive environment in North America, with a bounty of several kinds of salmon, sturgeon, steelhead, oysters, lamprey, seal, sea lion, ducks, geese, elk, deer, bear and edible roots, berries, seeds and greens. Materials for shelter, clothing and tools were at hand as well. The first people learned this environment intimately and developed sophisticated tools and ways to nurture and work with it. In fact, the Chinook often had food and other material surpluses, which led them to develop ways to preserve and store foods that rivaled contemporary Europe and to develop complex trading systems.

The Chinook's location put them in a position to become masters of trade, as they controlled the mouth of the Columbia River and breaks upriver at Celilo Falls and Willamette Falls. They traded with many different people from the interior via the Columbia River at The Cascades (The Dalles), western river valleys like the Willamette, and coastal communities of Northwest Coast and Pacific Coast. In fact, the official trade language used from

the Yukon to California was known as Chinook *wawa*, which combined Chinook, Nootka, English and French.

The trading system was so well developed that fur traders who came from Europe and Asia were able to join it, introducing global commercial exploitation of Pacific Northwest natural resources. Without the Chinook, the fur traders would have had much less success in so few decades.

The Chinook carved canoes from cedar trees (some six feet wide, others small enough to be carried underarm) and had legendary navigation skills, often guiding ships crossing the Columbia River bar. Their fishing tools and skills were highly honed, and included seine nets, weirs, gaffs, spears and clubs. Salmon were such a key part of their culture that the most important ceremony was the cooking over fire and eating of the first-salmon of the spring run. There were carefully prescribed taboos and rituals the people had to observe when salmon fishing that conserved and preserved the species.

There was leisure time for games like lacrosse and gambling. The Chinook considered it great fun to take something from

another and watch the victim try to figure out who had taken it and where it had been hidden. Unfortunately, when whites arrived they didn't understand the nature of the game and some considered the Chinook to be thieves.

But many early Europeans who observed and/or studied the Chinook noted their intelligence. Fur trader Gabriel Franchère wrote, "I believe them closer to a civilized state than any of the tribes living east of the Rocky Mountains. . . . They possess to an eminent degree those qualities opposite to idleness, improvidence,

This page: Willamette Falls, 27 miles upstream from the mouth of the Willamette River was an important fishing and trading site for the first people in what is now the Portland metropolitan area. Pulp and paper mills have made the river inaccessible to the public now, although there is a movement underway to restore the historic locks. On the right is a historic photo of fishing platforms used at Celilo Falls before The Dalles Dam flooded this entire section of the Columbia.

Pieces
of
Portland

and stupidity. The chiefs in particular distinguish themselves by their good judgement and their intelligence. Generally speaking they have quick minds and tenacious memories."

Hudson's Bay Company Governor George Simpson said the Chinook were "without exception the most intelligent and most acute and finished Bargain makers I have ever fallen in with."

The nobility among the Chinook were distinguished by their head flattening practice, which they accomplished by placing a board on the front of infants' skulls.

They created decorative art in the form of wood carvings, dentalilia and bead jewelry and painted their longhouse doors, often using the colors yellow, red, white and black. They pierced their bodies for dentalilia, and many had tattoos.

During much of the year, people of the Chinook wore little or no clothing, noted by Rick Rubin in his book *Naked Against the Rain*. When it rained, they covered their skin in oil so the rain would run off. This kept them warmer than clothing that got and stayed wet, although they wore animal hides and furs against the extreme cold. Even in snow, they were barefoot. Euro Americans who came to the area were surprised and sometimes scandalized by their nakedness.

They lived in longhouses that could be more than 200 feet long, made from cedar planks they cut and sliced, with roofs often made of tree bark. An extended family would live in one, with whatever slaves or people of lower status they used to help provide labor. Often the longhouses were collected into villages, sometimes of just three or four, but often 30 or so, arranged in rows parallel to the river and prevailing winds.

In some areas along the river, villages were inhabited year round; others grew or shrunk seasonally. One longhouse near the town of Scappoose was used continuously for at least 400 years. Four things accounted for most of the movement of villages—fish, food, floods, and fleas (moving toward fish and other foods and away from floods and fleas).

Each village was led by a man, selected by consensus. He was expected to be strong, wise, gentle, courageous, loyal, resolute, generous and responsible for the welfare of the people.

The Chinook living between the Coast Range and the Cascade Range were called the Multnomah (after the largest village Mahlnumax), and their language was different still. It was the most populous area in the land of the Chinook. Lewis and Clark mapped more than 15 Chinook winter villages in the vicinity of present-day Portland, most on or near Wapato (now Sauvie) Island, where the wapato (Indian potato) grew.

Lewis and Clark's Corps of Discovery and their very survival was greatly assisted by the Chinook. But, as Angela Sanders wrote in *Chinook Nation*, "If their journals are evidence, Lewis and Clark were ungrateful guests during the winter of 1805-06 they spent at Fort Clatsop. The Chinooks paddled in to Point Ellice and brought the Corps food when their own boats could not manage the turbulent Columbia. Lewis and Clark praised the Chinooks' skill and beautifully crafted canoes, then stole one on their way home....The Corps set up camp where the tribe had suggested and in one winter wiped out the local elk population....Lewis and Clark saw fresh salmon as unhealthy and instead preferred to eat dogs."

One of the notable local groups the Multnomah traded with were the Kalapuyan-speaking Tualatin who live on plains just over the hills from the Big River. Their language was Athabaskan, an entirely different family of languages than Chinook.

Above the Willamette Falls, Calapooyia Indians could not rely on salmon to the same degree as the Chinook. Their diet included game (especially elk and deer) and plants like camas bulbs, acorns and grain seeds— yield of the prairie, not the forest.

The Calapooyia improved their food yield by ridding the Willamette Valley of woods by repeatedly burning it. Fresh vegetation growth attracted game, and favored seed-producing grasses and plants. Repeated annually, fire eventually erased most trees from the valley except for stands of fire-resistant trees like oaks and those growing in areas too wet to burn.

The Calapooyia's response to the relatively fewer salmon upstream from Willamette Falls created remarkably different landscapes in a river valley that otherwise would have been fully forested. But their successful efforts to enhance their food supply ultimately sealed their fate as the prairies were deemed choice farm sites by the westward-looking, Eden-seeking whites who began settling the Willamette Valley in the 1830s. The agricultural surplus these farms produced created the need for a trade depot—the port that became Portland, where before long ships would cross oceans to come calling for Pacific Northwest wheat.

The earliest lasting incursion of whites into the lands of the Chinooks and Calapooyia was enticed by the profit to be made in fur-bearing animals. Although representatives of Russia, Spain, Great Britain and the United States all made claims to Pacific Northwest territory, only the British and Americans actually occupied the land. The first settlement was an American one—in Astoria in 1811—but it quickly failed. The dominant invading force in early Oregon Country was Great Britain, acting through its fur trading companies.

When Hudson's Bay Company directed its Columbia district to grow its own food supply, Astoria's coastal location was abandoned for the more hospitable, fertile interior on the north bank of the Columbia River just upstream from the mouth of the Willamette. Thus, in 1825, Fort Vancouver became the first white settlement in the vicinity of what is now Portland. A post at Oregon City soon followed in 1829.

The success of the agricultural experiment at Fort Vancouver prompted a number of early fur company employees to settle and farm the Oregon Country upon retirement. A fair number had married Chinook women. Because Britain had designs on the land to the north, Chief Factor John McLoughlin sent them south to the Willamette Valley.

Missionaries soon followed, but they had little success converting the original people to Christianity. However, they

publicized the region's agricultural promise, which encouraged overland migration into the Pacific Northwest that began modestly enough in 1840, but soon numbered thousands annually.

Before long, whites outnumbered native people, who had begun to succumb to European diseases almost as soon as Europeans set foot on Northwest soil. Diseases had once decimated European populations, and a herd immunity had developed to protect survivors. The timing of three smallpox epidemics are known: 1776-77, 1802 and 1824-25. Because the trading Chinook had so many contacts with people from overseas and those from the continent's interior, they were frequently exposed to diseases they for which they had no immunity. The Tillamook told of a ship that floated ashore leaving behind two sick men; they then came down with the same illness.

Lewis and Clark estimated the population of the Chinook to be 17,740 in 1805, but we know now that they missed counting several groups. Some researchers think about 80% of the lower Chinook succumbed to smallpox before Lewis and Clark visited. In 1829 an epidemic of what was thought to be malaria

killed 80% percent of the upper Chinooks, and by 1850, very few Chinook in the Willamette or lower Columbia river valleys survived to resist white settlement.

But their legacy endured. Fewer than a dozen farms in all of western Oregon had required significant clearing of forest as late as 1850. Most were on prairies that had been created by the Calapooyia Indians.

As for the Chinook, disease wiped out about 90% and white occupation drove them deeper inland. To survive, the Chinooks married into other groups and some were assigned to reservations of other tribes and nations. Those who were left in their *illahee* (land, country, world) lived in small clusters where they could still fish and carry out their traditions as much as possible. Bay Center, Washington, is the place most associated with the Chinook now.

From a low of approximately 500 in 1853, the Chinook population has been slowly rebounding. In 2011, there were nearly 3,000 enrolled members, although some are also counted by the Siletz, Warm Springs, Yakima, Quinalt and Grand Ronde.

As this was written, they had been denied federal tribal recognition twice, despite all the help they had given explorers, fur traders and settlers. It has been said that Hudson's Bay Company owed "its entire prosperity, nay, its very existence to commerce with the natives." Not to mention all the lives they likely saved, like Lewis and Clark and other members of the Corps of Discovery. What!? No good deed goes unpunished!?

And they're still missing a canoe.

Opposite page: This portrait by Paul Kane of a member of the Cowlitz Tribe (Caw Wacham) and her infant illustrates head flattening practiced by the Chinook people **This page:** This is a replica of a Chinook longhouse built on the Ridgefield Wildlife Refuge in Clark County, Washington, that is used ceremonially by local Chinookan people and is open to the public.

Several small communities were established on the lower Willamette and nearby Columbia in the 1840s. Following the lead of Oregon City, which became a town in 1842, Linn City and Multnomah City were founded just across the river in 1843; Linnton in 1843; Portland and St. Helens in 1845; St. Johns in 1847; Milwaukie in 1848; and East Portland and Milton in 1850.

At that point, Oregon led in population, trade and commerce on the Pacific Coast—California was claimed and occupied by Mexico and Great Britain had designs on the land north of the Columbia River. That left the rough equivalent of what is now the state of Oregon with a clearly American destiny.

But most settlements were accessible only by water as there was yet little overland travel within Oregon territory. Though supporters envisioned and vigorously promoted a lively overseas trade, only a handful of vessels actually dared confront the infamous Columbia River bar.

Then respected sea captain John Couch sounded the Willamette and declared Portland the head of navigation.

Portland's early boosters recognized the critical value of a link to the wheat fields of the Tualatin Valley, and immediately began work on a road. First used in 1846, the 12 miles of steep, winding, rough travel became a perpetual mud hole during rainy weather, but the region's dry summer climate ensured good conditions at harvest time. St. Helens and Milton were without Willamette River navigation problems, and even though the road connecting them to the farmland was about twice as long, its grade was much gentler and could be traversed in less time and more safely.

In response, Portland began surfacing its road with wood planks—the first such effort on the Pacific slope—to improve the most direct route to the plains. This inspired effort so impressed prospective investors that Portland continued to grow faster than its competitors. By 1850, Portland's population surpassed that of its neighbors once and for all, and it became known as the largest and most important city and port north of San Francisco. The City of Portland was incorporated in 1851 and was named county seat of Multnomah County in 1854.

The Gold Rush that began in 1848 in California created so much demand for supplies that in 1849, no fewer than 50 sailing vessels braved the Columbia River bar to carry loads of Oregon goods—mostly wheat and lumber—to California.

The discovery of gold in Idaho and northeastern Oregon created an average annual surplus of $15 million in the Pacific Northwest and stimulated intensive development of commerce and transportation in the interior via the Columbia between 1861 and 1867. Portland handled most goods to and from the

mines, and by the end of the decade the city's population had more than tripled to 9,600. The mining demand consumed the wheat and flour surplus from the Willamette Valley, but after the gold boom waned, Portland looked for other buyers and found them in Europe, where rapid industrialization had led to rampant population growth in cities. Crop failures like the potato famine caused them to increase their grain imports. Crops and goods from the eastern U.S. were going to rebuild the post-Civil War south. Shipping from Portland to England took at least five months, required crossing the equator twice and navigating through the treacherous, frigid waters of Cape Horn. The journey was so hazardous that underwriters refused to insure bulk shipments, so wheat and flour had to be sacked for transport, adding to their cost.

But Pacific Northwest fields were so productive (yield per acre was nearly double that of the Great Plains) and the wheat of such superb quality that it was competitive on the British market. The value of shipments increased sharply from $31,000 in 1869 to more than $4.6 million during the 1877-78 season. By the 1880s, more than 100 wheat ships called at Portland and "a literal forest of masts extended for miles along the west bank of the Willamette."

> Until 1910, Portland was the largest and most important city and port north of San Francisco.

Salmon canneries were built locally beginning in 1866, shortly after significant improvements were made in canning techniques, and by 1874 there were 13 canneries along the lower Columbia River. The industry produced 450,000 cases for export in 1878, the second item in value behind wheat/flour. By 1880 it was a $2 million per year business, with Columbia River canneries processing 80% of the world's supply of salmon.

Portland's 1880 population had swelled to 21,000, and the remarkable pace of growth continued for the next four decades, mostly due to growing wheat trade and associated businesses. As wheat farming became mechanized, production jumped from 50-75 bushels per day to 500 bushels. Acreage expanded greatly in the interior.

A federally-funded 2,500-foot breakwater completed in 1885 greatly improved navigation at the mouth of the Columbia River. The City of Portland had begun dredging the Willamette

Opposite page: A stone marker and plaque memorialize the wooden plank road early enterprising souls built to make a way to carry wheat from Tualatin Valley to the docks of Portland. It was enough to convince investors that Portland would become the city that was the center of commerce from the interior to the Pacific Ocean and beyond.
■ Quilt information on page 38.

Pieces
of
Portland

in 1864. Finally, a channel 40 feet deep and 600 feet wide from the Portland Harbor to the Pacific was achieved in the mid-1970s. Presently, any ship that can pass through the Panama Canal can penetrate the Columbia and Willamette rivers as far as Portland.

The watergrade route along the Columbia was selected for the first transcontinental rail line to reach the Pacific Northwest in 1883. By 1890, the thriving city approached 47,000 residents and was the third-fastest growing city in the U.S. from 1890 to 1900, when 90,500 inhabitants were counted. The Port of Portland was established 1891, signaling Portland's status as a world seaport. In 1901, Portland ranked fifth in wheat exports in the nation. Growth in the Pacific Northwest outstripped even California's, and prospects were bright.

Technological advances in both logging and transportation cleared more of Oregon's forests as demand for lumber rose in the eastern U.S., and most lumbering operations moved to the Pacific Northwest from the nearly exhausted forests of the upper Midwest. After the turn of the century, one-third of Portland's wage earners were connected with the timber industry. Employment in manufacturing increased tenfold between 1880 and 1920, much of it related to wood processing. A metals industry developed, mostly to provide specialized equipment for lumbering.

Economic growth brought considerable wealth into the Pacific Northwest in general and to Portland in particular. Incomes grew and fortunes were amassed, increasing regional demand for consumer goods, which began to be manufactured locally. The prosperity supported a strong service industry in Portland, and employment in professional, clerical and public service occupations grew substantially.

Portland's glorious optimism was reflected in ambitious plans to host a World's Fair to advertise the wonders of the city and its home state to millions of visitors. The Lewis and Clark Exposition of 1905 was a rousing success, and by 1910, Portland's population had surpassed 207,000, with nearly three-fourths of the increase due to immigration. But by the end of the first decade of the 20th century, and despite its phenomenal growth,

Portland was no longer the premier city of the Northwest. Seattle's growth had been even more remarkable, reaching more than 237,000 in 1910.

And even though it's been more than 100 years, Portland still hasn't fully recovered from losing first position. And it shows, as we will see.

Naturally, the Willamette River shaped the growth of Portland to a great extent, containing it mostly to the west side until a bridge was built to connect to the east. Streets in the downtown core do not conform to compass directions but are aligned with the river.

Floods were an annual event historically, with a severe one every decade or so and a catastrophic flood averaging once a century. Over time, the major north-south streets of downtown moved from beside the river to five or six blocks inland (where the transit mall is today) because of flooding.

The riverbank site where Portland first took root was big enough for a time, but before long the clearing was enlarged and trees felled over a 16-block area. Within a year there were some 20 buildings, including several businesses and a wharf. Downed trees provided all needed construction materials.

Settlement spread over the broad sloping river terrace, the population doubled, then tripled. Acre upon acre of forest was cleared, first to make room for farms, then for the town. Claims were laid to the north, west and south until they came up to physical obstacles—wetlands and shallow lakes to the north, steep and unstable hills on the west, the river to the east and the junction of the hills and river to the south.

In the earliest days of settlement, residents lived in apartments above their businesses or in nearby boarding houses or cabins. When business prospered, residential neighborhoods were established just west of the commercial area, including streets of palatial homes along what is now the South Park Blocks. When that area was filled, land to the northwest became a neighborhood of homes. Some were elaborate dwellings whose grounds occupied an entire block. By 1880, Portland's 18,000 residents felt crowded, and the city looked to expand.

Directly across the river there was a large, mostly flat plain that had been cleared of its forest most recently by a gigantic fire in 1846. Other communities had sprung up on the east bank—East Portland directly across from the center of Portland's business district, Albina and St. Johns to the north, Sellwood to the south. A ferry service, first established in 1852, connected both banks at four points, but exchange was limited until bridges were built. After bridge access was established, Portland began annexing neighboring communities—first East Portland and Albina in 1891, then Sellwood in 1893.

With the introduction of electric streetcars in 1889, settlement began to expand on the east side as a network of rails was built and existing ones electrified. Portland's population grew rapidly in the early 20th century, especially after the Lewis and Clark Exposition. It was a very big deal when the east side population surpassed that of the west in 1906. Blocks and blocks of houses were built quickly, first extending to 60th Avenue, then to 82nd Avenue.

The shape of growth during those years is still seen in Portland, with commercial zones located on streets where the tracks ran and intersected with other lines. Streetcars were relatively empty on weekends, so their companies developed recreation destinations—like Oaks Amusement Park and similar facilities on Council Crest and Jantzen Beach (that are now gone)—to fill cars and coffers on weekends. Longer distance interurban lines were built to Cadenza Park near Estacada and Chautauqua performances in Gladstone.

These leisure trips were so popular they are credited with creating a demand that the automobile could better meet. Cars greatly extended the commuters' reach, skipping over unincorporated areas lacking services like sewers. Bedroom communities much further out were more desirable, especially when federal funds became available to build urban highways. Once the Sunset Highway and tunnel opened in 1970, suburban development started taking over huge tracts of farmland in Washington County. Retail centers followed, threatening the vitality of downtown Portland's core.

Many wetlands and riverine zones were filled for industrial development and rail yards. In fact, the western shore of the Willamette has been extended and built up along the entire length of the city, both for shipping facilities and associated businesses, and to protect adjacent commercial areas, as in the case of the sea wall.

More recently, limits to the age of the automobile became apparent and Portland attempted to breathe new life into downtown by demolishing areas near downtown it considered blighted and replacing them with new civic, residential and office space and then building a transit mall and public square in the heart of the city.

The main stem of the Willamette once swung around Swan Island's eastern flank, but the river was rerouted west and the island joined to the mainland for railroad construction. Dock facilities have progressively moved downstream, accompanied by further filling on both shores of the Willamette to make room for larger yards required by larger ships and dockside rail connections. The Port of Portland's container terminal is located on the Columbia.

In recent decades, Portland's industrial growth has taken place away from the rivers, with footloose industries often locating in suburbs, where businesses can afford to erect park-like campus settings, as long as they tie into rail and highway networks, and the airport. Air travel has become more important, and Portland International Airport is one of only 14 in the country to have direct flights to both Europe and Asia; PDX is the smallest U.S. airport that does.

The Portland metropolitan area has an urban growth boundary and housing density targets to meet. There's been an epidemic of razing single-family homes and replacing them with multi-story apartment buildings in many neighborhoods. Their sudden appearance is jarring and they steal our sunlight.

It feels a little like we're being told, "Reach for the sky!"

Opposite page: Roads and streets along the Willamette River and placement of bridges joining west and east sides of Portland largely determined how the city grew and what shape it took in early decades. As new means of transportation developed, different patterns emerged, but the basic structure of the city west of 82nd Avenue relates back to streetcar lines.

■ Quilt information on page 38.

Pieces
of
Portland

Bridges to Somewhere

Once a certain threshold of people and activities was reached on both sides of the Willamette, there were a whole lot of reasons to cross the river, more than river ferries could manage. So Portland started building bridges. In fact, Bridgetown is one of our city's nicknames.

The first was the privately-financed Morrison Bridge, because it was at the center of settlement in 1887. During the rest of the 19th century, more bridges were built in the central part of the city. The private ones were so poorly constructed that the city took them over and rebuilt them within a few years. From then on, bridges across the Willamette were publicly financed.

In the 20th century, six more went up, increasingly distant from the downtown core. The last two were part of freeway systems that traverse Portland—the Marquam Bridge in 1966 and the Fremont Bridge in 1973. Oh yeah, there is one more bridge that is only for trains. It's called the Railroad Bridge. You probably haven't heard of it.

At this point, many of our bridges are old, with a few nearing the end of their expected lives. We are finally rebuilding the Sellwood Bridge, after it scored a sufficiency rating of 2 out of a possible 100 by the National Bridge Inventory.

But the most exciting news bridgewise in Portland for a very long time is the Tillicum Crossing, Bridge of the People, a gorgeous structure that connects southern downtown and the quickly cool South Waterfront with the up and coming southern industrial east bank. And here's the most Portland part about it. No cars allowed. Seriously. Only light rail, streetcars, bikes and pedestrians. It won't be ready for passengers until fall of 2015, but we can't wait. Oh, did I mention it's the first of its kind in the whole country?

If cars had been included, the bridge would need to be way bigger and would have required a whole lot of riverbank road building on both sides of the river. Which nobody wants, especially given all the returning-to-the-river momentum Portland has now.

There are a number of celebrations that involve our beloved bridges. The best known is the annual Bridge Pedal, when even the upper decks of the Fremont and Marquam freeway bridges are closed to cars so bikers can pedal in peace. Well, actually, the event became so popular with thousands and thousands of bikers, there were bike jams in some places, so a limit has been placed on the number of participants. With the Eastbank Esplanade, Springwater Trail and Waterfront Park, it's now possible to get up close and personal on foot or bike with all the non-interstate freeway bridges in an endless loop through Portland every single day of the year.

So we can cross any bridge when we come to it.

Opposite page: The beautiful St. Johns Bridge has been a favorite of most Portlanders for a very long time. **This page:** But I wonder if it will be eclipsed by the striking new Tillicum Crossing, seen on this page.

■ Quilt information on page 38.

Pieces of Portland

Must Be in the Water

If you live in Portland for a while, sooner or later, someone from elsewhere will ask you, "WTF is in your water??" Is the water, they wonder, perhaps the source of our endemic maverick and creative nature, our inexplicable activities?

Judging from our rhetoric and voting behavior, you would be forgiven if you think we believe our water has sacred qualities. A former mayor declared it to be the best water system in the world and began marketing a carbonated version for retail sale. I still have a bottle, in fact. It's prolly a collector's item by now.

Apparently we don't want anybody messing with our water, as witnessed by the repeated rejections of adding fluoride like almost every other American city does.

Soon after I moved to Portland in 1974, some work needed to be done in the city's pristine Bull Run watershed. To reduce the impact, the work was done by horses. Wearing diapers. Local TV news was all over it. Color me impressed!

Imagine my surprise, then, to later learn that, at the same time, very large scale commercial clearcut logging was underway in the watershed, diaper free. When I looked a little deeper, I learned that almost one-fourth of the watershed had been clearcut, and management of the basin was not being done by the Water Bureau, but by the US Forest Service, whose priority might be the forest rather than the water.

Along the way, I met Dr. Joe Miller, who filed a class action suit against the City and Forest Service in 1974 on the grounds that logging was violating the Bull Run Trespass Act, passed by Congress in 1904, that forbade entry into the Bull Run Reserve watershed by anyone except forest rangers and employees of the water district. Logging had been underway since 1940 because "Timber companies, Forest Service and others couldn't see the value of all that timber just left there going to rot." In 1957, the federal government ordered that Bull Run be logged commercially or the City would have to pay $1 million a year in lost federal revenue. That's when large-scale logging—and trespassing—took off.

In 1976, the Millers, joined by the Oregon Environmental Council, won the class action lawsuit and logging was ordered halted. But then, in the closing hours of the 1977 session of Congress, a bill slipped through that allowed any activity in the watershed "so long as it did not have a significant adverse effect on compliance with water quality standards."

So Joe Miller's work was only beginning. At that time I was teaching *Environment of Portland* at Portland State University and wanted to learn all I could about the water, a search that took me many places. One day, I went to the home of a retired Forest Service man on the recommendation of a retired Water Bureau man.

During our conversation, he told me that the Forest Service had decided to get support for logging by talking up the fire danger in a forest with so many trees. I asked him if he had anything in writing that demonstrated that. He gave me an internal memo written in 1952 by the district ranger that mapped out a plan to make money by logging the watershed. It read, in part, "For 50 years city officials and Portland residents have been ballyhooing pure Bull Run water from an unmolested watershed. Many are fully convinced that to keep their water pure the watershed must remain forever untouched. There is a tremendous P.R. job to change this thinking....The fire angle should be played up and revenue returns subdued in this initial discussion."

This was just a few years after Watergate, and when I read it, I thought, "OMG, where are Woodward and Bernstein? I think I just found the smoking gun!"

It was just days before City Council would hear testimony that logging needed to be ramped up to deal with disastrous damage to the forest from a December 1983 windstorm, caused by the highest atmospheric pressure recorded in the U.S. The Forest Service wanted to remove fallen and standing trees on 5,700 acres. Because of fire, of course. But when I looked at the map of the blowdown, it looked to me like most damaged areas were at the edge of clearcuts, or openings caused by past blowdowns that were next to past clearcuts. I read from the memo at the Council hearing and handed over a copy.

Joe Miller generously told me later he thought the memo had been an important turning point in the battle to save Bull Run. (It certainly was a turning point in my journey to question authority.) But it was actually the tireless advocacy of Joe and many other individuals and organizations, and other circumstances, that ultimately led Congress to pass the Oregon Resources Conservation Act in 1996, which prohibited logging on all National Forest land within the watershed and put the Water Bureau in charge of Bull Run.

The Bull Run watershed is a marvelous place for a water supply, as it is a completely isolated basin in the foothills of the Cascade Range about 30 miles from Portland that gets 130 inches of precipitation a year—more than three times Portland's total.

But distance also makes the supply vulnerable because it is delivered by pipe, and that could be subject to natural disasters and/or sabotage. Portland found a backup supply deep beneath eastern Multnomah County near the

---

This page: Simon Benson paid for the distinctive Benson Bubbler drinking fountains found throughout downtown Portland in hopes his workers would quench their thirst with water instead of at the many saloons in the city. **Opposite page:** This is one of the historic and picturesque reservoirs on Mt. Tabor that temporarily stores Portland's drinking water before gravity feeds mains and pipes to homes.

■ Quilt information on page 38

Pieces of Portland

Columbia River, and drilled wells that came on line in 1984. Some of the water in the aquifer is 40,000 years old.

The remaining vulnerable parts of the water delivery system are open reservoirs that store water at higher points in the city. The federal government has ordered Portland to cover the reservoirs or be forced to put in an enormously expensive filtration plant. After much back and forth, Portland officials have finally agreed. But some who live around the Mt. Tabor reservoirs and enjoy the park don't want that to happen and have vowed to continued to fight it. One person has raised the spectre of radon in enclosed concrete. Is that really a thing?

In the meantime, we gained international notoriety when the city emptied and cleaned one of the reservoirs after a security camera caught an 18-year-old man peeing in it. Alcohol was suspected to be involved. He later claimed he had actually urinated on the wall of the reservoir and said he was really pissed off about all the attention he was getting. He pointed out that birds pee in the water all the time and sometimes die there. And there's no flushing then. Personally, I was a lot more saddened and disturbed by the presence of a human corpse in the reservoir a few years ago, when a man chose to end his life by drowning there. Yes, that water was flushed, too.

Portland has constructed a massive underground storage tank within another volcanic butte a few miles from Mt. Tabor. Portlanders may never grow weary of the poop and pee and dead bodies, human and otherwise, in their water and don't want the covering to commence, but the City Council overruled them.

In the summer of 2014, a city-wide boil alert was issued when *e coli* showed up in test samples. Reservoirs were taken off line, flushed and cleaned and the nasty bugs were gone.

The city has laid out three options for the future of the reservoirs once they are taken off line and is collecting input from the public:

1. disconnect but keep water in them
2. disconnect and drain them, leaving large, empty bowls
3. disconnect and create a bunch of new water features.

Sometimes I wish government entities wouldn't eliminate ideas that aren't their favored options before the public is invited in. Like what if one of the empty bowls was kept as a little lake like it is now, another was turned it into the sickest skatepark on the planet, another was allowed to become a public art space, and we watch what happens to the canvas over time? C'mon now! I'm a granny and I'm asking these questions, so imagine how the young people feel. Or was I just born too soon? Or too late?

In any case, at this point it seems like disconnecting is going to happen. But then again, I wouldn't bet the farm on it.

Portlanders are pretty much determined that their Bull Run wild and free.

Pieces
of
Portland

Page 25

This is a detail from a quilt on page 170.

Page 31

Plank Road

Pieced and quilted by Marie Deatherage

I used Kaffe Fassett Collective fabrics in this quilt using the "Diagonal Brick" pattern by Judy Baldwin in Kaffe Fassett's book *Quilt Grandeur*. I got into orange leaning into purple that week. It's interesting to see the effect of fabrics that blend one into the other rather than contrasting colors. I'll probably make another in this pattern, it was fun!

Page 32

City Blocks

Pieced by Marie Deatherage; quilted by Nancy Stovall, Just Quilting

This is based on Cherri House's "City Green" pattern in her book *City Quilts*. I was so taken with her quilt that I tried to pick some of the same colors of Kona cottons, including shades of green, yellow, blue and a little purple. I put them together kinda randomly. I'm really quite drawn to the way the small blocks are dramatically set apart and stand out because of the little dark grey strips in between. Lots and lots of cutting and sewing... glad to be done. This pattern shows how striking simple can be.

Page 34

'September Garden'

Pieced by Joyce Brekke; quilted by Steve Ross

Pattern is "Sky Blue Pink" by Kaffe Fassett in Kaffe Fassett's *Caravan of Quilts*, uses many Kaffe Fassett Collective fabrics.

Page 35

Settlement Patterns

Pieced by Marie Deatherage; quilted by Pat Roche, Pat's Just Quilting

I was so taken with Malka Dubrowsky's Stitch in Color fabric that I bought it with no earthly idea what I would do with it. I love her use of bold color and graphics. This quilt (no pattern) was inspired by thinking about differences among neighborhoods, how some neighborhoods are walled and very private, protecting the residents by shutting out the rest of the world. They can feel somewhat staid and boring. Meanwhile, neighborhoods with smaller blocks, without walls, seem a little chaotic but more alive and interesting. It probably came from my geographer brain.

Page 37

Cool Clear Water

Pieced by Marie Deatherage; quilted by Nancy Stovall, Just Quilting PDX

This quilt started with a cloth napkin that caught my eye. I think its possibilities were inspired by Roberta Horton's "Brick Bracket Medallion Quilt" in Kaffe Fassett's *Quilts in the Sun*. I started adding strips of Kaffe Fassett Collective fabrics around the napkin to set it off. There's something about these colors that really soothes my soul, kind of like I feel when I drink a tall glass of cool clear water. And that is my very drinking water in the reservoir behind the quilt.

> Some of the quilts in this book are available for purchase from quiltlandia.com

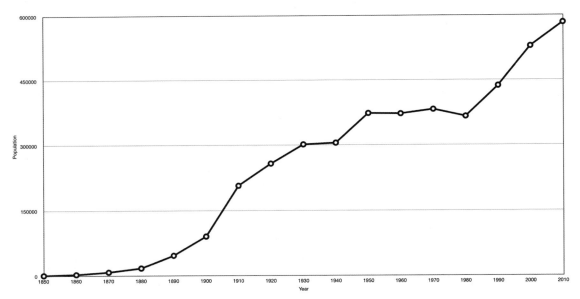

Portland Population 1850-2010

Graph by Jsayre64 (Own work) [Public domain], via Wikimedia Commons

Pieces
of
Portland

CONSEQUENCES

This page: The 2014 Big Float drew hundreds of participants, with a wide variety of kinds and sizes of flotation devices. And tutus. Opposite page: Tanner Creek re-emerges in Tanner Springs Park in the Pearl District. It's one of the more interesting small parks in the city, and you just might spy a Great Blue Heron.

Quilt information on page 46.

Up a Creek, Who's Got the Paddle?

It's no fun to be little Debbie Downer amidst all this joyous celebration of our river, but we still have some troubled waters.

In 2000, the Environmental Protection Agency declared much of the Portland Harbor from the Broadway Bridge to the Columbia Slough a Superfund site. Federal budget cuts are delaying its cleanup, which is projected to cost millions, if not more than a billion, and take years. Planning won't even start for several more years.

Toxic industrial waste was dumped in the river for more than a century. According to the EPA, "Water and sediments along Portland Harbor are contaminated with many hazardous substances, including heavy metals, polychlorinated biphenyls (PCBs), polynuclear aromatic hydrocarbons (PAH), dioxin, and pesticides. These compounds have been found to be harmful to human health and the environment. Because of the contamination, some types of fish found in Portland Harbor, such as bass, carp and catfish currently pose a health risk to those who eat them." This is why we can't have nice things.

The EPA expects responsible parties to pay for any cleanup their activities require. That would be awesome and the legal and ethical thing to do, and I hope they're actually held accountable. In the meantime, I noticed a line item on my water bill that reads "Portland Harbor Superfund," explained as "funding the city's required participation in the ongoing federal Superfund investigation into historic pollution of the Willamette River."

In the meantime, it's no surprise that all river events like the Big Float take place far upstream.

Returning to the sunny side of the creek, Portland has come to better terms with some of the streams that ran over the land in the early days. Tanner Creek (named after the tannery built beside it in 1845) used to flow from springs in the West Hills down into wetlands at the edge of the Willamette. As the city's population grew in the last part of the 19th and early 20th centuries, the wetlands were filled and Tanner Creek was piped and rerouted underground.

The buried part of Tanner Creek is as much as 50 feet below the surface, though it flows only seven feet below the Timbers Army section of our frequently renamed soccer stadium (known as Providence Park in 2015). In fact, it is said that the seats in some sections dip because of a former collapse in the underground system.

Both the stadium and the Goose Hollow Max station pay tribute to the glory of Tanner Creek, and I'm told that if you listen really closely, you can hear the water rushing underground from manholes at the Max station. Please try this and report back.

As Portland has been mending its ways, it created Tanner Springs Park, a block about 20 feet above what had been the surface of Couch Lake wetland in the Pearl District. The water in the park is from Tanner Creek.

Other cities have tanning beds. We have tanning water.

Sh*t Happens

Early in the city's history, Portland troughed its waste products downhill directly into the Willamette River. Things like human and industrial waste, for example. As the city grew, it piped the waste underground and developed it into a sewer system of pipes that has now grown to close to 2,500 miles long, ranging in diameter from four to 144 inches.

Whoever in the latter half of the 19th century decided that Portland's sewerage system should be combined (carrying both storm water runoff and unsanitary waste) created a messy problem for Portland. Because it rains a lot here, pipes carrying the combined load were often overwhelmed, so raw sewage poured directly into the Willamette River and Columbia Slough dozens of times a year. Like whenever it rained more than one-tenth of an inch within 24 hours. Do the math.

The large outlet pipes were always identifiable from a distance by the flocks of seagulls feeding there. Yuck.

Portland finally took a huge step toward fixing the problem with the Big Pipe project, spending $1.4 billion to install pipes gigantic enough to hold the combined wastewater and storm runoff so it could all be piped and pumped (by 96 pump stations) to a treatment plant near the Columbia Slough in northeast Portland. And the pipe is certainly big at 22 feet in diameter. You can get an up-close feel for its size by walking through the Big Pipe Portal sculpture that Ean Eldred created near the east side pumping station on Swan Island at the entrance to the North Portland Greenway Trail.

Mind you, there are still a few times a year that even the Big Pipe can't handle all the volume, and overflows happen. But one whole heck of a lot less often than before.

Our sewer bills have increased by nearly 43 percent over the last 10 years, as a result. With more to come, I'm sure.

Now the city has embarked on a Pipe Rehab program to replace the worst of the more than 2,200 miles of aging water pipes beneath our streets before they fail. Many are approaching the end of their lifespan. So money's still too tight to mention.

But the most talked about Portland waste issue in recent years is the Portland Loo. The brainchild of former City Commissioner Randy Leonard, the Loo is a public toilet with a patented design that "addresses the needs of the masses to relieve themselves, while making forward thinking efforts to curb the crime that accompanies so many public bathrooms."

Portland now has seven Loos, all located downtown, from the Pearl District's Field Park in the north to the South Park blocks near Portland State University.

Portland hoped its Loos would generate income by selling units to other cities. As of 2014, four units had been sold to cities in Alaska and Canada, and five more have been ordered.

Among its selling points, the Portland Loo promises to offer accessibility (large enough for wheelchairs, strollers and even bicycles), easy cleaning and maintenance (rust resistant fixtures, anti-graffiti surface), energy efficiency (solar powered) and economy ($90,000 is said to be a fraction of the cost of other stand-alone models). It claims to solve the crime problem by putting the handwashing station outside to discourage "loitering" and designing the bottom with louvered slats so the occupant has privacy but his or her or their feet are always in view.

I believe many of us appreciate the Portland Loos. Actually, considering how long we had to wait for the pictured Loo to empty so Joyce could photograph it, I would say multitudes of us love the Loos.

In 2014, a Multnomah County judge found that Portland misspent $618,000 of Water Bureau funds on the Loo project. Soon afterward, the City handed over marketing and selling of the Loos to the company that manufactures them, reducing the City's ongoing annual cost by about $60,000. The agreement preserves an eight percent royalty on sales—or about $7,200 per unit at its present price—for the City.

Many in Portland remain optimistic about the future of Portland's "unique solution to a universal problem." Soon after the Loo arrived in Victoria, Canada, it was named "The Best Public Restroom in Canada." Doesn't it suck that you have to leave town to be appreciated sometimes?

But maybe it's only a matter of time before demand for the Portland Loo explodes and royalties begin dropping a serious load on Portland's bottom line.

Portland is also home to an international organization called PHLUSH, which stands for Public Hygiene Lets Us Stay Human. This volunteer group works to protect toilet rights across the world and in Portland. It publishes a newsletter (*Pee, Poo and You*) and participates in World Toilet Day and the World Toilet Summit. Perhaps its most immediate value is the Portland Public Toilet Locator on its website.

For the rest of the world, there's an app for that. It's called Sit or Squat.

You're invited to contribute to its growing data pile.

Opposite page: The Portland Loo, our city's innovative and unique solution to a universal problem. **This page:** A sculpture that shows just how big a 22-foot-diameter sewer pipe is, with enough room to carry Portland's combined sewage and storm runoff except during biggest rainstorms.

■ Quilt information on page 46.

Pieces of Portland

Everybody knows you can't have good fauna without good flora. And Portland has a plethora of plants. Not to mention more garden clubs than any other city in the U.S.

Portland is a gardening paradise. Its long growing season (average 236 days, but frequently longer) and plentiful moisture create a most favorable environment for flora. We're technically in Zone 8, but many (including both Joyce and me) can't keep ourselves from pushing the limit. And sheltered areas can add another zone of safety.

It is impossible to keep things from growing in Portland. Turn your back and plants take over. That was visible in the primeval forest that covered the hills and valleys west of the Cascade Range before humans came to northwestern North America. Willow, cottonwood, maple, ash and alder grew along the streams, and western hemlock, Douglas Fir and red cedar were plentiful in forests, with scattered oak and pine. There are some remaining remnants of that original forest, even inside the city's Forest Park.

But today rampant plant growth is best seen in the invasion of native habitat by introduced species. English ivy is choking out trees in the forests of the West Hills, for example. Purple loosestrife and reed canary grass are crowding wetlands at Oaks Bottom and Wapato Lake on Sauvie Island. Wapato (or Wapatoo), the Chinook word for "tuberous plant," was a staple for indigenous people living along the Columbia River, who say it was here "before the salmon came to the Columbia."

Later in these pages, we'll meet a few notable gardens and gardeners in Portland. But first we must acknowledge how many people and groups are needed to remove invasive plants and restore the native flora and its ecosystem.

Probably the best known plant predator group is the "No Ivy League," now a program of Portland Parks and Recreation Department. The league has been at work removing English Ivy from forests in Portland since 1994. And it has piled up some impressive stats:

- Work sites visited: 118
- Total site visits across all sites: 1,803
- Workers and volunteers involved: 25,377
- Ivy removal work hours logged: 88,537
- Full lifesavers performed: 16,784 trees
- Lifesavers and girdles performed: 11,472 trees
- Square feet of ground ivy removed: 4,504,905
- Acres of ground ivy removed: 103.42

To prevent more yard dwellers from escaping to run wild in the woods, several organizations help Portlanders preserve and protect the native ecosystem (native plants and the species of fauna they support because they evolved together).

Audubon Society of Portland has a wildlife habitat certification program with silver, gold and platinum levels and resources to help homeowners achieve them. Its website has a gallery of example yards to provide inspiration.

The Native Plant Society of Oregon has a Portland chapter, whose members inventory plants and remove invasive species.

The earliest white settlers brought plants from their native land with them, especially fruit trees at first. By 1850 at least one local nursery had introduced ornamental plants as well, and before long, Portlanders were planting pleasure gardens. By the 1870s, bamboo and gingko native to Asia were available locally. The Lewis and Clark Exposition introduced Portland to South American species like the monkey puzzle tree.

A survey in the 1970s by Portland's first urban forester found that less than five percent of Portland street trees are native species. There were 29 species of native trees in pre-urban Portland, and now there are more than 130 species—a 450% increase in diversity from trees introduced from other areas.

But diversity does not necessarily imply ecosystem health. In the city, dead or decaying trees are removed, which means they don't reintroduce nutrients into the soil or support bugs and slugs and all the other things that crawl that feed the birds that pollinate the plants that spread their seeds and live with the other animals in perfect harmony. In the house that Jack built.

The urban forest has a discontinuous canopy, so some species' habitats are gone. An urban forest has more numbers and species of flowering trees and fruiting species, attracting certain birds and insects, but not necessarily native ones. The native forest had a series of vertical zones—upper canopy, middle canopy, shrub and ground cover. The city forest has canopy and ground cover, but most of the middle layer species are gone.

Oregon is the leading state in the U.S. in nursery production of shade and flowering trees, which means we now grow many species from other places because most of them grow better here than where they came from.

That's why you never want to turn your back on a plant. You are encouraged to trust the people, but not the introduced plants.

Opposite page: The photo on the left shows English ivy vines crawling up native trees in the West Hills. If you look closely at the photo on the bottom right, you'll see a lonely wapato that's made its way through the purple loosestrife covering Wapato Lake on Sauvie Island. **This page:** the photo shows a panorama of Wapato Lake on Sauvie Island. It used to have wapato as far as the eye could see, but now it's mostly covered in invasive species like purple loosestrife and reed canary grass. Major bummer.

■ Quilt information on page 46.

Pieces
of
Portland

Index to Quilts

About the quilt on this page, below.
Mother and Child
Pieced and quilted by Marie Deatherage

Several years ago, we were watching HGTV and saw a house that had a model replica bird house out front. My husband is an Internet shopping sleuth (his motto is "Where do I click?"), so he tracked down who made it, ordered one and put it on a post. I decided they both needed quilts to round out the look. You can't actually see much of the house, probably because Parker Sanderson proclaimed me a "plant whore."

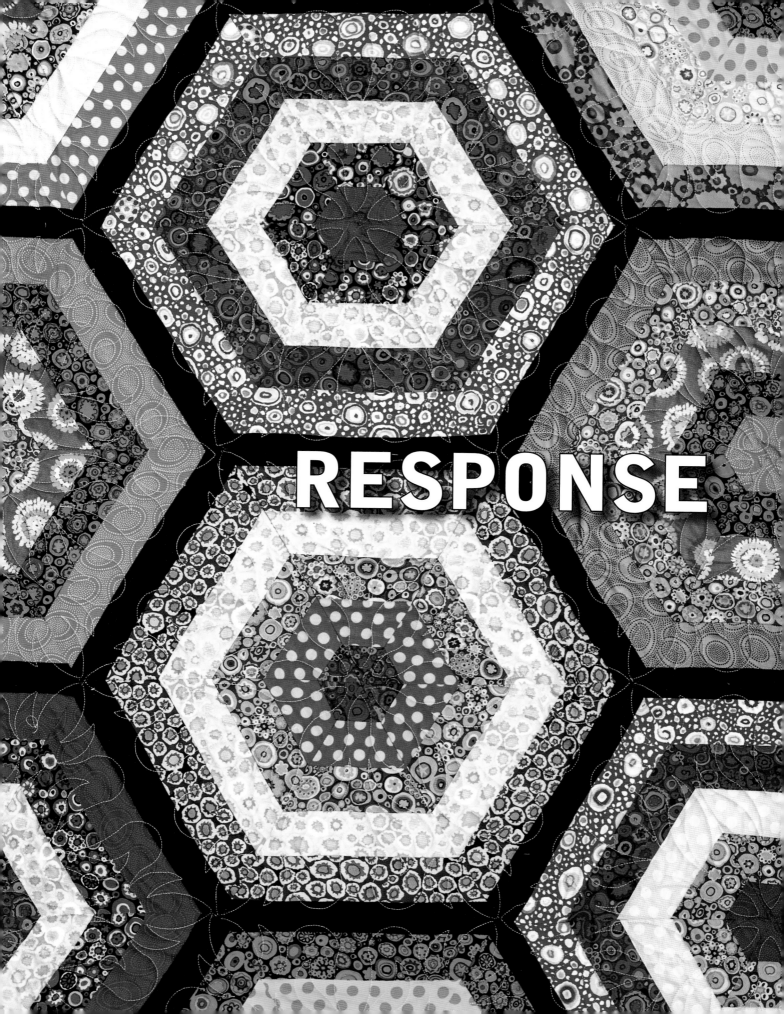

RESPONSE

Put a Bird On It!

Many people have used the intelligence, imagination and cooperation called for by Lewis Mumford to be good enough to have this country in their possession. None more so than Mike Houck, Portland's first urban naturalist, most acclaimed environmentalist and favorite bird whisperer (and whistler).

Mike was born in Portland but moved to several other places across the country as a Navy brat before settling in Estacada, a logging town 30 miles east of Portland near the Mt. Hood National Forest, in high school. He went to Iowa State University on a track scholarship (he ran a 4:06:2 mile), then studied biology in graduate school at Portland State University.

Along the way he directed field programs and a research center for OMSI and taught high school biology before being hired by Portland Audubon Society in 1980. In 1999, he founded the Urban Greenspaces Institute to "promote the integration of urban green infrastructure—parks, trails, streams and wetlands, fish and wildlife habitat, urban forest canopy, and greenspaces—with the built environment."

Mike's combination of knowledge, insight, selflessness, chutzpa, charisma and relentless doggedness was instrumental in saving Oaks Bottom as Portland's first wildlife refuge and convincing Portland to adopt a city bird.

Portland Park Bureau planned to fill the city's largest wetland into a combination theme park, sport fields, motocross course and a giant marina with boat docks. Despite conservation efforts in the 1960s, the bottoms had already begun to be destroyed when things came to a head in the 1970s.

Though it seems unlikely now, Portland's Park Bureau did not welcome interference from Mike and other activists. So Mike decided to take some guerrilla action. "I knew Oregon Department of Fish and Wildlife had large yellow signs with 'Wildlife Refuge' printed in impossible-to-miss black text," Mike remembers. "I asked for 40 signs and cut off any markings that could be traced to the agency and spray painted 'City Park' using a hand-made stencil on the bottom of the signs."

"Jimbo Beckmann and I took a tall ladder, nails, a hammer and a fifth of Jim Beam and posted all 40 signs around the perimeter of the Bottoms, high enough that no one could remove them. Within a couple weeks *The Oregonian* began referring to Oaks Bottom Wildlife Refuge in stories related to the area. It was only a matter of time until Oaks Bottom was called a wildlife refuge by local residents, other media and refuge advocates."

Mike also helped form the "Bottom Watchers" group that rallied to preserve the wetland.

After the successful Oaks Bottom preservation efforts, momentum in city bureaus shifted entirely from a development-oriented future to a preservation and restoration model. Presently, the Parks Bureau has a City Nature Division, and natural areas have the same status as recreation facilities.

Mike also led efforts to get a 50 by 70-foot mural of a Great Blue Heron painted on the west wall of the Portland Memorial Mausoleum overlooking the wetland in 1991. Other birds have been added to what is now the largest hand painted mural on a building in North America.

At the same time, Mike led work to get Portland to adopt the Great Blue Heron as the official city bird in 1986. Now, Portland's City government even has an official bird agenda.

Every May, Portland celebrates the Great Blue Heron as an icon of integrating built and natural environments in Portland. These huge birds—with a wingspan of almost six feet—have a nesting colony on what's left of Ross Island and can be seen about town swooping down on backyard koi ponds. Including mine.

It's also common to see bald eagles, osprey and other birds of prey around Portland, especially in and near wetlands. Because the city is along the Pacific flyway, many migrating birds pass through and in 2003, Portland was the fifth city in the nation selected as a pilot city for the Urban Conservation Treaty for Migratory Birds.

No wonder we put a bird on everything!

But get this: Every year, Portland's urban naturalist par excellence—who has made enormous contributions to the city, enormous personal sacrifices and done as much as any single individual to get Portland on all the Best of and Most and Favorite lists and national/international recognition—constantly faces the challenge of funding his work. Way too much of his time is taken seeking funding for his next year. Ain't nobody got time for that! Although he has no plans to retire anytime soon, eventually the financial challenges will make any retirement moot.

I wonder what Lewis Mumford would think and say about that?

Opposite page: Mike Houck, Portland's urban naturalist, led the movement to save Oaks Bottom Wildlife Refuge and frequently visits to check on its welfare. **This page:** Mike was also instrumental in raising money and for the initial design for the murals on the nearby building. The murals were painted by father and son, Mark and Shane Bennett.

■ Quilt information on page 46.

Pieces of Portland

"I left my regular bone awl in the car," Peter Bauer apologizes as he works to connect the ends of a headband he has fashioned out of the bark of Himalayan blackberry, an invasive species that has overtaken so many spaces once held by native plants.

Peter is Portland's most passionate and outspoken rewilder, and his Rewild Portland organization works to actively create a rewilding community in Portland through earth-based arts, traditions and technologies.

He was drawn to rewilding after reading Daniel Quinn's *Ishmael* in high school. "The plight of the planet and the future survival of the human race felt very urgent—and still do today—so I dropped out of high school to do what I thought was more important: learn wilderness living skills." He intensely studied survival skills and got to the point he could do pretty well on for his own.

At the same time, he was becoming very adept at modern technology, especially creating digital videos and using the Internet. The two worlds—ancestral and modern—met in the form of Urban Scout, a character Peter created in summer 2003 that became an alter-ego and muse for the next few years, developing into a persona who blogged. A lot.

Maybe you saw Urban Scout in those days, hanging out downtown somewhere around Pioneer Square, in his loin cloth, using his bow drill to light cigarettes for people waiting for the bus.

Urban Scout's mission was to promote a culture of rewilding through the spread of ideas, mostly through a blog. In 2010, he published the book *Rewild or Die*, but by the time he did his book tour the following spring, Peter was growing a little weary of his muse.

"I had to get my own identity back," Peter explains, "and learn to interpret what Urban Scout says and filter it through my own head rather than just give him the reins. My heart just couldn't take it anymore. I'm a nice person and I want people to like me. I had to shut him up because his spirit is one of 'truth-speaking' and generally people don't want to hear the truth, especially when it comes from an angry sounding dude."

"Now that I don't give him total creative control, so to speak, I feel much happier and I've made a lot more headway in creating the kind of life I want to live."

Peter's long-term goal is to live—as closely as he can—a hunter/gatherer/gardener way of life and to inspire and help others to do the same. "We are creating a new culture," Peter says, "and that starts with building a bridge from this one to the next. I'm a bridge-keeper."

Some are surprised to find Peter using obnoxious invasive plants in his rewilding work, but it seems totally obvious when he explains it. "To me, the most resilient you can be is being able to get all the things you need for your mind, body, family, and culture, with your own hands, from your landbase, and all in a regenerative way."

And sadly, as we've seen, what could be more plentiful in the urban land base but invasive species?

Not long ago, Peter was surprised when he was hired by basket makers he considers his elders to teach them how to process blackberry bark into a wearable fiber. "It felt great to be able to give something back to them after learning so much from them."

"After spending an afternoon harvesting and processing blackberries, we were driving back to our meeting point and one of the students said, 'Oh, that's a good one!' She was pointing at a blackberry vine growing in an alley," Peter recalls. "This made my day. It exemplifies what I want to do: connect people to their landbase and the plants growing right here. None of them had used blackberries in that way, and now they were seeing them in a completely different light."

A lot of Peter's crafts use English ivy vines, removed from trees the vines are choking and girdling. We met up in Washington Park, where he and his wares sat on a quilt made by one of my own ancestors. I had no idea ivy could grow to such a massive size until Peter held up a section of trunk next to the basket he was making.

Why does he rewild in a city? "Cities are the most domesticated places on the planet and so need the most rewilding," he explains. "Humans will 'voluntarily' rewild when they have no other choice but death."

In the meantime, he says, those who feel oppressed by the dominant culture or have empathy for the planet and all of its species or have a lot of foresight are the ones who will rewild now.

The first three things (but certainly not the only things) Peter advises to begin rewilding are:

1. Learn and plant native plants.
2. Learn to identify, process and cook weeds.
3. Learn your ancestral way of life before civilization killed it.

Peter thinks that if he had been born in any other place, he wouldn't be the same person. "I didn't realize until I moved away that Portland was like The Shire (in Middle-earth). I grew up here. Every time I try to leave I realize just how shitty the rest of the country is." And he keeps coming back.

Personally, I'm very glad to hear this, because when the hammer comes down and it starts getting real, I'm looking for Peter. His survival skills that are honed for this environment will make him the last man standing.

Peter is working on a revision of Urban Scout's *Rewild or Die*. Its title shows that Peter really is speaking for himself these days.

It's called *Rewild and Live.*

Opposite page: The two sides of Peter Bauer. In the top photo, Urban Scout warns of the impending end of civilization in earlier *Rewild or Die* years. Below, he's a kinder and gentler rewilder helping Portland *Rewild and Live,* using ancestral tools and skills to turn invasive species into useful things. The piece of trunk he holds shows the breathtaking size of the ivy plants running rampant in forests of the West Hills. **This page:** Peter works on an ivy basket while surrounded by many items he's made from local plants, roadkill and other found resources.

■ Quilt information on page 62.

Pieces of Portland

Park It Here

Portland has killer parks. I'm sure you've noticed. It didn't hurt that we had the likes of the Olmsted Brothers planning and designing some of them. And they are so varied! Our city park system has been proclaimed one of the best in America and is one of the things residents report liking most about the city. About 80% of Portlanders live within a half mile of a park, and more than 16% of Portland's city area is parkland. The city is working on creating spaces for the 20% not close to a park, but we have a ways to go. Here's a sample of several different kinds of parks, clockwise starting from top left:

- **Top left:** Washington Park Rose Garden, a formal international test garden established to protect European roses threatened by WWI destruction.
- **Top right:** Mt. Tabor park, a large park with significant landform features that include natural areas prized for their views, like the one looking toward the Portland skyline.
- **Bottom right:** The worlds smallest park—Mill Ends Park—inside a traffic circle on a major thoroughfare.
- **Bottom middle:** Laurelhurst Park has majestic trees and fresh green glades that remind me of the *Avatar* setting.
- **Bottom left:** Cathedral Park relates to the built environment, under the St. Johns Bridge, home to many community events from a Jazz Festival to the Trek in the Park Star Trek celebration.

■ Quilt information on page 62.

53

Pieces
of
Portland

Other Worlds Are in Us

Maybe you've noticed that a considerable number of our parks are gardens. What else would you expect in a gardening paradise?

Gardens are a way Portland meets and gets to know other cultures worlds away.

Take the Japanese Garden, for instance. In 1958, Portland became a sister city to Sapporo, Japan. A growing interest in Japanese culture followed, and city leaders decided it would be wonderful for Portland to have a traditional Japanese garden.

The City leased 5.5 acres of Washington Park to the Japanese Garden Society, which raised funds for the undertaking. Professor Takuma Tono, one of the most important Japanese landscape architects of his time, designed the garden, which opened in 1967. Japanese ambassador to the U.S. Nobuo Matsunaga said, "I believe this garden to be the most authentic Japanese garden, including those in Japan." Seriously?

Several decades later—again following a sister city relationship, this time with Suzhou, China—Portland got a Chinese garden. After all, Suzhou is the Garden City of China, which is the mother of all gardens.

Lan Su, or Garden of Awakening Orchids, was built by artisans from Suzhou who were here for nine months, using the traditional tools and techniques from the Ming Dynasty (14th through 17th centuries). While it was being built, I walked by from time to time, watching them at work, meticulously choosing a pebble at a time to place in a courtyard or placing elaborate wooden structures joined without nails or screws.

Lan Su opened in 2000, occupying a city block in Old Town. Lan Su Garden is based on gardens in Suzhou that were the homes of Chinese officials and scholars, with a design meant to honor and nurture the *qi* that flows through all things and awaken all our senses. In addition to plants, Chinese gardens integrate large beautifully eroded rocks (ours are from Lake Tai west of Suzhou), buildings and other structures, along with calligraphy of significant

quotes (e.g., "Listen to the Fragrance") and poetry. Every single thing has great meaning, which is one reason visitors discover something new every time they return. It's never twice the same.

For example, inscribed on a panel in the "Flowers Bathing in Spring Rain Pavilion" is a poem that tells it like it is:

> *Most cherished in this mundane world is a place without traffic;*
> *Truly in the midst of the city there can be mountain and forest.*

And sometimes that's exactly what we need.

Opposite page: A quilt accompanies the three friends in winter (pine, bamboo and plum) featured just outside the front gate of Lan Su Chinese Garden in Old Town in northwest Portland. **This page:** A quilt draped over a rock mirrors the Japanese maple in brilliant fall color at Portland's Japanese Garden. Visitors go to both gardens in search of tranquility within the city. Both gardens reflect the important trade and cultural connections between Portland and Asia, including sister cities in Sapporo, Japan, and Suzhou, China.

■ Quilt information on page 62.

Rose City

Portland has ideal conditions for growing roses, weather-wise and soil-wise. It's only natural we are known as the City of Roses. Our biggest civic celebration is the Portland Rose Festival, which began in 1907, and is probably best known for its Grand Floral Parade, where everything is made out of plant parts, presumably including tons of rose petals. I'm actually not sure because, would you believe, I have never been to a single Grand Floral Parade? I've been to the Junior Parade and lots of Starlight Parades and Runs, though. Is that too weird?

Early white settlers brought rose cuttings with them to plant beside their new homes. The first rose in Oregon Territory is reported to have been a wedding gift for missionary Jason Lee's wife in 1837.

Roses began to be an official thing in Portland in 1888, when a prominent woman invited her friends and neighbors to display their roses in a tent set up in her garden. The next year the Portland Rose Society was formed, and the rest is history.

By 1905, rose bushes had been planted along more than 200 miles of Portland streets, thanks to a campaign to rosify the city for the Lewis and Clark Exposition.

Few of these rows upon rows remain in parking strips, however, as they were thorns in the sides of people exiting the passenger side of cars. Literally.

Local attorney Frederick V. Holman was on a mission to brand Portland the Rose City, as it had not yet developed an emblematic nickname. The case he presented—reported by local writer Christen McCurdy in the Summer 2014 issue of *Oregon Humanities* magazine—is rather, uh, astonishing: "The rose is the flower of the dominant white races of the world, and it has been from the beginning. It is interwoven with their traditions. It is in their poems and songs from the beginning of civilization."

Please don't let that be why Portland decided to be Rose City.

In 1915 Jesse A. Currey, rose hobbyist and author of a gardening column in the *Oregon Journal*, convinced city officials to create a rose test garden to serve as a safe haven during World War I for hybrid roses grown in Europe. Rose lovers feared that these unique plants would be destroyed in the bombings.

In 1924, Portland dedicated its International Rose Test Garden, which has 7,000 bushes of 550 varieties of roses. It's still found at the center of Washington Park within a series of other gardens, art installations and facilities.

Portland has a number of other rose gardens, including ones in Peninsula Park and Ladd's Addition. And the rose continues to be a favorite among Portland's gardeners. Although I confess I look at mine a bit differently after knowing about the "white dominant race" thing.

But it's not the rose's fault. Clearly, their perfection here exceeds that of the humans who plant and grow them.

Both pages: The International Test Rose Garden in Washington Park is a place of popularity and pride in Portland and one of the most photographed. And sometimes it's hard to tell the real flowers from those in a quilt.
■ Quilt information on page 62.

Pieces
of
Portland

The Day Everything Changed

Portland clearly established its credentials as a city that would go against the grain during the 1970s, electing young maverick Neil Goldschmidt as mayor in 1972, who supported what many viewed as counterculture ideas, like dropping plans to build a freeway from downtown though southeast Portland neighborhoods to the eastern suburbs, spending money on public transit instead. But to me it still felt like the old guard was standing by behind the scenes, ready to snatch back power at any moment.

So when Neil Goldschmidt left Portland to become President Carter's Transportation Secretary in 1979, I was pretty worried for Portland's future. Then in 1980, Frank Ivancie was elected mayor. In his campaign, he put up billboards in outer southeast Portland that read, "If Frank Ivancie were mayor, you would be home now." (Suggesting that the freeway bulldozing a wide swath through southeast Portland neighborhoods was still on the table.) What a slap in the face. The fact that he won the 1980 election told me that a substantial part of Portland was not like me and the people who thought like I did. Which was pretty much everybody I knew. It felt like the city wasn't ours anymore.

> ## Bud Clark was eccentric even by our standards. He wore lederhosen, yelled 'whoop whoop' while commuting on his bike.

I confess that I was one of those who viewed Ivancie as the epitome of moneyed interests that were accustomed to running the city. It didn't help that he just seemed so rigid and uptight—like he had a pole up his butt. I think his 1980 victory shook progressive Portland, but we weren't sure how to deal with it. Before the 1984 mayoral election, it took a long time for an opponent to emerge to oppose Frank. I guess most people figured the incumbent would win, so just let it go. That view was reinforced when the opponent who finally emerged for the May primary turned out to be someone most people had never heard of—Bud Clark—who media referred to as a tavern owner with no political experience.

"In 1983 I was asked by several people to run," Bud Clark remembers now, "but my first thought was, 'Who in the world would want that job?!' But when it looked like Ivancie was going to run unopposed, I decided I would do it. I remember it was December 28th. There was an ice storm as bad or worse than any previous storm. I announced I was running and promised the city there would be no ice storms when I was mayor. And there weren't!" He throws his head back and out comes his infectious laugh.

I think a lot of people, including me, had thought his candidacy was a lost cause. When it was first announced, I didn't know what to think. The guy who owned and ran the Goose Hollow Inn? Couldn't we find someone who would be taken seriously?

Then one evening I participated in a focus group convened by a local news station testing out potential advertising campaigns. The guy who sat across the table from me had a Bud Clark button on the lapel of his jacket. When I asked him about Bud, he told me how smart he was, how much he cared about people, how he recognized the importance of neighborhoods in Portland, how his life and business experience made him such a good fit for mayor, how much he believed in him, enough to devote himself to working for the campaign. Wow, I thought, maybe I should get behind this guy after all!

It turned out Bud Clark had become a neighborhood activist upon seeing the effect of urban renewal in the South Auditorium site. According to *Oregon Encyclopedia*, the South Portland/South Auditorium displaced some 2,700 people—including many low income, elderly and minority residents—along with 141 businesses, including several labor union offices, 17 hotels and rooming houses, six taverns, and so forth. One of the taverns belonged to Bud Clark. "We fought it but weren't successful. It got me interested in neighborhoods coming together to fight City Hall. When the city came to impose urban renewal on the Northwest neighborhood where I lived, I joined the neighborhood association."

At one point during the campaign, Bud told a story about how his neighborhood had tried to have a Recycle Sunday block party and City Hall was making them go through all kinds of red tape. In describing the Kafkaesque ridiculousness of it, he said, "So we finally gave up and just parked a truck across the end of the street." He had me. Now I got it: we actually had the opportunity to elect a real person. Someone who knew what living in the city and being part of a neighborhood and making things work meant. And I learned he had been delivering meals for Meals on Wheels for more than a decade and had started a neighborhood newspaper.

I don't mean to reduce all my and our thinking to a couple of small anecdotes, but OMG, what a refreshing change! He was someone who was comfortable in his own skin. We could trust him. He wasn't going to make a bunch of empty promises, then go right back to standard operating procedure. Hell, he didn't even know standard operating procedure!

Now pay attention here, people. This is a key moment in Portland history, and I think it's precisely when Portland permanently pivoted in the direction it's been going ever since.

Because not only did Portland elect Bud Clark mayor. We did it in the primary, when he got a majority of the votes (54.6%, 13 points ahead of Ivancie), which meant there wouldn't even be a runoff in the fall election. Holy epic smackdown! Think about it. That's pretty unexpected. Brave even. Risky maybe. And weird!

What city does that??

I cannot begin to describe the joy in the city that night and the next day. It was pretty much a coming of age moment for Portland. Bud Clark was not only a tavern owner who had never run for anything, he was eccentric even by Portland standards. He lived in a big old house in funky (at that time) northwest Portland, he got around town by bike, he wore lederhosen, he had a flamboyant mustache, he was the poster child for supporting the arts when he posed as a flasher in front of a nude statue on the transit mall, he had described himself as a born-again pagan, and he was so gregarious that he yelled out "whoop, whoop" frequently.

"I wasn't really surprised when I won," Bud says. "I had so many volunteers going door to door, it was a grassroots thing. I took out a $50,000 loan against my house for ads, otherwise it was

just person-to-person. We held coffees in houses all over the city, I asked people what their issues were, and their concerns made my platform."

"Frank Ivancie didn't take me seriously," Bud continues. "He didn't know he was in trouble until we were in the St. John's parade a few days before the primary. He was at the head of the parade and the crowd booed him, but when I came by, they cheered me. His campaign put out a very negative ad about me the next day, (characterizing Bud as 'someone who considers that it might be fun to be mayor, someone without credit, without a belief in God'), but it worked against them."

It made perfect sense that Bud Clark was seen out on the Willamette River in the center of the city the morning after the election, standing in his canoe, paddling with his pole, slowly making his way through the city. Making much better use of a pole than Frank Ivancie ever had.

The celebratory feeling led to the Mayor's Ball after his inauguration, whose story was memorialized by one of its founders, the late musician Billy Hults. Held all eight years while he was in office, the Mayor's Ball became a ginormous night of music at the biggest venue in town at the time, Memorial Coliseum. One year

This page: Bud Clark reunites with Kvinneakt, the statue by Norman J. Taylor on the downtown transit mall he famously flashed for the "Expose Yourself to Art" poster. It was an early sign that Portland is weird and has a zany sense of humor. We wonder if she prefers sharing a colorful and cheerful quilty moment with the former mayor over seeing inside his trench coat. ■ Quilt information on page 62.

Pieces
of
Portland

it made the *Guinness Book of World Records* for most bands under one roof in one night: 88 bands on eight stages in eight hours. And it raised $375,000 for charity over the years.

"Winning in the May primary gave me several months to prepare for office and advertise Portland," Bud says. "We were working against how some interpreted Governor Tom McCall's message to visit but not stay in Oregon. Going on Johnny Carson's 'Tonight Show,' I hoped to turn the perception of unwelcomeness around and put Portland 'back on the map' to bring visitors and businesses to the city and state."

"It also gave me time to study issues and possible solutions," he continues. "One of the first big things I took on was the convention center. We were deep in one of our worst recessions, and I saw it as a way to bring business to Portland. I was warned I was putting my head on the chopping block, but I did it anyway. And we were successful."

One of his biggest surprises was discovering the city only had $500,000 in reserves, when it had been $27 million when Ivancie took office. "And it shocked the hell out of me to see how bad the drug problem in Portland was. I went on a ride-along, and we had people stopping cars on the street to sell drugs, openly doing drug deals in public. On Mississippi Avenue there was a stretch where it was so bad there was only one retail business open (it's still there), otherwise it was industrial or boarded-up buildings. The police knew about it but said they couldn't do anything about it, so I asked 'What is the police department for then?' We went around the bureaucracy at the higher levels of the bureau and got the neighborhoods involved, and look at Mississippi Avenue now."

"We also started confiscating the cars of people with multiple driving violations who were still driving, then we started doing the same to johns in a crackdown on prostitution. Oh, what an outcry. Men love their cars more than their wives." Again his marvelous laugh.

In 1992, after he had been at the helm of the city for eight years, Portland was named the best-managed city of its size in the United States by AMCAC, an international insurer of cities. And the city had $20 million in reserves. Although there are plenty of enduring achievements from his years in office—from the first collective plan to address homelessness, to making community policing official police bureau policy, to developing and opening the Oregon Convention Center—there's something else his election and service meant and still means in Portland. We learned it was okay to trust our instincts. We could do what no other city our size would do, and it would be okay. Being ourselves was a good thing.

His election really showed us we could embrace our quirkiness. Being eccentric just made things more interesting. More fun. We still got our homework and chores done, and they didn't even feel like a burden when we made them fun. These are truths that are evident throughout our city and this book. In fact, it's that very spirit that fuels my decision to just be myself in writing this book, even though being myself is not what you might expect from a grownass woman.

Days after Bud took office in January 1985, a *New York Times* headline proclaimed that "Portland, Ore., has a new mayor and a new style." Yeah we sure did. And we've been headed in that direction ever since. How does Bud think the show *Portlandia* has affected Portland? "Well, we're moving forward at warp speed now," he says. "You know, back in 1985, after we got the Portlandia statue, I suggested to friends that the city change its name to Portlandia," he says, "but they said thumbs down. There are dozens of Portlands across the country and the world, but there would only be one Portlandia."

Well, actually, at this point it would be one of three Portlandias. There is the aforementioned IFC television series, of course, in its fifth season when this was written, with two more seasons on order. But first was sculptor Raymond Kaskey's statue, Portlandia. She is based on the female figure in the City's seal.

Portlandia is the second-largest hammered copper statue in the U.S., after the Statue of Liberty. She was built in sections in Maryland, shipped to Portland, then assembled in a barge-building facility. One Saturday morning in October 1985, the city's residents gathered on the streets to watch her be carried up the Willamette on a barge, then loaded onto an enormous truck that slowly made its way to the front of the Portland building, where she was placed on a platform above the entrance to welcome visitors.

Somehow it feels so very Portland as a place of contradictions to have this would-be famous statue remain understated and somewhat unknown because much of the time it's hard to find her through the trees. As we've already seen, trees win in Portland.

For years and years I have been puzzled about why it hasn't acquired the blue-green patina like the Statue of Liberty. When it arrived, it was such a shiny coppery color—just dazzling! Then it turned the brownish color it has been ever since.

Finally curiosity got the better of me, so I asked Keith Lachowicz, Public Art Collections Manager at the Regional Arts and Culture Council, the group charged with maintaining the sculpture. He explained that it's because Portlandia is not exposed to a big body of salt water like the Statue of Liberty, which is located in the middle of New York Harbor and "is bathed 24/7 in an environment with a high concentration of chloride salts."

"Ray Kaskey initially wanted Portlandia to be green like Lady Liberty," Keith explains, "but upon consultation with art conservators it was suggested that she would never develop an even green patina across the entire surface in Portland's environment. Some natural oxidation would probably cause her to only go green in places, but sections would remain brown permanently. So the decision to wax the sculpture's surface was made. Waxing bronze sculpture (which weathers very similarly to copper) is the traditional method of arresting oxidation. Waxing Portlandia would preserve an even patina, albeit a brown one, not a green one. Apparently Mr. Kaskey agreed that an even, brown finish was better than an uneven brown and green one."

Le sigh. That makes sense, I guess. But did the experts consider *all* options? Like could we get volunteers to bathe her 24/7 when it's not raining? Could we install sprayers like the produce departments in grocery stores? Could we put a moat around the Portland building or turn the streets into canals? Is it too late to crowdsource this question? Asking for a friend.

Oh, just one more thing. In our photo, is Portlandia reaching down to pick up the quilt to warm herself after a solid week of January rain, or is she is dropping it into the outstretched arms of someone who will spend the cold night on the streets with a bit more cover than usual? I guess it could go either way, but my heart totally tells me it's the latter.

Opposite page: Portland's iconic Portlandia statue, by sculptor Raymond Kaskey. ■ Quilt information on page 62.

Index to Quilts

Some of the quilts in this book are available for purchase from quiltlandia.com

The Coolest Picnic!

Pieced by Marie Deatherage; quilted by Nancy Stovall, Just Quilting PDX

This quilt was made from a single April Cornell layer cake. It seems to beg to be taken to a picnic. I just put half square triangles together, and in the end, made it look like the picnic quilt was going on a picnic. I tried to get the inventor of the Coolest Cooler (of record-setting Kickstarter campaign note) to pose for a photo, and it looked like it might actually happen, but in the end I think he is focusing on getting the cooler made and shipped to supporters. As he should be. Those of us who supported the campaign were invited to purchase tiny replicas of the cooler to give as teaser gifts. So that's what we used for the photo. I can't wait to get my real coolest cooler and picnic it.

Pieces
of
Portland

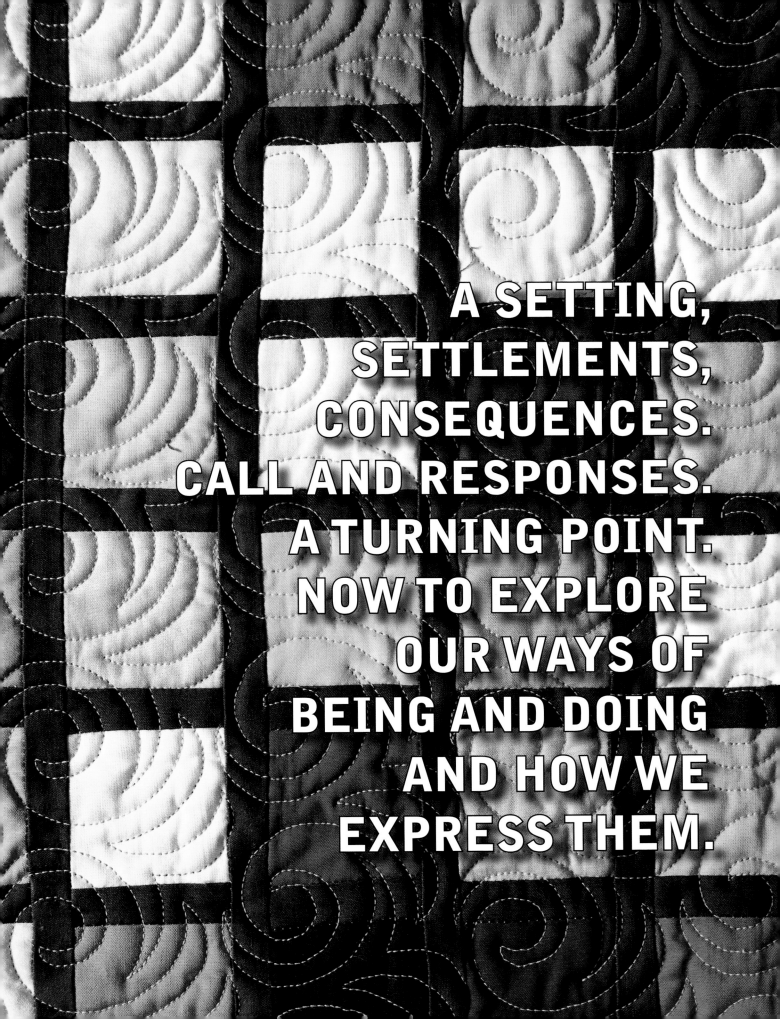

A SETTING,
SETTLEMENTS,
CONSEQUENCES.
CALL AND RESPONSES.
A TURNING POINT.
NOW TO EXPLORE
OUR WAYS OF
BEING AND DOING
AND HOW WE
EXPRESS THEM.

Ball Don't Lie

In the early decades of the City of Portland, the actual legal entity, I could find little evidence that newcomers were reading the landscape and seeking ways to honor it. Instead it seemed they were trying to turn the wilderness pastoral, by recreating what they left behind. Even the name Portland was chosen because Portland, Maine, was the hometown one of our city's early founders. Early plats looked a lot like New England towns and cities, with small blocks (20 per mile) and narrow streets built for pedestrians and muscle transport.

As Portland grew, it began to emulate what other big cities were doing. On one hand, this led to Portland's beautiful park system, partly designed by the legendary Olmsted Brothers.

But it also accounted for the city beginning to cater to auto-based living in the mid-20th century, when city dwellers escaped to the suburbs, where lots and blocks were much larger and even sidewalks weren't required, so one really had to go by car.

In the 1950s, 14 freeways were planned through and around Portland, carving deep gashes through its neighborhoods. That's how we came to have Interstate 5 that cut through the center of the city, I-405 near the West Hills that provided a way to avoid downtown, the Fremont Bridge that connected I-405 with I-5. Later, I-205 was built along the eastern edge of the city proper back then. It was first envisioned to run somewhere along 52nd Avenue, but was actually built near 92nd Avenue. Entire sections of downtown were removed and replaced through urban renewal.

And we could always hear the voice of the little underdog icon sitting on our shoulder, whispering in our ear, "Nobody knows you exist, they can't even pronounce the name of your state. They don't think there's anything between Seattle and California." If we were known at all in the mid-20th century, it was for having been eclipsed by Seattle early in the 20th century. Portland may have been asking itself, "Is being forgotten how we want to be remembered?"

Oregon exhibited a strong populist trend during the first century of its statehood, and many reforms that carried across the nation began here. There were some noteworthy attempts and acts to do the right thing to save our magnificent setting from the beginning. For example, Governor Oswald West led the state to establish a public highway along the entire coastline in 1913 (along with a public park every 10 miles or so) in order to establish the beach as public property. There had been cries to clean the Willamette River for decades, and it was no accident that it was the will of the people that made it happen.

I remember when a motel owner tried fencing off sections of sand at the coast when I was in high school, prompting the Oregon Beach Bill in 1967, which established that the public "has free and uninterrupted use of the beaches" up to the line of vegetation. The first time I visited another state's beach and saw parts fenced off, I couldn't believe my lying eyes. How could such a thing be tolerated? Another big step came with the passage of the bottle bill in 1971, when we decided to charge ourselves if that's what it took to clean the litter from our highways and byways. From then on my college classmates from all over the country stopped asking me if Oregon had indoor plumbing and started visualizing it as an unspoiled garden populated by fully enlightened people.

As a child, I remember overhearing some grownups say Oregon was becoming the laughingstock among the landed gentry, who believed all land should be available to them at a price for their personal profit and private projects, and that nobody from the world of financial shakers and makers would ever invest in such a state who followed these hippie, if not communist, ways. But at some point, we realized we could do without them and be brave enough to determine our own future, to depart from the herd, and create a world we actually wanted to live in.

So look who's laughing now.

We must never lose sight of what this place started with and all the work it took to put us on a better path, giving credit where credit is due. Neighborhood groups in southeast Portland put great pressure on officials to kill the Mt. Hood freeway, and Mayor Neil Goldschmidt and others from the City, along with leaders of Multnomah County like Don Clark and Mel Gordon, got permission to use federal funds that had been earmarked for the freeway on public transit instead. It was close, in fact, it seemed things were on the verge of reverting back, and they could have gone astray, but Bud Clark's election was pivotal in setting us on our current path.

The call from Lewis Mumford had some people asking out loud if we were good enough, and perhaps it planted a subliminal message in our collective unconscious. In large part, our ways of being and doing grew from our collective response to what we saw happening to our setting, when we realized how much we had to lose.

In hindsight, if only we had learned from the ways of the first people, who proved to be deserving of the setting. They provided a living model, which could have saved us a lot of time and pain, if only we had paid more attention and shown more respect.

We didn't set out to become the weirdest city in the land. That happened because we came to a place where we dared to be different, dared to be ourselves—doing what feels good and right, joyfully expressing ourselves because we found we had created the right conditions for creativity, courage, freedom, joy and seeing the world as more than this moment on this block. But we also understand that we create our world one block at a time, and we're not finished making that right. There have been some great efforts and successes in saving what nature gave us and restoring what we damaged. But there is no rest for the weary, who find they need to apply relentless pressure relentlessly.

More recently, we have turned our attention to weighing the human cost of our settlement and actions. Do we even know how to measure that? Does anyone know how to restore that? We are struggling with that now. It finally has our attention.

I hope for social justice to enjoy the same kind of groundswell of popular will the environment did. I want it to be what Portland is known for next. And I believe we can do it if we really want to. But we have to make that choice. It won't happen without a deliberate collective decision. We can't dilly-dally around the margins.

As Rasheed Wallace used to remind us, "Ball don't lie."

BEING
AND
DOING

To get Portland, you need to start by understanding Oregon. If you aren't sure you get the Oregon independent streak, which is plenty in evidence in Portland, I think I can help you out because I'm pretty sure I have it. Here's my take: We don't really care for anybody telling us what we can and can't do. We have a lot of common sense, we use it on a daily basis and we expect you to exercise yours as well. We have no patience for shady back room deals or you-scratch-my-back-I'll-scratch-yours politics. We want you to treat us as you would have yourselves treated. Tell us the truth. We, the people, expect to be heard and treated with respect. We speak plainly and we expect you to as well. We don't mind being first to try something—somebody has to. Just because nobody else is doing something doesn't mean we aren't willing to try. We don't mind being different. We don't like being pigeon-holed or put inside your neat little box, because as soon as you do, we'll defy your expectations. And despite all these predictable things, we can be pretty unpredictable.

Oregonians have put civic participation on the map time and time again. For example, we developed a system of governing in 1902 that enables citizens to directly initiate new statutes and changes to the state's constitution and to overturn actions taken by the Oregon Legislature through referendum. It was approved by voters by an 11:1 margin! It also allows the Legislature to refer legislation directly to the people.

We actually use these powers, too. According to the Initiative and Reform Institute, Oregon holds the record for the most statewide initiatives (there were 363 between 1904 and 2013), the highest average initiative use, and the most statewide initiatives on the ballot in a single year: 27 in 1912.

Oregon was the first state to elect its U.S. senators by popular vote, an initiative of the people, of course. In 1910, Oregonians passed an initiative to establish the first presidential primary election system in the nation.

Oregon is one of two states in which women gained the right to vote by initiative, the seventh state to grant women's suffrage. The same year, 1912, another initiative established the eight-hour work day for public works projects. Two years later, Oregon became the first state to decree a minimum wage. In 1930, an initiative established people's utility districts for water and power. And although the 1937 Oregon Legislature had approved a law to clean the Willamette River, the governor vetoed it, so the people passed an initiative to clean it in 1938.

Another significant use of the initiative process was in the passage of the Death with Dignity Act in 1994 that allows mentally competent, terminally ill adult Oregonians to obtain and use prescriptions from their physicians for self-administered, lethal doses of medication to determine the time of their own death. The Oregon Legislature referred its repeal to voters in 1997, when voters once again showed their support of death with dignity, by a greater margin than three years earlier. It was like voters were saying, "Hey, we already told you what we wanted. So shut up and do it."

There were additional efforts to block the law by just about everybody, including Congress, a federal judge and the Bush administration. Finally, in 2006, the U.S. Supreme Court upheld the law by 6 to 3. Followed by exactly none of the dire predictions of death squads coming to pass. Now we're comfortably living with dignified dying.

Oregon was the first state to hold all elections by mail ballots, and the fourth state to allow online voter registration.

It also consistently has one of the highest voter turnout rates in the country, attributed at least partly to vote by mail. However, we don't have so much to brag about when we consider that only about 75% of eligible voters are registered in Oregon. But that's about to change. Counter to a trend toward making voting more difficult in many states, in March 2015 Oregon adopted an opt-out voter registration system. When you get a driver's license or state ID, you are automatically registered to vote unless you choose to refuse. I can't wait to see how this affects our democracy.

Another truly big thing to come out of Oregon's election system is the Citizen Initiative Review. In 2003, Tyrone Reitman and Elliot Shuford met in graduate school at the University of Oregon, where they were studying public administration and citizen deliberation. They founded Healthy Democracy in 2007, a "nonpartisan nonprofit organization dedicated to elevating the public's voice in our democracy." They heard about a citizen initiative review process from Ned Crosby of the Jefferson Center in 2007 to "present voters with clear, useful and trustworthy evaluations of statewide ballot measures." After a field test in 2008 was found to be "fair and unbiased," the Oregon Legislature agreed to a pilot project in 2009. A National Science Foundation-funded evaluation found the pilot to be of high quality and useful to voters. In 2011, the Oregon Legislature made CIR a permanent part of elections in Oregon—the first time a legislature has made voter deliberation a formalized part of the election process.

This summary does not do justice to the work that Elliot and Ty did over the four years that led up to 2011. "We put on suits and met with every member of the Legislature and their staff for two whole sessions (except for a handful who refused)," Elliot remembers. The moment that made all the work worth it came on the third day of the first CIR panel. "We saw the panel taking control of the whole process," Elliot says. "They were really owning it. That's when the magic happened. That first year, these random citizens had no reason to show up for five days to be in a hotel listening and talking about ballot measures. But they did it. I just thought, 'This is democracy!' It felt so good!"

Oregon's CIR was selected as International Project of the Year by the International Association for Public Participation in 2013.

A panel of 20 citizens for each ballot measure is randomly pulled from voter rolls, and then a selection process picks a representative sample of Oregonians who have an open mind about the issue they will consider. They hear arguments from campaigns on both sides of the issue. "We see that panel members walk in with a degree of skepticism," Ty says. "Randomly selected voters have great BS detectors." Panel members are allowed to question non-partisan experts and campaign representatives and cross examine them.

"When a panel member asks a question and the campaign reverts to its sound bites rather than answering the question," Ty continues, "we see the panel get frustrated. And they ask follow-up questions to try to force a straight answer."

It's the goal of the CIR to get neutral experts for the panel to hear so the inquiry can move beyond the campaigns. However, politics has become so polarized that in the 2014 election, the campaigns would not agree on neutral experts as in past elections.

After the panels hear arguments and finish their questioning, they construct key findings most grounded in fact that all members agree on. Those findings are what goes in the voter's pamphlet that is sent to every household in the state with a registered voter. Panel members then vote yes or no on the initiative and the final tally is also provided to voters.

An evaluation of the 2014 election found that 54% of voters were aware of the CIR, and two thirds of those had consulted it in their decision-making. In addition, three to four percent (and possibly up to eight percent) said their vote was directly affected by the CIR's findings.

Healthy Democracy is now working with other states, beginning with Arizona and Colorado, to export yet another Oregon civic innovation.

The Citizen Initiative Review is established in Oregon now, it has legitimacy and documented impact. But when the Legislature approved the CIR, it provided no funding. Healthy Democracy has only raised enough charitable funding to review two initiatives per election cycle; the goal is to review all of them.

That means the CIR remains somewhat fragile when its staff has to devote time, energy and resources to fund-raising rather than focusing solely on the work of the CIR.

Oregon has found something that is nonpartisan, unbiased and very helpful to voters, but now the CIR has to dial for dollars and cast about for charity to continue. Seriously? Is this the way Oregon supports democracy? Not the way I remember it, growing up in this state.

Just after Tyrone finished explaining his concerns about the future of our democracy, Joyce started taking photos. Suddenly the Healthy Democracy banner on the wall behind them came loose and began to fall.

We trust it was only a coincidence.

This page: Elliot Shuford and Tyrone Reitman met with us in Healthy Democracy's office in downtown Portland, discussing 2014's Citizen Initiative Review. When the sign behind them suddenly gave way, they couldn't hold back their laughter.

■ Quilt information on page 164.

This Club Will Have You As a Member

In the midst of all the political reforms and progressive changes taking place in Oregon in the first two decades of the 20th century, a new kind of club was formed in Portland in 1916. It was organized by a small group of men who were "well-educated, eager to foster positive change, and dissatisfied with the operation of the city's public institutions."

Their new City Club was to serve as a community watch-dog—not to merely gripe about things but to do something about things they thought mattered. "No mossbacks or drones are wanted," the first secretary said.

The first constitution and bylaws set down seven purposes:

- To bring together congenial, forward-looking men of divergent beliefs, politics and occupations.
- To assemble a library of information relating to all phases of civic life.
- To study and discuss impartially Portland's civic problems.
- To work for the improvement of the city's economic and social conditions.
- To encourage fellowship which would breed ideas and to endeavor intelligently to discharge the obligations of citizenship.
- To work with all high-purposed organizations for a greater Portland.
- Ultimately to have a club house in which hospitality could be extended to all other civic organizations.

Well, right away we can see there's a problem. City Club was exclusively male, and could be joined by invitation only. Women were not allowed to become members until 1973, in a very contentious struggle that took three years. Portland men, what were you so afraid of? Seriously.

Now membership is open to everyone 17 and older, and the club is actively working to make its membership more representative of all parts of the community.

One of the valuable services the City Club has performed for Portland has been its study of and reporting on many, many issues in Portland. City Club research "examines issues of community importance through a rigorous citizen-based process. The research board chooses topics and oversees the research with strict protocol designed to assure impartiality and thoroughness."

Well over 1,000 such studies have been done since 1920, and many have directly influenced public policy. *Oregon Encyclopedia* author Ted Kaye credits City Club's reports with leading Portland to establish Forest Park, defeating a mayor's election after a vice investigation, transferring the Multnomah County Library system from the county to the Library Association, and contributing to reforms of Portland's fire and police disability and retirement system and Oregon's public employees retirement system.

City Club members still point with pride to the time Supreme Court Justice William O. Douglas cited a City Club report on jails in his 1951 dissent in *U.S. v. Carignan*.

Not every report and recommendation meets with success. City Club's 1995 study of and recommendation for fluoridating public water failed to sway voters. The club recommended passage of each of the six more times it appeared on the ballot, but each attempt was rejected by voters.

Apparently we like the *qi* of our water far too much to put more chemicals in it.

There's been no shying away from difficult topics and unpopular recommendations. A 1984 study recommended legalizing prostitution and is said by some to have resulted in the report's lead author losing her job.

Some issues have required further study. For example, City Club made early and influential inquiries into race relations, beginning with *The Negro in Portland* by Dr. Unthank in 1957 and continuing with studies in 1968, 1980 and 1991. And there is undoubtedly more that the club can contribute to this issue that continues to need attention and diligent action in Portland.

Recent research examples include a report on what needs to be done to give high school dropouts a second chance at a prosperous life, an analysis of Portland's rising water and sewer rates, restructuring Oregon's tax system, no turning back on bicycle transportation, reducing toxins in Portland's airshed, improving mental health services, reducing excessive partisanship in Oregon politics and so on.

Sam Adams, who was Portland's mayor from 2009-13 and was a City Council staffer for a long time before that, led City Club as executive director until early 2015, when he took a position with a global organization based in Washington D.C. It will be hard to find anyone who knows more about how the city works than Sam did. One of his first efforts was to increase and diversify club membership, so the club doesn't become yet another civic organization where one looks out over an audience that is a sea of grey hair. He reported that membership grew by more than 50% over the past two years, and new member orientations are attended by younger, more racially diverse people.

A core focus for the club in 2014 was racial equity, which included expanding its programs to high school students and residents of east Portland.

City Club plans to continue the tradition of watchdogging the city, keeping windows open so the people of Portland have a good clear view of the way of things from where they look. The work to strengthen the impact of City Club's research, advocacy, events and programs continues.

Mossbacks and drones are still not welcome here.

Especially drones. We don't want no stinkin' drones.

Opposite page: Portland City Club Executive Director (when the photo was taken in 2014) and former Mayor of Portland Sam Adams stands in Pioneer Courthouse Square—Portland's living room—holding a quilt with window views that symbolize the transparency and accountability that the City Club seeks for Portland, standing in Pioneer Courthouse Square, Portland's living room.

■ Quilt information on page 164.

Pieces of Portland

I think Portland is greatly relieved to feel it has an actual identity now and won't just be remembered for being forgotten. Even those who don't personally identify with the most popular current persona of the city are reassured by discovering that others think of us, look to us, come to us. And many of our natural tendencies make it easy for us to find ways to contribute to our civic life and show our love for our city, or call its attention to something we want to fix or change.

Portland is a city of neighborhoods that act as representatives of their residents on shared interests and concerns. Working through and with neighborhood associations is an important part of getting things done. Some neighborhoods are more vocal and visible than others, of course, but the structure exists for all to use.

Portland has also gained fame for less formal and more grassroots doings within neighborhoods. One organization that has organized many community building events is City Repair Project, a nonprofit group that helps residents create spaces and places for gathering, communicating and creating community. City Repair began in Portland with the idea that localization—of culture, of economy, of decision-making—is a necessary foundation of sustainability.

One of the most popular ways City Repair accomplishes its work is through intersection repair—transforming intersections with the sole purpose of moving cars through into public places for all kinds of community gatherings and activities. The repaired intersections become places that are more human in scale and encourage people to gather and connect.

Here's how City Repair describes it: "The community works together to make the place special. They make it a place where people want to go to, where they feel safe and welcome. They make it beautiful and interesting. They make it meaningful, an expression of their own local culture... One neighborhood may paint a giant mural on the intersection and stop there. Another may go through many phases: painting the street, installing a community bulletin board, building a mini-cafe on a corner, reconstructing the intersection with brick and cobblestones, opening businesses to make it a village center....and on and on!"

The intersections also slow down cars and make drivers more aware of pedestrians and cyclists.

Many projects take place during Village Building Convergence, a 10-day event held every May and June in Portland, based on natural building and permaculture design. The 2015 convergence is the Urban Permaculture Extravaganza where people look to "Thrive It Up!" with more than 40 simultaneous repairs and lots of other things "on the edge of vision and participation."

One of the first and most fully developed is the Sunnyside Circle in inner southeast Portland. If things keep going this way, someday I expect the whole city to pretty much be totally repaired.

The Village Building Convergence was preceded in 1996 by the Share-It Square on Sherritt (get it?) Street in the Sellwood neighborhood of southeast Portland. This project came about when neighbors just decided to make it happen and were reportedly told by a city official, "That's public space, nobody can use it."

Share-It Square includes a painted street intersection, a tea station, a community bulletin board kiosk, a bench for resting and conversation, a children's playhouse and lots of other features. One of my favorites is a beehive shaped structure that houses the local neighborhood newspaper, *The Bee*.

Construction was done using reclaimed and recycled materials, so the cash outlay was only $65. And it's still there after nearly 20 years.

Neighbors near the intersection added other features to expand the community space, such as an outdoor oven for cooking pizza, fruit trees and bushes so neighbors can graze while spending time outside together. Organizers report that since the square was developed, traffic slowed, crime decreased, there was less litter and much better communication among neighbors.

Now Portland has a process for these kinds of city repairs and is officially in favor of the public using public spaces.

This page: The Sellwood neighborhood's Share-It Square's T-Station stands ready to quench all thirsts.
Opposite page: The Sunnyside Circle is another of the City Repair Project's traffic calming and community-building projects. The paint is periodically refreshed by volunteers.

■ Quilt information on page 164.

To Share Is Human

Sharing is a very big deal in Portland. Generosity is a widely held community value, and you are pretty much expected to give of yourself. As you will find others give to you.

Maybe it's in the water or soil, as sharing was at the core of this area's first cultures. Potlatch, or gift-giving feast, was an economic system and means of preventing hoarding of wealth among the people of the Northwest Coast, including the Chinook. And according to Wikipedia, federal governments in both Canada and the United States banned potlatch when they took over. They said it was "contrary to 'civilized values' of accumulation." Yikes! I checked Snopes and this does not appear to be an urban legend. OMG, does this mean we can blame hoarding on the federal government!?

There is an old story that at a fork in the Oregon Trail, those who sought riches turned left to the California gold mines, while those looking for something more meaningful headed to Oregon.

Whatever the reason, over time I've come to believe we have less cutthroat competitiveness, fewer turf battles, more sharing and collaboration here. I'm not the only one who thinks so.

"I firmly believe that Portland has an underlying culture of collaboration and that folks are far more collegial than competitive," says Rick Turoczy, who should know as he's spent the last 20 years observing and participating in Portland's startup and tech scenes.

He cites two quick examples:

1) PIE (Portland Incubator Experiment), an ongoing collaboration between Portland startups and Wieden+Kennedy, the largest privately held creative agency in the world. "We've been working together for five years on this experiment, trying to determine how a global corporation can work to benefit startups and how those startups can work to benefit a larger company," Rick explains. During those five years, PIE has assisted more than 40 startups with $20,000 each, mentoring and office space. The project has grown so much it had to move into larger space in Spring 2015 at CENTRL Office, a nearby co-working space that houses Oregon Angel Fund and is designed to bring investors and entrepreneurs together.

2) Calagator, the aggregated calendar for the Portland tech and startup scenes. "This resource—which is built and maintained by the Portland community at no cost—is our way of sharing what's happening in town. It's the first site I recommend to Portland newcomers."

"Bridgetown is all about bridging gaps," Rick says. "We're a successful port, conveying products between parties. We were a

Photo by Reid Beels

lumber hub, providing the raw materials craftspeople needed to create things. We're a hub for open source development, because of the ethos of contributing to a project to make it better for everyone. Even our most successful tech companies —Mentor Graphics, Intel, and Tektronix—are about helping others make better products. We are collaborators and enablers. It's just what we do."

Sharing isn't just for tech companies. Portland has a long history of making it so every single person doesn't have to buy every single thing of their own. There's a thriving sharing economy, sometimes called collaborative consumption. Mesh or peer to peer economy. Disownership. We're not just a DIY place, but also a good place to DIT (Do It Together).

For example, we have five tool lending libraries—way more than any other city in the land. If you need a drill to screw up some shelves, we've got you covered. Want to weed your garden? Come check out our hoes. The city's first tool library was the Northeast Portland Tool Library (NEPTL), and it subsequently helped the one in southeast Portland get going, donating its surplus tools. Then when a volunteer at Southeast Portland Tool Library (SEPTL) developed custom tool library software, SEPTL gave it to NEPTL. Naturally.

According to Stephen Couche, who helped found SEPTL, it has about 4,000 members and about 3,000 tools. It operates from a small storage space at St. David of Wales Church. There is no fee for borrowing items, but if you are late returning them after the one-week loan period, there's a small fine. On the night we visited, there was a steady stream of people returning and checking out tools. At one point, it was so busy that two of the people in line to return tools stepped up to perform library duties. It was all just so neighborly.

Just down the hall, Robin Koch was volunteering for KitchenShare, a kitchen tool library she started up two years ago. Besides loaning tools, it also offers classes in food preparation, from mead making to coffee roasting.

And since this is Portland, we keep seeking the next level. Like Repair Cafes, which are "free events that bring volunteers who like to fix things together with people who have broken items that need fixing." We were so excited to hear a Repair Cafe was scheduled at SEPTL later in the week!

Portland is the birthplace of car sharing, which began in 1998. We also share homes, yards, bikes, food, toys, books, clothing, plants, seeds and pretty much everything else you can name. Some of the peer-to-peer sharing is global, like couchsurfing and vacation rentals. Others are local and particular to Portland.

The sharing economy is based on the same principles as Open

Source Software, where the talents and resources of all contribute to making something better everybody. And it just keeps going here because it makes so much sense to us.

It's not just for products. Portlanders participate in bartering exchanges, gift circles and time banks, where time credits are earned when time and skills are contributed. Co-housing is big here as well, along with intentional communities that have private living space and communal gathering and event space.

A lot of skill sharing goes on, too. For example, Resourceful PDX ("Buy Smart, Reuse, Borrow and Share, Fix and Maintain") connects people who offer classes in what they know and do to those who want to learn. For example, in November 2014, there were classes on pie baking, Thanksgiving side dish preparation and upcycling jars into etched glass Thanksgiving decorations.

Many of us also take part in buying clubs and community-supported agriculture, where we purchase an up-front share of a farm's crop and get weekly deliveries of fruit, vegetables, eggs and so forth that are of the greatest quality you can imagine. As it turns out, it's a great way to discover new produce you might never have thought to try. Sometimes farmers give recipes and instructions for preparing the more unusual items.

Farmers get up-front investments to support their farm, making for more predictable cash flow, and buyers get food directly from farm to table, as fresh as can be.

It's important to make sure we have enough members in our buying clubs though, as the club needs to purchase quite a lot of something to qualify for bulk purchasing. As my friend Abby's husband Tom said once after she placed her making-up-the-difference order, "I'm not sure we can afford to save this much money."

Opposite page: Rick Turoczy talks about the Portland Incubator Experiment he leads to help early stage startups. **This page:** Below, Laurie Sugahbeare repairs jewelry for Ann Pernick and her daughter. Repair cafes are often held at tool libraries like the one Stephen Couche (top right) helped start in southeast Portland. Dadgummit, we forgot to bring a quilt.

Collectively Speaking

The whole time I've lived in Portland, I've been aware that there is a strong collective vibe in the city. Workers aren't to be exploited, everybody gets an equal share, we are all in it for the collective good. Power to the people.

Well, actually, in the 1970s and 1980s, even part of the 1990s, it was all about co-ops. There would be a thing, everybody interested would volunteer, and stuff would be divided up equally. Preschool co-ops. Food co-ops. Baby-sitting co-ops. You know the drill.

Sometime around the beginning of the new millennium, it was less co-ops and more collectives. Worker-owned collectives. It somehow sounded more serious or more militant than co-op. Yes, there were a few using the word collective in the Portland way earlier, like the Maoist Lesbian Roofing Collective that replaced the roof on our house in 1978, but that's a whole other story for a whole other lifetime. Just ply me with alcohol first.

So as I was doing research for this section, trying to figure out the difference between co-ops and collectives and when and why things switched over, I googled Worker Owned Collectives Portland, and the first entry that appeared was Worker Owned Cooperatives Portland in portlandwiki. Now I'm really confused.

Then I noticed there is a law firm in Portland called the Portland Law Collective, and I merrily clicked on its website link to "What Is a Collective?" thinking I would get the inside legal scoop, and got this answer: "A collective is a team of equals working toward a common purpose." Well, then.

So yeah, Portland has a lot of things that call themselves collectives and they may or may not mean remotely the same things and now I know words don't always matter. I am quite intrigued by a number of collectives in the Google results. For example, did you know Portland has a Winter Solstice Puppet Collective? And a Black Cross Collective that is currently on hiatus of unknown duration? A Rose Hip Medic Collective of street medics and healthcare activists who operate from an anti-oppression framework? I didn't either.

I wasn't at all surprised to find an Urban Farm Collective in Portland. But I didn't necessarily expect a Portland Meat Collective that describes itself as "an up close and personal traveling butchery school" that delivers meat directly from small ranchers to meat eaters who then butcher it themselves. We can be so very hard core! I suppose the fact that more than 1,000 students have attended butchery classes speaks to the popularity of Paleo in Portland.

There are some well-known Portland groups that are on the list of Portland Cooperatives/Collectives/Worker Owned things. Like Citybikes, a "worker owned cooperative bike shop." KBOO, a "Volunteer-Powered, Non-Commercial, Listener-Sponsored, Full-Strength Community Radio for Portland, Oregon, Cascadia & the World!" Red and Black, a "vegan, worker-owned, collectively managed, IWW closed shop cafe."

Red and Black might be the one that is most familiar to the general public because local news is all over the story every time workers made it clear police were not welcome there. Most recently, when a customer was experiencing a heroin overdose,

Red and Black called 911 to request medical help but asked that police not come with them, as is customary. I thought about trying to feature Red and Black in these pages but their hours have shrunk so much I couldn't find it open, and then its website up and disappeared. Then in March 2015, it announced it was closing down. A sad end to what used to serve a great community need back when it was on southeast Division Street.

When I asked around, People's Food Co-op was mentioned as maybe the best representative of a cooperative/collective in Portland today. It's such an important Portland institution that its history was chronicled in the *Oregon Historical Quarterly* in 2011.

People's Food Co-op began in 1970 as a food buying club, a counterculture alternative to corporate grocery stores. I remember unpacking produce and cutting chunks of cheese as a volunteer there in 1976. The store found ways to survive over the years, but when a financial crisis developed in 1991 and only two board members remained, they decided to start fresh with new management and staff and develop a long-term plan for success, which slowly came over the ensuing decade.

The store doubled in size in the early 2000s, adding a lot more space and green features: energy efficiency (ground source heat pump and solar chimney), zero runoff of stormwater (ecoroofs, porous ground surfaces, buried runoff cistern, bioswales), eco-building materials (cob structures, wheat board, stone bases, reclaimed and certified wood and other structural materials), non-toxic materials. Containers are reused and recycled, food scraps are composted by worms, items are offered in bulk rather than packages and so forth.

People's prioritizes certified organic and local sources for food items and includes fair trade practices in its product selection guidelines, avoiding growers or businesses that exploit workers. It does not carry meat or other animal products that require an animal to be killed, except in pet food, where chicken and fish are allowed. The store doesn't sell products with artificial color, flavor or preservatives.

It's the co-op's scrutiny of the ingredients, policies and practices of its goods that makes it so popular among Portlanders. The most recent survey of its shoppers revealed that its strict product guidelines are the single most important reason people shop there. "People see their own values reflected in the care we take in selecting what we sell, they can trust what they buy here," explains Development Manager Shawn Furst, who has been part of the co-op's co-management team since 2010.

And it's not just about environmental and social justice. People with food allergies—and we certainly have a lot of those—also need to be able to trust labels and screening for ingredients that pose health risks.

In recent years, People's has been consistently at or very near the top among U.S. food cooperatives in sales per square foot, which Shawn thinks shows that People's needs more space.

Shawn credits much of its success to its "staff/management structure that creates conditions for efficiency, empowerment and accountability." First, after it became a cooperative corporation, in 2000 it created ownership shares costing $180, attracting 500

Photo by Bryn Harding

owners within the first five months. By late 2014, it had 10,000 member owners, with 4,000 active. The sale of shares allowed People's to build up equity that greatly strengthens its financial position.

But in many ways, the success of People's seems to be about the workers. When I first laid eyes on the staff photo above, I thought, "Holy blissed-out!! People's must be the happiest place on earth. Those are some 'joy to the fishes in the deep blue sea' people."

People's is a "co-managed" workplace. All workers, no matter the job title, begin at the same hourly wage. After nine months, workers are "confirmed" as "co-managers" and thereafter raises go according to seniority. After three months on the job, everybody gets four weeks paid time off. Benefits include full health insurance coverage and partial subsidy for family members and a 19% discount on co-op purchases. Any meeting that lasts three hours or more includes a meal of healthy, nourishing food.

Thirty co-managers use consensus to manage operations and implement the big picture guidance from the board of directors, elected by member-owners. At its best, People's holds that

"Consensus acknowledges that all participants have a piece of the truth. It encourages participants to share those truths, to listen openly to the truths of others, and to work toward decisions that reflect the whole group intention and serve its greatest good. Consensus embraces individual perspectives, while emphasizing the good of the whole."

Shawn points out that for the past seven or eight years, two-thirds of the co-managers have been female. If I may be permitted a bit of editorial commentary [and why wouldn't I, it's my effing book :-D], I daresay that's at least partly responsible for the listening and sharing that needs to happen for consensus to work.

People's has a courtyard outside its entrance, and on Wednesdays, it and the adjacent street are used for a farmers' market managed by the co-op. Upstairs is a community room that hosts a number of events for neighborhood groups and activities.

It's no secret that "natural food" has become big business in Portland and other cities. While it was once hard to eat organically, even in Portland, now even the biggest supermarket chains sell things they call organic.

A lot of consumer education is needed for stores like People's to stand out amidst the growing crowd. Fortunately, Portland is full of people not only willing to learn, but who are actually a little obsessive and compulsive about what they buy. And our fair city is full of people who are allergic to certain foods. And injustice.

What we don't know can hurt us. What we do know can keep us from hurting others. Hey, not bad, I just made that up.

Unless you already thought of it.

This page: Sorry, Disney, but I think the happiest place on earth must be People's Food Co-op. Check out those smiling faces on its workers. People's is consistently at or near the top of food co-ops in the country in sales per square foot. Its popularity is largely due to the environmental and social justice scrutiny it applies to what it sells. Shawn Furst is the one in the middle wearing a teal scarf, which is standing in as understudy in the role played by a quilt, since we used the co-op's own photo.

Pieces of Portland

Garbage In, Geek Out

What you do with things you don't need or want anymore is a very big deal in Portland. Well, of course you recycle—duh, that's so very last century. Actually, recycling is sorta disdained. A much better approach is to consume less, buy less, do with less. If you already have something and don't need it anymore, give it to someone who does. If it's past that point, use it in a piece of art. Make something out of it. As a very very very last resort, put it in the recycling bin so it can be broken down into parts and manufactured into something new again.

You need to start by rethinking your entire existence. Stop acquiring stuff. You don't actually need to buy anything. Clothes you wear? Go to a clothing swap. Or mend and make do. Food scraps? Put them in City-provided compost bins. Or your worm bin. You do have a worm bin, right? Plastic? Wait, what? You bought something with plastic packaging? There's a special place in the landfill for people like you. Look at the number on the bottom to see if the plastic recyclers will take it. If not, at least upcycle it into your next craft project. Before you put a bird on it.

And you don't really need to buy your own tool. Borrow it from the tool library, for Earth's sake, every part of town has one. You already have a car? We hope it's at least a hybrid, but whatever it is, you should share it. There's an app for that.

It's hard for me to imagine a place devoting more time and attention and organizations to garbage than Portland. And frankly, it's a little intimidating. Every so often we get large infographics in our snail mail that try to explain our ever-adapting system, with "27 8 × 10 color glossy pictures with circles and arrows and a paragraph on the back of each one explaining what each one was to be used as evidence against us." (Remember, that was a garbage case, too!)

I can't tell you how humiliating and self-esteem destroying it is to find you can't even do garbage correctly and put something in the wrong colored bin or tried to dispose of something in a way that is outright banned. I find myself doing the slink of shame out to the curb after the trucks have been by to face that dreaded moment where you might find a note from the garbage collector left on one of your bins announcing your mistake(s), which are all lying there on the curb for all the neighbors to see.

But seriously, it's all worth it and we wouldn't have it any other way. Because the planet.

A great place to witness Portland's reduce, reuse, recycle ethic is Free Geek, where volunteers take apart cast off computers and related hardware and reuse the good parts to build perfectly wonderful new computers and responsibly recycle parts that can't be reused. Who builds the new computers? People

who need computers and can't afford to buy them, taught by volunteers who have already been through the program and want to help others.

Some of them do it for a very long time. Richard Seymour has been a Free Geek staff member almost since the organization began in 2000, and Blaine Deatherage-Newsom had been a volunteer build instructor for more than 11 years when this photo was taken in summer 2014. And it goes to show that even geeks appreciate our arty and crafty wonderland, because they are holding a quilt that spells out FREE GEEK in binary code.

The ReBuilding Center is another iconic Portland reuse and recycle success. Since 1998, the north Portland nonprofit has been accepting the region's large volume of used building and remodeling materials; it then makes them available to those who need them. One of its services is DeConstruction, an affordable and sustainable alternative to conventional demolition. Its EPA Lead Safe Certified crews salvage materials by hand so that up to 85% of a building's major components can be reused.

DeConstruction Services complete about 200 residential and commercial projects every year, ranging from bathrooms and kitchen remodels to entire city blocks. In one sample project, for instance, 240 tons of material were salvaged and reused from 8,000 square feet of deteriorating buildings. Before the ReBuilding Center came along, it would have been landfilled. When salvaged materials are donated to the ReBuilding Center, their value can be claimed as a charitable donation.

And they have a lot of fun doing it. For example, on Paul Bunyan Denailing Day, they invited volunteers to remove nails from wood while wearing their favorite plaid shirt, with a photo booth to record the event. And who knew there is a National Macaroon Day? The ReBuilding Center does, and they built another denail session around it.

ReBuilding Center revenues support the programs of Our United Villages, whose mission is "Inspiring people to value and discover existing resources to strengthen the social and environmental vitality of communities." Its work has earned a number of awards, and it is one of the most authentically Portland organizations to be found.

If I had to pick two all time fave groups in town, these might win. Since I don't have to pick two now, I won't say them out loud. But if you come to a book signing, I might whisper it in your ear.

Opposite page: Two geek standouts—Richard Seymour and Blaine Deatherage-Newsom—who have worked and volunteered at Free Geek for well over ten years each hold a quilt that spells out FREE GEEK in binary code. This page: The community gathering space at the entrance of the Rebuilding Center is made entirely of cob construction and recycled materials.

◼ Quilt information on page 164.

Pieces of Portland

When the Best Grade Is a B

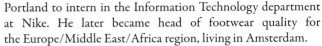

The Portland metro area is not known as the home of big business. In fact, only two Fortune 500 companies have headquarters here. There used to be more, but several moved to other parts of the country. We're pretty much a place of independent small businesses. Not that we don't have big businesses, chain stores and shopping malls in both the city and suburbs, but they're not necessarily the go-to places for a lot of us, and they don't always achieve specimen form here.

The poster child for local business success and paying it forward might be Bob's Red Mill, a company that produces one of the largest lines of organic, whole grain foods in the country. And guess what owner Bob Moore did on his 81st birthday? You might want to sit down for this.

He actually gave his business away. To his employees. No, I am not making this up, and he has not lost his mind. He gave them total ownership of Bob's Red Mill through an Employee Share Ownership Program. "It was just the right thing to do," he said. Geez, maybe we are a bunch of hippie communists after all.

You could say that Bob Moore set a pretty high bar for community-minded businesses.

Though it's hard to find anything that quite compares, a number of businesses are establishing themselves as B (for Benefit) corporations. B corps are designed to enable for-profit companies to create general public benefit by making a positive impact on society and the environment, in addition to generating profit. A triple bottom line. Public benefit is defined as "a material, positive impact on society and the environment, taken as a whole, as assessed against a third-party standard, from the business and operations of a benefit company."

B corps legislation was first proposed in 2010, but Oregon didn't pass its law until 2013. B Corps must report on their public benefit and apply a third party assessment each year.

§

Justin Yuen is what can happen when you grow up as a digital native and are willing to think about doing business in a new way.

When he was very young, he did a lot of graphic design and desktop publishing, and in high school had access to Princeton University computers in his New Jersey town. His early exposure to the Web made him realize the potential for increasing communication and knowledge for anyone anywhere.

Justin came to Oregon on a family vacation while he was a student at Johns Hopkins University. While here, the Yuens toured the Nike campus (his mother had worked for Nike in Shanghai). When he finished college, he moved to Portland to intern in the Information Technology department at Nike. He later became head of footwear quality for the Europe/Middle East/Africa region, living in Amsterdam.

He returned to Portland in 2001 as Nike's senior manager working to integrate sustainability into business practices.

His global work taught him the value of virtual tools, and he saw a need for group communication and project management options while working on teams at Nike—a solution that would supplement face to face meetings and be more like a social network.

He had $10,000 his grandmother had left him when she died, so he hired software engineer Eric Rath and they spent day after day in Portland's Urban Grind coffee shop designing software. When it reached Version 3 in 2005, he launched his startup called FMYI (a play on the acronym FYI, changing Your to My). Nike became his first client.

Given his work and passion around sustainability, Justin wanted to figure out what it would mean for a software company. Not just how to reduce printing things on paper and what to do with obsolete hardware, for example, but to instill it into the very fiber of the business. Instead of the standard for-profit corporation, he decided to make it B Corp. FMYI met the certification developed for other states in 2010, the first software company in the country to do so. As soon as Oregon adopted legislation, FMYI registered and became certified in Oregon.

FMYI hosts over two million workspaces for small teams and large organizations around the globe. FMYI adapted its software in developing and hosting Oregon Unlimited, which is available at no cost to Oregon nonprofit organizations and people working for the common good. Its new quick conversation tool–Grouptrail–is available to them for free as well.

Justin feels strongly that his benefit company support work-life balance for its workforce. In 2013, FMYI won the Alfred P. Sloan Award for Excellence in Workplace Effectiveness and Flexibility for the third year in a row, given to companies that

> **This page:** Justin Yuen started FMYI [For My Innovation] in 2005; it became a B corp in 2010. FMYI builds and supports software that helps groups communicate and work on projects together. FMYI has earned Excellence in Workplace Effectiveness awards for how well its employees are able to balance home and work life. **Opposite page:** Staff members in the Portland office take a break from their computers to share conversation and treats.
> ■ Quilt information on page 164.

Pieces
of
Portland

are innovative, flexible and effective. "Employees need to be able to take time to care for their families," Justin says. "It's important for employee retention."

He credits his parents for much of his own success and honors their sacrifices to give him a good education and life.

"I also think there is a value to travel and time off," Justin says. "People need time to reflect and come up with ideas. That's what I want for myself, and it's a value held by the local community." Justin commutes to his office and business meetings and events by bike from his home in northeast Portland, where he lives with his wife Katrina and two young children. "My bike IS my transportation."

"I appreciate the natural beauty here," he says. "It seems to foster an appreciation for and desire to preserve the environment."

Justin acknowledges that Portlanders are surprised when they find out he grew up in New Jersey. "I don't have an accent, and I have a more west coast attitude. Maybe it's because of my Chinese heritage. I like the collaborative nature of doing business here over the in-your-face ways of the east coast."

He thinks much of Portland's quirkiness can be traced to our deep and abiding love of fun. What a fun idea!

He contributes his own time and talents to a number of community groups and projects, serving on the board of trustees of the National Crittendon Foundation and being a board member of Bicycle Transportation Alliance and the Northwest Earth Institute (and many others over the years). "There is a lot of civic energy here," he says. "We can't rest on our laurels, we need to be looking for what happens next. The most important

and hardest part is getting people to agree. Collaboration takes longer than top down decisions." He's aware that conversations can go on too long, and must lead to action at some point.

FMYI outgrew its first office near the east end of the Broadway Bridge and recently moved to a new building in a neighborhood in northeast Portland that is transforming into a denser, more upscale and expensive place. He's first to point out that neighborhood development has to take care of the needs of the people already living there.

"Development itself is not necessarily bad," he says. "But to preserve the neighborhood, it has to include financial incentives, less than market rate options and workforce development outcomes for the people already here." He spent the next several minutes talking about ways neighborhood development could include public benefit, social and environmental goals in a time of fewer government resources, from purchasing office supplies from local businesses to using technology to connect neighbors.

As we left, it occurred to me that people like Justin and B corps like FMYI should be among those who can find solutions to rapidly rising housing costs that drive out long-time residents in Portland neighborhoods. Even though they moved in just a few months ago, FMYI is already working with neighborhood school and youth organizations on STEM (science, technology, engineering and mathematics) activities and entrepreneurship. They've hired an intern from nearby Self Enhancement Inc.

While so many talk the walk, Justin and others at FMYI walk the talk.

Well, except when they're on their bikes, of course.

Pieces
of
Portland

Start Me Up!

According to Rick Turoczy, director of Portland Incubator Experiment, "The Portland startup scene has become a thriving community of collaborative companies in a relatively short period of time. It seems that everyone is willing to contribute time. And it doesn't matter how busy they are. They want to give back. And to help other people succeed."

As he is generously taking time from his own very busy day to answer my questions.

"That's why accelerators and incubators are thriving here. Because they're able to serve as the bridge between startups and the mentors who would like to help them, connecting those in need with those who can help."

One notable recent startup is Little Bird, founded by Marshall and Mikalina Kirkpatrick in 2011. I met Marshall in 2008 after posing the question, "Who's the best blogger in Portland?"

Besides his personal blog, Marshall was the first writer hired by Tech Crunch and from 2007-2012 was lead writer for ReadWrite Web, one of the key places I read to keep up with what was going on with the Web and technology. I learned a lot of what I know about the Internet from his posts.

One thing that set his posts apart from the gazillions of other bloggers on the web was his ability to use search and reputation tracking tools to identify the best sources and resources for the topics he covered. He started consulting for businesses who wanted access to trusted experts and the most reliable information in their fields.

Marshall said he pretty much hacked his way to his reputation tracking and influence measuring system. When he described his work to software engineer Tyler Gillies, Tyler told Marshall he thought he could build software to make it more efficient.

Mikalina was finishing her undergraduate degree, which she did with a 4.0 GPA. She planned to go to nursing school, but was turned down. Weird. But an okay thing, in the end.

Soon afterward, Mikalina and Marshall were in Ireland for an international Web event, and at a pub one night, they decided to take the leap and start a technology company around the networking software. At first it was evenings and weekends because they didn't have funds to quit other jobs.

The first help they got was from Portland Ten (now called TenX), a startup accelerator that helps "high potential organizations and individuals" generate growth in early stages, like learning how to pitch a business to investors. One of their assignments was to make a list of the richest people they knew.

Mikalina remembered that several years earlier, Mark Cuban (tech billionaire after selling Broadcast.com to Yahoo, Dallas Maverick owner and Shark Tank investor) had written Marshall about something on his personal blog. So Marshall applied his methods to a subject he thought Mark Cuban would be interested in (viz., analyzing Mavericks coverage by sportswriters/

sportscasters, compiling data from Twitter about players' use of social media, etc.) Marshall pulled up Mark's old email with his personal email address and sent him that analysis and told him about the software he was creating, then called Plexus Engine.

Mark was impressed. Three-quarters of a million dollars invested impressed. His was the funding that germinated the seed. As they put it, Marshall and Mikalina could then hire people who knew what they were doing. They both laugh now about how much they had to learn, the mistakes they made, the importance of the roles each of them played.

"Blogging, which I describe as working out loud in public, brought me lots of good things," Marshall says. He continues blogging now at marshallk.com.

Their startup was then selected for a class at PIE, where they had access to space, other startups, tech help and the brand and marketing expertise of Wieden+Kennedy. That was when Plexus Engine became Little Bird (as in "a little bird told me"—a clear reference to Twitter). In fact, the reference almost kept Marshall and Mikalina from adopting the name because they feared Twitter would object. But when they contacted Twitter and told them what they were doing, the response was, "Oh good, we were hoping someone would build something like that."

Little Bird has grown a lot, especially in the past year and now has a staff of 17, with a nest—I mean office—overlooking Portland's downtown transit mall. They have a lot of big-name clients, but are mostly working through early adopters within giant companies. The next stage will be helping these insiders convince their bosses that Little Bird will make them money.

Marshall's role now is primarily focused on taking the company to the next level by finding new investors and enterprise customers. Mikalina served as chief operating officer until recently and is now continuing her education to become a counselor.

There are plenty of other ideas and businesses being launched here. And now companies that started in other places are coming to Portland to incubate and accelerate. In October 2014, *Business Insider* featured three companies moving from San Francisco to Portland, citing fresh points of view, affordability, right size, talent, quality of life, great food and culture among reasons for relocating. Larger companies like eBay, Airbnb and Salesforce also recently opened offices here.

Portland has a number of co-work spaces, like NedSpace, where companies like Puppet Labs, POWR and Second Porch came to life. Oregon Entrepreneurs Network and Startup PDX have similar resources. OEN's Angel Oregon has an annual showcase, where more than $2.9 million had been invested by 2014. Portland Seed Fund has helped 36 companies raise $23 million in outside capital, creating more than 200 jobs. Even Nike has developed an incubator program.

Pitchlandia is the world's first completely crowd-sourced, crowd-based and crowd-selected startup pitch event. The top 2014 winner was GRASP, a company that makes customized, affordable, Open-Source 3-D printed prosthetics. Producing a prosthetic hand this way reduces the cost from $5,000 to $250.

So Portland. So cool.

And so very handy!

Opposite page: Marshall and Mikalina Kirkpatrick and their two canine companions shortly after moving into Little Bird's larger nest downtown. Their startup identifies and connects people with the best sources of information.
■ Quilt information on page 164.

Pieces
of
Portland

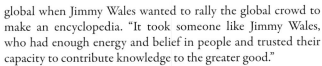

Well, of course, Portland has produced rock stars. From back in the day, the Kingsmen and Paul Revere and the Raiders, then later on, Nu Shooz and Quarterflash. Everclear. The Dandy Warhols. More recently, the Decemberists, the Thermals. And others not in the rock genre, like Nancy King, Esperanza Spalding, Curtis Salgado... I know, I know, I'm leaving out so many great ones.

But here's my point. If you took combined all their fame, it does not begin to touch the effect Ward Cunningham has had on the world. Because without Ward Cunningham, there would be no Wikipedia. Nor anything else on the Web that uses wiki.

Wiki is a website that allows collaborative editing of its content and structure by its users. When we met with its inventor, I was expecting a very technical conversation about software. Instead, we mostly talked about people.

Ward developed wiki to solve a common human dilemma: people working together on a big project or solving a problem in common—in his case software engineers—needed a way to share their work and invite others to collaborate on it in real time. Wikis make interactions open and transparent and allow users to edit one another's work.

As Ward acknowledges, this way of working can cause culture shock in people who are accustomed to working alone and not revealing the outcome until they think it's finished. I have watched a considerable number of people freak out a little or a lot when they watch projects develop using the wiki way. Some of them never recover. But the horse is out of the barn and we all better get used to it if we want to do the most good with the time we have, because that's pretty much how it's gonna roll in Portland. IMHO.

Ward grew up in Indiana and earned bachelor's and master's interdisciplinary degrees in engineering and computer science from Purdue University. He developed an interest in how engineers share ideas when he was working as Principal Engineer of Research and Development at Tektronix and found that even the most innovative engineers were very cautious with decisions they made. Such caution didn't always help. Later, as an independent consultant, he had time and opportunity to explore the matter.

"Let me see if I can solve it," Ward told his peers. He pulled together something that tracked the flow of ideas in about a week, then launched it in 1995 on his own website for the Portland Pattern Repository and invited other programmers to contribute. "Well-known programmers started contributing, which brought along a lot of others who wanted to be where the famous people were."

"I knew I had made something," Ward remembers. "But it took about five years to prove itself of lasting value." It went global when Jimmy Wales wanted to rally the global crowd to make an encyclopedia. "It took someone like Jimmy Wales, who had enough energy and belief in people and trusted their capacity to contribute knowledge to the greater good."

For Ward, the power of wikis is that many people get to contribute, which creates something more interesting. While websites and blogs provide content, a wiki creates community. Wikis rely on people trusting one another more than they have any reason to and believing that you don't have to have all the answers before you start a conversation.

"It was a turning point in my programming career when I realized that I didn't have to win every argument. I'd be talking about code with someone, and I'd say, 'I think the best way to do it is A.' And they'd say, 'I think the best way to do it is B.' I'd say, 'Well no, it's really A.' And they'd say, 'Well, we want to do B.' It was a turning point for me when I could say, 'Fine. Do B. It's not going to hurt us that much if I'm right and you do B, because, we can correct mistakes. So let's find out if it's a mistake.'

"I can't tell you how much time is spent worrying about decisions that don't matter," Ward says. "To just be able to make a decision and see what happens is tremendously empowering, but that means you have to set up the situation such that when something does go wrong, you can fix it."

Which is exactly how wikis are designed. Ward has a way with words; in fact, there is a wiki page of his quotations that others have posted. One of Ward's most memorable and insightful observations is a statement now known as Cunningham's Law: "The best way to get the right answer on the Internet is not to ask a question, it's to post the wrong answer."

I can see all of you knowingly nodding your heads.

"One's words are a gift to the community," Ward explains. "For the wiki nature to take hold, you have to let go of your words. You have to be okay with that. To collaborate on a work, one must trust. The reason the cooperation happens is we are people, and it is deep in our nature to do things together."

Ward points out that allowing everyday users to create and edit any page in a website is exciting in that it encourages democratic use of the Web and promotes content contributions by nontechnical users. Wikis and other free open source software that is openly shared with others so they can use and contribute in turn is pretty much part of Portland's DNA.

Wikis have also crossed over to the business world. "Private wikis are replacing intranets. It's a low-cost solution that can stay alive instead of a clunky intranet. It can be a transformative experience."

After leaving Tektronix, Ward worked for a number of software companies and did consulting. He served as an Open

Pieces of Portland

Data Fellow at Nike. Now he works at New Relic, a software firm that occupies two floors of Portland's Big Pink. "I was getting obsolete," Ward says. "I wasn't having to stay current and learn new stuff. Here I appreciate those around me who are pushing the envelope, thinking six months to a year ahead."

"It's pretty easy to get ten years ahead if you don't mind being ignored," he laughs.

"Portland will never be Silicon Valley," Ward says. "We don't have the depth of talent of research universities, CEOs, CFOs and so forth, to please the venture capitalists. People here don't want a new job. We're not about growing and selling companies. We want to do something of value for the world."

This page: Ward Cunningham, the man who invented the wiki, explains the federated wiki project he's working on now at New Relic in downtown Portland. He presented his work at the Open Source Conference at the Portland Convention Center in July 2014. Opposite page: The annual event is held here because many consider Oregon to be the center of the Free/Open Source Software movement.
▪ Quilt information on page 164.

"If you're an original thinker, you can pursue your idea here," he continues. "You can afford to live and find a community that will support you, but you won't get rich. You'll find the living good here."

Another of Ward's commandments: "Ask yourself, 'What is the simplest thing that could possibly work?'"

Here's the thing about true geeks: they use the best tool for the job, not the latest bright shiny technology when a three- ring binder will do.

So when I asked what he's working on now, Ward held up a three-ring binder with graphics illustrating his current work on federated wikis. The new project enables people to develop smaller wikis by borrowing from other wikis in a process called forking. Not only does this enable wiki contributors to control their own contributions, it allows disagreement to exist, with opposing viewpoints connected so they can be explored. He planned to show the binder to visitors to his booth at the 2014 Open Source Conference (OSCON), the largest gathering of Open Source folks in the world that is held in Portland every July.

It was the simplest thing that could possibly work.

Pieces
of
Portland

A Super Colossal Crafty Wonderland

Portland is a flat out crafty wonderland. For reals. In fact, twice a year the Oregon Convention Center fills with more than 200 vendors displaying their art and craft in events called, what else: *Crafty Wonderland: Super Colossal Spring Sale* and *Crafty Wonderland: Super Colossal Holiday Sale.* The events are "meant to bring together crafty people with those who appreciate cool handmade items, to support artists, and to spread the joy of craft throughout our community." These extravaganzas are very popular in Portland. You probably should be getting in line already.

The two women responsible for Crafty Wonderland met at Portland Super Crafty, a women's craft collective that produced the book *Super Crafty: Saving the World from Mass-Production.*

When you meet someone in Portland, especially a woman, there is a very good chance she creates some kind of art and/or craft. It's almost a prerequisite for admission at the city gates. Men can get a pass, but it's way better if they have at least a bit of the maker in them.

There are plenty of makers at Portland's Saturday Market, which is the largest continuously-operated outdoor market in the U.S. The market is a mutual benefit corporation of 400 members (with 252 on site at a time), and all items must be handmade by the person selling them. A committee of members screens items for quality. The market attracts an estimated one million visitors each year and generates an estimated $10 million in annual sales.

Let's take knitting, for example. Portland has an enormous and strong knitting community. Knitters meet in brewpubs, coffee shops, private homes, community spaces and pretty much everywhere else. Check out just a sample of groups listed on

Meetup: Sip and Knitters (to have support in knitting and life while eating great food and sipping beverages), Pints and Sticks (knitters who meet at Portland brewpubs, bottle shops, homebrew and beer hubs), Veggie Knitting (for vegans/vegetarians and others who treat animals and the environment with respect), Prime-Time Knit Wits (for mature, liberated women), Queer Craft Night (come hang out and pretend to work on projects while meeting awesome fun people and making new connections, or for reals work on things if you have sh#!t to finish), Westside Make and Cake (crafters who believe "a party without a cake is just a meeting!"). I tried to count all the knitting groups and subgroups and cross groups and Meetups with knitting as one of its activities, but my head exploded.

There is also an active community of yarn bombers, where colorful knitted or crocheted pieces are incorporated into infrastructure and most anything above ground. Most of our city's bombs are relatively small, affixed to bike racks, small trees, street signs and so forth. Keep your eyes open in north, northeast and southeast neighborhoods, and you'll see one soon. Every winter holiday season, Portland knitters create "ugly sweaters" for sculptures and statues around Pioneer Square and Courthouse (see photo on page 5). We think the festive sweaters and leg warmers they make are anything but ugly. Beautiful, in fact. Which might explain why they disappear sometimes.

The most organized yarn bomb project we've seen in Portland was an art installation that was attached to the Broadway Bridge in July/August 2013, to commemorate the bridge's 100th birthday. Some 150 volunteers created four 18x21-foot superblankets in a rainbow of colors that were hung as banners that looked like colorful sails poofing in the wind. Once the exhibit was over, the superblankets were divided into 42 6x6-foot afghans and given to local homeless shelters. The knitters wisely used non-felting wool so they won't be damaged by rain or laundering.

Let it be known that while we love yarn-bombing with all our hearts, we wonder if another trend is bubbling under the surface, ready to emerge. The world might not be ready for quilt bombing, but we bet Portland is.

> **Opposite page:** The magnificent rainbow yarn bomb project on the Broadway Bridge marked the bridge's 100th birthday in 2013. The large spreads were divided into smaller blankets for homeless shelters. **This page:** Informal yarn bombing shows up pretty much across the city, this one on a bike rack in Kenton. You can find them on sign posts, trees, and pretty much everything else.
> ■ Quilt information on page 164.

Pieces of Portland

When I thought of all the artists/crafters I've met in Portland to pick one to represent the rest, I immediately thought of Rose McCoy, who does just about every kind of arts and crafts and is always learning something new.

Rose comes by her creativity honestly, being from a family with a long line of artistic talents. Her extended family includes a painter, a sculptor, knitters, quilters, a landscape designer, a classical music composer, a music producer, an anime cartoonist, an illustrator and seamstresses. And that's just the list off the top of her head.

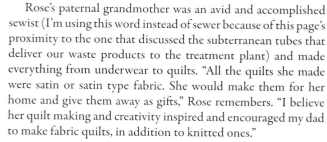

We met at SCRAP's Creative Reuse Center in northeast Portland, as she was in the market for some supplies. SCRAP began in 1998 as a place for teachers to share classroom materials and has outgrown its space four times, most recently moving to a larger place in 2015. In 2013 it diverted 140 tons from landfills. The organization now has satellite locations in California, Michigan, Louisiana, Texas and Washington, D.C.

Rose can hardly remember a time she wasn't making some kind of art or craft. She grew up in Eugene, where her parents lived after they were married. Her father's family already lived there, and her mother met her father when she came up from southern California to visit her brother.

Her first memory of making something is when she was five or six. She dug clay from her yard, made a pinch pot, then let it dry in the garage.

Her father, Grant McCoy, was her artistic role model. He painted, sculpted, knitted and quilted. He learned to knit in the army, while he was based in Okinawa during the Vietnam War. That's where soldiers stayed before being sent into battle in Vietnam. "He learned to knit during his time in the army because to keep the soldiers sane, they would supply them with all sorts of things like guitars, bibles, arts and crafts like yarn."

Rose notes that, "He never made it to combat because he fell gravely ill and was sent back to the U.S. and honorably discharged."

By the time her parents were married a few years later, Grant had knitted his first quilt, a block pattern.

Opposite page: Rose McCoy shows the first quilt she made in a class at Portland's Modern Domestic. She chose the fabric for the pieced front, the backing fabric is from her late father's collection. **This page:** SCRAP uses its mobile unit at community events. The creative reuse center recently moved to a much larger space.

■ Quilt information on page 164.

Rose's paternal grandmother was an avid and accomplished sewist (I'm using this word instead of sewer because of this page's proximity to the one that discussed the subterranean tubes that deliver our waste products to the treatment plant) and made everything from underwear to quilts. "All the quilts she made were satin or satin type fabric. She would make them for her home and give them away as gifts," Rose remembers. "I believe her quilt making and creativity inspired and encouraged my dad to make fabric quilts, in addition to knitted ones."

Her father made two quilts for Rose, but after he became ill when she was 15, he no longer quilted. When he died in 1999, Rose was "inspired to pick up where he left off, and my mom gave me the large box of fabric he had collected over the years so I could make some quilts."

Rose took a class at Portland's Modern Domestic, where she made the quilted wall hanging she's holding in the photo. She has another one in the works that is no doubt finished by now. She uses some of her father's fabric in her own quilts now, carrying forward his legacy. The backing fabric on her first quilt is from her father's stash.

Quilt making is a small part of the arts and crafts Rose creates now, including painting, mixed media using recycled items, paper arts, sewing, knitting, repurposing, photo transferring, and more. She makes art and craft because she likes beautiful things and the creative act is soothing for her, something she turns to when the walls start to come in. Her artistic talents also extend to music, as she plays autoharp.

Soon after our interview, Rose spent a sabbatical in several cities, including Seattle, San Francisco, New York and Pittsburgh. "It was a transformative experience," she says after her return. "Even though I have always loved art and incorporated it into my life, I had begun to lose the sense of where it played a role in my life. During my time away, I was able to rediscover why art is so important in my life and how it is a permanent fixture in what brings my life meaning. While away, I completed several paintings and haven't stopped even though I am back to my regular 9-5 job."

Rose finds Portland to be very open to and supportive of creative minds. "It's literally a gathering place for creativity," she says. As she sorts through a bin of wood at SCRAP, she explains that she likes Portland's emphasis on reuse, recycling and upcycling. "I like the openness to seeing everything as a resource, as something that can be used rather than thrown away."

So crafty.

So Portland.

So real McCoy.

Pieces of Portland

It's kind of strange that a city known far and wide for people not wearing any clothes is also a very big deal for fashion design. On a per capita basis, Portland is many runways ahead of any other city when it comes to Project Runway. In 13 seasons, four people from the Portland metropolitan area have won the fashion design competition. That's almost one third! And on a per capita basis, a nearly impossible achievement. As Tim Gunn would say, Portland designers know how to make it work.

Our most recent winner—Michelle Lesniak—says that's no accident. "Portland is such a free-thinking city," she says. "Portlanders are taught from early on to not be afraid of who you are. Here it's okay to be yourself. We are rule breakers by nature."

She attributes part of our creativity to the weather. "We don't get gloomy about the rain here," Michelle explains. "We're thinking, 'Oh, good, it's raining so I can get to work now.' In the summer, when it's sunny all the time, I'm outside sketching, looking for inspiration so I will be ready when the rain comes."

We met Michelle in her southeast Portland studio on a sunny day in November. The airing of the 2014 season of Project Runway All-Stars was a couple of weeks in, and Michelle was competing. I didn't ask her for any inside information, because, 1) I didn't want to put her on the spot, and 2) since I've convinced my son and husband to watch with me, I didn't want to know the ending of the story before they did. All three of us are sure she should win, and that she will. [Actually, she came in third, but she represented Portland well!]

Michelle was born and raised in Portland and graduated from Cleveland High School. She's lived in other places, including New York and Chicago, but finds none can compete with Portland.

"I love this town," she says. "There's nowhere else in the world I'd rather be. There are so many designers here and people support local businesses and buy local. It may not be huge amounts of money, but we do what we can afford."

Some call Portland an incubator for slow fashion, comparing it with the slow food movement, where there is care and attention to detail at every step rather than producing as much as possible in the shortest time.

"Even the big marketing agencies do things differently. We're a little cheeky, we take a different approach, we don't take things so seriously that we can't make them fun. We're very confident in who we are and what we do. It's just how we are, and people who can take that stay here, those who can't move."

The mannequins in her storefront window featured pieces from her Decay collection, telling a dark, moody, emotional fairy tale that creates something beautiful, representing her feelings about her marriage ending while she was creating

it. She also designed the fabric in the collection, which has exquisite images of decaying leaves printed on the softest silk chiffon. Then when you look more closely, you see the rats among the leaves. That's where the cheekiness comes in.

Since Decay, Michelle has designed two more collections. The most recent is Weather Worn, inspired by photographs and stories from the Great Depression. There is a lot of layering, mixing of different textures and fabrics. If I were Heidi Klum, I'd totally say, "This is very exciting, we really haven't seen anything like this sectioned plaid shirt before. It truly represents who you are as a designer. I want to wear it!"

Everything in Michelle Lesniak Design is locally manufactured. She purchases fabric (when she doesn't design it herself) from a wholesale four-story, football-field-sized warehouse in Los Angeles. A collection has 25-30 pieces. She makes all the patterns and cuts the fabric herself to ensure its most frugal and accurate use.

Between three and five pieces in every size of each piece are sewn locally. Her designs are featured in a number of boutiques, and she makes sales from her studio and online, where she has customers from around the globe.

Before winning Project Runway, she had a day job and did design and sewing on the side. Now she works on her collections full time, and her designs are featured in museums. "I am living my dream life," she says. "Designing is my therapy. I wake up designing, I go to sleep designing."

Recently, she designed costumes for Oregon Ballet Theater. She also enjoys public speaking, recently talking with an audience of 5,000 about how she finds inspiration.

Michelle grew up sewing because she grew up among women who sewed, including her grandmother, who made Michelle a quilt she keeps with her in her studio for inspiration. It wasn't that many years ago that she saved up all year to attend the annual Sewing & Stitchery Expo in Puyallup, Washington. Her life changed a lot after winning Project Runway.

"Project Runway was both the most horrific and most rewarding experience I've ever had," she says now. The horrific part was the sleep deprivation and physical, mental and emotional exhaustion. The best part was the creation of a family bond among the designers. Michelle says the drama that sometimes seems to be the leading character on the show is mostly the result of exhaustion and stress.

"Everybody ends up with a little Post Traumatic Stress Disorder," she admits. Watching the show later gave her little heart palpitations.

But the designers form one big support group. "As soon as everybody gets a good night's sleep and a little distance from the drama, we are all one big family," she says. "We're actually very close, it's a little like surviving combat together. We stay in

Pieces of Portland

touch with one another long after the season ends. Fashion design is such a hard industry. Many of the people who were on Project Runway are out of the industry now. Three or four of those on my season, which was only two years ago, are already out."

Of course, Portland (and Oregon) has a solid textile and apparel industry heritage. An ideal place for raising sheep, woolen mills were built in Oregon soon after white settlement began. Pendleton Woolen Mills first made trading blankets and robes for Native Americans. In the early 20th century, the company breathed new life and color into the men's wool plaid shirt. Jantzen gained fame by revolutionizing the bathing suit into a swimming suit (for serious swimming as opposed to leisurewear) when it brought the rib-stitch to swimwear in 1919. Langlitz Leathers' amazing jackets are world famous.

Columbia Sportswear's founders came to Portland after fleeing Nazi Germany in 1938 and, inspired by the great outdoors in their new home, created an outdoor apparel company for all kinds of recreation. Nike, the world's largest designer and supplier of athletic shoes and apparel, grew from an experiment to create track shoes using a waffle iron in 1964. The company

has brought designers from all over to its headquarters in the Portland metro area, and they have made revolutionary design changes in shoes and clothing for athletes. Portland is also the home of Adidas' North American headquarters. There are a growing number of small specialty activewear labels in Portland now, some founded by alumni of the larger companies. Portland Development Commission named footwear and activewear as one of the industries it targets for economic development.

Portland's growing apparel industry provides jobs to significant numbers of immigrants and refugees, who worked with textiles before coming to America and continue the folk art traditions of their homeland. The current vibrancy of the local fashion design scene is partly credited to Seaplane, a Portland boutique that featured local apparel and jewelry designers from 2000-08 before it was purchased, then closed. It provided an important showcase for local designers. Portland's apparel industry is growing, supported by the Portland Apparel Development Co-op, "a shared studio with access to industrial machinery for all textile applications...to help members of the textile industry bring their ideas and projects to reality within a productive community."

There was one more thing I had to ask Michelle before leaving. Is Tim Gunn as wonderful as he seems? "Tim Gunn is even more wonderful than he seems. He's so generous, he's better than Santa Claus. He's just the most genuine, wonderful human being ever."

Don't you just love it when that happens?!

Opposite page: Michelle Lezniak, winner of Project Runway Season 13, holds a beloved quilt her grandmother made for her outside her southeast Portland studio. This page: While we talk, she prepares materials for her next fashion collection. ■ Quilt information on page 164.

Pieces
of
Portland

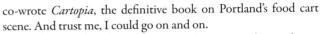

Manufacturing probably isn't the first thing that comes to mind when you think of Portland. That's more of a Rust Belt thing, and we think of ourselves as a more Green Belt kind of place. But making things has always been pretty big in Portland. In fact, almost one-third of the Portland area's gross domestic product comes from manufacturing, according to the U.S. Department of Commerce's Bureau of Economic Analysis, which is a larger percentage than cities in the country's largest industrial centers.

The first people who lived here made things from raw materials for their own use and to trade with others. White settlers quickly began processing raw materials like timber (e.g., sawmills, tanneries) and food crops (e.g., flour mills), first for local consumption, then for export. Through the 19th century, additional industries were developed, ranging from the manufacture of tools and equipment to ramp up raw material processing (e.g., steam engines, paper mills) to more specialized economic activity (e.g., rope factory, pickle works, printing). By 1890, Portland had 600 firms converting raw materials into manufactured goods.

In the 20th century, Portland became known for ship building, especially during the two world wars. The relative low cost of energy supported a thriving metals industry. Electronics manufacturing began in 1946 and has now grown to more than 1,200 high tech firms in the Portland metropolitan area, earning us a new nickname—the Silicon Forest. Portland also manufactures trucks and complex metal components and products. Portland Development Commission has designated "advanced manufacturing" as one of its initiatives.

§

An interesting new concept has appeared on the local manufacturing scene in recent years. A "maker movement" was launched in the mid-2000s by people who want to make things themselves, rather than take part in a mass production consumer culture driven by planned obsolescence. While manufacturing an item used to take an enormous expenditure of resources from industry and big business, technological advances have made manufacturing possible for regular people, as long as they have access to knowledge, skills and tools. That's where ADX comes in, providing a space where people make and learn by sharing tools, knowledge and experience. (The AD stands for Art and Design; adding the X makes it a play on Portland's airport code, PDX.)

ADX was founded by Kelley Roy in 2011 in a 14,000-square-foot warehouse in inner southeast Portland. Kelley is basically a whirlwind wonder woman. She grew up in Virginia, where she was well on her way to becoming an Olympic equestrian when her parents redirected her to college. She got her undergraduate degree in geology, then a graduate degree in urban planning. She co-wrote *Cartopia*, the definitive book on Portland's food cart scene. And trust me, I could go on and on.

Kelley thought she might like living in the Pacific Northwest so she visited Seattle in 1994, but it just didn't connect with her. So she tried Portland. "As soon as I drove into town," she remembers, "I felt like I was home. I found my people." Just before starting ADX, Kelley was working with raw spaces in Portland, setting them up for events and galleries, when she heard about an all-encompassing work studio and art space in Brooklyn, New York. She looked into the concept and decided Portland needed a place where people could make things using sophisticated tools and expensive equipment that they couldn't afford to buy, and ADX was born.

There are four ways to use ADX: become a member and use the large selection of tools and equipment; sublease space and use ADX resources as needed; take classes to learn new skills and how to use new tools; hire ADX to manufacture something for you.

"We have hardware and software needed for 3-D design and printing. Members make prototypes, then reiterate as needed, and go to production," Kelley says.

In the three-and-a-half years since it opened, 200 businesses have launched from ADX. Items made range from handcrafted straight razors and strops to award-winning Scandinavian-influenced furniture. The day we visited, we saw a teardrop shaped travel trailer that had been built there.

Kelley also founded Portland Made, a self-sustaining collective of makers, artisans and manufacturers that advocates for and supports its members by providing education and marketing, a shared resource hub, and a brand that promotes their products locally and globally. "Why go it alone," Portland Made asks, "when you could have a whole community behind you?"

ADX has become a popular tourist destination, and all of that traffic provides a lot of organic promotion for Portland Made. "We are definitely on a lot of radars," Kelley says. "We've had 75,000 people come through, including people from Japan, Australia and South America. ADX and Portland Made businesses get exposure to media, politicians and consumers."

While many other maker spaces across the country have failed, ADX's business plan projects that it will reach profitability this year, although it faces ongoing financial challenges due to huge up-front investments it made in equipment and staff. ADX and Portland Made had more than 700 members in November 2014. Kelley says ADX is thriving because of its business model and because it's in Portland. "I don't think we would be where we are today if we didn't offer design, fabrication and production services," she says. "Being tied to the local design and manufacturing sector is critical to our success. ADX is incubating Portland's artisanal manufacturing sector, and providing much needed services to

locally grown companies throughout the state of Oregon," she says, pointing to parts ADX is manufacturing for two breweries.

"I'm a business person, not a maker," Kelley explains, "so I've hired people to do the things beyond my expertise. We are a social impact business that takes care of people first, then profit. What brings me joy is seeing people believe and invest in themselves. It's really hard to trust oneself, but when you have a built-in community of support, it makes it easier to take the leap. That's what ADX is: a resource for risk takers."

"We're tapping into the desire to make only what's needed and reducing how much waste is created in the process. Making just enough, just in time. There's a lot of thought given to how to design and produce to avoid waste."

As Kelley points out, a lot of us have become more conscious about how the things we buy are made, who's making them and under what conditions. She likens it to what has been happening in the food movement for the past 20 years.

When she was dreaming up ADX, she looked at companies like Portland's Leatherman Tool Group. "Their bylaws say they have to stay in Portland," Kelley points out. "There are a lot of companies, B corps and business alliances in Portland that have a deep commitment to the community, manufacturers that are dedicated to high quality and have a sensibility around sustainability. Portland Made acts as a business alliance for companies with these values. People, planet, then profit."

> **Opposite page:** The ADX sign on its southeast Portland home for designing and making. **This page:** Founder Kelley Roy has made a lot of things happen since she came here in 2011. The well-worn signs on the floor of ADX are evidence of its 700+ members and the 75,000 visitors who have toured ADX in the last three-and-a-half years.

"There is so much creativity in Portland," she continues. "People are pioneers, they move here to start something. The lifestyle is very active. There's a strong work ethic, but we also like to enjoy life and have fun."

Kelley says ADX gets constant inquiries about how it works; people want similar places in their cities. "We want to help them, but it's such a place- and culture-based thing," she admits. "We are super connected with the manufacturing sector in Portland. And everybody in Portland wants to know how to do and make things."

"There's something about Portland. We are so curious and so ready to geek out over things. Sometimes it goes a little over the top," she laughs. "I'm kind of the den mother here. I try to keep things real."

Pieces
of
Portland

This page: Portland transportation modes compete for attention in this city where it really matters how you move. **Opposite page:** There are so many tiny cars on the road that groups of them gather in some parts of town. Our PDX airport is best in class and its 1970s carpet—whose design was based on its runway configuration—attracted a cult following. It has photo galleries on Facebook, Instagram, flickr and who knows where else. It has inspired the making of many items for purchase. Its replacement in 2015 was widely mourned, so much so that it was given away in 1,000 yard lots to local makers. And it's the grand marshal of the 2015 Starlight Parade.

■ Quilt information on page 164.

L et's face it, Portland is completely obsessed with how people move about. Head down one street, we're told to Go By Streetcar. Before long, we're approaching a bridge that confronts us with a plea to Go by Train. Later, we are implored to Go by Bike. Then, Go by Tram. Go by Tram?? What city transportation system would tell us to go by tram??

We see these exhortations all around town and begin to feel guilty that we may be neglecting one or more. We even count the number of people who commute by skateboard!

We are for any transportation that does not include automobiles. Well, I mean, sure, you can have a car, but it's probably best if it's either old enough to be considered vintage (as long as it passes DEQ), uses biodiesel or is electric powered or at least a hybrid and is as small as you can possibly have it and still fit inside somehow. We're seeing more and more of those really teeny cars that look almost like toys, especially in some neighborhoods. You know that company that brands itself as the nation's only eco-friendly auto club (Better World Club)? It's headquarters are in Portland, of course.

Even our airport has a cult following. Much higher powers than me have declared PDX to be the best airport in the country. It's not just about the free wi-fi or that most of the shops there are local businesses that don't gouge customers because they set prices the same as their in-town locations.

It's all about the carpet cult. Yes, you heard me. There is an online vault of photos people have taken of their feet standing on it. I am serious. And in our explorations for this book, Joyce discovered...wait for it...the carpet has more than one pattern. Wait til this gets out! There has been great wailing and gnashing of teeth of late because the beloved carpet is being replaced in 2015. I halfway expect subversive action. But not to worry. You can still get T-shirts, socks, beer and any number of things exhibiting the old pattern. And there's a waiting list of people who want souvenir pieces of the acres that have been removed and I fully expect it to support cottage industries that upcycle it into useful items for our buying pleasure. Calling all makers!

The Portland jury is still out on the design of the new one.

Our train station is not half bad either, and I've heard there is actually a Portlandia car on Amtrak's Cascade line between Eugene and Vancouver, B.C. Can anyone confirm this? And have you heard of the Bolt Bus? I've heard it's actually owned by Greyhound but is rebranded for hipsters. Can that be true?

Did you know that the first long distance transmission of electricity happened here between a powerhouse at Willamette Falls and a string of lights in downtown Portland in 1889? Local interest in electricity is one reason Portland was the third city in the country to have electric streetcars, also beginning in 1889. Portland's first streetcar was horse drawn and traveled along First Avenue between NW Glisan and SW Carruthers streets. A round trip took one to two hours, depending on the horse. Walking was faster.

During the 1890s, Portland's electric streetcar network extended to about a five-mile radius on Portland's east side, or the distance the cars could travel in about 30 minutes—the maximum time commuters were willing to spend traveling

to and from work. Streetcar use rose sharply in Portland until about 1920, when they began to be replaced by buses, which could take more flexible routes. The last streetcar left Portland streets in 1950. When the Ross Island Bridge was built in 1926, it didn't even have streetcar tracks. But things have a way of repeating themselves, and now Portland is laying streetcar lines again.

The first automobile arrived in Portland in 1898, and by 1912, Portland had the highest per capita car ownership rate in the country! How bizarre is that?

Because cars can go so much faster than streetcars on roads built with them in mind, after World War II the commuting limit reached much further, all the way to bedroom communities that became suburbs. Lots and lots of paradise was paved over for all the freeways and places to park all these cars. Often, space in-between was skipped over and remained unincorporated.

A uto emissions became a leading cause of air pollution, but air quality has greatly improved over the last few decades. In the latter part of the 20th century, when temperature inversions kept cold still air hanging at the surface, carbon monoxide was a problem. But with improvements in auto emission controls and the Portland metropolitan area's auto emissions inspections program that began in 1975, carbon monoxide is rarely a problem in Portland now. The ban on open burning and wood stove certification has reduced particulates in the air. Portland's investments in public and alternative transportation are given partial credit for reducing ozone pollution, along with vehicle inspections.

I guess this means being obsessed with movement is healthy for children and other living things.

WELCOME TO AMERICA'S
BICYCLE CAPITAL

The Bicycle Way

Many in the baby boom generation became disillusioned with a culture thoroughly dominated by the automobile, a trend that was accelerated by the oil embargoes of the early 1970s and ever increasing prices of gasoline. Cities began to rethink their transportation services and plans. So Portland aborted a plan to keep building freeways right through neighborhoods and spent the money instead on improving public transit and building one of the country's first modern light rail systems.

The Trimet mass transit system is considered among the nation's best, combining buses, light rail, streetcars and commuter rail. You really don't need to own a car here. In the 1970s, Portland completely rebuilt two avenues in downtown into a transit mall that restricted auto traffic in favor of buses. It now stretches 1.2 miles along 57 blocks, from Union Station in the north to Portland State University at its south end. All light rail lines and the city's bus lines connect here. The American Planning Association named the Transit Mall one of 10 Great Streets in 2014 (with the likes of Broadway in New York City and Pennsylvania Avenue in Washington, D.C.) And of course there's a killer app to help us use it.

Portland's tram came about because OHSU (Oregon Health and Science University), one of the region's biggest employers, was running out of building room at its West Hills (Pill Hill) location. To keep its expansion in Portland rather than in a suburb, the City partially funded a tramway to quickly and efficiently move medical staff and patients from the hill to a new development on the south waterfront with outpatient clinics and other facilities. Making the trip by road is very time consuming and a big pain in the butt. Unless you are on a sightseeing jaunt.

As we saw on page 36, soon the most exciting transportation structure in Portland will be the Tillicum Crossing, where no cars will be allowed. Bikers are thrilled, to say the least. And speaking as an older person, I get a little freaked out in bike lanes when cars are speeding by me only inches away. I prefer to have enough room to spare so that, if I tip over, I won't become road kill. My balance ain't what it used to be.

When you talk about bikes in Portland, it's important to know which biking community you're dealing with.

There are the bike commuters—the ones who view cycling as the best and most sustainable way to travel on wheels. They are hardcore, and neither sleet nor hail nor dark of night shall keep them from biking to and from work. Portland has so many of them that our city has the highest per capita commuting by bike rate in the U.S., which is one reason why Portland has called

itself America's Bicycle Capital. It seems we've been surpassed by other cities this past year, and it hurt, but we have people planning our comeback and calling for better bike infrastructure.

The recreational biker mainly rides for pleasure and exercise and uses her or his bike to explore and play outdoors. Many in this group are families, and parents are instilling good environmental and social values in their children through biking. There is a lot of overlap among commuters and recreators, but they may have different bikes for different uses.

Then there are the bicycle racers, the ones who push themselves to their fitness limits in order to win. They may also commute and recreate on bikes, but their racing machine is a finely-tuned thing of beauty and you probably shouldn't touch it.

But there's been another category of Portland bikers that might be most Portland of all, and most fun to write about. I'm not totally sure what to call them. They are the ones pushing the limit out beyond the edge. They combine bike craft with fun and adventure and not a little mayhem. Those who view bikes as a way to express their freedom. Bike anarchists. Bike remakers. Bike pornographers.

You might be surprised to learn what many Portlanders do to and with their bikes. Some make them 15 or more feet tall. Bikes capable of carrying huge cargo. Bikes outfitted with pontoons for amphibious travel. Bikes on fire. Bikes tested for surviving the apocalypse. Bikes with charcoal grills. Bikes with picnic tables attached. I sense that very few people in these biking circles actually ever buy a bike, they make everything from things found lying on the street or in dumpsters. There is much creativity on display.

As one biker lamented back in 2006 on the C.H.U.N.K. 666 website, "The Ross Island Explorer, the world's first fully amphibious human-powered tallbike-paddleboat. What? Crap, what does a guy have to do to be original these days?"

C.H.U.N.K is a hard group to describe. Some say it is a mutant bike or freak bike group. I couldn't find a mission statement anywhere, but its website looks like a legit biz selling polo shirts and bike accessories, but clicking on links takes you anywhere but there. Go ahead, you try. Here's a blog entry from 2004:

> "It started to rain just as we reached the river. We convinced ourselves that we knew what we were doing and floundered across. All the rides, people, and supplies made it to the island, although some were more submerged than planned. Once we arrived, we agreed that it was one of the stupidest things that we had ever done. This new world was very entertaining. We looked for treasure, sang around the fire, swam, and ate and drank well. Sandy made a spooky burning will-o'-the-wisp raft and towed it around the river, and the prince of the hydrochuds visited. It rained all night, which means that there were floaters in the river on our way back due to the 'combined sewage outflow. Riding the Willamette made us feel free and strong."

One can't help but wonder about the effect this might be having on wildlife that takes refuge on Ross Island. We wonder if the bikers are aware of them? I bet if they knew, it would appeal to their caring side. And trust me, they do have a caring side, witness below.

Opposite page: This photo fills us with sadness and longing because it is only a memory at this point. In fact, the day after we took it, and watched tourist after tourist come to take a picture, the words and image were painted over by order of the City of Portland because it was deemed to be an ad for a bicycle shop nearby. Gonna have to part ways with city officials on this one. Think it was a dumbass move. In this photo, you can't help but notice how much space downtown is reserved for automobiles. Even when they're not there.

■ Quilt information on page 164.

"What is it like to ride with us? One can learn of the phases of the typical foray. From thence the perils of the night delivery, recovery mission, rain rides, aquachopper expeditions, and Flaming Bikes of Deth might be comprehensible. If not, there's always an ordinary ride to the Mass…Danger cannot be avoided by staying close to home, either, as shown by our local operations, construction workshops, the West Side Invite, the Chunkathlon of 2002 (and the Chunkathlon of 2003 in Brooklyn), the Organ Donor Invitational, and the Mutant Bike Proving Grounds. Our caring side is made evident by our community service record, parade participation, children's crusade, neighborhood outreach program, and reflections on riding during wartime, while our more fabulous aspects are mentioned in our dress code article."

There have been no blog posts since 2011. Frankly, I'm worried.

Zoobombing may be the best known bike activity in Portland. Zoobombers ride minibikes down from the top of the most impressive hill above the zoo to the flat part far below, in the middle of the street. In the dark. My favorite zoobombers have all been hospitalized at some point. The police used to try to stop zoobombing for safety reasons, but you can't really put a lid on this form of revelry.

It's important to understand that zoobombing is not just an event, it is a culture. Some call it a religion. Zoobombers are behind many other interesting bike things in Portland, including Mini Bike Winter that features "craft night, torch night, chariot wars, big ass party, winter olympics, cupcake challenge, badass challenge (can you make it up the hill backwards and become a badass?), tour de bomb, mini bike bomb, freak bike bomb, gravity bike bomb, family bomb." They are also connected to bike polo, and it is said there are games every Sunday afternoon at Alberta Park rain or shine. You can see jousting matches and tall bike parades at the right community events.

SHIFT 2 Bikes is another decidedly Portland group, which "revels in expressing Portland's creative culture through performance events and bike fun intended to highlight the positive contributions of bicycling for the community at large." SHIFT promotes events like Pedalpalooza (a month long series of bike activities), Midnight Mystery Ride, Breakfast on the Bridges (free food and drink for bike commuters). Their community tendencies extend to things like helping bike people move.

"Shifties love to help when it comes to moving the belongings of other bikers. It's a big social event. Typically the movee provides coffee and light snacks before the ride, and beer and a meal at the end. The move doubles as a house warming party. You should definitely help on somebody else's bike move before asking for help on your own move, partly so you know what you're getting involved in and partly for karma. This is not a moving service for hire. We do this for friendship and good times, not for money. Knowing this, if you would like a herd of bike trailers to show-up at your place to assist your move in a pedal-powered way, then email movebybike. Please give at least a week's notice."

One of the most joyful among Portland bike groups is the Sprockettes. In 2004, a group of young women who met

zoobombing and had fantasized about starting a mini-bike dance crew made it happen, and they kept it going for 10 years.

Some 40 women have been involved over the years, wearing hot pink and black outfits and "performing their wild and wily acrobatic bike tricks in parking lots, dirt patches, city parks and warehouses."

On the last day of Pedalpalooza 2014, the Sprockettes celebrated their 10th anniversary by assembling past and present members for a performance in Colonel Summers Park, the site of their first gig. They promised that "past Sprockettes will dance some of our greatest hits, and current Sprockettes will perform new jams." We were there. They delivered!

Jonathan Maus, founder and editor of BikePortland.org pronounced it "one of those moments that will be talked about for years...an emotionally charged and historic performance." He should know, as he is one of the best-informed reporters on all things bike Portland.

Many former members who had moved to other cities returned for this anniversary performance. Over time, the Sprockettes have became known nationally, and even across the globe, with performances in different cities and many performance videos on YouTube. They've held summer camps for young prospective Sprockettes.

> **Opposite page:** Portland's incomparable Sprockettes in action at Pedalpalooza June 2014, when they performed some of their greatest hits to celebrate their 10th Anniversary. **This page:** They pose for a photo opp for adoring fans after the legendary performance at Colonel Summers Park.
> ■ Quilt information on page 164.

In addition to their bike energy and entertaining choreography, the group's purpose as described on its website was to present "an alternative to the dangerous mono-culture of what the ideal body type is; and promote female positive perspective that celebrates women's empowerment.'"

The global appreciation of the Sprockettes is reflected in a love letter from a young woman in Japan:

Dear my hero the Sprockettes,
*   I have only seen the Sprockettes on youtube so I really want to see them in live!!!!! and I am very interested in Portland, Oregon.*
*   I've heard the place there is so beautiful and Portland is the motherland of Bicycle. yeaa, my friends from Nagoya, just went to SSCXWC and saw you guys in Live!! My friends told me that you guys were so awesome! getting into muddy with great smiling!!*

That letter? It's only the best thing ever.

Sadly, there is little evidence the Sprockettes can still be seen "in live." Their website no longer comes up, and the group has gone radio silent. I could find no communication after its Pedalpalooza performance. Maybe it was the last waltz?

Lately, other zany biking events seem smaller and less visible too. I can't remember the last time I saw a Critical Mass. Then on February 2015, @dieselbol plaintively tweeted, "Is zoobombing still a thing?" Although the answer was in the affirmative, the fact that someone posed the question at all is enough to cause real alarm among the populace. And where is C.H.U.N.K. anyway?

Who's gonna pick up the bike freak flag and fly it now?

Pieces
of
Portland

Pieces
of
Portland

The Naked Truth

There are a lot of eyes focused on nudity in Portland, and for good reason. Our state constitution is pretty big on freedom of expression, and removing one's clothing is considered a form of expression. We are masters of expression.

I am told we have the greatest number of strip clubs per capita of any city in the country. And we are talking full on nudity at many, I am told. And oh, yes, we reportedly have a vegan strip club, but you probably knew that already because of Cory Booker's tweet that got crazy inexplicable coverage by national mainstream media.

For this aspect of this topic, we had to rely on reports from others because we didn't think that a couple of grannies showing up with a pile of quilts at a strip joint would make it past the bouncer. Some things just don't pair well. We also hear there is a well-known nude beach on Sauvie Island. We didn't actually go there ourselves because we didn't want to get sand on our quilts. Mainly.

Not to mention the fact that we have a sculpture downtown that is commonly known as "Three Groins in the Fountain" for the full frontal exposure the three figures display right there at eye level. For both adults and children. What's interesting is that it was commissioned by Georgia Pacific for the opening of its world headquarters. It's not clear if the sculpture had anything to do with GP's subsequent vanishing from Portland, but that's what happened and we're not at liberty to say more.

With all that said, we are 110% in favor of people letting it all hang out or air out whenever and wherever they are so moved, but we trust they will not be offended if we hold up a sufficiently-sized quilt to shield our own eyes. We are from the peace and free love generation, after all, but we've reached the age where nudity is just somewhat less interesting to us than it once was. Can you dig it?

I personally learned a lot about nudity when I made a short documentary film about Rev Phil Sano. He taught me that it is actually not illegal to be naked in public in Portland as long as you aren't being sexually provocative about it. He said this in defense of his dropping trou and streaking the field during a Portland Beavers game, and yes, that was the actual name of our minor league baseball team that left town when our baseball park was reconfigured as a soccer stadium. A sign of the times.

But back to nudity and Rev Phil. After I heard that the Rev was inclined toward spontaneous nudity, when we worked together on a subsequent documentary film about Free Geek, I was worried enough about seeing his junk that I insisted our little company be named Pants On Production. Fortunately, that kept anything from cropping up along those lines.

There are random moments of nakedness to be seen in Portland at random places. It's as easy as keeping your eyes open. For example, I have often spied naked people standing beside their bikes in the circle around the Joan of Ark statue that appears on page 150. Actually, in my Hawthorne neighborhood, nudity isn't really the exception, it's more like a rule. Spontaneous naked events happen in the streets, on the sidewalks and during Strip Jeopardy games in public places. You just have to know which ones. There's probably a wiki about them by now.

It didn't feel at all weird that we were invited to participate in skyclad croquet at the Deluxe Mystery Hole when we visited. Just another lazy afternoon in southeast Portland. Seriously, if you hang around the right people in Portland long enough, clothing begins to seem so—optional?

But of course the nakedest granddaddy in the buff of them all is the annual World Naked Bike Ride. Portland totally goes balls out for World Naked Bike Ride. Thousands and thousands of people of all shapes, sizes, ages and persuasions shed their textiles, hop on their bikes and ride like the wind. It's quite astonishing and must be witnessed. Being in the audience is challenging though because the route is not announced ahead of time. So how do people know where to go? What's the frequency, Kenneth? You have to know somebody who knows somebody who knows.

Once again, the right Rev Phil makes an appearance. Part of his fame comes from being arrested during the 2006 Naked Bike Ride when he was facilitating the flow of traffic but the driver of a large SUV did not believe in facilitation and ran into him. Yes, he was arrested, and yes he was vindicated. You should ask him to tell the story sometime, if he ever gets back from his global jaunts that feature films and performances illustrating the connection between bicycles and nudity and sexual freedom of expression.

You should ask him about that, too, he can explain it way better than me.

Some things are just outside my wheelhouse.

This page: Count Alexander von Svoboda carved "The Quest" from a single 200-ton piece of Italian marble, intended to be "symbolic of man's eternal search for brotherhood and enlightenment." Its street name is "Three Groins in the Fountain." **Opposite page:** Thousands of bikers gather as dusk falls for Portland's 2014 World Naked Bike Ride. We were advised to blur body parts that could be identified, and we kept a quilt handy just in case. Photo courtesy Jonathan Maus, bikeportland.org.

■ Quilt information on page 164.

Pieces of Portland

How Does Your Garden Grow?

There's a comfortable and funny banter between Bruce Wakefield as he and his partner Jerry Grossnickle tell the story of the amazing two-acre garden the two of them have created on a hidden hillside only minutes from downtown Portland.

Bruce was eight years old when his grandmother came to live with his family in California's San Fernando Valley. She was a gardener and recruited young Bruce to help her out for the next several years. The seed was planted, as it were, but it didn't germinate until after Bruce moved to Portland, where he met Jerry. In 1987, Bruce heard about the Hardy Plant Society of Oregon and decided to attend a meeting to absorb some gardening knowledge.

"From then on I went full throttle, it was a total immersion in gardening," he grins. "And Jerry and I formed a team." Growing up in Oregon City, Jerry's family always had a vegetable garden.

They bought their property in 1988. It had been on the market for four years, and Bruce describes it as a "steep scraggly woodsy marshy soggy piece of land that nobody wanted." After Jerry found room for a house near the top of the sloping acreage, they bought it for $25,000 and spent the next two years clearing the site by hand. "Neither of us was made of money," Bruce explains. "Jerry cleared vegetation growing wild so we could garden."

The large Douglas Fir trees on Bruce and Jerry's property had been logged in the early 20th century and not replanted, so there was a chaotic free-for-all among the vegetation left behind, with

countless trees mixed in with undergrowth up to 20 feet tall. "Plants were coming up by the tens of thousands. Trees wouldn't even fall because they were caught by branches of other trees. Jerry had to cut eight trees to get one to reach the ground." If the hillside had not already been logged, Bruce and Jerry would never have planted their garden. "We would never cut old growth trees to make a garden," Bruce says.

They designed the house themselves and found a builder. While the house was being built, they started creating the garden. They partitioned it into sections and laid out a lawn in the middle. Because their space was so large, they needed lots and lots of plants. For economy, they grew hundreds of perennials from seed. Over the years they kept adding sections of plants.

"When you live at a place as long as we have, you learn the microclimates and through trial and error, end up knowing what plants will thrive in what place," Bruce explains. "We didn't start out with a grand vision, we just made up our garden over time."

The two have a definite division of labor. Jerry is the designated garden engineer; he does the hardscape, vegetable garden, lawn and pathways. Bruce is the plant nerd. "I get to do the shopping!" Bruce laughs. "I don't have complete free reign, and I'm not as bad as a friend who writes all her gardening purchase checks as

Safeway in her ledger so her husband won't know how much she's spending."

Their garden now has a deer fence to keep out the plant predators who can destroy a garden in short order. "Jerry got tired of me moaning and finally put one in."

"He's smarter than I am," Jerry replies. "He uses a subtle strategy to get what he wants." "No, you're the smarter one," Bruce retorts, "because now that we have a fence, we have a perimeter. I can't expand now." They both laugh.

Besides still doing all the work on their garden themselves, Bruce has also devoted a breathtaking amount of his time and skills to the Hardy Plant Society of Oregon (HPSO). He's been on the board of directors for 20 of the group's 26 years and held every official position in the organization. He's now serving as the volunteer office director, and does all the back end work on the group's website. He started HPSO's travel club and organizes its international tours, which sell out in mere minutes. He still supervises the Hortlandia plant sale, in which more than 100 nursery owners and garden artists participate.

People like Bruce and Jerry are what make organizations like HPSO thrive in Portland. HPSO has more than 2,300 members and is one of the largest nonprofit gardening groups on the west coast. It hosts lots of gardening events, open garden tours, plant and garden art sales and many other programs and activities year round. It publishes a quarterly magazine and provides a home for nearly 20 garden blogs on its website.

Oh, and by the way, the fact that we obsess over hardy plants that last over the years does not diminish our interest in acquiring new plants. We keep seeking out even more exotic and interesting specimens. Once addicted, resistance is futile.

Opposite page: With an easy, loving and funny banter, Jerry Grossnickle and Bruce Wakefield tell the story of the amazing garden they've created over the past 25 years on a steep hillside north and west of downtown Portland. The bottom left photo is the view from the deck of their home. **This page:** A quilt that was a gift from a gardening friend, Nancy Stober, covers a table in one of the many lovely landing spots within their garden. ■ Quilt information on page 164.

Pieces
of
Portland

Another Roadside Attraction

As one might expect, with this many plants, Portland is bound to have to some floral oddities—even some genetic weirdness. Why, I've seen it in my own yard.

In 1997, we had a 65-foot long concrete wheelchair ramp built in our small front yard because our front porch was 65 inches above the sidewalk. I decided on a concrete rather than wooden one because I knew we could pile soil up to the edge of concrete, and that meant we wouldn't have to install handrails. And it meant I could garden in all the spaces between the ramp segments, as the yard was now a veritable clean slate.

It was a bold move, but I had a feeling I was on the right path when a *très chic* couple walked by with their standard poodle and stopped to chat as I was putting the first plants in the ground beside the concrete. "What an interesting design element you've incorporated into your yard," the woman asked. "What was your inspiration?"

"Uh, I guess it would have to be my son's wheelchair," I replied. Which did not seem to be the answer they were expecting.

I gave each section of dirt a name, and in the lowest part, I planted a lot of different colorful, unusual and exciting plants. I called it the Zone of Exuberance. Two of the varieties were *Amaranthus caudatus* and *Amaranthus hypochondriacus*. They expressed their exuberance that summer and died down in winter. Come spring, literally hundreds of volunteers sprouted up where they had been and not knowing what they were, I decided to give them free reign and see what developed.

The picture on the opposite page shows what happened. At first I wasn't sure if it was plant or animal. It looks exactly like what you're thinking it looks like. You're not going to make me say it out loud, are you? Good.

The new specimen was unlike any of the plants I had put in the prior summer. My best guess is that the two Amaranths had shared more than sunshine and water while they cohabitated and created a new life form. Our parking strip has been full of them ever since! Kind of a phallic urban forest, if you will. About as tall as, er, well, the average groin. They die back every winter, but just like the swallows of Capistrano, they return every spring. True to form.

We thought it was our private little joke until we overheard the embarrassed titters, admiring whistles and outright guffaws from passersby.

Then one day I was telling someone I had just met where we lived, and her eyes widened, her voice raised 12 registers, and she said, "YOU live in THAT house?!? The one with the PLANTS???"

"You do realize that people make pilgrimages from all over the city to see those plants!?" she exclaimed.

Uh, no, not exactly. But come to think of it, we had noticed people—especially tastefully attired, impeccably groomed, well toned men—lingering on our sidewalk, admiring the view. Some have shown up with landscape cameras and tripods and spend long periods taking portraits. From every angle.

We have viewed our plants with renewed respect ever since. And watched them more closely. They're almost like family.

We call the section below the Vienna Boys Choir.

On this day, two words: Lorena Bobbitt.

They are hardy to at least Zone 8, because they keep coming back every year. And they're starting to spread! There are some in our neighbors' yards now and we've spotted them elsewhere in the neighborhood, probably because we've happily shared seed that spills from the shafts.

And even though we've planted many other fine plants in the parking strip in years since, and every spring I swear I'm going to make room for new plants and not let these highly erect specimens crowd them, in the end, I don't have the heart to whack back these purple giants.

I'm not even sure I have the right tool.

Opposite page: Despite never planting plants that look like this, our parking strip has become a triple x-rated zone for many years now. No matter what we do, they keep coming up so we've learned to embrace them. In fact, they've become a roadside attraction. ▪ Quilt information on page 164.

Pieces of Portland

Farm Your Yard or Farm My Yard

I've watched an anti-lawn sentiment grow like weeds during my 40 years in Portland. Lawns take too much water, people use too much pesticide and they're not creating enough value in the community. And then there's the mowing. I guess they're better than pavement, but not by much.

Now very few of the yards in many neighborhoods, especially in close-in locations, have lawns. I haven't had one for more than 25 years in the back and close to 20 in the front.

Some of the lawn's demise can be traced to increased interest in home food gardening. The organization Food Not Lawns was founded in Eugene, Oregon in 1999 by a group of activists who handed out free meals at Food Not Bombs in a city park. They decided to grow some of the food for meals they provided.

According to its website, "Soon we started hearing about other chapters and realized we had spawned a powerful, inspiring part of the growing sustainability movement."

When member Heather Flores published the book, *Food Not Lawns: How to Turn your Yard into a Garden and Your Neighborhood into a Community*, in 2006, new local FNL chapters starting popping up all over. "Now we are a global community of avant gardeners, working together to grow and share food, seeds, medicine, and knowledge."

We found three active chapters listed for Portland. Even City Hall has joined the movement, with a small vegetable garden planted on the unpaved part of its grounds.

The City of Portland also has 50 community gardens around the city; many have wait lists. The closest one to my house has 99 plots and 125 people waiting.

§

Portlander Albert Kaufman has taken things a step further with Farm My Yard, the volunteer service he formed in 2011 to match people who wanted to grow produce but didn't have yards with people who have yards but don't have time and/or interest in growing fruit and vegetables. Total win-win.

A Portland resident since 2002, Albert's FMY work is strictly volunteer. In his day job, he teaches people how to improve their online business presence through social media and email marketing.

"It's always nice to hear people who have heard of your idea, and then you tell them that it's your idea, and smiles happen," Albert says. "Mostly, the outcomes have been good. There have been people who have come forward as farmers who haven't stuck with it, but what I really love is the 1,000 different kinds of relationships that can come from each connection. That's what excites me, most. Plus, saving the planet."

Albert was inspired by the activities of City Repair Project and its annual Village Building Convergence (see page 70-71).

"I love living in Portland," Albert says. His favorite part is meeting interesting people. But he's pretty sure he would have fun anywhere. "I have a pretty good time wherever I am, so I suspect I'd do okay elsewhere, if I chose to move."

Albert is not one to brag about Portland. "I don't really talk Portland up too much," he admits. "I tend to encourage people who have never been here before to borrow what is working here (like Farm My Yard!) and bring it to their neck of the woods. I think we Americans move around way too much."

§

Portland's spirit and earnestness is also on full display at the Fruit Tree Project, best captured in its own words:

"Portland Fruit Tree Project is a grassroots nonprofit organization that provides a community-based solution to a critical and growing need in Portland and beyond: Access to healthy food. By empowering neighbors to share in the harvest and care of urban fruit trees, we are preventing waste, building community knowledge and resources, and creating sustainable, cost-free ways to obtain healthy, locally-grown food. Because money doesn't grow on trees... but fruit does!

"We organize people to gather fruit before it falls, and make it available to those who need it most. We register fruit and nut trees throughout the city, bring people together to harvest and distribute thousands of pounds of fresh fruit each year, and teach tree care and food preservation in hands-on workshops."

In 2012, 75 harvest parties picked about 60,000 pounds of fruit that would have otherwise rotted on the ground. If needed, one can borrow canning and preserving equipment from the local kitchen tool library to put the fruit up for the winter.

Yes, we really have thought of everything. It gives us life. The only things we haven't thought of yet don't exist. But rest assured we have people already working on them.

I'm sure there's a wiki. And a waiting list of volunteers.

The food grown in this garden is donated to local charities who feed the hungry.

This page: Top photo, Albert Kaufman, founder and leader of the Farm My Yard movement, which began in Portland. Bottom photo is a little piece of the City Hall garden in early spring. Opposite page: So far, nobody has stepped up to farm Albert's yard, but in the meantime, he uses it to display signs the all-volunteer group creates for people with yards to use to invite would-be farmers to get their hoe down.

■ Quilt information on page 164.

Loco for Local

"My grandfather lived in the Portland area since he was five. He told me once of having to carry water up from the Willamette to where they were staying. He, his brothers and sisters and parents lived on a campground that later became the family farm in 1938," says Ian Winter as he sets out fruit and vegetables for the Farmer's Market at King School in northeast Portland. "The farm is now run by my father and uncle."

Crops include beets, carrots, potatoes, cabbage; green, yellow, red shell and purple shell beans; corn, spinach, kale, chard, peppers, tomatoes, eggplant, onions, zucchini, broccoli, cauliflower, romanescue, winter squash, pumpkins, strawberries, raspberries, blackberries, leeks, rhubarb, stinging nettles, parsnips, jostaberries and quince.

While Winters Farms once sold exclusively to the wholesale market, stores and processors, its harvest is now split 60% to farmers markets, 40% to wholesale, stores, bakeries and restaurants.

Doing things this way takes a lot more work. Ian describes a typical week for market vendors:

"Monday through Friday is harvesting and restocking of our crops, jam, and honey for the weekend. Friday afternoon we begin loading the two trucks for the Saturday markets. The week's harvest has to be divided between the four markets we do on the weekend, though not always evenly as some markets have a larger customer draw than others. The size of our trucks, booths, weather, events on the day of the market can also be a factor in distribution. Each market takes roughly two-and-a-half hours of setup, much of which is physical labor. We then enjoy the company of our customers for the next four or five hours, then proceed to tear down as quickly as possible so that we may: a) go back to the farm, b) unload the trucks, c) distribute the next day's supplies, d) reload the trucks, e) and then finally go home for the day. Other farmers have it worse than we do, having to drive for hours coming to and leaving the market."

Winters Farms is located in the Troutdale area on the bluff overlooking the Stark Street Bridge.

The schedule has ramped up as Winters Farms attends more markets. "It's much busier than it used to be," Ian says. "Instead of doing two markets on Saturday and harvesting during the week, we now harvest during the weekend and have to work five markets during the course of the week (one on Thursday, two on Saturdays, and two on Sundays). With the proliferation of farmers markets, long gone are the days of working a half day on Sunday (if at all) during the summer. And there is more competition at each market, so we have to do more markets to sell the same amount of produce as in years past."

Portland Farmers Market was established in 1992 to set up marketplaces for local farmers who wanted to supply fresh produce, meats and prepared goods to the people of Portland. The original market—held in a parking lot at Albers Mill— had 13 vendors on opening day. Before long, the main market moved to the Portland State University campus on Saturdays, and a second downtown market was added on Wednesdays in 1997.

Each year the number of vendors has grown, and today more than 250 vendors sell their goods at six sites in Portland. And now there's even a farmers market at our airport! Total sales for all vendors are nearly $6 million annually, with the majority of that income going directly to vendors themselves.

According to Ian, applying to a market and meeting requirements is relatively painless, and fees are reasonable. "Market staff are very easy to get along with," he says, "and they are much nicer than we are as they do not have to sell people turnips."

His biggest challenges? "Crop loss, transitioning from the previous generation to the next, making much-needed changes to our practices, meeting the demands of our customer demographic (and learning to live with those demands), figuring out our customer demographic, and most importantly: staying in business."

Biggest rewards? "Happy customers. Learning from your customers, learning new things to share with your customers, making a sale to someone who a minute ago had never tried what you were offering them (let alone tried it raw). One of my favorite rewards is knowing that some of the choices I make now will outlive me and still be a benefit to my family for generations to come."

Ian thinks farmers' markets make customers more aware of where their food comes from, but not as much as previous generations who grew up working as seasonal help on local farms, like my generation did. Back then, every summer we picked strawberries and other crops to earn spending money as adolescents and young teens. "But with the change in labor laws, shifts in labor demographics, and decreases in balanced diets, now there's less connection between consumers and the farming community," Ian says.

He concludes on an optimistic note. "Humans are a very curious, inquisitive, and enthusiastic lot, and the desire to re-establish this bond with their local farmers is quite strong. We field questions from our growing practices, to how best to prepare an unusual vegetable for dinner, or why a customer's rhubarb stalks are green (probably needs to be fertilized, FYI), or if they can come and take a tour of the farm sometime."

Given their weekly schedule, it's hard to figure out when the farmers would have time to give tours, but farmers are passionate enough about their work they very well might try to manage it.

But they probably wouldn't mind if we showed up wearing our farming clothes, ready to lend a hand.

Opposite page: Ian Winters of Winters Farms sells his wares at King Farmers Market in northeast Portland every Sunday, and at other farmers' markets across Portland the rest of the week. The farm has been in his family since 1938.
■ Quilt information on page 164.

Pieces of Portland

Voodoo Magic

If you were sitting in a Portland restaurant in the early 1970s and stepped into a time traveling DeLorean that delivered you to 2015, you would have to believe you had entered a new universe named Whiskey Tango Foxtrot. That's how drastically the food scene has transformed in the intervening years. It used to be there was Jake's and the Ringside and a few other gems, but mostly places that served up food like our moms' cooked. And there were a few Chinese/American places.

Since then, there has been nothing short of a food revolution in this town. When he was here for FEAST 2014, the editor of *Bon Appetit* called Portland "the hottest food city in the country right now." We keep getting put on "Best of" lists by foodies from all over. Portland was named one of the 11 greatest foodie cities in America in 2014. Some days it feels like our food scene presents an embarrassment of riches.

But after all, James Beard—the celebrated chef, cookbook author, teacher, columnist and personality sometimes described as "the face and belly of American gastronomy"—was born in Portland and grew up eating Pacific Northwest foods, with an emphasis on seafood, game, fruit, nuts and greens. So maybe we come by it honestly.

What's behind our great food? First, we have access to spectacular ingredients, partly because of the mild climate. We enjoy a very long growing season for lots of vegetables, berries, orchard fruit, nuts and so forth. There is wild fish and game, along with abundant space on the range. The presence of plentiful moisture that flows into streams and rivers give us fertile alluvial soil.

Given our rep for serious fine dining, it's a bit weird that the most famous or infamous food location in Portland is probably Voodoo Doughnut. Open 24/7. Cash only.

It might actually be more fitting to describe these doughnuts as art rather than food. Like more about the fascinating concepts, strange ingredient pairings, gasp-inducing shapes, unusual icing colors and decorations. Voodoo turns out an astonishing 90 different kinds of doughnuts! Even some that are NSFW.

It's a simple story, really. Two guys—Kenneth "Cat Daddy" Pogson and Tres Shannon—wanted to start a business together. They learned how to make doughnuts and opened a shop in downtown Portland. Many of their doughnuts were on the weird end of the spectrum. They sold like, well, I was going to say "they sold like hotcakes," but given their wild success I'm thinking that expression should be changed to "they sold like doughnuts." Officially. Who sells this many hotcakes? Nobody.

Its trademark doughnut is a voodoo doll, with a pretzel stake though the heart. If you stick the stake in far enough, blood red jelly oozes from the doughnut. Their Maple Bacon is also a crowd favorite. Then there's the Portland Cream doughnut: raised yeast filled with Bavarian cream, topped with chocolate and two eyeballs, representing the vision of our great city. (This might be kind of an inside joke, poking fun at the frequency of our city's visioning exercises. Or maybe it is a brag about Portlanders' great eyesight. Or a public service reminder to get our eyes checked more often. I guess I could ask them but sometimes it's actually more fun to speculate.)

I did break down and ask why the magic is in the hole, though. I was shocked that it wasn't a Frequently Asked Question on their website. I emailed the question because I didn't want to have to stand in line for hours to ask it.

The answer came quickly.

"The doughnut hole is very magical. It's not what you can see, but what you can imagine. :)"

Alrighty then!

Please do not expect a restaurant guide or a foodie tour in these pages. That would not work because I don't have enough years or money left. It's really more about what I notice about food in Portland, what it represents, what we are known for and why. In other words, the magic of what we put in our pie hole.

But before I go, I'll drop this one insider tip. If you're looking for a more gourmet Portland doughnut dining experience, you might want to check out Blue Star. Brioche recipe from southern France. Sustainable flour. Eggs from cage-free chickens. No artificial anything. Organic everything. Vegan version available. Cooked in rice oil.

Rice oil? You can get oil from rice?!? Do you know how frickin' dry rice is? Where's the oil hiding?

What the heck else is in there?

Pieces
of
Portland

The Ethics of Eating

If you have people over for dinner in Portland, bear in mind that most of your invitees will have at least one food allergy, along with several strongly-held food beliefs.

And OMG, potlucks. One cannot depend on sheer luck. Hell no. Not only should you keep your dish at the right temperature for food safety, we will greatly appreciate your listing all the ingredients on a card so we can determine what hidden dangers might be lurking in your food.

It would not surprise me to learn that Portland has more Paleo Practitioners per capita than any other city. Nor would I be shocked to hear that we have proportionally more Vigorous Vegans than elsewhere in America.

Just as we consciously track what we do with everything we use and digest and send to the sewers, many people here pretty much obsess over what they ingest. I'm not referring to calorie counters. Oh, no. We're way more meta than that.

It's about applying your overall belief system and grand theory of everything to eating.

Should we be eating like hunters and gatherers because it really wasn't all that long ago that humans lived that way and there hasn't been enough time for our digestive systems to evolve fast enough to keep up with the range of things available for people to eat now?

Is wheat really the source of all dietary evil, poisoning us and making us bloat? And what about soy? Here we thought tofu (it's pronounced dofu, people, please stop saying tofu, I let a lot of things go, but this one has me on my very last nerve) was the answer to everything but now we're hearing that it has too much estrogen in it?

And meat and dairy and eggs all involve the exploitation and/or killing of animals, so that can't be good, right?

Except that we are beginning to hear that plants might just have consciousness, too. And many are still alive when we eat them. That's even worse than eating dead things, right? Just because you can't hear their screams doesn't mean they're not shrieking in fear and pain. Knowing these things changes you as a person.

Questions like these are much debated in Portland. And there's a whole lot more where those came from.

You drink alkaline water, right? Don't you know that it removes toxins, super hydrates, scavenges and neutralizes free radicals, balances your pH and enhances your immune system? Okay, so I'm being a little over the top here, but I'm trying to help you prepare for conversations about things like this.

There is a place, pictured on the opposite page, that I like to think of as Ground Zero of Alternative Everything in Portland. I encourage you to read all the signs in the photograph. It's important for your education. Feel free to google the terms that are new to you.

Portland's Vegan Mini-Mall isn't far from Ground Zero. You won't believe how much vegan junk food there is. Some of it is even imported.

Which brings up another point. Have you traced the geographic origin of what you eat so you can calculate its carbon footprint?

And then there are the freegans, who are appalled at how much food we waste and respond by refusing to buy food, but subsist on all the perfectly good stuff that is going to waste. In Portland it's become something of a system, with people assigned to make the rounds when local food establishments close so they can pick up and distribute that day's remainder.

Freeganism reflects an anti-consumerist and somewhat anarchistic ethic about eating and, according to a "Why Freegan" pamphlet, includes "dumpster diving, plate scraping, wild foraging, gardening, theft, employee scams, and barter as alternatives to paying for food."

Okay, I'm sorry, you lost me at plate scraping. Some things even I am not ready to try. Employee scams and theft? Whoa now.

There's nothing more shameful about living in Portland than discovering you are unable to embrace or even meet some kind of minimum radical readiness threshold.

We Portlanders are very mindful about what we eat because we are what we eat. At opposite ends of the spectrum are vegans and those who eat like cavemen. There are plenty of other stands to take on dietary ways and sources of food. It pays to pay attention. **Opposite page:** The Cultured Caveman cart that serves up Paleo food on SE Hawthorne is at the very center of alternative everything in Portland. **This page:** The vegan mini-mall isn't far away. Perhaps they regard one another with disdain, but I've never seen them come to blows.

◼ Quilt information on page 164.

Pieces of Portland

Like Mom Used to Make

When you grow up in the City of Eternal Spring but you prefer to live in Portland, you know there has to be something special here

Javier Hurtado was born in Cuernavaca, Mexico, in 1973. Dubbed "City of Eternal Spring" by Alexander von Humboldt (18th-19th century scientist/explorer of Latin America who wrote five volumes unifying all scientific knowledge) because its climate stays in the 70s all year long, Cuernavaca was first established by the mother culture of Middle America about 3,200 years ago. Aztec emperors had summer residences there. Hernan Cortes of Spanish conquest fame built his palace there.

Javier's family had come to the city from a farm that could only be reached by two days on horseback. His mother's family had a restaurant in Cuernavaca, and his father's family had a cattle ranch with a slaughterhouse located near the restaurant. That's how his parents met.

Javier grew up around food making, working in the family businesses as a child and shopping his family's bread, cheese and sausages around the neighborhood.

Preparing and eating food was at the center of the many gatherings and celebrations of his extended family. Farming and ranching gave them access to the highest-quality ingredients, which went in to making healthy and delicious food.

One of Javier's cousins started attending the University of Portland, and because his mother wanted them to get a good education, Javier and his brother Luis were sent to Portland when Javier was 15. "My cousin thought I should make the move in secondary school so my English would be better when I started college," Javier remembers. "I went to David Douglas High School for a year-and-a-half. After I graduated, I was supposed to go Concordia College on a soccer scholarship, but the grant did not come through. So I took classes at Portland Community College, Mt. Hood Community College and Clackamas Community College."

When he got his associate's degree, Javier went back to Mexico. "But I missed Portland, so I came back."

Why did he miss Portland? "Because it's weird," he laughs. "I like the rain, and having nature so close. Skiing at the mountain, hiking trails everywhere. It's so clean, the people are so nice."

After thinking for a moment more, he gives his final answer, "I missed the order and the serenity."

He enrolled in Portland State University and got his degree in business with a focus on finance in 1999. He became certified as a stockbroker and worked as a financial advisor for a year-and-a-half. "But I didn't like it," he says. He was spending a lot of time in the cafe his brother and cousin had opened.

Opposite page: Javier Hurtado enjoys a glass of wine at the South Waterfront Cha!Cha!Cha! location shortly after it opened in 2014. The wine is made for his menu, which is based on the food his mother cooked in Cuernavaca, Mexico. His was the first Mexican restaurant in Portland to use local organic ingredients in all its dishes.

■ Quilt information on page 164.

"Food and eating are in my blood," he says. "It gives me the space to be creative."

When he went to visit a friend near PSU, he saw that an Indian restaurant was for sale.

He thought it over and decided to go for it. "They gave me the best deal ever," Javier says. "I bought it in 2001 on contract. It happened very organically, it was meant to be." His brother Luis joined him in the business and they changed its name to Cha!Cha!Cha!

The Cha!Cha!Cha! brand is now known in Portland for healthy, delicious, freshly-prepared food at a bargain price. "I am a cook, not a chef," Javier laughs. "I didn't go to culinary school. But there is a lot of family influence in our dishes."

He bought the building that housed it in 2003, then along came the Portland streetcar and eminent domain, and he was forced to sell the building and close the restaurant in 2007. By then, he had opened locations in the Pearl District and on northeast Broadway, so he focused on those, then opened on southeast Hawthorne, northeast Fremont, north Lombard, a taqueria in northwest Portland, and in summer 2014 at South Waterfront. In October 2014, Cha!Cha!Cha! opened in the Moda Center for Trailblazer games.

The food business has changed a lot over the nearly 15 years since he began. "When we started, Portland was not so much into local sourcing and sustainable food," Javier says. "It was much more conventional."

"We were the first Mexican restaurant to start sustainable sourcing. We make healthy Mexican food, and that's why we've been successful." No doubt the business degree has helped, too.

"You have to stay ahead of trends," he continues. "We have gluten free dishes, and we use non-GMO ingredients, they are organic. All these things are important here."

Luis, Javier's brother and business partner, has a 57-acre farm, with 20 acres under irrigation, and is growing and raising more and more of the produce and meat Cha!Cha!Cha! uses.

Javier also works hard to find the best sources of ingredients he can only get from Mexico. He described a recent visit to a tequila house in Jalisco that makes the spirits from hearts of seven-year-old blue agave plants that are steamed, extracted, fermented among citrus trees, distilled, then aged in oak barrels.

Cha!Cha!Cha! also has its own pinot noir and pinot gris wines made specially for its menu by a Willamette Valley winery and three kinds of beer from local microbreweries.

He fields a lot of requests to open new locations, and hopes to have a downtown space again before too long. "We have to be careful about expanding as we've been self-funded so far," Javier says. "It's important to keep it in the family, to keep our integrity."

"We've come full circle," Javier marvels. "The food we offer at Cha!Cha!Cha! now is as fresh and healthy and delicious as the food my mom used to make. In fact some of it is the very same food my mom used to make."

And we don't have to ride two days on horseback to get it.

Pieces
of
Portland

PDX671
#guamfood

AS SEEN ON THE
FOOD NETWORK'S
DINERS, DRIVE-INS, & DIVES.

Follow us for UP-TO-DATE info
pdx671
@PDXSixSevenOne
PDX Six Seven One

you see I owe to spaghetti

ASK NOT WHAT YOU
CAN DO FOR YOUR
COUNTRY. ASK WHATS
FOR LUNCH

I always cook with wine.
Sometimes I even add it to the food.

Cheese - milks leap toward immortality

CHOCOLATE
IS THE
ANSWER
who cares what
the question is

Life is uncertain. Eat dessert first.

you are what what you eat eats

Welcome to
ROSE CITY
FOOD PARK

BSSST - Bacon, Smoked Salmon,
Spinach & Tomato, with fresh dill

Kalua Double Pig Sandwich

Build-a-BLT

BACON
PDX

Located: NE Sandy Blvd & NE 52 Ave

Cackalack's
HOT CHICKEN SHACK

Jalapeño Poppers

Bacon Wrapped Potato Wedges

Candied Bacon Pineapple Bites

ROSE CITY FOOD PARK
"From the Farm To the Table". www.rosecityfoodpark.com

FruiTea Bubble

Snapshots from Rose City Food Park on Northeast Sandy Blvd., one of the many food cart pods in Portland. There are so many individual carts and new pods opening it's hard to keep track of them all. Reading foodcartsportland.com will help. ■ Quilt information on page 164.

Vivi's YUMMY Rolls
Vietnamese Food 503-810-7051

THRILLIST
Ranked Us
TOP 7 Finest
Food Cart

Kaffe

OPEN

All Cart, No Horse

If there's one thing you already know about food in Portland, it's probably that every single person has a food cart. Well, okay, that's a slight exaggeration. Some of us are still planning our food cart, so we can't really be counted yet.

Seriously, you have to plan your route through the city carefully if you don't want to run into food prepared and served out of something that looks like an extremely tiny house or a modified erstwhile RV or delivery truck. Tourists want to be all over them.

Here's a conversation that happened while we on a photo-taking mission in the Pearl District.

Tourist couple walking along: "Where can we find the food cart?"

Marie and Joyce: "Well, there are a whole lot of them. Are you looking for one in particular?"

Tourists: "No, we've just heard about the food cart."

M&J: "So are you looking for a pod?"

Tourists: "What's a pod?"

M&J: "It's where there's a cluster of food carts."

Tourists: "Yes, that would be good."

M&J: "Well, there are several downtown."

Tourists: "What's the one that takes the fewest directions?"

M&J: "That sidewalk you're on, start walking in that direction and keep going until you run into food carts."

Tourists: "Oh, thank you! We wanted to make sure we saw the food cart while we were here."

Others have thoroughly documented the food cart story and/or revolution elsewhere. For example, if you want to grok the food cart scene, and I am sure you do, there's nothing better than *Cartopia* by Kelly Rogers and Kelley Roy.

In this small space, I'm going to offer up the things that especially fascinate me. Things like Why Did This Happen? What Does It All Mean? Where Will It Lead?

I have a few theories to toss out and see what sticks to the wall:

- We get lots and lots of ideas and we like to make our ideas happen.
- An entrepreneurial maker spirit flows pretty much through all veins and arteries in Portland.
- Food carts are a relatively quick and inexpensive way to start a business.
- Food carts are a relatively quick and inexpensive way to get a delicious meal.
- Cooking and preparing scrumptious meals is one way to practice one's art.
- When immigrants and refugees come to our city, one thing they can do fairly quickly for work is cook the food of their homeland.
- When you go to a pod, it's like you're accessing several restaurants at once, so the menu is ultra-varied.
- In today's technological society, many of us crave one-on one-experiences, up close and personal.
- We love to support others' creative impulses and art/work because that's how things will work in the Cascadia many of us believe in and hope will come.

So enough about my theories. Let's deal in facts.

Oddly enough, experts Kelly and Kelley agree with some of my theories, and they discovered a key thing I hadn't. It seems the stance of the city bureaucracy in Portland has been an important part of the whole scene.

Portland considers food carts to be vehicles rather than buildings (even those without wheels) so they aren't subject to the building code, which can open a ginormous can of worms. And who wants any size can of worms opened in the presence of their food? When vendors push the limits, like the time one built an attached outdoor deck with a roof, the city steps in and draws the line (the deck had to be removed). Overall, Portland's departments and bureaucrats are mostly complaint-driven about carts on private property. If nobody complains, everything's chill.

Food carts are subject to health regulations and get inspected just like brick-and-mortar restaurants do. The carts have special challenges, because many aren't hooked up to city services, like water and sewers, so they have to pack clean water in and waste water out in totes every day. Health inspectors watch for these things, of course. Some of the newer pod locations were created specifically for food carts and have water and sewer hookups.

There has been grumbling from restaurant owners who think there's a double standard because they are subject to building codes, and the carts represent unfair competition. Some restaurants have added carts to their repertoire. Some carts have been so successful they've turned into brick-and-mortar operations. Much of the time it seems like there's enough demand to go around; if you have delicious enough food, people will come, no matter where you serve it.

New pods are still being born. But some are disappearing because the landowner wants to develop the space into something that produces a lot more revenue. Cartopia, the first pod to stay open into the wee hours, will be replaced by a multi-story apartment building soon.

The latest pod closest to my house suggests something more might be happening. It includes a double decker London bus that is a vintage clothing and accessories shop. Nearby is an Airstream trailer that offers flowers, vintage things and cultural gifts, presumably with a French flavor since it's name is Dragonfly Monet. On the other side of the pod is a produce stand. So there may been changes afoot in the cart revolution, going way beyond food. I can't wait to watch what happens.

Another foodie trend has emerged in Portland that goes beyond carts. I'm talking about the food pop-ups I keep hearing about. Somebody goes in and occupies a space for a day or a night, offering up a special meal, sometimes one-of-a-kind. I have yet to attend one of these, so I can't really give you the 411.

But it's kind of intriguing that the hottest restaurant in Portland right now is a popup that's kind of a *Chronicles of Narnia* experience, because you have to enter it through a bookcase in another restaurant. And you can't eat there because it's totally booked for as long as its calendar goes.

But there are always other options. No need to stay hungry and thirsty, my friends.

Pieces of Portland

This two-page spread features an assortment of snapshots at carts and pods from different parts of town. We went behind the scenes a bit to show you some of the infrastructure needed for a successful cart and pod. It's interesting to see that carts are branching out beyond food. For example, at one of the newer pods on southeast Division Street, a double decker bus houses Lodekka, a vintage clothing and accessories shop. Bringing a bit of the London look to Portland. At another location on SE Hawthorne Boulevard, Anna Gale has a hair salon in a Bambi Airstream.

■ Quilt information on page 164.

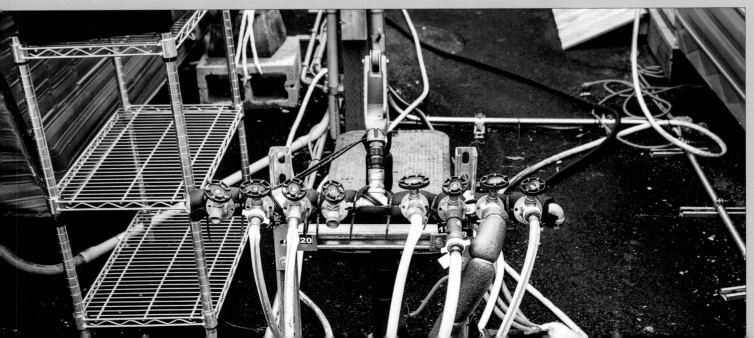

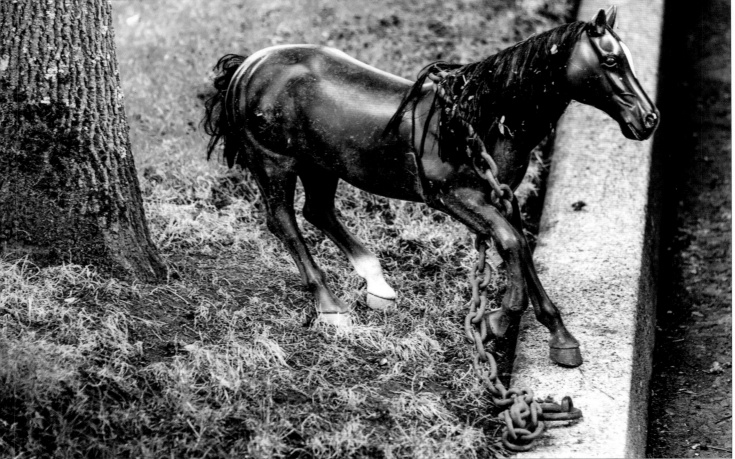

In January 2015, Purrington's Cat Lounge opened in northeast Portland. One side of the cafe is a lounge area for humans that serves a limited menu of food and drink, with large windows looking onto the other side where the cats hang out. For an hourly rate of $8, up to 15 people at a time can head into the kitty side to get some "purr-therapy" from hand-picked friendly felines.

Naturally, since this is Portland, the cafe will feature rescue animals and encourage adoption. Here's how it works, as expressed on the lounge's website:

> Visitors can hang out with cats and get to know them in a different way than one could at a shelter. This is essentially their temporary living room while they wait to be adopted into their forever home. To promote a stress-free environment, we do have rules posted in the cafe and lounge and we do limit visitor capacity to 15 people per hour. The cats are hand-picked by our shelter partner, Cat Adoption Team, to ensure cats can benefit from being in this environment. The cats have a private area where they can go to if they need to take a breather from visitors. Also, there is a custom structure with high areas they can go to if they don't necessarily want to go to the private room, but maybe just want to people watch or sleep. Basically, they are free to do what cats do.

Humans are not necessarily free to do what humans do.

> We want everybody to enjoy their visit with the cats. Their safety and comfort is priority number one. Your help in observing the rules posted in the cafe and cat lounge regarding the cats is not just appreciated, it's required. Cats can be very unpredictable. To avoid scratches or bites, we ask that cats are not picked up at any time or disturbed while sleeping. Sudden moves or loud noises could also startle the cats. Please consider your actions while in the Cat Lounge.

In other words, no horsing around!

Speaking of horses, they are also well loved in Portland. A great public outcry is raised every time it looks like budget cuts will eliminate the mounted police patrols, with offers of private fundraising—not to keep the human police but the horses they ride.

Portland's favorite horses, however, are probably the diminutive ones found tethered to the curb throughout the city. These Portland ponies have their own official website and a page in Wikipedia.

When Portland neighborhoods went up, and streets and sidewalks paved, the city was still a horse and buggy town. Brass or cast iron rings were routinely attached to the curb to provide

a place to tether horses. The rings were sturdy things, with many surviving decades and decades longer than the horses did. I'm told the rings began to be systematically removed at some point "for safety purposes." I am unable to visualize what kind of horsing around would make them hazardous, but then I'm not in risk management.

In the late 1970s, a citizen complained to the mayor that Portland was losing some of its history with the loss of the rings, so the city passed a law to protect them, requiring them to be saved and/or replaced when curb repairs are made (see the box).

But that wasn't enough for Portland. Portland artist Scott Wayne Indiana thought it was a shame that we don't tie our horses to our rings anymore, so he started the Portland Horse Project. "I loved the rings, and felt that people just weren't noticing them," he said. "This was an attempt to shake people out of their routines and get them to notice their surroundings."

Scott tied his first toy pony to a horse ring in the fall of 2005 in the revitalized Pearl District in northwest Portland. He invited others to follow his lead, which they did in herds. Rumor has it that one person has tied 150 horses. A map showing the horse locations was put on the website, and they became a tourist attraction.

Lots of Portlanders have joined in the fun, leaving saddles and lassos, blankets, water and hay, etc.

Current City of Portland Regulation

(6) Horse Rings – Salvage any metal horse rings encountered during curb removal. Reinstall horse ring assembly back at the same project stationing or as close as practical. If no new curb is constructed, deliver horse ring assemblies to the City's Maintenance Bureau at Stanton Yard located at 2835 N. Kerby Ave.

But just like on the 19th century frontier, wherever there are horses, we find horse thieves and many of the horses go missing, their tether cut or undone. The Horse Project has a thoroughly Portland appeal to address the thievery problem:

> "If you happen to see someone removing the ponies, ask them why and tell us or send us a picture of this incomprehensible act. We will protect your identity! Or you can post anonymously to our guest book. We would really like to understand the why, but we will keep putting our horses out until and unless we can work out some compromise. We have had a report of one horse thief (from a guest book entry–since lost) in the Lloyd Center area...Hopefully if the police ever find a bunch of horses that seemed to be displaced, they'll give them to us, rather than throwing them out. We'd love to put them out again! I'll update this space if I get more information about this or other horse thieves. Stay tuned.

While horses are the most frequent animal to be tied to Portland's curb rings, wikipedians report that pigs, dolls and other species have also appeared.

Somehow our favorite curbed horse has survived over the years, although his mane and tail could use a good brushing. See how he loves frolicking with the children at play in the quilt. At an undisclosed location.

We could tell you where but then we'd have to corral you.

Opposite page: The horse with the rather unkempt mane in the top photo frolics on a quilt at an undisclosed location in a Portland neighborhood. Too many of Portland's curbside horses have gone missing and we don't know why. The horse in the bottom photo turned up across the Columbia River in Vancouver, where presumably it had been sent out to pasture for its own safety.

■ Quilt information on page 165.

God Is Dog Spelled Backward

It must be said that Portland is mad about all fauna, not just birds, cats and horses. For example, when a bear was spotted up a tree in a northeast Portland backyard at 3 a.m. recently, it had at least two Twitter accounts and a hashtag by the time I woke up three hours later.

But among all fauna, it's dogs that are top dog in Portland. In fact Portland has been named America's Number One City for Dogs. I tried counting the number of dog rescue/adoption organizations in Portland but I ran out of digits. Let's just say they range from Another Chance Rescue to Pawsitively Pit Bull to Senior Dog Rescue to Other Mothers Animal Rescue and Rehab. The city has more off-leash dog parks than all but NYC, which is a whole lot bigger.

Portland offers doggie day care and overnight lodging, doggie dental clinics, massage, portraits, sitters, walkers and stylists. For your dog's health needs, you can choose among holistic health care, integrative chiropractic care, naturopathic treatments, acupuncture, reiki healing, Chinese and western herbal medicine, laser therapy and homeopathy. Oh, and there are some traditional veterinarians too, I think.

To get inside your dog's head, you can access tarot card readings, psychic readings, behavior therapy and animal communication, in person or by phone. Portland also offers dogs K9 nose work, play groups, pet blessings, rehab and fitness classes, heated swimming pools, breed walks and parties, and so much more.

But perhaps the most impressively weird dog item in our fair city is a dog bowl art installation in the North Park Blocks. Commissioned by the now-defunct Pearl Arts Foundation, the cast iron dog bowl with bubbling water (an homage to our Benson Bubblers seen on page 38) placed on stone tiles that simulate kitchen linoleum was designed by noted Weimaraner photographer William Wegman. Did I mention it cost $176,000? In private donations, thankfully. We tried convincing a number of dogs to drink from it for our photograph but we learned you can lead a dog to water but can't make it drink.

Dog owners...oops, let's pause for a moment to consider the word owner. It's not the preferred term here, because while you are responsible for the care of your dog, it is somewhat offensive to imply that you own a dog. It's probably better to call yourself a dog companion or parent or guardian or caretaker or keeper or steward, etc.

By any name, let's say Huparents for now, Huparents can attend bonding classes, pug crawls, arf in the park, loose leash walking seminars, canines uncorked wine tours, dogtoberfest, paws in the park, bow wow bashes, strut your mutt parades, doggie dashes, mutt mixers, tails of summer run, tour de lab (ride a bike with your dog from one Lucky Lab pub to another) and grief support groups after they make that trip over the Rainbow Bridge. And of course pet burial and cremation services are available.

The Oregon Humane Society was formed in 1868, only 23 years after the city was founded, and is one of the first animal welfare organizations in the country. A local doctor witnessed a brutal beating of a horse and in response, organized a group of prominent citizens to protect draft animals.

Some question whether Portlanders care more about dogs than children! In fact, in 1891, Oregon Humane Society added children and companion animals to its protected classes. OHS remained Oregon's child and animal protection organization until 1933.

Oregon Humane Society's save rate for dogs is 99% and for cats 98%. Its campaign to "End Petlessness" seems to be succeeding because Portland is a transport-to destination for a number of rescue organizations from other regions where shelters have high kill rates. People in Portland who apply for dog adoption should expect a great deal of scrutiny and even be prepared for rejection.

What was once animal welfare is now animal rights. I predict that in the not-too-far-off future, animal rights will be similar to human rights, and living beings will be treated as one. And I will not be surprised if it happens first in Portland.

In fact, in August 2014, the Oregon Supreme Court found that animals can be considered "victims" legally, which increases sentences for those who neglect or mistreat them and does not require a search warrant to rescue an animal from private property if it appears to be in imminent danger.

But I doubt animal rights will take the vision of the cofounder and president of People for the Ethical Treatment of Animals (PETA), who sees a future where companion animals would be phased out and dogs would live a feral existence, pursuing their natural lives in the wild. Because, quite simply, we cannot imagine life without our dogs at our sides. Everywhere we go. Yes, even there.

Opposite page: A dog looks suspiciously at the William Wegman-designed bubbling water bowl in Portland's North Park blocks. Apparently it wasn't that thirsty. Below a man takes his dog paddle-boarding on the Willamette. Please note that the dog is wearing a life jacket, but the man is not. **This page:** To the people who pick up their dog's poo in a bag then leave the bag for we peasants to deal with, STOP IT! Yes, that was a read. ■ Quilt information on page 165.

Pieces
of
Portland

Getting Our Goats

Urban farming has become a really big deal in Portland. We have an Urban Farm Store, an Urban Farm Collective, a seven-month training program for Beginning Urban Farmer Apprentices, backyard farming consultants and a whole lot of urban farms. Community supported agriculture is very big. As you already know, Portlanders buy shares of local farmers' crops and farmers markets are plentiful.

Portland residents can keep up to three hens, ducks, doves, pigeons, rabbits, pygmy goats and miniature pot-bellied pigs without applying for a permit. If you want to keep turkeys, geese, doves, pigeons, peacocks, cows, horses, burros, sheep, llamas or bees, no matter how many of these animals, you need to apply for a permit. (Yes, I realize doves and pigeons are on both lists, as they are on the City's website. Ask them to explain.) To keep bees, you need a permit and the consent of all your neighbors.

Chickens are by far the most popular animal for Portland backyards. The city holds a Tour de Coop each summer, where people trek coop to coop to see fowl in action. It has been said that there are chickens within hearing range of every block in the neighborhoods of inner southeast and northeast, along with much of north Portland.

Local news outlets cover the shenanigans of Portland's farm animals with some regularity and much enthusiasm. No activity is too small to cover.

In August 2014, for example, pretty much all local news reported that someone had called Portland's non-emergency line to report that a chicken was crossing a road and traffic had come to a halt. Police reportedly investigated but were unable to locate the chicken and ascertain its intent. So we still don't know why the chicken crossed the road.

Local news also reported, with accompanying video, that on June 3, 2008 "at approximately 9:45 p.m. last night, an unattended pygmy goat walked onto a Line 14 Hawthorne bus. The bus was on layover at SE 94th and Foster, and the operator was standing outside her bus with the doors open. The operator was concerned because of the freeway nearby and busy street traffic, and closed the bus doors. She immediately called dispatch and TriMet's dispatch called 911. A Portland police officer responded and transported the goat. 'The 35-pound goat was wearing a nylon collar.'" An update was added later that the goat had been reunited with its owner. Or herder.

But the most faunal publicity in the city of late has been about the Belmont Goats.

Portland's Original Urban Goat Herd lived in a two-acre space where a fire had leveled a warehouse and the Monte Carlo and Lido restaurants. The buildings, vacant by then, burned down in 2002. For years the two blocks were overgrown with weeds and from time to time, goats were temporarily brought in to clear the overgrown plants.

Eventually, the business across the street, Creative Woodworks NW, acquired a permanent herd named the Belmont Goats, and they became a community touchpoint.

"Would you like to get inside and meet the goats?" asked Christopher Frankonis, one of the herd's owners who had arrived that Saturday morning to feed them.

"Would we ever," we replied. Joyce had been struggling to get a photo that included both goats and a quilt over and through a chain link fence. We draped the quilt over the goats' wooden shelter. Chester immediately hopped on top and walked over to check it out.

"These goats changed my life," Christopher said quietly as he spread out some hay.

He told us how the presence of the goats had been the impetus for a spontaneous community that formed in the neighborhood.

"I didn't know that goats had so much personality," he said. "The interactions and connections I've seen have been amazing."

The goats have a website at thebelmontgoats.org, which includes a number of testimonials from goat friends, like Alison Bingham who wrote, "A day cannot suck if you have sat with a goat." It also has short bios of all members of the herd, with a set of horns rating scale from one to five describing their approachability. Five horn sets mean "Very, very friendly. Will approach you, loves getting petted and scratched. May jump on you," while one set of horns is "Mean, aggressive, nasty. Hold on to your wallet." None of the goats have this rating. In fact, none of the goats score less than three and most are fives.

Christopher has noticed that the goats provide a kind of therapy for their human visitors. "People come here to decompress when they're stressed." We later learned that two goats went to Reed College to help students during finals week. At this point, Bailey was beginning to eat our quilt so we bid the herd adieu, but not before we fell in love a little.

In early 2014, the developer who owns the goat field wanted to begin work to construct multi-level apartments and retail space, so the goats had to go. Their new home is in Lents in outer southeast Portland.

The owners conducted a successful Indiegogo campaign to raise funds for moving and resettling the herd. A chain link fence went up around a space that Portland Development Commission owns on SE 91st Avenue near Lents Town Center.

I recently spotted queries for places to live close to the new goat space. The new home may be temporary as well, if the PDC decides to develop this piece of property.

We visited the herd at the Lents Park location to see how they were doing. They looked healthy and it seemed like they felt comfortable, but there were no visitors while we were there. I hope they're not too lonely and have made new friends.

Time will tell if our city is able to provide a long-term home and support for an urban goat herd. But if any city this size can get with goats, it'll prolly be Portland.

Opposite page: Before being moved to a new location in the Lents area of outer southeast Portland, the goat herd lived on an empty lot on Belmont Street in an inner southeast Portland. The block had been vacant for a number of years after a huge fire. In 2014 the lot began to be developed. Neighbors mourned the goats' loss. Alison Bingham said it best: "A day cannot suck if you have sat with a goat."

■ Quilt information on page 165.

Pieces
of
Portland

Portland's Vitamin C

A lot of people think our winter weather explains our caffeine addiction. That may well be part of it. Anyone could use an extra jolt or two to achieve a fully-awakened state on mornings where one cannot actually tell if the sun has arisen. The days with the heavy dark grey that never lifts, the ones Henry Adams said "would gorge a glutton of gloom."

But our coffee intake holds firm in summer, so there must be something more. Maybe it's just that our coffee is so damned good. You can explore this question further by reading *Caffeinated PDX: How Portland Became the Best Coffee City in America*.

When I moved to Portland, there was Kobos. It was in John's Landing, and you could tell the coffee was special because it was in those jute bags like ships carry across the seven seas. That's when I first got serious about buying whole beans and grinding them fresh for each pot (Chemex of course). The only downside was that I had already used my hand cranked coffee grinder to artisanly grind all the spices to make my own authentic curry powder and nothing ever overcame the lingering flavor of the subcontinent. Did I inadvertently invent chai coffee?

Now Portland has dozens and dozens of roasters, and some have called our city the center of "third wave specialty coffee" or even said that we are creating a fourth wave. As *Willamette Week* said, the history of coffee in Portland is one of "constant, obsessive refinement." You could say it's our vitamin C.

Coffee cafes are everywhere. Just start walking and you'll find one. Some have called coffee houses our third place, after home and work. I love several, especially those with wonderful light, a friendly owner who might also be the roaster and barista, with comfy places to sit and work that are spacious enough to not feel claustrophobic. Free wi-fi is a given. The background noise is just right for keeping my focus on writing while intuiting when the house gets crowded and I am using up more than my share of space/time to keep the business running.

I can't reveal their actual names, because then you'll go there and I won't be able to find a seat. Okay, fine, I'll be Portland about this and share. The one in the photo is Oblique Coffee on southeast Stark. It's where *Portlandia* coffee scenes are filmed. Please limit your visiting hours, and the chair in the window is mine.

The *New York Times* called our coffee culture intimate and relaxed. But then, everything in Portland seems intimate and relaxed to the NYT. I think what they mean by relaxed is slow, like Jerry Seinfeld thought when he had coffee with Fred Armisen on *Comedians in Cars Getting Coffee*. But it's really true that we always seem to find a way to totally nerd out on things out of genuine interest rather than to be pretentious. So they have to be done on a small scale (a cup at a time) and take a while (if you skimp on the pour time, you'll cheat the flavor notes).

And believe me, when it comes to coffee in Portland, there is no end to the nerding out. Yes, of course there is an algorithm.

First, pick a name whose pronunciation must be learned and whose meaning must be explained. Its origins must be traced to a garage, of course. Every step and every step inside every step must be traced to its most fundamental and basic element. Its pure essence.

For example, let's take another of my favorite coffee places: Coava. Pronounced \ko-vuh\. An ancient word that means unroasted or "green" coffee. Began in Matt Higgins' garage in 2008. Uses single origin beans from farms he visits. Opened brew bar and roasters in 2010 in inner southeast Portland space shared with Bamboo Revolution, "a collective of designers, product developers, craftsmen and innovators that believe bamboo has unlimited potential to create a better built environment" that is also working to create a bamboo timber industry in Oregon.

Coava has not only worked to perfect the brewing of a perfect cup of coffee, producing many prize-winning baristas along the way, they have also developed recipes and tools to perfect the grinding/brewing/pouring process. Like the Kone, a perforated steel cone to replace paper and/or mesh filters.

Coava shares its coffee-making ways on its website, telling you exactly how many grams of beans to measure out, exactly what temperature the water should be and how much time the pour should take for each kind of brewing device.

It has developed a spectrum for describing coffee, distinguishing between flavor notes and taste notes, whether the coffee is rich or delicate, earthy or fruity, and how it feels in the mouth. I'm going to have to let them explain it, because every coffee has a story, and this degree of simplicity can get very complicated.

Two key players in the Portland coffee scene for decades are Jim and Patty Roberts, who opened their first coffee establishment in northwest Portland in the 1970s after selling coffee at Saturday Market in Eugene for several years. The Roberts family lived in an apartment upstairs and at first they sold only beans. "I was a coffee psychiatrist," Jim laughs. "I would talk to customers to determine what combination of our 30 kinds of beans would help them reach their inner coffee bliss." He shared his knowledge to help folks learn how to make the best coffee possible at home. He sold grinders below cost to encourage them to grind beans fresh.

"The single most important thing you can do to improve cup quality is to grind your beans immediately before brewing," he says. "When you slash the beans open, it releases the beautiful pockets of oils inside. If you don't protect the oils, they spoil and turn rancid." In 1983 he opened a small store, Coffee People, that served coffee in various drink forms. One day a big limo pulled up

outside and Howard Schultz (Starbucks owner) and his posse of six came into the store. He told Jim he was going to be opening a few places in Portland. "It won't hurt you," he promised.

"And it actually helped us," Jim explains. "They bought full-page ads to educate people about how to pronounce latte. That's partly what led to our tagline: 'Good Coffee, No Backtalk.' We didn't want coffee to turn into something snooty, where you would be judged by what you ordered, or your pronunciation." They might be Portland's proletarian purveyors of coffee. "I don't care if you put ketchup in your coffee, if that's what makes you happy," Jim says. Coffee People were pioneers in several ways, opening the first drive-through coffee establishments in the country, for example. And even though Jim and Patty don't roast their own beans in their Jim and Patty's Coffee shops now, they select beans and direct Kobos how they should be roasted.

At this point, the best-known coffee in Portland is Stumptown. Its founder looked all over the world for the best farmers who grew the best coffee and insisted on paying them a living wage and offering complete financial transparency of the supply chain. So we're not just about delicious coffee, we want our coffee to be ethical. Stumptown now has several cafes in town and supplies coffee to a large portion of the others. It has also expanded to other major U.S. cities.

In a profile of Stumptown, *Entrepreneur* magazine wrote that "the company's commitment to direct trade practices means paying two or three times more than fair trade prices to ensure real sustainability and structural improvements at partner farms." Stumptown pays its baristas family wages and full benefits. As *Entrepreneur* puts it, the company has "elevated the barista from a part-time gig to a real occupation."

Even while making coffee at home, we keep visiting shops to see what new and exciting next big thing has come along. A few years ago, cold brew (letting coarse grounds steep for hours and hours at room temperature) was the new thing. It could be delivered in stubbies—the beer bottles of old. Now there is cold brew on nitro, coffee delivered through a nitrogen tap like those used to pour a proper pint of Guinness.

So are coffee and beer becoming one in Portlandia? Yes, they certainly are, and I must be the last one to know. There's actually an annual NW Coffee Beer Invitational at the Goose Hollow Inn.

Pro tip: Travel Portland isn't just for tourists. We home girlz and boyz should monitor its website for all kinds of fun we might not be hearing about in time. Finding out about the coffee-beer connection this late is almost enough to give me a case of FOMO.

Opposite page: Jim and Patty Roberts stand outside the latest incarnation of their coffee business. You can tell how long they have been part of the coffee scene (since the 1970s) by comparing their before and after images. **This page:** Oblique Coffee on southeast Stark Street practically lures people in with an inviting ambience. Everybody except hippies, that is. But that rule seems to be loosely enforced. They let me in.
◼ Quilt information on page 165.

Pieces of Portland

Making Tea the Hero

For all the fuss we make and attention we get over coffee in Portland, you might be surprised to hear we are also very big on coffee's caffeinated cousin. Not related by blood, but by marriage.

It is said that America's modern tea culture actually started in Portland when Stash Tea launched in 1972.

At this point, are you starting to catch on that pretty much every single thing, or at least every single important thing, began or caught fire in Portland? And oh yeah, did I mention we invented the Internet? Well, part of it.

In fact, a surprising number of nationally-known teas got their start in Portland because it's the home of Steve Smith. He was one of the founders of Stash Tea, which was sold to a Japanese company that has been in business for more than three centuries. He and two other guys named Steve started Tazo Tea in 1994. Even if you haven't tried the tea, you likely noticed its brand marketing, with the tag line "the reincarnation of tea" and every box labelled as "blessed by a certified tea shaman." It played well in Portland!

Starbucks bought Tazo in 1999. The shamans are gone, but its website still promises green tea enlightenment. Steve continued with Tazo for a time, then he and his wife and son moved to France. After a year, he got restless.

You have to understand that in addition to his main business, at any given time Steve usually has at least one and sometimes several projects going on the side. He decided he wasn't quite finished with tea; he'd always wanted to do something in retail tea, so they came back to Portland and started Steven Smith Teamaker. What would be different from other retail tea endeavors?

"We make tea the hero," Steve says. "It's where all our focus goes." He's had his fill of show business retail, where a product is marketed as "authentic" but only a small part of the process is visible, while the real operation is trucked in the back door at night. He decided to just keep it simple and focus on making the best tea he could. His tasting room, in an old blacksmith shop in northwest Portland, didn't even have a sign on it for the first 18 months it was open.

The business of tea is on a rapid growth spurt in Portland, especially when it comes to specialty teas like the 75 or so that Steven Smith Teamaker makes, with 13 in its core line, 13 loose leaf, 30 different flavors of single origin tea. They also scent teas in barrels that held liquids like whiskey and pinot noir wine, and are working on smoking tea.

Ritual handling, pouring, steeping and drinking is at least as important in tea as it is in Portland's coffee culture. We are guided, mostly, by those from Asian cultures where tea originated. Being on the Pacific Rim no doubt nurtured our taste in tea. Both Portland's Japanese and Chinese gardens have tea houses that are popular among visitors and locals alike.

After hearing from Steve, it's clear our household has been doing tea completely wrong. And this was without even admitting that our microwave is sometimes involved. Steve convinced me that if you're going to drink tea, you want to get the most out of it, which means you need to store it correctly, use filtered water, heat it to just the right temperature before pouring and let it steep just the right amount of time. Some teas require boiling water, while the best temperature for others is 190 degrees. We were surprised to hear that Steve recommends buying tea in sachets inside packets, rather than using loose leaf tea. "With loose leaf tea, you keep opening up the container, exposing the tea to more oxygen," he explains. "And you won't necessarily use the right proportion of tea."

His sachets are made of very fine material, with a very cool look and feel. They just seem so right somehow, a great tactile experience. But you really shouldn't handle them much.

"When we first opened our shop," Steve says, "we were only going to sell tea within our zip code, so it would be as fresh as possible. But we've obviously expanded way beyond that and now have operations in other nearby buildings." He'll be opening a second tasting room and retail space in inner southeast Portland soon. He also ships his teas around the world.

Fresh ingredients are crucial to his process. Steve used to buy mint from Egypt, but wasn't happy with the ground-flour-like texture. One day he was driving near Madras in central Oregon and smelled fresh mint. He convinced the farmer growing it, who had been exporting it in oil form, to let the crop dry on the ground and sell it to him. He filled a VW van and a U-haul truck with leaves, stems, sticks and all, and after cleaning, sorting and grading the mint, began selling it and started using it in his tea making.

Steven Smith Teamaker buys tea from China, India, Sri Lanka, Kenya, Tanzania and Ethiopia. I may have missed a few from his list. He's visited every farm he buys from and logged a lot of air miles over the past several decades learning more about tea than, dare I say, any other American. With the possible exception of Tony Tellin, his head buyer and taster, who started with Steve back in the early Tazo days.

After our visit, I learned that Steve has worked closely with Portland-based Mercy Corps to improve the quality of life of the people in India's tea-growing regions. It seems this very modest man downplays almost everything about himself.

When I picked up the three sachets from the packets Steve had opened for us to smell and asked if I could take them home and try them, he quickly swept them up and said, "Oh, no, these have been exposed to the air while we've been talking, my hands touched them, I put moisturizer on a couple of hours ago, your hands touched them, they've been sitting on the table, they've been contaminated." He insisted on sending me home with hermetically sealed packets.

Steve usually drinks about 12 cups of tea a day but has cut back to six cups recently. I asked him if he ever drinks coffee and he says he does, but lately maybe only half a cup a day. Which is a shame because part of the Starbucks sale included free coffee for the rest of his life. He probably would prefer Coava anyway, but that's just a guess, and he probably wouldn't be able to tell me if he does.

I am told that one reason tea making and drinking are prized in Portland is that our Bull Run water—delivered straight from the lake in the forest reserve with very little treatment and no filtration—is considered to have great *qi*, to be "very full and alive" by those who most closely observe and contemplate the bond between nature and culture.

That trend may well be enhanced now that it's been shown that *Camellia sinenses*, the tea plant, can be successfully grown in the Willamette Valley, as it has the right combination of temperatures, precipitation and acidic soil. The Minto Island Farm research plot was planted from 1988 to 1992 and now has 200 varieties. Farmers report the plants "not only survived, but they thrived."

Its 2014 pickings—processed into green, oolong and black tea—were said to be "the most delicious yet." And as its website suggests, this may well be "the beginning of the Oregon-grown hand-crafted tea movement." It would fit us to a Tea.

Some people think green tea is better for you than black tea. The difference is that green tea is quickly processed after picking before oxidation occurs.

Another interesting thing about tea is that it readily picks up flavors from other things, which is why we have things like Earl Grey tea, which contains oil extracted from the rind of the bergamot orange.

Oregon Chai began making its version of chai (black tea with spices used in traditional Sanskrit medicine) in 1994. Now we see chai in supermarkets. Even Oprah is in favor of it and has put her name on a chai that is sold under Starbucks' Teavana label.

There are no end to the plants that are made into teas that don't contain actual tea plant. Wikipedia lists almost 100 major varieties of herbal tea, from A to Y. Many are used for medicinal purposes. Did you know that the leaves and fruit of the coffee plant are used to make coffee cherry tea, while the beans (seeds, actually) inside the fruit are what's used to make coffee?

Many Portlanders I know refuse to drink tea from the tea plant because they don't believe in caffeine, but they are happy to drink tea made from pretty much anything else.

That brings us to kombucha, which is a "lightly effervescent fermented drink of sweetened black and/or green tea produced by fermenting tea with a symbiotic colony of bacteria and yeast." Kombucha has become a very big deal in Portland. Maybe it's part of the fermenting obsession, our quest to pickle every single thing. The idea is that plant parts that are left to sit out at room temperature for a long time will rot and turn into microorganisms. You know, germs. Bacteria. The kind that do good deeds in our digestive tracts. Allegedly.

The problem with this approach, as I see it, is that you have to smell and taste these super germs in order to reap rewards. Because they must smell and taste like rotting food, right? I'm pretty sure I don't want my tea to taste like rotting food.

Have we reached the point in Portland where we have to pretend that refrigerators haven't been invented??

Yes, apparently we have. And, yes, I do realize this time I've gone too far and I am totally going to be exiled.

This page: Teamaker Steven Smith relaxes in the garden outside his tea shop in northwest Portland, after a long day of making tea the hero. He's had a hand in all the leading tea-making businesses in Oregon (and the nation) since the 1970s. ■ Quilt information on page 165.

Days before this book went to press, we learned that Steve Smith had passed away. Our sincere condolences to his family. We are happy to hear his business will move forward with his wife and business partner Kim DeMint at the helm.

Pieces
of
Portland

We're So Beered (and full of spirit)

In November 2014, Thrillist put a big pile of data into a "statistically infallible" formula and discovered that Oregon is the booziest of the 50 states. Check out their findings:

"Standout stat: 6.3 craft breweries per 100,000. It leads any booze-related national conversation on the strength of its unassailably dense beer scene, but OR's also third in wineries, fifth in distilleries, and 13th in bars per capita. Oh, did we mention craft beer and wine alone account for $4.6 billion in economic impact each year, and Oregonians drink 2.65 gallons of booze? Because it does, and they do...The Beaver State is America's Booziest."

It's largely Portland's fault.

Just how beered is Portland? Very very beered! Actually, it's the most beered city on the planet.

We have more breweries (58 in 2014) than any city in the world. Yes, the entire planet. We're also first in the percent of beer dollars we spend on craft beer. We don't mind paying a bit more for things artisanal, remember. And don't get me started on our beer festivals, like Collabfest (brewery collaborations), Zwickelmania (a backstage affair), StormBreaker Brewstillery Festival (perfect storm of microbreweries and micro-distillers, Malt Ball (featuring local bands and brews at Wonder Ballroom), Puckerfest (sour beer), Handmade Bike and Beer Fest, Portland Craft Beer Festival held during Oregon Craft Beer Month, Oktoberfest and festivals celebrating fruit beer, rye beer, organic brewers, international beers, nano beer, fresh hops, beer and cheese and holiday ales. I told you not to get me started!

One of our city's newer nicknames is Beervana, because we have so many great microbreweries. Beervana is also the name of probably the leading blog about beer in Portland. And quite possibly anywhere. Portlanders love beer. Almost as much as coffee. I used to think I didn't like beer, but now I understand there's a huge difference between old school beer and the incredible variety in craft beer. People, this beer is ridiculously delicious! You just have to find the right one(s).

Oregon has a good wine rep as well. The first pinot noir grapes were planted in 1965 in the Dundee Hills, about 30 miles southwest of Portland. And the rest is award-winning history. But then you've no doubt already heard that story, so I don't have to go into it here.

This is about beer. Craft beer. Brewed in small—or micro—batches. That's the way Portland loves it most. A significant reason for this development is that, in 1985, Oregon began allowing beer to be sold where it is brewed.

Of course, we must acknowledge the role PBR (Pabst Blue Ribbon) plays among a certain demographic among us. Because it's somewhat hip to eschew a crafted beverage for a blue collar one. You know, part of resisting the leading paradigm.

One of our beery advantages is how well hops grow in our climate and soil. No kidding. We planted a hop plant in our backyard one summer and almost before we had blinked our eyes it had pretty much covered all the shrubs and vines and trees on that side of our yard. We are still pulling little shoots that creep through the cracks. This is a plant that cannot be killed here.

The Willamette Valley used to produce the most hops in the country, and fields with wires and poles nearly 20 feet tall supporting the sturdy vines stretched for miles, or so it seemed. Beginning in the 1950s, markets have increasingly turned to places like eastern Washington and Idaho that grow hops more cheaply. But our hops are special because they are aromatic hops, with something like 350 compounds in their essential oils that give both taste and scent. Boutique hop fields are popping up. This is beginning to sound like something that is worthy of crafting, does it not? Locally. At the hippest edge of beerdom.

Craft beer uses a lot more hops than mass produced beer, up to 20 times as much. And hops are the most expensive ingredient in beer. A new Oregon business, Indie Hops, has invested in a hop processing plant so it can be processed in Oregon, and Oregon State University has a hop research program studying aromatic hops to optimize their use and develop new varieties. Hillsboro Hops is the name of a Portland suburb's minor league baseball team.

OSU also studies barley and is home to Barley World. Even more important for Oregon craft beer, one of the biggest malting plants in the western states is located just across the Columbia River in Vancouver. How convenient! It's like beer is our destiny.

Now we are hearing about something more artisan than microbreweries. Nanobreweries don't usually brew more than one batch at a time and are served only very locally. They're one step above home brewers, which are also plentiful in Portland.

More and more, people are buying beer in growlers, which are like little brown jugs (not necessarily brown or juggy) that can be cleaned and filled again and again. Reused. So Portland. Now you can get beer at bottle shops and growler stations.

Brewpubs are important gathering and meeting places in Portland. While one might go to a coffee shop to get work done, to a teahouse for quiet time, brewpubs are for socializing. Because there are so many and humans can be indecisive, people often go pub-crawling from one to the next. There are many ways of accomplishing this. One is by pedalounge or brewcycle where a bunch of people sit at a bar and pedal, like on a bike. And somehow it goes forward. It's hard to explain. Portland also has a brewbarge where you grab a growler and take to the river.

And then there are the Portland distilleries making handcrafted spirits in small batches. We have six distilleries all in a row in inner southeast Portland. They make vodkas, gins, rums, whiskeys and even more specialized spirits like aquavit and flavored liqueurs.

Some of the flavors are very interesting. Like New Deal's Mud Puddle Bitter Chocolate Vodka and Hot Monkey Pepper Flavored Vodka. New Deal does not have a mission statement but it does have a manifesto. It's very touching and very Portland:

> "New Deal is about Hope. We want to capture the spirit of progress and hope for prosperity. We want to go in a new direction where the individual matters...We're offering vodka that's high quality, a good value, big bang for the buck. It represents the fruits of our hard labor and reflects our individual style. We think you should treat the people around you well, because we're all in this together. And we know that you can get ahead without screwing everyone over. We think of Ken Kesey's bus. If you meet someone you like, offer them a ride and if they stay on the bus for a month or a year—so much the better. Throw a good party and people will come—and we aren't talking about a corporate, from-the-top-down kinda party. We want the real thing. We want to sell the real thing and know the real people."

House Spirits has a different vibe. You have to type in your birthdate to see the website. Weird! Apparently there wasn't an upper age limit because they let me in. !

I've also heard that Portland is the birthplace of the craft cocktail movement. And though I cannot offer you any proof, I'm pretty sure this is something nobody would lie about.

In fact, this whole section presented me with such a dilemma. So many breweries, so much to drink, how do we figure out where to take our photo? I was in a panic because I didn't want to favor anybody over anybody because where would it end?

Then I discovered the Oregon Public House. It doesn't brew but it's a pub that claims to be the world's first nonprofit pub, whose mission is "to EAT in community, DRINK to a new way of giving back and GIVE to those changing the world." As founder Ryan Saari explains it, "I was sitting in my backyard with friends and we were talking about what kind of business we could start as a nonprofit. We were drinking some beers and I just said, 'What about a Pub?' And we all laughed...and then got really serious. And we thought, 'Why not?'"

The pub has a board of directors who volunteer their time to oversee and support the organization. All the money that isn't used to cover operating costs is shared among the 10 nonprofit groups the pub supports, $46,913 since May 2013. It invites other 501(c)(3) organizations to apply to be on its charity list.

Drinking beer with a good conscience because you're helping the world? A drunkard's dream if I ever did see one.

Pieces
of
Portland

I See Where You're Coming From

With the exception of some 6,000 Native Americans, all the residents of Portland in the latest census (2010) are immigrants or descended from immigrants. For the purposes of this page, I'm defining immigrants as those who arrived and settled in our land after it was already occupied by the First People.

The founders and early residents of what became Portland were from the eastern parts of the U.S. The coin toss that determined the name of our city was between men from Portland and Boston, who had come here by sea. Substantial immigration into Oregon Country started when the Oregon Trail opened, bringing Americans from the Midwest and east who came west to "settle" the "frontier" and take part in the westward expansion that many in the United States considered justifiable and inevitable, because it was America's "manifest destiny."

At first, Portland's foreign-born immigrants were from Europe, primarily Great Britain, Germany and Scandinavian countries. There were considerable numbers of immigrants from China in the 1870s and 1880s when workers were needed to build railroads and work in the salmon canning industry. Between 1880 and 1910, when Portland's population boomed, most international immigrants were from Canada, Germany and Italy. Because they were often mistreated, Chinese immigrants tended to cluster in the eastern part of what is now Old Town in downtown Portland. Japanese immigration grew in the early 20th century, locating near Chinatown.

Immigration from Mexico and Central and South America has ebbed and flowed, depending on whether the U.S. needs agricultural workers, and how much political pressure there is to deport them when Americans resent them as economic threats. As immigration policies became more and more restrictive during the last part of the 19th century and first half of the 20th century, Portland's immigrant population declined and began to rise again when refugees began arriving in the 1970s. Oregon was one of the early destinations for those fleeing Vietnam, Laos and Cambodia who were in danger after the U. S. military withdrew upon defeat.

I remember in 1975, when I was teaching an *Environment of Portland* class at Portland State University, a gentle young man came in to my office to ask me a question about something in class he didn't understand because he was not yet fluent in English. When I saw he was upset, I invited him to sit down and asked if he was okay. He told me he was from Vietnam, had no way to reach his parents and family. He hoped they were in a refugee camp, but he didn't know if they were even alive. Imagine trying to take a college class in a new language while living with that kind of fear.

Over time, I heard many similar stories from those who would likely be dead had they not escaped from their home country. They have experienced so much fear and loss, it warms my heart to think they can find safety and feel welcome in Portland.

What is now the Immigrant and Refugee Center of Oregon was first established to serve those from Southeast Asia, then expanded in the mid-1980s to add programs for refugees from

other areas of war, political repression and/or forced relocation. Refugees included Afghans, Ethiopians, Eritreans, Iranians, Romanians and other eastern Europeans.

Since then, refugees have come to Portland from other parts of Africa, Asia, former Soviet Union, eastern Europe and Central America.

The African population in the Portland metropolitan area has grown by 110% in the past decade, coming primarily from Congo, Ethiopia, Somalia and Sudan.

Asian and Pacific Islander populations in our area have grown by 90% in the last 10 years, with more than 100,000 making their home here now, creating communities of Vietnamese, Laotian, Cambodian, Hmong, Mien, Burmese, Filipino, Pacific Islander and Chinese. Asians are populous in east Portland and Washington County and are dispersed through the rest of the metro area. While part of Old Town has traditionally been Portland's Chinatown, many businesses and people from that area have moved to outer southeast Portland.

There are an estimated 100,000 people from the former Soviet Union in the Portland area. In the 1970s and 1980s, several hundred Jews arrived from the Soviet Union. More recently, arrivals have been evangelical Christians. There are a number of groups and festivals where all the Slavic groups come together, usually in eastern parts of Portland where the majority live.

Southeast Asia still accounts for the largest regional area of origin of refugees in 2013 in our area (43%), with those from the former Soviet Union in second place (31.5%). Others (>1% data shown) come from Afghanistan (1.2%), Bhutan (1.3%), Myanmar (1.7%), Congo, Cuba (4.8%), Czech Republic, Ethiopia (1.5%), Haiti, Hungary, Iran, Iraq (1.9%), Kosovo, Poland, Romania (3.4%), Somalia (3.1%), Sudan and other African countries.

Once refugees settle here, other family members may be able to join them if they are able to provide financial support.

The most recent arrivals in Portland come from former Soviet republics, Cuba, Burma, Iraq and Somalia.

Nearly 13% of Portland's population was born in foreign lands. About half of them have become naturalized citizens. According to PSU's Population Research Center, about 90% of net in-migration between 2000 and 2009 in Multnomah County was international.

The minority population of the Portland metro area grew by 41% between 2000 and 2008, seven times faster than the overall population growth. Latinos are the fastest growing minority population because of both domestic and international migration, as well as fertility levels above the Oregon state average. The Hispanic population in Portland grew by 52% between 2000 and 2010, an increase from 36,052 to 54,840.

People of the Karen ethnic minority group in southeast Burma fled prosecution and spent years, sometimes decades, in refugee camps in Thailand before being resettled in Portland. Luba Gonina created a weaving group for Karen women, with the assistance of Ladella Williams of the local Handweavers Guild. **Opposite page:** Standing: Kaw Kleh Wah, Baby Win, Ya Htoo, Ma Ma Aye, Htee Kve, Ladella Williams, Ra Day, Luba Gonina. Seated: Keh Lay Htoo, Ree Thu, Lucy Htoo, Kah Mar. **This page:** Baby Win uses the hand weaving tools and techniques from her homeland to make decorative wall hangings, scarves, purses and clothing. No quilt was necessary because of the beautiful weaving.

I wonder if we Americans truly understand how hard it is to escape or be forced to leave one's mother country, often separated from family members, then being held virtual prisoners for years and years in crowded and ill-equipped refugee camps before being assigned to another country halfway across the world, not of their choosing. Understanding and navigating the different ways of a new place and culture is so challenging, not to mention finding employment to support themselves and their families. The best possible outcome is to mix our cultures so the better parts of each are introduced and known among all. But it's not so easy.

I remember when I was in graduate school, I met some wonderful students from Iran. They were, and still are, among the kindest and smartest people I've ever known. I repeatedly invited them over for dinner, and they repeatedly refused. I didn't understand why and was beginning to take offense, when I read an article about cultural differences that explained that in Persian culture, it is considered rude to accept invitations readily, and they must be repeated many times before it becomes permissible to accept. When I told Fereydoon, Habib and Riaz about the article, they immediately laughed and said, "Yes, yes, that is true!" and we all felt so relieved that we had reached an understanding... and they no longer considered me rude for accepting their first invitation when they had issued it weeks earlier.

There are some very innovative programs that people in Portland are trying out to address cultural challenges. Women in many refugee

Pieces
of
Portland

families are particularly isolated. There are tensions between parents who want to preserve their native cultures and teens who feel pressured to adopt American culture to fit in with their peers. If these problems aren't addressed, they can have tragic consequences.

Luba Gonina came to Portland from Kiev, Ukraine. She had never heard of Portland and had no choice about where she was sent as a refugee. "Until maybe 10 years ago, refugees were sent to large cities because the perception was there would be more opportunity there," she said. "But it turned out refugees did much better in smaller cities, so Portland was a more common destination when I left Ukraine." Luba got her undergraduate and graduate degrees in the U.S. in mental health counseling and art therapy. After finishing her studies and becoming a citizen, she lived in different parts of the world but returned to Portland because she thinks it's the best place for her and her work.

Building on her own refugee experience, her art and counseling training and observations, Luba decided she would try using art therapy as a way to help refugees deal with the post traumatic stress from their past and the anxiety about their loss of identity in trying to decipher and understand the new culture they had to negotiate.

The Karen ethnic group in Burma (aka Myanmar) was repressed and threatened with death after the country became independent from Great Britain in 1948. Over the years, many Karen escaped into Thailand where they spent years and sometimes decades in refugee camps. At Lutheran Community Services in Portland, Luba began working with Karen refugees.

"It all started with one client about two years ago," she remembers. "To help the client start unwinding from these horrible and scary experiences, I sought a safe environment in which to begin exploring common threads and build a therapeutic relationship."

When she asked questions about cultural traditions that had been joyful, Luba learned about the weaving Karen women had always done. In fact, weaving had been especially important while

they were living in the refugee camps, because they were able to provide clothing for their family. While in the refugee camps they were surrounded by fences, they could not leave the camp, and the only work they could do was weaving. To help women get through the stress of very rapid forced assimilation and to help them develop coping skills, Luba decided to use weaving as a form of art therapy, gathering all the materials and tools needed for weekly weaving sessions.

"Our 'Weaving Together' group not only became a safe place to express feelings and relieve post-traumatic symptoms," Luba says, "but was also a way to tap into natural resilience, restore a sense of trust in oneself and bolster support mechanisms."

The women began to make hand woven scarves, bags, pouches, shirts and more. Luba contacted a local handweaving guild that worked with the group to begin marketing their work at local art fairs and markets. The sales provide them with income and build relationships with others beyond the Karen community.

When Joyce and I visited the Karen weavers, they welcomed us and readily posed for the group photo but did not smile without some prompting. Later, the translator explained that in their culture, smiling only happens when there is something funny going on, something to laugh about. To smile for a photograph is to be fake, because it is not an authentic smile. They are puzzled about why Americans smile so much. We found it hard to come up with a satisfactory explanation. How would you explain it? We were so touched when several came over to hug us goodbye.

Luba explained that very often refugees are oppressed three times over. First, because of their minority ethnic status in their own country, then in refugee camps, and then in the U.S., where they face discrimination and resentment. Many remain isolated and cultural norms are turned upside down (e.g., children replace elders as leaders of families in communication in official settings because they are the ones who learn English most easily and quickest).

Luba is also using art therapy with mothers and children from the former Soviet Union to work together on folk art projects and improve their communication and understanding of one another.

The day we visited was a special one because they celebrated International Women's Day as they had done in their homeland. Think of it this way: take Mother's Day as celebrated in the U.S. and pretend like our nation actually honored women on Women's Day and you would begin to understand what their experience was like. Children and men prepare breakfast in bed for all the women, who don't have to do any work that day but are treated like queens. The children in the group worked on making special candle holders for their mothers and prepared cards and stories to perform at the meeting.

It was also the day of the festival of Purim that commemorates the salvation of the Jewish people in ancient Persia through the actions of Queen Esther. Lovely Aviva Zelkind told the story to the group and we all played our parts, cheering and booing at the appropriate moments. It warmed our hearts to see the closeness of the children and their mothers.

We felt honored to be welcomed by both groups, who are adding so much richness to our community. I hate to have to tell you they are treated badly by some, even in Portland. I have to believe those Portlanders would be ashamed if they knew what the refugees and immigrants go though before coming here. If not, I am ashamed for them.

And apologize to one and all on their behalf. Which is not nearly enough, I know.

Opposite page: At top, Ra Day, wears a number of scarves with very intricate patterns she has woven in the Weaving Together group. Below, Aviva Zelkind tells the story of Queen Esther for the Festival of Purim. **This page:** Elizabeth Chumak reads a card she wrote to her mother Nataliya after she gave her handmade flowers to celebrate International Women's Day, which is a very big deal in their culture.

How Much Do You Know About How Immigration Actually Works?

Current immigration and refugee policy in the United States is determined by federal law and is a highly regulated and tightly controlled system. Current federal policy is designed to re-unite families, admit people with skills valued by the U.S. economy, protect refugees and promote diversity.

Immigrants: For much of its early history, the United States allowed unrestricted immigration until 1875 when Congress established direct federal control of immigration and prohibited entry by prostitutes and convicts. Over the next several decades, laws were adopted that allowed the U.S. to exclude other categories of individuals (e.g., Chinese people, "lunatics, idiots, people with physical or mental defects or tuberculosis, persons of psychopathic inferiority, illiterates, alcoholics, stowaways, vagrants, and other persons likely to become public charges.")

In the 1920s, the federal government began setting quotas for countries of origin. Britain was allotted 50% of the number of slots. Immigration from southern and eastern Europe was limited. Asian immigration was almost entirely prohibited. During the Great Depression, immigration dropped dramatically and continued to decline until the U.S. faced labor shortages in WWII, when agricultural workers from south of the border were admitted and Chinese exclusion laws were repealed.

In 1952, immigration and naturalization were joined into a comprehensive federal law, upholding quotas and former restrictions and tightening security for people considered subversive (viz., Communists).The Immigration and Nationality Act of 1965 ended the national origins quota system and replaced it with a preference system emphasizing family reunification and immigrant skills. The Immigration Reform and Control Act of 1986 was intended to control and deter illegal immigration. The Immigration Act of 1990 raised the ceiling of the total number of immigrants per year to 675,000 and revised grounds for prohibiting immigration and deportation.

As of 2014, federal law allows a limit of new 675,000 permanent immigrant visas annually, based on family reunification (480,000 visas), employment, (140,000) and a diversity lottery system (up to 55,000). The lottery is available to people in countries with historically low immigration to the U.S. Family sponsored immigrants represented 66% of all individuals granted legal permanent resident status in 2012. Immigrants admitted under an employment based visa were 14% of the total, refugee and asylee immigrants were 15% and the diversity lottery immigrants were 3.9%.

Except for visa lottery winners, immigrants must be sponsored by a close family member or an employer. People who win the diversity lottery must show that they have reliable means of support and are unlikely to become public charges before they will actually be approved for entry as legal permanent residents. Eligibility for federal benefit programs like financial assistance (SSI, TANF) and SNAP (food stamps) is severely restricted or denied for most immigrants for at least the first five years.

Refugees: After World War II, the U.S. began admitting displaced people and refugees, the first being 400,000 Europeans in 1948. Later laws admitted people fleeing persecution, primarily intended for people escaping communism. Today, refugees must prove they have a "well founded fear of persecution" in their country of origin due to religion, political opinion, race, nationality or membership in a particular group. The United Nations determines which countries have conditions that produce refugees. U.S. officials determine whether a particular person qualifies for admission. The number of refugees the U.S. accepts varies from year to year (58,000 in 2012) and there are regional ceilings. Upon arrival, refugees are connected with a voluntary agency that helps them find housing and other resources and that offers support for up to eight months. Although refugees are eligible for public assistance when they first arrive, the U.S. emphasizes early economic self-sufficiency through employment to speed their integration into American society.

Pieces of Portland

When You Wish Upon a Tree

Sometimes somebody starts a random thing in a random place and it catches on to an astonishing degree. The Wishing Tree in northeast Portland is a sweet example. Before leaving town for the weekend in November 2013, Nicole Helprin and her two kids wrote a few wishes on tags and hung them on a tree in front of their home. While they were gone, a local news station reported it, and when the Helprins returned, the tree was covered in wishes.

It has become a total thing. Shipping labels and markers are provided so anybody can keep adding wishes. We contributed ours when we dropped by.

In another neighborhood, a family started putting a bucket of water out near the sidewalk to quench the thirst of dogs passing by. Then one Easter, they hung ornamental carrots with dog treats inside from branches of a dogwood tree (naturally!) near the water. The neighborhood dogs caught on, and insisted on being walked in that direction for a treat. Humans had to start bringing their own treats so their dogs would move on. Over time, the thing became a movement and now the carrots filled with treats hang year round. Anonymous donors drop off boxes of treats as replacements. And this has been going on for 20 years!

While writing this, I found a website for another Portland magic tree, led by an organization that exists to actually grant wishes. Is there no limit to where Portland takes things? Do we pretty much just do every single thing any of us thinks of? And keep it going and going and going?

Yes. Yes, apparently we do. And probably always will.

Opposite page: Besides trees for hugging, Portland has at least one tree for wishing. **This page:** Below, you can read some of the wishes passersby have left. New ones appear all the time. Apparently there is a lot of wishful thinking in Portland. I wonder if anybody is tracking outcomes to see how many wishes come true. Above, a Dogwood tree dispenses treats for passing dogs, causing Portland dogs to wish to be walked in its direction.

▪ Quilt information on page 165.

It's Way More Than a Game

To fully understand Portland, you must grasp the Underdog Complex. The one where you lose so often, you begin to expect it. And way too frequently, you actually come in dead last. It probably started in Portland a few years after the beginning of the 20th century. For more than the first half a century, the city of Portland stood head and shoulders above the city of Seattle, with way more people, more business, pretty much more everything. But then we got eclipsed and people forgot we existed. And I don't think we've ever really recovered, because we are still looking for ways to convince others (but mostly ourselves) we are better than Seattle. I suppose we will get over this someday, but you need to have that as background to understand an essential part of our character.

For the longest time, Oregon was simply not known in the rest of the country. If we were known at all, it was as a vague place between Seattle and California. I've received mail addressed to Portland, Oregon, Canada. And does anyone east of the Rockies ever pronounce Oregon correctly?

It seems that the longer we've lived in Oregon, the more acute our Underdog Complex is. Take someone like me, for example, who has lived in Oregon for six decades give or take. That many years with a complex means it's chronic. Acute too. It helps to understand this in order to grasp how we view games and sports.

As a teen, a cousin from another state (I'm looking at you Bill D.) asked me at a family reunion in 1965 if I had ever heard of the Beatles. As if I weren't totally in love with George. Or maybe it was Ringo. When I got to Chicago for college in 1967, upon meeting other students, I was asked in a serious tone if Oregon had indoor plumbing yet. One guy wanted to know if we still had cowboys and Indians out on the range. I am not making this up.

My first year as a graduate student at the University of Oregon was the beginning of the Dick Harter era and the introduction of kamikaze basketball to the world. Looking back, it was the weirdest thing ever. Players diving halfway down the court to go for a ball that was already out of bounds. Players just standing there holding the ball or bouncing it every now and then for minutes at a time. Until the other team gave up and called a time out or committed a foul on purpose, just to make something happen. (There was no shot clock then, and this kind of basketball is surely why one was invented.)

Despite its utter ridiculousness, we fans ate it up. You have to remember that this was at the height of the John Wooden UCLA basketball dynasty, and most of the other Pac-8 conference schools were much larger and better funded. California teams and the Huskies expected to waltz in and crush little old wagon train-riding Oregon without breaking a sweat. Which is pretty much what always happened. They didn't hide how much they looked down on us hicks from the sticks, so anything Oregon

did in Mac Court to shake things up, to throw other teams off their stride, made us cheer our pea-pickin lil ole hearts out. And then one day the kamikaze weirdness worked, and Oregon beat UCLA. Yes, that's what I said. They beat the team led by Bill Walton that became national champions.

What a fluke! But for a few moments, we let ourselves believe we were that good. It felt hugely awesome! The campus actually levitated. Of course the following weekend we started losing again and reclaimed our underdog status.

This complex was not confined to Eugene, but carried over to Portland as well. In 1970, the Rose City got an NBA franchise as an expansion team. Naturally, the first few years were unremarkable, but in its seventh year, led by none other than UCLA alum Bill Walton (we loved him instantly when he became a Blazer), the Portland Trailblazers became NBA champions.

Understand this: Portland was a one-sport major league city. We had minor league baseball and hockey, but the Blazers were the shizz. Portland was electrified to infinity power. Our day had come! Finally, at long last, people from Oregon were getting champagne dumped on them in a locker room. We were coming unglued, all over the city. Those of us unlucky enough to not be at the game, that is, and who had our eyes glued to the television.

And then you know what happened? CBS, the network that was broadcasting the game, almost immediately cut away to a golf tournament whose name I can't even remember. There is no way to convey the collective outrage that swelled up from our city. And we knew in our hearts, that it was because we were underdogs. That's what happens to small market teams and towns. We're just lil ole Portland, we can't get no respect. We got dissed, and we were pissed.

And, naturally, being underdogs, we knew our championship reign couldn't last. Things fell apart the following season when Bill Walton was seriously injured.

But here's what underdog Portland does when it wins. For what they accomplished in that one season, for bringing so much joy to the city that all our hearts grew seven sizes that day, we showered the Blazers with love so great that from 1977 through 1995, the team sold out 814 consecutive home games, the longest such streak in American major professional sports. We even stayed with the Jailblazers, but they eventually overtried our patience.

We went to the finals twice more during the Drexler/Porter/Kersey era, but there have been some pretty lean years since the mid 1990s.

Now I'm going to tell you the truly heartbreaking part, the part that will always haunt us. And I think it directly relates to the Underdog Complex. Because there's no other way to explain what happened. In 1984, the year that Michael Jordan was in the draft, the Blazers had the second pick. Houston took Hakeem Olijawan so there was Michael Jordan, sitting there waiting. The Blazers took him, of course. A clear no brainer. Slam dunk. But that's not what happened. We took Sam Bowie. You've probably never heard of him. Nobody has. BECAUSE HE BROKE HIS LEG EVERY TIME HE TOOK THE FLOOR.

Well, twice. That I know of.

> **Opposite page:** The Rose Garden, now called Moda Center, is the home of our beloved Portland Trailblazers. We know the challenges of being a small market town. Often our players are under-appreciated outside Portland, but they are never under-loved here at home. We're Rip City, baby!
> ■ Quilt information on page 165.

He never even really had an NBA career.

How could the Blazers brass live with themselves?!?! Michael Frickin Jordan! Slam junk!

Oh, but it doesn't end there. Then in 2007, 23 years later, having been one of the teams with the worst record in the season that had just ended, Portland had the NUMBER ONE PICK IN THE DRAFT! Picture an entire city—a city filled with people with depression caused by seasonal affective disorder because of the perpetual winter grey—rehabbed off antidepressants in one day. We were gonna get this one right! So who did we pick? Greg Oden. Who could we have had? Kevin Durant. Can you spell MVP? And what happened to Greg Oden? Oh, HE BROKE HIS KNEE BEFORE THE SEASON EVEN BEGAN. As soon as one knee healed after the first season, he broke the other one! And kept on breaking things. We stuck with him and tried to help him heal for a very long time, but finally gave him up. He's not really had an NBA career either. And our franchise player—Brandon Roy—who filled us with hope for a time had his knees crap out after six years.

Here's how it works, people. Fans and teams and cities with serious Underdog Complex don't really believe they will ever win—secretly even feel they don't deserve to win—so they unconsciously self-sabotage. I fear it's now in our DNA and will be passed on to future generations.

Either that or it's some kind of Tonya Harding curse on all things sporting. Ever wonder why it's almost always the knees?

But we are beginning to believe again. Last year gave us hope, we are head over heels in love with our players again. Did you see Damian's three-point shot at the buzzer that won the first round playoff series over Houston in 2014? Was that not everything?!? And Robin Lopez? Was he not made for Portland?!?

§

Now let's turn our attention back to the Oregon Ducks, this time to football. We were serious underdogs in football too. Even when we had players who later became NFL stars like Dan Fouts, Ahmad Rashad (known then as Bobby Moore), we lost more than we won. We couldn't seem to get a break.

Oh, it got really bad. I was at that Civil War game against the Oregon State Beavers that ended in a 0-0 tie. Imagine sitting in relentless cold rain, wearing a leaking slicker while the person in front of you keeps tipping the water that collects on their umbrella back into your lap, watching a game where your team's most effective offense is the forward fumble. It was tragic and I thought it would always be that way.

The very thought that the Oregon football team would be ranked in the top 25 in the nation, let alone in the top 5 (number 2?!), is nearly beyond our imagination. It's like I suddenly looked up and there were the Ducks, winning, crushing in fact. It felt like there was a bit of wizardry at work, they hardly huddled and the coaches on the sidelines held up huge posters with weird pictures, like they had entered another dimension somehow. I think I saw them in the national championship game even. But maybe it was a dream.

I'm so afraid to wake up. I prefer the surreal version of Duck football. And when I saw an ESPN map that showed there are Duck fans all over the country, that the Ducks are beloved everywhere now (well, except in the SEC), I get vertigo and have to take to my bed. That's an alternative universe I'll never dare believe in. I know that my Underdog Complex is still alive and well because I cannot bear to watch an Oregon football game until the Ducks are up by 30 points. Then I can begin to look without being hooked up to life support.

And their uniforms! Don't you just love them?? The saturated colors, the greens, the yellows! The Oregon Ducks have turned the football field into a runway. They are so very fashion forward. No matter what the score, no matter how quickly they start losing again, I'll have that to hang on to.

That's how underdogs think. They pretend the score doesn't matter. And it's just a game. Yes, I do realize I went on a bit of a rant here, but I wouldn't have done it if I didn't think it was important. And I had no idea I knew so frickin much about sports! Okay, okay, my son filled in the gaps. :)

Opposite page: Despite being in the 2015 national title game and Marcus Mariota winning the Heisman trophy, some of us will never totally overcome our underdog expectations that were once associated with Oregon Duck football. But we're trying. Please give us more time to get used to winning and go see the saturated colors at the Duck Store.

◼ Quilt information on page 165.

It Takes an Army to Join a Global Village

I'm just going to say it. I don't get soccer. I try to watch it, but I don't know enough to understand what's going on, because surely it can't just be a swarm of players randomly running about the field, randomly kicking the ball to random places without ever scoring. Can it? And whose idea was it not to use hands? Why? No hands, but heads? How does that make sense on any level?

I get that Portland snagging its second ever major league franchise is a very big deal. So I'm really happy for the Timbers Army and everything.

Actually, I find Portland's response to the Timbers very fascinating. I know part of it reflects the fact that a lot of present-day Portlanders grew up playing soccer. We didn't have it back in my day, but I don't think children are allowed not to play soccer in their youth now. I see it everywhere, and my grandkids have all played, with at least one granddaughter playing on a select team.

But that's not enough to explain the Timbers. So I shall offer up my theories.

We consider it a compliment of the highest order when someone says Portland is like a European city. I'm not contending that it actually is like a European city. But I do I think it's one of the few cities in the U.S. that has European qualities. Like it's kind of civilized, in certain ways. We have good public transit. It's possible to experience our city without seeing any strip malls. A lot of people actually walk and bike places, and much of it seems not to be dominated by combat-ready Humvees and SUVs. We have lots of cafes with sidewalk seating. We keep things somewhat clean and orderly.

Soccer, of course, has been the most popular global sport for decades. People in other countries thought it was weird that we didn't have professional teams, like it was some kind of fetish comparable to rejecting the metric system the rest of the world uses.

Portland is a port. It connects to the Pacific Ocean. The city has been trading with Europe and Pacific Rim countries since the mid-19th century. The Chinook people did so in the 18th century and likely much earlier. Yeah, yeah, I know Seattle/Tacoma has much deeper ports and are ahead of us in exports now, brag brag brag.

We are anxious to be seen as a global partner. We have the most awesome Japanese and Chinese gardens of all space and time. So when a GLOBAL sport comes to Portland, don't you think we are going to jump on it and show the world how GLOBAL we are, and even already were? Loving soccer is a way we show how cosmopolitan we are—I mean already were.

So the Timbers Army was inevitable, I believe. And yes, it's true. Crowds of soccer fans gather at the soccer stadium hours before games—I mean matches—begin. Which doesn't begin to compare with what they do all game long.

The spectacle blew *New York Times'* reporter Joe Rhode's mind:

> "The crowds gather at Providence Park hours before the matches begin, and the intensity of the Timbers Army — before, during and after the matches—is something to behold; hours of nonstop singing and chanting and synchronized taunts. They erect huge section-covering canvas banners... elaborately painted fluttering billboards, some of them covering 16,000 square feet and weighing more than 1,500 pounds. The Timbers Army, which takes up 6,000 seats, stands and screams for the entire match, the roar reverberating from the covered stands.
>
> "These don't look like traditional sports crowds. The stadium is full of technology nerds and hemp-wearing hippies, nose-pierced punks and artisan soapmakers. There are, to be sure, suburban soccer moms and children in their youth league uniforms, but, for the most part, it's a 'Portlandia' casting call come to life."

He also noted that Portland fans don't march before the game or do face paint, because that's what Seattle does. See what I mean?!

When Portland scores a goal, a logger named Joey fires up his chain saw and saws a slice off a log. "OMG, I hope it's not old growth," I find myself reflexively thinking. But fear not, I have been assured that only logs are used that have already fallen or have become injured, diseased or hazardous. There's a "Blessing of the Log" ceremony at Lumber Camp 18 in the Coast Range during pre-season every year, in hopes that it leads the Timbers to more goals scored and more crosscuts made.

"Oh, I hope they are turning the sawed off piece over to Urban Lumber to put it to good use afterward," I can hear lots of people in the stadium thinking to themselves. The Timbers Army website reported that the 107ist (107 Independent Supporters Trust) planted 325 trees on February 15, 2015. Presumably to help make up for the log sawing.

We also have a professional women's soccer team—the Portland Thorns—that played its first season in the National Women's Soccer League in 2013. They have almost as impressive a following at Providence Park as the Timbers, with their own Rose City Riveters. They are apparently quite good and won the first-ever national championship game in 2013.

Another way we reveal our character through sport is by openly expressing love and loyalty to our teams. We are genuinely shocked when we see fans in other cities boo their own players and teams. We would never do that. We only boo our own players when they harm dogs. Or tell us they hate us. But it has to be three times in a row.

Portland has a lower ratio of cynics than many other cities. We can still admit we love things, we can still show enthusiasm and wear our hearts on our sleeves and get stars in our eyes. We like being nice and friendly. We want people to like us and we want to like other people. So, in many ways, we are grateful to our sports teams because they give us opportunities to feel our joy and express our love and admiration.

Hands down, we are the best damn fans a team could wish for.

Period. Amen.

Opposite page: *Facing the Crowd* sculptures by Michael Stutz stand at two corners of what is now called Providence Park (earlier it was PGE Park, then Jeld-Wenn, the name may change again before you read this?). Perhaps foreshadowing the name changes, the two silicon bronze sculptures are of a boy and a man, representing two stages of life. This one is the laughing man, who is somehow able to keep laughing while his tongue hangs all the way out.
■ Quilt information on page 165.

It must be said that many Portlanders have no interest in, or knowledge of, professional sports teams whatsoever. We do, after all, have our share of representatives from the too cool for school movement, although I bet most aren't actually from here. Some find the spectacle to be a bit unseemly. Others find professional sports to be indefensible from a social justice perspective. Many find it boring, because they must stay in the stands and watch, rather than join in the action. (This is what leads to streaking, I think.) Others just have more compelling other interests.

Portland has lots of the usual sports and games going on, with leagues for things like roller derby, rugby, lacrosse, tennis, and things played with every kind of ball you can imagine, and some you can't.

Some of our more unusual sports may well be unique to Portland, or at least reach their full manifestation here, like the Urban Iditarod, Big Wheel Championship, Adult Soap Box Derby (which you'll meet shortly) and I'm running out of room.

Out of all the quirky sporty choices, we want to tell you about Mondo Croquet. The mondo part is that it's played with sledge hammers and bowling balls, with bent rebar for the wickets.

"The idea came from my business partner Bernhard Masterson," says the man who introduces himself as Lord Peter, who seems to be somewhat overseeing the World Championship Tourney in the North Park Blocks on a summer Sunday afternoon in 2014. "I was very active with the Portland Cacophony Society at the time"—SCREEEEEEECH!!!

HOLD ON NOW, I've been looking for the original source of all the weirdness in Portland, perhaps this particular rabbit hole will contain the motherlode. The Portland Cacaphony Society? How have I never heard of this group? Must take a quick detour!

OMG, it has a website! Caco, as it calls itself, is "a randomly gathered network of free-spirits seeking new adventures beyond the pale of mainstream society." Apparently they are the ones behind SantaCon (where thousands dress up as Santa and do revelry) and Burning Man Portland (where folks share fond memories of the mothership Burning Man and are invited to bring an art car to burn out in the parking lot.) Actually, I think it's best to let them explain in their own words:

"Our events may involve costumes and drinking, we are NOT a pub crawl company. We're not even a company, although we'll keep you company. Any events we have involving costumes and drinking are usually ABOUT something else, there's just some tangent and surface things the public pick up. For every Santacon there are twelve small mindf■ks which the masses do not find as easily joined or co-opted. For every massive crowd we create, there are numerous small interactions. We're not going for WOO HOO, we're going for 'I don't know what just happened, but you should have seen it!' "Nobody is 'in charge', there are no official 'representatives', we're a do-ocracy and friends. If you don't do things, and you're not friendly, you're not a Cacophonist. We value contribution, self-expression, self-reliance, and participation. Caco events are experiences, not spectator-based entertainment. Life not only isn't a spectator sport,

it's not a tour."We're not recruiting, we're welcoming. We're not here to entertain you, we're here to help you entertain yourself, or make you think…or maybe just enjoy ourselves and maybe count you as part of the 'us' in 'ourselves,' if that makes sense. Then again, what does? We may be your guides, your catalysts, your bad/good influences, we could very well be the people your mother warned you about. We're the people Tyler Durden was based on, but real… sorta. We're a lot less intense and more huggable. We don't want to sell you anything, we just want to go on zany adventures with you.

"Portland Cacophony Society – making you think and not charging you a dime – since 1996.

"You may already be a member…

Is this the motherlode? Well, it's probably a chicken and egg thing. But hey, Caco is awfully close to Cacao! Just sayin.

Okay, back to the Lord Peter interview:

"They provided a group of fun people ready to take on something new. A certain Cupcake McFastlane had a lawn full of bowling balls, so all the pieces came together."

Did I mention that everybody playing in the Mondo Croquet World Championship Tournament that day was dressed as a character from Alice in Wonderland?

"We decided early on that it would add to the fun of the event to be dressed formally in traditional British lawn games style," Lord Peter explained. "That quickly led to a tea party, which in turn lead to the Mad Hatter Picnic. It all goes together quite nicely, don't you think?"

But of course!

While games can be held in other places, the championship is always in Portland. "Many people have been coming back year after year. We've had people come from as far away as Florida to participate."

Lord Peter hopes to make Mondo Croquet an event at the Summer Olympics. "There are not enough sports in the Olympics where you can be old and out of shape and still be a contender." And to prove he's serious, he earnestly adds, "It would also be fun to do a celebrity tournament as a nonprofit fundraiser."

In Portland, even the weirdest things and people have good and pure intentions.

When I interviewed him later, I forgot to ask Lord Peter who won the tournament. That's probably because I know it's not about the points.

As Lord Peter said as he bid me goodbye, "It's all about the fun."

> **Opposite page:** In the top photo, Lord Peter prepares to slam the bowling ball through the rebar wicket in this peculiarly Portland game of Mondo Croquet, which was invented here. It's not clear it's played anywhere else on the planet. As if that weren't enough, players wear costumes from the tea party in *Alice in Wonderland*. In the bottom photo, the group takes a short break to pose for a portrait.
> ■ Quilt information on page 165.

Creating Recreation

"You prolly shouldn't lay that there," one of the skaters warned as we spread our quilt on the smooth sloping concrete. "No telling what kind of filth there is."

We had come to the skate park under the east end of the Burnside Bridge—the one we had spotted on *Portlandia*. We had heard that Portland is considered the best skateboarding town, and we wanted to capture some of the lesser known, more alternative sports in our city. Because, of course, the major league teams, even in Portlandia, pretty much appeal to mainstream folks. Who can afford the ticket prices. There are a lot of other less organized, more individual ways to get exercise and have fun outdoors in Portland.

A notable thing about the skate park is that it was built without permission by skaters. They wanted a place where they could do their thing out of the rain in a place nobody was using where nobody would be bothered. So they created their own recreation place under the Burnside Bridge. Now it's legendary in skate circles.

The fact that we have such a great outdoor environment with a rather dizzying array of recreational opportunities is what makes this place so special to a whole lot of Portland people.

Within about an hour of Portland, you can reach world-class skiing, snowboarding, windsurfing, mountain climbing, bicycling, kayaking, rafting, camping, fishing, you name it, we have it. Well, I guess I've never seen anyone snorkeling hereabouts.

A lot of these things require a considerable amount of equipment, so there are barriers to entry. If the Subaru wagon is the preferred vehicle of the recreating class, the roof rack is the mandatory accessory piece. Because so much equipment.

The best part of equipment requirements might well be the additional opportunities they offer for nerdgasming. Don't get these enthusiasts started on their equipment unless you are prepared to donate the next few hours or days of your life. And don't ever accompany them to REI or Patagonia unless you share their obsession.

This being Portland, many of these equipment needs lead folks to build their own versions, which sometimes even lead to artisanal craft manufacturing startups in their garages. Well, I mean, they would if their garages weren't already filled with recycling, worm bins, brewing and fermenting equipment, crafting supplies and books to take to Powell's.

The one activity most anyone can do—partly because some paths are even paved for wheelchair access—is hiking. Yes, hiking is something that can be done alone, without special equipment, within the city limits. So I'm going to declare it the official recreational activity of Portland. Our city has more than 150 miles of hiking trails, and a 40-mile-loop trail around the metropolitan area is close to being finished. And our varied topography presents us with a wide array of hiking opportunities, depending on how flat or steep you want your walk to be. Not to mention the many amazing and wonderful vistas you can behold when you pause for breath or take a sip of water from your water bottle or hydration pack. Hydration pack? Whatever happened to bota bags and canteens? I feel so old school right now.

And with the coming of our new car-free bridge, we'll have safer and more pleasant ways to cross the river in our hiking adventures.

So go take a hike!

Recreational opportunities abound in Portland and environs. **Opposite page:** Hiking in the mossy woods of the temperate rainforest of Forest Park is a popular way to get close to nature. **This page:** Contrasting with the soft moss of the woods is the hard concrete of the Burnside skate park, used by both skateboarders and bikers. Portlanders find many ways to recreate. If we don't find them, we create them.
■ Quilt information on page 165.

Pieces
of
Portland

There are a few important things to know about Portland's Adult Soap Box Derby:

- The event is said to have been inspired by something witnessed in the Mission District of San Francisco, with the plan for the Portland version hatched over beer at the Horse Brass Pub.
- The first derby was held in 1997 with only six entries.
- Entries are called vessels.
- There is a race every four minutes.
- Only adults can race, all ages can watch.
- It's always the third Saturday in August.
- There is apparently no limit on time and imagination people devote to their vessels.
- Some participants reportedly spill blood. This is taken much less seriously than the spillage of beer.
- The racetrack is on the side of a volcano and racing is called "tickling the spine."
- Several thousand people turn out to watch each year.

In 2014, we saw a wide range of entries from a Priscilla of the Desert inspired wagon to recognizable cartoon/toy characters. There were two entries from folks at ADX—one for speed, one for style. Some 15 people worked on ADX vessels, with a few months of planning and preparation before the first weld was made. They used free or inexpensively-sourced scrap metal.

The stylish vessel was inspired by the perennial favorite of kids' everywhere, the rubber ducky. Donated bike frames served as the foundation of the speedy racer. "On race day, the duck car accomplished its singular goal—looking awesome," an ADX blogger reported. "The speed racer, dubbed 'Falcon Arrow 5000', performed admirably during its first two preliminary heats, but prior to the third heat the steering column broke..."

One of our favorites was Mr. Potato Head, who wore a derby hat and a hipster mustache as he zoomed down the mountain, his arms in a "hands up don't shoot" position. What impressed us the most was the fact that he apparently underwent gender reassignment after the first heat, appearing as Ms. Potato Head in the second, with a broad smile, bright red lipstick, volumizing mascara, a pink smock and a scarlet hat festooned with a daisy.

Not exactly fashion forward, but still.

Opposite page: Transgender Potato Head entrants are easily spotted in action in their Radio Flyers as they tickle the spine. That looks like Lewis and Clark in their canoe next to Ms. Potato Head. **This page:** Look closely to see the wire rubber ducky in the ADX-made cart (38) near the top of the course. You'll notice there's no quilt in any of the photos. We couldn't figure out where to put a quilt so it wouldn't be in the way. We certainly didn't want to create any road hazards.

Losing Our Religion

urveys consistently find Portland to be a relatively unchurched place. A 2015 study, for example, found that 42% of our city's residents are not affiliated with a church, almost twice the national average of 22%, and nearly 10% above Seattle and San Francisco, the second and third place cities. Compare that with Nashville's 15%, the lowest percent unaffiliated. Forty percent of Portlanders said they never go to church, and 17% said they are just not religious.

This is kind of odd when you consider that a fair number of early settlers in Oregon Territory were missionaries who came to "save the heathens."

Even some evangelical Christian churches and organizations are different here, perhaps because they have to adjust to Portland's relatively progressive stands on social issues. That's not to say churches don't exist; it's just that the rigid doctrinaire houses of worship don't fare so well. Some think it's because we are surrounded by landscapes so beautiful they have us falling to our knees, worshipping nature. Or that we celebrate community and life itself, unattached to a place or institution.

To get an inside read on Portland's unchurched ways, I turned to Marilyn Sewell, who was senior minister of Portland's First Unitarian Church for 17 years before retiring in 2009. "I think that might be because many people come here to start over, disillusioned by the institutions they grew up with. The West has always been a place of renewal and new starts. Also, Portland is very progressive politically, and progressives often equate church, any church, with conservative social values. That

is not true of First Unitarian, and I believe that is why the church grew and flourished."

Marilyn continues her work as an author and speaker. Her memoir, *Raw Faith: Following the Thread,* is the back story to the documentary film made about her, also called *Raw Faith.* The memoir describes the personal journey that led to her ministry at First Unitarian.

"I had never been to Portland before I arrived for my initial interview at the church," Marilyn remembers. "What I noticed was the grand and noble landscape, and the green, which infused everything. It was spring when I arrived, and blooming flowers greeted me everywhere, and lofty trees shading streets. The church itself was classic, and beautiful.

"Several things were going against me, as a prospective senior minister," she continues. "I had just finished seminary and had never served a church, and therefore was not expected to be called to a large church like this one. Secondly, I was a woman. The church was founded in 1866, and I was the first female minister. I told the search committee after my first meeting with them that 'this is where I am called to be.' I had an inner conviction that I was meant to be here. I told them, 'You are great church and you have forgotten that. I can help you remember that you are great church.'

"There was a nationwide search, and so I had to wait for their answer," she continues. "But I knew, somehow, that they would choose me, and so when they called two months later with their answer, I was not surprised."

Marilyn feels at home in Portland, and finds peace in the view from her home beside the Willamette River. "The city streets are full of a great variety of people, food carts are flourishing everywhere, young people line up every day at Voodoo Donuts, and Powell's books is filled with locals and tourists. Demonstrations draw young and old. People fight for tickets to the Portland International Film Festival. We have light rail and we have the trolley. So I would say Portland is a very alive and interesting city!"

She also sees its flaws. "I have been disappointed, however, with the lack of bold leadership in civic matters. Our recent mayors have been weak, and Charlie Hales has yet to prove himself. Police brutality is an ongoing and very distressing problem. I am appalled at the amount of poverty seen in our city, and the number of homeless people who die on the streets every year."

If Portland is not religious, is it spiritual? "Many people who would not call themselves religious feel comfortable calling themselves spiritual. I think this is because the institutions of religion, being led by flawed human beings, have so often let people down. They believe that these institutions should be on a higher moral order, and indeed they should. But the leaders and members of churches are simply human beings, and subject to error, like other human beings. Everyone has spiritual needs, I believe, and so most people will continue to look somewhere for the answers to the big questions: What is the meaning of my life? How do I find love? What can I do to find fulfillment? How do I handle the fact that I will die? They may read books, they may go to retreat centers, they may find a guru to follow. These are religious questions they are attempting to answer."

Lewis & Clark College sociologist Monica Miller, in an interview in the *Portland Mercury*, said a lot of Portland's young people don't even consider themselves spiritual. "For them, meaning happens where social, culture, and political issues lie. They're very focused on the importance of community. Art. Music. People saying, 'I believe in feeding the hungry, I believe in sharing.' That takes the place of what we would consider religion. It's more like a post-modern individualized spirituality."

She thinks the openness about cultural issues in Portland lends itself to critical thinking, so "you can walk around with horns on your head or pink hair, people aren't going to look at you twice. On the East Coast, we have higher levels of diversity, but also higher levels of conformity."

Wait, what? Did she just say pink hair?

> **Opposite page:** This outdoor labyrinth, often used in meditation, is in a southeast Portland church parking lot. I wonder if the cars benefit when parked there. **This page:** Marilyn Sewell finds evening peace on her deck looking over the Willamette River and Ross Island.
> ■ Quilt information on page 165-6.

Pieces
of
Portland

JOAN OF ARC
MAID OF ORLEANS

1412 — 1431

It felt like something sinister was happening in or to the women's movement in Portland. I mean, assuming there still was a women's movement in Portland.

First, Old Wives Tales suddenly closed. Then the building it lived in for all those years was demolished and another multistory apartment building appears to be replacing it. It used to be the center of feminism here. Then Feminist's Agenda posted this on its website:

"As of June 2014 Feminist Agenda PDX is on indefinite hiatus. Due to personal reasons we are no longer able to maintain the organization." In explaining the launch of the website in 2012, founders pointed out that, "We have this critical mass of people who understand how feminism intersects with different forms of oppression, but one of the big things we see is lack of engagement. To each their own, but we hope this will give people a way to get engaged."

And then in August 2014, In Other Words, the feminist bookstore and community center that *Portlandia* uses as a location for its Women and Women First bookstore scenes, announced it was in dire financial straits and was in danger of closing, for lack of volunteers and income. It called a general assembly to figure out its future and held a crowdfunding campaign to meet immediate financial needs. Afterward, the board decided to commit to one more year of operations.

And only three feminist Meetups? One discussion topic was "Where is the anger? When do I suppress my anger through rationalizing, laughing it off, etc.? How can I use anger as a tool to empower myself and others? Bring your own brunch, eat, drink and bash patriarchy."

I found this surprising and confusing. I had come of age when the modern women's movement was just getting traction. I assumed we would always have one—I mean, as long as women are still paid significantly less than men for the same work. We still don't have an Equal Rights Amendment (?!) and we are still not fully represented in many fields, especially technology, where women receive truly vicious verbal abuse and death threats when they are outspoken online.

Have we reached a post-feminist state where misogyny is a thing of the past in Portland? We wish.

Opposite page: The Joan of Ark statue in the traffic circle at northeast Glisan and Cesar Chavez Boulevard honors her historic importance. It has also become an important meetup place in Portland. I have seen more naked bike riders there than anywhere else outside the World Naked Bike Ride parade. **This page:** The mural below was created by Robin Corbo to honor history-making Portland women. In fact, two of them are featured in this book.

▪ Quilt information on page 165.

Here's what Marilyn Sewell, the first woman to head Portland's First Unitarian Church had to say:

"People always underestimate women, full stop. There are very few women who lead large churches, and so sometimes people, asking me what I do, would simply not believe me when I told them I was a senior minister. They might say, 'You mean you teach the children in Sunday school?' As the leader of an institution, I was assertive, and women are supposed to be compliant and keep everybody happy. That is not possible, if you want to be an effective leader. So I was criticized sometimes for being strong and controlling, judged harshly in a way that a man would not be. However, I felt my leadership was almost always accepted and appreciated in my church."

There's no doubt things are better than they were in the late 1960s and early 1970s when I attended consciousness-raising groups and protests. In 2015, Oregon's governor, secretary of state, attorney general, speaker of the House, president pro tempore of the Senate, and majority leaders of both houses are women. Nearly one-third of Oregon legislators are women, compared with 24% nationally. (But we are 50.5% of the population, so yeah.)

Oregon has a foundation dedicated to women's issues now, with plans to engage in grantmaking, research and advocacy.

I think a big breakthrough came from Title IX, the federal law that prohibits spending more on males than females in schools that accept federal funds. Its most visible presence is seen in equal access to athletics, but its reach has been much wider.

When I was in high school, I competed on the girls' basketball team. This was back in the day when girls were limited to three dribbles before we had to pass the ball and we couldn't cross the center court line, for our own good. If you are under age 40, I'm sure you aren't even believing me right now. The only time we got to practice was when the high school boys' basketball teams were at an away game. Oh, the high school had a boys' gym and a girls' gym, alright, but the boys' varsity practised in the boys' gym and boys' junior varsity team practiced in the girls' gym. As a girl, I got the direct and distinct message that our sports didn't matter. And that meant we didn't really matter much either.

When I was in graduate school, in a field that had considerably more males than females, an important bonding experience took place at weekly basketball games that the male students and faculty (which was all male) played. We women students would hear the collegial banter following the games for the rest of the week.

Well, I loved to play basketball and had a decent outside shot, so I showed up and joined in the fun. The next week there were more women. But not all the men on the floor wanted us there, so I got to experience shunning. There were two men who suddenly

couldn't hear me, see me, or experience me in any dimension back in the department office. I got the message and stayed away. There was no one to go to who would have my back.

When Joyce was in court as a lawyer, a judge told her to "Sit down, you are represented by counsel," and another judge called her "bunny" from the bench. It seems important to remind us that these things really happened in our adulthood.

Before Title IX, one in 27 girls played varsity high school sports. By 2001, one in every 2.5 girls did. This is important because according to the Women's Sports Foundation, "Women who are active in sports have more self-confidence and are more outgoing than women who do not participate."

Harvard Business Review reported a 2014 survey finding that 52% of female business executives had played college sports. It discussed the importance of having experience with teamwork and competition. Competing at a high level is something women didn't have many opportunities to do back in my day. I cannot find words powerful enough to explain how happy I feel when I see my three granddaughters participate in sports to an extent that was not possible for me. Calla does gymnastics and swimming, Caitlyn plays soccer and basketball, and Ellery is a gymnast and a runner. Watching their strength, self confidence and skills grow eases the lingering pain of the unfairness I encountered when I was their age.

There are other organizations and activities in Portland that build strong, confident girls and women. Like Girls Inc., Rock'n'Roll Camp for Girls, Building Girls at Oregon Tradeswomen and Girls on the Run, to name a few.

Before Title IX, it was legal to exclude women from admission to colleges. Women were not admitted to Harvard College until 1972. That was a year after Joyce and I graduated from college! Seems like yesterday.

In my research, I came across a thing that's been termed "cupcake feminism." According to writer Meryl Trussler, it's "the cute-ified new face of feminism. The opposite of the angry, hairy feminist stereotype of the 1970s, the cupcake feminist wears an adorable vintage cardigan while reclaiming baking, knitting, apron-wearing and the like in the name of women's empowerment....It's all about cute dresses, felten rosettes from Etsy, knitting, kittens, vintage lamps...and yes—a lot of cupcakes. Rouged, lipsticked, cinched at the waist, she performs big-F Femininity as the drag-show that it is. Her 50s-housewife shtick sets off everything about her that is radicalized and new. And, importantly, she emphasizes that typically 'feminine' pursuits are no less worthy or important than their 'masculine' counterparts."

Is this why there are so many women in Portland big into knitting and wearing/making vintage dresses and aprons like my mom and aunts used to wear? Whoa. I doubt any woman in a consciousness-raising group in the early 1970s would have foreseen this development, and I admit to being very puzzled.

§

So what's going on here? To sort out my confusion, I turned to Sarah Mirk at Portland's Bitch Media to get some insight on 21st century feminism. Sarah previously was a reporter for the *Portland Mercury*. She and Know Your City have already published a series of comic books of marginalized events and people ignored in the usual telling of Oregon history. Sarah has also published *Sex from Scratch*, a guide to relationships and dating that is revolutionary because it is based on honesty! She's accomplished so much so fast and is involved in so many Portland things that she's been called "the hardest working person in Portland." And that's saying something in this town.

Bitch Media is a nonprofit feminist media organization best known for publishing the magazine *Bitch: Feminist Response to Pop Culture*. Bitch Media's mission is "to provide and encourage an engaged, thoughtful feminist response to mainstream media and popular culture." Sarah does reporting, writes and edits blog posts, curates a feminist news roundup, manages its social media, creates Popoganda podcasts and I'm pretty sure I'm forgetting at least 17 other things.

"I think conversations about feminist issues are as vibrant as ever now, if not more so," Sarah says. "But they're not taking place in physical spaces. Intense discussions are happening online now, communities of very diverse women are growing there. Women who would never have connected before—from rural South Dakota to rural Texas to cities all over—are having conversations on Twitter, Tumblr, other social media."

Another difference Sarah sees is a desire to see sexism not as a siloed issue, but as a form of oppression that connects to others in a larger discussion of equity and social justice. "There's a strong interest in looking at how issues of sex, race and gender can be better understood in a common context."

Sarah sees the funding problems in organizations like In Other Words all across the country. A recent issue of *Bitch* magazine explored the causes.

"It's a little hard to parse," she explains, "but we found some common themes. One, bookstores everywhere have financial difficulties because the book-selling business has completely changed. It's not a feminist issue, it's a bookstore issue."

Bitch also found that volunteer-run community centers all over are facing problems because younger people often seek and find communities online. Funding is a constant challenge because passion-fueled causes frequently don't have a well-planned income strategy to carry an organization forward once the founders and early joiners burn out.

A few years ago, Bitch Media faced serious financial issues of its own when it relied solely on magazine subscriptions and newsstand sales. That revenue was steadily decreasing while costs of producing it (paper, printing, mailing) went up. Bitch reorganized as a nonprofit organization that is member-supported, much like National Public Radio. It also raises funds through a "Bitch on Campus" program that makes it easy for schools and colleges to bring *Bitch* editors and writers to their campuses for lectures, workshops and events. It began accepting online donations and beefed up its online presence, hiring Sarah as its first full-time online editor in January 2013. The print magazine is published quarterly and has 10,000 subscribers in 46 countries. Five stories from each issue are offered free online. *Bitch* online also posts two or three articles each day and regularly connects with its 100,000 Facebook fans, 67,00 Twitter followers, 23,000 registered users and 25,000 email subscribers.

Recent topics getting a lot of attention and conversation online are street harassment of women and sexual assault on college campuses. Sarah watched a Reed College student's 2011 guerrilla art project go viral. It featured a toilet placed in the middle of the campus cafeteria with names of male students women had reported as rapists. Sexual assault on campus was picked up by national media and has traveled all the way to the top, as President Obama announced in 2014 the "It's On Us" campaign to put an end to sexual assault on campus.

Bitch Media is our local source with a global perspective for keeping up with issues like these.

§

One of the issues I hear more about these days is gender identity. It seems that the more we explore and examine ourselves and our world, things that seemed simple and binary are getting more complicated. And as people feel more free to express themselves, and have tools to do it, our usual categories are failing us.

When Facebook began, for example, there were two genders to choose from: Male and Female. People started pointing out grey areas. *The Daily Beast* put it this way: "Gender is more about your personal sense of who you are (e.g., man, woman, transgender, etc). Gender primarily refers to qualities that are masculine or feminine or neither or both. Just as sex is often talked about as male/female, gender is often thought about as being a man or woman. However,

this binary gender system is inadequate for understanding the gender of all humans, especially across cultures. Many societies are now expanding their use of gender terms."

Since humans begin their uterine existence with both female and male bits, there's more variation in human babies at birth than male and female. Some have both parts, and parents choose which to keep. Some children are born with no sex organs, and gender decisions are made by looking at chromosomes. After spending a few years volunteering in preschools with both infants and toddlers, I couldn't help but notice how blurred gender lines are at that age. This isn't a new thing, but the attention to and allowance for it is.

Now Facebook has three options in the pull down menu: Male, Female and Custom. If you choose Custom, there's a blank field to fill in, and you are asked what pronouns you prefer. He, she or them. Them (or it, ze, ou, hir, they) is available for people who identify as agender or non-binary. They don't feel like a he or she. Argentina allows residents to choose their own gender, without any legal or medical procedures. Think Pat on *Saturday Night Live*. Why did others try so hard to figure out its gender? What difference would it make to know?

Some "radical feminists" resist the notion that a male-to-female transition should be considered a "womyn" because growing up male, he did not experience misogyny. And that gender identity is caused by culture, not nature. Many disagree and accuse them of discriminating against transsexuals. When In Other Words announced it would remain open with new board members, it also mentioned it is "building stronger relationships with...transgender people and people of color."

And the beat goes on. If we haven't yet, I expect we will be challenged to expand our understanding and vocabulary to include words like agender, bigender, cisgender, gender fluid, gender queer, intersex, neutrois, pangender and so forth. Is gender mostly a cultural construct, like race is, after all? So much to ponder, so much to consider, so much to discuss.

Although not at the top of the list among cities, Portland has had a reputation for being LGBT-friendly for decades, with the second largest percent of LGBT residents in the U.S. in 2015, at 5.5% of the population. San Francisco is highest among major cities at 6.2%.

Maybe someday we will figure out we're all just people.

Pieces
of
Portland

Water World

In Portland, we live in a water world. It defines our sense of place. Portland is awash with water, mostly in the form of rivers. So Portland has floating homes. An estimated 1,100, as it turns out. Only 87 are on the Willamette, most are along channels connected with the Columbia River.

I think living on the river is the most quintessentially Portland kind of address one can have. Often I wish I lived there.

Apparently a lot of people share my interest, because there is always more demand than supply, which drives prices up up up, and is why people like me can't afford it. There are moorage fees too, and a lot of expensive upkeep, what with being so exposed to the weather and water and all.

The most expensive location is the Oregon Yacht Club, near Oaks Bottom Wildlife Refuge. We tried to get a look and take a photo with a quilt, but it is a highly-gated community and our access was denied.

We visited a floating home (no, they are technically not houseboats because they are on flotation logs, rather than being actual boats big enough to be a house) on Multnomah Channel and found it to be a way of living closer to nature than most of us can imagine. Witness the birds in their own home mere inches from the sliding glass doors that were only a few more inches of decking from the water. My friend Carolyn Lee spends a lot of time in the water, swimming or kayaking. She finds peace there. Who wouldn't?

As it turns out, these homes have special challenges.

One is the way sewage is handled. Carolyn explains that there is a "honeypot" attached to each floating house, with a pump that flushes the contents out when it gets full, into a pipe that runs along the boardwalk and then to a treatment facility.

It's not just human poop that presents a challenge, I'm told. Many kinds of birds share a love of the river and make their own homes there or are frequent visitors. Evidence of their presence is easy to find.

It's more difficult to keep water pipes from freezing in a cold snap, so cold weather can be a pretty stressful time. Walkways and ramps can be treacherous in winter.

Homeowners also have to make sure the float is at least six inches above the water, "not too much, not too little, as we watch for log decay." There's more moss along the water, as well.

"It's very very quiet living with birdies and nature," Carolyn says. "There is constant entertainment with nature flowing by."

Yes, nature flowing by is our highest form of entertainment. There is no need for any other kind when this is your view of the world.

Opposite page: Carolyn Lee has a front row view of Portland's water world, living in a floating home community. At any moment, she can hop into her kayak and take to the water, or simply jump in. **This page:** The top photo shows birds living in a house just outside her sliding glass doors. In the bottom photo, we see that the view out the back along the walkway where the infrastructure is housed can't compete with nature flowing by in front.

■ Quilt information on page 166.

Where Size Matters

Kol Peterson and Deb Delman hooked up because they both think size matters. And when it comes to houses and hotels in Portland, at least, tiny is better.

They built a tiny house—technically called an Accessory Dwelling Unit (ADU)—in their backyard in northeast Portland. That's where they live now, renting out the regular house on the lot.

They also own and operate Caravan, the Tiny House Hotel on Alberta Street in northeast Portland. The week we visited, they were doing interviews with us, *Wall Street Journal*, *Nightline*, HGTV and a *Portlandia* segment was about to be filmed there.

I think it would be fair to say that in 2014 at least, tiny houses are one of the biggest things in Portland.

According to the City of Portland's Bureau of Planning and Sustainability, nearly one-quarter of single dwelling development permit applications in the city these days are for Accessory Dwelling Units. Currently, there are about 800 of them in Portland.

Kol came to tiny houses through his study of urban planning (he has a master's degree). "I'm interested in efficient use of urban space," he said, "and tiny houses are a good way to achieve density." He just may be the country's leading expert on ADU requirements and how to achieve them.

Deb loves creating beautiful spaces and the challenge of achieving great interior design solutions in limited square feet. She has figured out how to make the spaces functional and beautiful, reusing materials like copper pipe to create shelving and compartments. She's decorated all the Caravan's tiny houses, and we were very pleased to discover that they all have quilts on the beds, so we used one of those instead of our own.

"We've traveled all over the world. We love to travel, love meeting people," Deb says. "We love Portland and we wanted to offer visitors a unique, authentic Portland experience. Tiny houses give us the coolest and funkiest design opportunities."

"We love to show people what's possible and give tiny house builders a place to showcase their talents," she says.

In tiny houses, extra care must be taken to prevent pipes from freezing during Portland's infrequent cold snaps. Most tiny houses have composting toilets to handle waste.

But Caravan is completely sewered, and that makes it unique. "This is the only completely permitted collection of tiny houses in the country, and it took us a year-a-half to work out all the zoning and permitting issues," Kol explains. "All our units have flush toilets, and waste goes into the city's sewer system."

"We wanted to appeal to mainstream people, not just the Portland types who are comfortable living an alternative lifestyle." It must be working. Caravan was at nearly 100% occupancy all summer in 2014, when it had been open less than a year. "Guests come from all over," Deb says. "We've counted 13-14 countries and most of the 50 states. The demographics are across the board, with a broad range of ages and lifestyles. We've had families with children and older people. People come here for honeymoons, weddings, business retreats, family reunions, and we've even hosted a surprise birthday party."

Their hotel has been so successful, Deb quit her day job as a high school teacher to manage it. Kol still works for the U.S. Forest Service.

Caravan's houses are arranged in a circle, with a community space in the central courtyard. They recently had a beautiful rain canopy/sun shade installed so that guests can stay dry and make s'mores in the fire pit all year long.

Because of their experience and knowledge, Kol and Deb have become tiny house advocates and educators, helping the growing numbers of people interested in ADUs. In 2014, for example, they offered a tour of 12 houses on a Saturday in June. When the number of people who registered reached 850, they had to cut it off. In 2015, the event will run for two days.

They think the tiny house movement is exploding partly because young people would rather have experiences than stuff. "Thirty-year-olds don't want 30 year mortgages," Deb explains. "They want a sense of freedom. And maybe they remind them of tree houses and forts they built as children. Tiny houses have existed for a long time, as gypsy caravans, wagon trains, and so forth. This is the modern iteration."

Deb has a background in teaching and social justice work, so she looks for ways tiny houses could help solve social problems.

"There are all kinds of potential applications," she says. More than 4,000 people in Portland sleep on the streets or in shelters every night. Why not use tiny houses to help solve homelessness?"

I think that idea may be catching on in Portland, actually.

"And they are so fun, creative and cute," she adds. "You have to be a serious grouch to not think they're cute."

This page: Kol Peterson and Deb Delman, owners and operators of Caravan, the Tiny House Hotel, know more about tiny houses than just about anybody. They also live in an ADU they built outside their traditional home, which they rent out.
Opposite page: Deb has developed special skills for making the best use of the space inside a tiny house. The interior of the Caboose unit illustrates some of her approaches, including the use of repurposed materials.
■ Quilt information on page 166.

Portland is often included in lists of cities with a proportionally large population of people who don't have permanent addresses and sleep on the streets, in parks or other outdoor areas, under bridges, in cars, in emergency shelters and—in well-watered Portland—even on old boats or rafts on the river.

There were a large number of homeless people during the Great Depression, of course, and Portland had its own Hoovervilles, the name given to "shantytowns" made by the great numbers of Americans migrating from the Dust Bowl.

The destruction of the southeast end of downtown Portland during the 1950s and 1960s displaced 2,300 people, many with limited incomes. Many were older single men. I wonder how many of the homeless men I saw on West Burnside when I came to Portland in 1974 were among those displaced by Portland urban renewal?

According to City authorities, replacing the low-value structures multiplied the assessed value of the property by 25, and added 15,000 jobs. The area now includes Keller Auditorium and Fountain, parking garages, large- and mid-size office buildings, high-value and luxury apartments, and so forth.

Another boost in homelessness emerged after 1965 because Medicaid (created to make federal funds available to states to help them meet the medical needs of poor and disabled citizens) excluded reimbursement for patients in "institutions for the treatment of mental diseases," such as state psychiatric hospitals. To qualify for reimbursement, states moved many people with mental illness into single-room-occupancy housing, nursing homes or other settings without adequate treatment and follow-up care. This trend became especially prevalent in the 1970s. Many ended up on the streets, leaving their care to hospitals, public shelters and jails.

Chronic homelessness became a societal issue during the 1980s, as the Reagan administration slashed federal support by half for public housing and a housing voucher subsidization program. Housing and Urban Development's budget was reduced from $74 billion to $19 billion. It was also a time of economic recession and high unemployment.

That's when homelessness became widespread and reached unprecedented numbers. In 1970, there were 6.5 million low-cost rentals in the U.S. By 1985 that number had dropped to 5.6 million units, while low renter households rose from 6.2 mil to 8.9 million. A national news weekly magazine put a homeless family on the cover in 1985, because families had joined the ranks of the homeless in large numbers by then.

Portland was actually one of the first cities to address homelessness, when in 1986 Mayor Bud Clark's 12-point plan on homelessness increased the city's efforts to find solutions and end it. "He was the first mayor to put homelessness at the front of his agenda," City Commissioner Nick Fish said later. "That 12-point plan laid the foundation for all the work we've done since."

His plan got all the organizations and agencies with programs for homeless people to work together. Portland was also early to shift resources from managing the symptoms (through homeless shelters, soup kitchens, etc.) to programs that aimed at addressing the cause. For example, Burnside Project (established by Portland church leaders to "provide lodging, food and other assistance for poor and homeless men") changed its name to Transition Projects in 1991 to signify its changed mission of moving people into housing. Central City Concern also expanded during the 1990s to address the root causes of homelessness: addictions, mental illness and unemployment. JOIN emerged as another nonprofit organization to transition folks to permanent housing, and Human Solutions helps low-income and homeless people move out of poverty.

Many of these programs are working. Over the past eight years, some 17,000 people without homes in Portland were moved into stable housing using an array of tools like rapid re-housing, flexible rent assistance, permanent supportive housing, and so forth. And now Portland is exploring using tiny houses to help solve the problem.

But despite these successes, programs, organizations and initiatives that came out of multitudes of meetings, planning groups and task forces, there are more homeless people in Portland than ever.

The latest point-in-time count in January 2013 found 3,000 living on the streets or in emergency shelters in Portland, with another 1,500 in transitional housing. Everybody thinks the number is actually much higher, because many people who are homeless are hard to count. People in the know estimate there were nearly 16,000 under the broadest homeless definition (people who would be homeless without rent assistance, people living in motels, people couch surfing, in doubled up housing, and so forth.)

Why so many? Half of them had been homeless for less than

This page: Some of the shacks where homeless people lived in Portland in the Great Depression. Looking south, that's the Ross Island Bridge in the background. **Opposite page:** Right2DreamToo's village in downtown Portland and a close-up view of the quilt.

■ Quilt information on page 166.

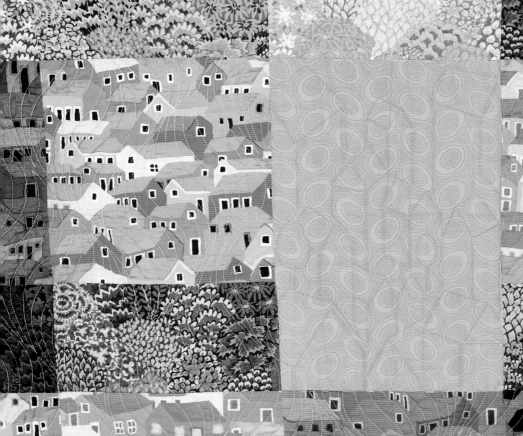

a year, showing that as people leave the ranks, they are more than replaced by newly homeless, demonstrating that the recession has not ended for a significant portion of the city's people who have lost jobs and exhausted all resources and benefits.

The numbers are bleak: the minimum wage would need to be $24.27 per hour of full-time work to support a family with one adult and two children in Portland's rental housing market, which has a low vacancy rate of 3.4%. To put it another way, the fair market value of a two-bedroom apartment in the Portland metropolitan area is $912 per month, which would take 64% of a full-time minimum wage worker's income. (To be considered affordable, housing should take only 30%.)

Sixty-five percent of those living on the streets have a disability that significantly interferes with their ability to work. People of color are also overrepresented among the homeless. About 30% of Multnomah County's population are people of color, but they are about 50% of its homeless population.

The number of homeless living on the streets is 38% higher than in 2011, is 16% higher for those in emergency shelters, and is more likely to be families with children. Even the number of chronically homeless increased by 27% over the past two years. One-third of chronically homeless are veterans. The number of homeless families with children increased by 18%.

Since the beginning of the 21st century, a "housing first" model has come into favor, with independent housing provided immediately without requiring treatment or stability before transitioning to housing. It's housing that creates conditions for stability. For example, among mentally ill people who live on the street, 63% don't take medication as prescribed. When living indoors, 82% take meds as prescribed.

In recent years, the City of Portland has authorized two permanent camps. These consist of tents, tarps and small abodes made from all kinds of materials, where people create communities through self-determination and holding themselves accountable.

"We don't use the word homeless," Ibrahim Mubarak says as we start our conversation at Right2DreamToo, a camp on Burnside Street. "The home is where the heart is, and we have hearts. So we use the word houseless."

Ibrahim started living on the streets after he was divorced 35 years ago. He traveled around the country and world. Along the way, he studied cultures and learned that his heritage is Choctaw Indian, Somali, German and Irish. While in Somalia, he converted to Islam. "It helped my depression," he explains. "It helped me learn to control myself." His self-control is manifest in the two communities he helped found in Portland: Dignity Village, a 60-person community near the Portland airport and R2DToo. There are strict rules excluding drugs, alcohol, violence, sexism, racism, etc. Each member must contribute his or her time to the community. Ibrahim lived there for 4-1/2 years.

Much of his advocacy and activism are directed at ways society is "criminalizing houselessness."

"There's a fine for sleeping on the streets," he points out. "When there's no public restroom, at some point you have to relieve yourself. If you get caught doing it three times in public, you are arrested for indecent exposure, and you're classified a sex offender. If you are houseless and are pregnant or have kids, Children Protective Services can take your kids away."

"If you don't get proper sleep, you can't function fully. People use drugs to self-medicate, and you can't get addiction treatment unless you commit a crime."

Ibrahim's words get right to the heart of the issue. What shape would I be in if I never got a good night's sleep? What if I had nowhere to take a nap when I wasn't feeling well or was just plain worn out? My brain would quickly turn to mush, and I wouldn't make good decisions or figure out how to turn things around. How would I avoid a continued downward spiral? Likely, I couldn't.

While the City of Portland supplies the land, Dignity Village has to pay its own water, electricity, garbage pickup and portable toilet cleaning and maintenance that comes to about $2,000 per month. It's a nonprofit organization, so is eligible for tax-exempt donations, and residents run micro-businesses. Portland police and fire departments have been impressed with the lack of problems in the village, and fire fighters have donated space heaters in winter.

Ibrahim points out that through help from Right to Survive, 190 have found permanent housing, 130 found work, 10 are off drugs and 10 completed online education through its computer lab.

Some suspect that Dignity Village is tolerated because it is so far away from any commercial or residential area, which also means it is far from services. But R2D2 is right smack downtown, hidden behind a wall of doors residents painted to beautify the space. At some point the lot will developed. R2D2 has been looking for a permanent location for two years. It met with neighborhood resistance from the Pearl District and property developers when the city agreed to let them relocate in a sheltered area beneath the Broadway Bridge. Now it may move to the east side near OMSI.

Both Ibrahim and Israel Bayer pointed out another fly in Oregon's particular ointment that has been in the way of creating affordable housing, more than most anywhere in the country. Oregon is one of only two states—the other is Texas—that prohibits any agency from requiring that affordable housing be

included when housing is developed. In 48 states it is permitted, but not in Oregon. While Portland may probably be willing to require it, it's against the law to do so due to heavy lobbying by the Homebuilders' Association. So the lack of affordable housing across the community keeps getting worse.

In the 2015 session, the Oregon Legislature took up the issue, and when we went to press, a bill to permit inclusionary zoning had passed the House and moved to the Senate. Affordable housing advocates are optimistic about its chances, but there is well organized opposition. I was hoping we would know before we went to press, but it was not to be.

I've also heard folks discussing rent controls, fee waivers and other ways of making housing more affordable.

Now we are under a new federal Ten Year Plan to End Homelessness, which began in 2010 with the goals to:

- end chronic homelessness by 2015
- prevent and end homelessness among veterans by 2015
- prevent and end homelessness for families with children by 2020
- set a path to end all types of homelessness

In his role as executive director of the weekly newspaper, *Street Roots*, Israel Bayer meets a lot of people without houses. He's worried about something he fears is coming as Portland changes. "It's like we're seeing a different expectation of urban life. All these outside forces are piling up. Cities are becoming places where the very affluent and the very poor live."

"The middle class is disappearing," he says. "Over time, the affluent become less tolerant of poverty issues. Over time they are less focused on ending poverty and more focused on keeping it out of sight."

Israel thinks it's important to be realistic about solutions. "We already have an overeducated workforce doing food service," he points out. "I don't think we're going to see a mass entry of our people into the work force." That's why he is more excited about improving economic standing through entrepreneurial efforts like Street Roots' vendors and micro loans where people without housing use their skills to create income. He also says federal and local governments have to do their share to care for people whose challenges are more than they can handle alone.

And make no mistake about it. People who are houseless need our help. They don't, as Ronald Reagan told the *New York Times* when cutting housing funding, "make it their own choice for staying out there." And now we know what works.

As the 20th century began, America's public conscience was stirred when it was revealed that people with mental illness were being housed in local jails and prisons. The public considered it to be inhumane, so states built mental hospitals. Ironically, closing mental hospitals without providing services in the communities where patients were sent has meant we are seeing history being repeated. Jails and prisons now have more people with mental illness than any other kind of housing.

Oh, the humanity.

How does Israel keep hope alive in the face of the hardships he witnesses and the daunting size and complexity of the issues?

"I'm a constant optimist," he says. "The collective resilience of street people is pretty phenomenal."

There was nothing more to be said.

Pieces of Portland

One That Didn't Get Away

Many of us live in the 100-year-old-plus houses in inner city neighborhoods that were built during Portland's rapid growth in the early 20th century. We love their charm and craftsmanship. But they are disappearing as developers buy them singly or in multiples, tear them down and replace them with McMansions, large-scale apartment buildings or condos. In April 2015, the *Oregonian* reported that 2,100 homes in Portland had been demolished since September 2003. It breaks our hearts, but once in a while things take a better turn. Neighborhood groups have sometimes stepped in to purchase properties and developers are now required to give earlier and better notice of their plans to demolish old homes.

Here's an example that happened on my street. A developer bought about half a block of land facing Hawthorne Boulevard with two grand old homes that had been divided up and rented as office space to small businesses for decades. When the neighborhood heard he planned to raze the houses in order to make way for a 77-unit, four-story apartment building, it jumped into action to do whatever it could to save them.

Beth Bonness and Jeffrey McCaffrey didn't set out to be neighborhood heroes when they got the call asking if an empty lot they owned could be used to store the largest and grandest of the two houses until a new home could be found for it. They had planned to build rowhouses on the lot but their project finances had stalled.

Beth and Jeff had purchased their nearby family home in 1983, and had completed a duplex infill project on an adjacent lot and an accessory dwelling unit above their garage. These construction projects were done while they both held down their day jobs— Beth was Vice President of Program Operations at a high tech firm and Jeff is Vice President of Design and Engineering at a furniture manufacturer—and raised three daughters.

To make a long story short (the long version will be told in the book Beth is writing about the whole saga, which I can't wait to read), the house was hauled across a block-long lot, then across a street and through a parking lot on the next block to its final resting place on Beth and Jeff's lot. Not to mention that the drive-up kiosk at the credit union next door had to be removed and rebuilt. There were a few snags along the way, and it took longer than was first anticipated. Trust me, it's not something you want to rush.

It was the most exciting event our neighborhood had witnessed in the 35 plus years I've lived here. The morning the big move began, neighbors were tailgating and the smell of bacon was everywhere. There was a collective sigh of relief when it finally settled into its new space.

Now the house has been completely remodeled into seven apartments, and it looks like it's always been there. This outcome is providing a hopeful alternative to other inner city neighborhoods that lose character every time an old home dies.

The other house was reportedly deconstructed by the Rebuilding Center, so it was by no means a total loss. Let's hope some of the wonderful wood features from it are already showing up in other Portland homes. Because they don't build homes with wood like that nowadays. Back then a 2x4 was actually 2x4.

Opposite page: In the top photo, Jeff McCaffrey and Beth Bonness relax on the expansive front porch of the Montgomery House after their moving/restoration project was completed. The large house took a rather treacherous journey across a block, street, parking lot and into its new space on the street to the north. This page: The top photo illustrates just how challenging the moving project was as it made its way into the space where the ground had been removed for the basement and foundation. Then voila, a grand old home was remodeled into seven tasteful apartments that retain wonderful features of the original home.
 ■ Quilt information on page 166.

Pieces
of
Portland

Tramside Living

The Emory Apartment building on Portland's South Waterfront had a marketing campaign I'd never seen. Or expected to see. It invited us to say hello to tramside living—the tram being the gondola that connects South Waterfront to Oregon Health and Science University and its hospital up the hill. It's even identified as OHSU affiliated housing. At first I thought it was an appeal to those who already are or expect to be very ill, requiring near immediate access to the emergency room. Which seemed a little, oh, I don't know, maybe insensitive. Even cold-hearted. A constant reminder of their incurable and hopeless status?

But then I noticed that amenities included things like secure bike parking and a pet washing station, so I realized it's reaching out to those who work or study at OHSU. Offering them a sky-riding take on live/work space.

I can totally get behind that.

This page, photo at right: The office where you can sign up for tramside living.
■ Quilt information on page 166.

163

Pieces
of
Portland

Page 118
Playtime
Pieced and quilted by Marie Deatherage

I was just horsing around with some Aneela Hoey's Little Apple fabrics. I didn't have a pattern in mind and only a few fat quarters, so I just used what I had and invented blocks. Now it's a baby quilt or playmat.

Page 120
Keep Flowers at the Center
Pieced and quilted by Marie Deatherage

Sometimes I find simple is best. I love these big bold orange poppies and found some fabrics that seemed like they were meant to be together.

Page 122
'Out and About'
Pieced by Joyce Brekke; quilted by Nancy Stovall, Just Quilting PDX

The pattern is "B2" by Maple Island Quilts and the fabrics are mostly from the 'Folklorica' collection by Julie Paschkis

Page 125
'Under the Stars'
Pieced by Joyce Brekke; quilted by Nancy Stovall, Just Quilting PDX

Didn't use a pattern, fabrics are from Oceanica by Julie Paschkis.

Page 127
'RickRack'
Pieced by Joyce Brekke; quilted by Steve Ross

Pattern is "Parquet" by Kaffe Fassett in his *Quilts in Sweden*.

Page 134
More than a Mystery
Pieced and quilted by Marie Deatherage

This was a mystery quilt that took place in a Facebook group online. First I chose the print, then added complementary batiks. The origin of the pattern is still a mystery to me.

Page 136
Cinderella Story
Designed and pieced by Marie Deatherage; quilted by Nancy Stovall, Just Quilting PDX

This quilt tells the story of never giving up hope, even when the odds are overwhelming. It was inspired by Blaine, on many levels. The design came to me in a dream after Blaine and I had been talking about March Madness brackets. The entire story is told in the quilt, with the lowest ranked team in the weakest bracket winning the championship. The audience in the stands and on television is represented around the brackets. It took second place in the large quilt category at the Northwest Quilting Expo in 2013.

Page 139
Take Me to Your Autzen
Pieced by Marie Deatherage; quilted by Nancy Stovall, Just Quilting PDX

I intend for this quilt to accompany some lucky fan to Duck Football at Autzen. I used wool batting so it would be extra warm for cool night games. The pattern is Scout by CluckCluckSew.

Page 140
Quilters Just Wanna Have Fun
Pieced by Marie Deatherage; quilted by Nancy Stovall, Just Quilting PDX

I started this quilt in a class with Gyleen Fitzgerald, using a pattern from her *Trash to Treasure Pineapple Quilts*. Gyleen is cut from fun-loving cloth. Her exuberance made it into the quilt. And the photo.

Page 143
All Colors Found in Nature
Pieced and hand tied by Marie Deatherage

Nature is not shy about using colors. Why should we be? I know Granny would have loved the brilliant jewel tone colors and rich textures. I decided to experiment combining velvet, silk and satin fabrics. This house had never heard such swearing. Things just kept moving on me, velvet and satin are not a great sewing match, so there are lots of the corners that don't match perfectly. That's why I added buttons and tied this quilt with thin silk ribbon.

Page 145
'Wedges'
Pieced by Joyce Brekke; quilted by Nancy Stovall, Just Quilting PDX

Pattern:"Rosie's Charm" in Fons and Porter's *Easy Quilts*, Fall, 2009

Page 148
Some Things Just Go Together
Pieced by Marie Deatherage; quilted by Nancy Stovall, Just Quilting PDX

My mother bought me this "Cinnamon & Ginger" pattern from Allison Quilt Designs and fabric for my 60th birthday. So very fitting. These Kaffe Fassett fabrics are my people, we go together, like cinnamon and ginger.

Pieces of Portland

Page 149
Made You Look
Pieced and quilted by Marie Deatherage

I found a set of strips of wonderful hand dyed Gee's Bend fabrics. There was something about the colors, I couldn't take my eyes off them. The pattern was inspired by the blocks in Gwen Marston's Mexican Hat Dance in her book, *Liberated Quilting II*. She nudges us to not try to match things up perfectly, because the imperfections create more interest. Or excuses. :)

Page 150
Liberté, Egalité, Fraternité
Pieced by Marie Deatherage; quilted by Nancy Stovall, Just Quilting PDX

This is another quilt that started with a napkin. It reminded me of the wonderful trip Joyce and I took to Paris in 1990. It was the most French of our quilts, the better to accompany Joan of Ark.

> Some of the quilts in this book are available for purchase from quiltlandia.com

Page 152
Title IX
Pieced by Marie Deatherage; quilted by Pat Roche, Pat's Just Quilting

This quilt is a tribute to Title IX, the law that means my strong and awesome grand-daughters have much better opportunities in education, including sports, than I did. Calla is demonstrating her gymnastics form, Caitlyn's strength is on display holding her. Ellery's flexibility is completely amazing. The quilt pattern is Sweet Garden by Carolina Patchwork and it's made entirely from one layer cake and white fabric.

Page 154
'Forever Blue'
Pieced by Joyce Brekke; quilted by Nancy Stovall, Just Quilting PDX

The pattern is "Yellow Potpourri" from Kaffe Fassett's *Simple Shapes, Spectacular Quilts*. Most of the fabrics are from Kaffe Fassett Collective

Page 156
Caboose quilt
Caravan, the Tiny House Hotel, has quilts on all of its beds. All are custom made by Marita Wallace, whose Etsy page is https://www.etsy.com/shop/RatherBeeQuilting.

Page 159
Home Is Where the Heart Is
Pieced by Marie Deatherage; quilted by Pat Roche, Pat's Just Quilting

This quilt features all colorways of Brandon Mably's Shanty Town and Kaffe Fassett's Oriental Trees fabrics. I was feeling grateful for having a home and a yard for a garden, and wishing everyone did. The reality that they don't is represented in the center block quilting, where the houses are only a dream.

Page 163
Granny's Flower Garden
Hand pieced and quilted by Ethel Deatherage

My mother made this quilt for my 40th birthday, the pattern is the traditional Grandmother's Flower Garden. I recognize many of the fabrics from my childhood, including from a dress she made me for my ninth birthday. What a precious treasure!

Page 163
Sepsis Derailed
Pieced by Marie Deatherage; quilted by Nancy Stovall, Just Quilting PDX

I made this quilt to regain my equilibrium after Blaine recovered from a serious infection and came home from the hospital. It uses Karla Alexander's Plaid Passion pattern from her book *Color Shuffle*. I was deep into my purple and orange phase.

EXPRESSION

It's Been an Honor

There's a lot to be discerned about Portland's changing culture through who or what the city chooses to honor in its public sculptures and statues through the years.

Presidents were common traditional subjects of civic sculpture in the 19th century. This one, in the South Park Blocks, shows President Abraham Lincoln during the Civil War years, "somberly reflecting the divided state of the Union." It was a gift donated to the City of Portland by Dr. Henry Waldo Coe, who donated several notable sculptures to beautify the city. This one is the work of George Waters and was cast at the famous foundry of Claude Valsuani in France on Lincoln's birthday in 1927.

■ Quilt information on page 214.

This statue of Paul Bunyan was designed and produced by the Kenton Business Association to pay tribute to the timber industry in Oregon in 1959 as part of the state's centennial celebration.

■ Quilt information on page 214.

Forecourt Fountain and the Portland Center behind it were the result of urban renewal in downtown Portland in the late 1960s. Designed by Angela Danadjieva, the Forecourt Fountain was completed in 1970. Thirteen thousand gallons of water per minute cascade through its terraces and platforms, suggesting the Northwest's abundant waterfalls. The concrete fountain became an instant city landmark and an internationally-acclaimed open space. In 1978, the fountain was renamed after Ira C. Keller, a civic leader and first chairman of the Portland Development Commission who was behind the renewal plan for the South Auditorium area of downtown. It has been said that "it was Keller's enormous energy that made urban renewal work in Portland." It's an important symbol of the time when Portland was proclaimed the country's most livable city.

■ Quilt information on page 214.

Pieces
of
Portland

The most photographed man in Portland is said to be this guy, who stands ready to help in Pioneer Courthouse Square, often referred to as Portland's living room. Called Umbrella Man by most Portlanders, the sculpture's actual name is *Allow Me*. He is said to be hailing a cab. Excuse me? How often do you see anyone hailing a cab in Portland? If we do, we likely use an app. We think it's more likely he is offering shelter under his umbrella to someone who is houseless. And we're pretty sure he would want to offer up a quilt for its comfort and warmth. *Allow Me* is the work of John Seward Johnson II, and was donated anonymously to Portland in 1984. Pioneer Courthouse Square is emblematic of the changing transportation emphasis that took place in Portland during the 1970s and 1980s. The square is located on the city's transit mall, which was designed for the TriMet bus system, with restrictions on auto traffic. The block the square is on was a two-level parking lot. We think this is a much better use.

■ Quilt information on page 214.

A statue of Vera Katz was added to the south end of the Eastbank Esplanade on the east side of the Willamette River in 2006. The esplanade was named for her in 2004 to honor her vision and leadership in serving as mayor of Portland and in seeing the construction of the esplanade through. Construction began in 1998 and was completed in 2001. It was an instant hit and is heavily used by pedestrians, bikers, skaters and more. The esplanade is 1.5 miles long, extending north from the Hawthorne Bridge, past the Morrison and Burnside Bridges, to the Steel Bridge with connections to eastside neighborhoods as well as across the river to Gov. Tom McCall Waterfront Park. The Esplanade is a demonstration project for improved habitat areas for fish and wildlife and riverbank restoration. At 1,200 feet, its floating walkway is the longest one of its kind in the United States, and offers the sensation of walking on water. The adjoining 120-foot public boat dock provides moorage for recreational boaters as well as space for a future river taxi and other commercial uses. The bronze sculpture is the work of Bill Bane.

■ Quilt information on page 214.

The Peoples Bike Library of Portland is a functional bike rack, bike 'lending' library, and monument to the vital bike culture of Portland. Erected by artists Brian Borrello and Vanessa Renwick in 2009 in collaboration with Zoobomb, an iterative design process led to the current sculpture. An accumulation of small kids' bicycles are locked to the sculpture, lent to the public for weekly zoobomb rides.

■ Quilt information on page 214.

Pieces
of
Portland

Above and left: One day a few years ago, someone (from nearby Reed College perhaps?) decided to defy the "Post No Bills" sign that rather oddly and inexplicably rests on a cyclone fence in SE Portland. After the first few Bills began appearing, somebody tweeted a photo. So of course we had to get in on the action. Bills upon Bills were added, covering much of the fence, before a killjoy returned it to a Bill-free zone. **Below:** Portland is infamous for posters stapled one on top of another and another and another on utility poles. We are talking multiple inches, as is illustrated in the cave that was carved in the bottom right to get to the pole's markers. Sometimes an industrious person removes them, to no avail. They just return, like moths to the flame..

▪ Quilt information on page 214.

Signs, Signs, Everywhere Signs

Portland has a sign fetish. Maybe you've noticed. It's really the most remarkable thing and could be the best and most authentic grassroots expression of ourselves in the whole city.

We wantonly put up our own signs here there and everywhere, we add our own stenciled words to very official signs, we post bills where we're not supposed to, and even some of our official signs...well, are open to interpretation.

We thought we'd take you on a little tour.

Let's start with one of my personal favorites. We were driving down Lombard Street one day when we spotted a reader board that said, "Please ignore last message."

Having our curiosity piqued, we parked and peeked in the windows of the building attached to the sign to look for clues

It can be so satisfying to get to the bottom of a Portland thing. It took us several tries over a few months, but we persevered and finally met the man responsible for the mysterious sign below that's been on a building on northeast Lombard for quite some time now. As with so many of our adventures documented here, we met another wonderful person who does what he can to make our city just a bit more interesting and wonderful than it already is.

■ Quilt information on page 214.

to its meaning. It was dark inside. Nobody was there, so we were left speculating.

Then weeks later, when we spotted an open door, we went in and met the owner, Howard Barney. We asked him what the last message had been. "STAND BY FOR IMPORTANT MESSAGE," he sheepishly grinned. "But then I couldn't come up with one." A friend later gave him the bumper sticker he is standing beside: DISREGARD THIS BUMPER STICKER.

Then there was the meme I spotted on Twitter, where people were taping pictures of guys named Bill on a fence that had a sign ordering everyone to "Post No Bills." Joyce found the fence and photographed it for posterity. But we think the quilt takes star billing. How many Bills can you name?

Ever since I've lived in Portland, the utility poles have been plastered with posters. One upon another upon another and so on. You wouldn't believe how deep it goes, if we didn't have photographic proof. Try to count the layers someone carved out to expose the official utility markers.

From time to time I see people painstakingly trying to remove the paper and even the staples. Can you possibly even imagine how long that would take? And for what purpose? New signs will be up before the remover reuses or upcycles the removed fiber in a craft project or adds it to the compost bin.

Above and right: Most of the signs within this array of stenciled stop signs are within a small radius of my home. There are many things my comrades would like to see you stop doing. I think I get most of them, but I'm not smart enough to know how to stop entropy. I don't even really know what outcome it seeks. But I'd like to meet the person who thinks we can. I don't know if it relates to entropy, but these sign alterations are getting more complex. After the Stop Driving sign was removed and replaced with a brand new regulation sign, someone considered it an invitation to step up the level of sophistication and added a three line song lyric. It's the one on the right. I confess I had to google the phrase to get the reference. I'm still not sure what it means, but I'm pretty sure it matters.

On left: Because Portland has so many cyclists, we have discovered hazards that are specific to traveling on two wheels. In one case, there is a potential clash between streetcar tracks and bike tires, so a special sign was developed to alert cyclists to that danger. Sometimes those signs are embellished with additional warnings, like maybe in case any land sharks are out and about on the other side of the tracks. **On right:** There's a whole different warning sign for the place where streets and bridges meet on a bike path. I'm not sure which is more dangerous. And I'm tempted to devise an Olympic-type rating system for the dismounts, with points for artistic merit and flat out badassedry.

We look for ways to improve pedestrian signs as well. **On left:** We're not sure if this is a Halloween costume or a crime-watcher warning. **On right:** We are convinced the person on the right is very grateful that somebody shared a creamsickle on such a hot day.

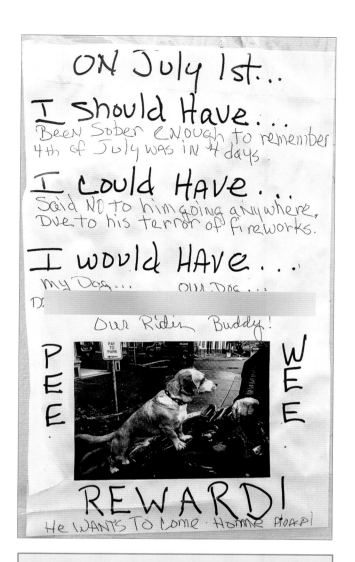

ON July 1st...

I should Have...
Been sober enough to remember
4th of July was in 4 days.

I could Have...
Said NO to him going anywhere,
Due to his terror of fireworks.

I would Have...
my Dog...   our Dog...
D,
Our Ridin Buddy!

P
E
E

W
E
E

REWARD!
He wants To come Home ploApl

Above: I'm frankly astonished by the degree of self-disclosure on signs in very public places in Portland. Witness the lost dog sign above, which included a confessional and cell phone numbers before Joyce's redaction. There is a certain amount of radical transparency mixed with naive lack of social filters on display. I know this because I have been guilty of this myself, like the time I found all my underwear missing from a load of laundry in a housing project laundromat that I had left for an hour or so. Upon discovering the loss, I posted a plea for their return that included my apartment number. I was too lacking in experience with the darker, seamier side of life to know that underwear thieves are not moved by appeals to conscience, and you certainly don't want to give them precise directions on where the hell to find you for follow-up purposes.

On right: Yes, it's true. Portland has official routes designated for people who commute on skateboards.

SKATE ROUTE

SW SECOND A   SW TAYLOR ST

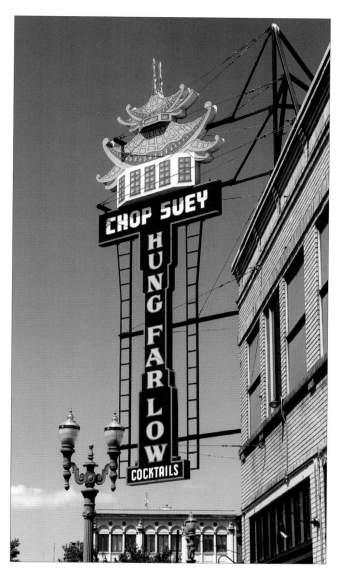

CHOP SUEY
HUNG FAR LOW
COCKTAILS

Above: This sign is such a favorite in Portland that it was saved after the restaurant it advertised closed down. The titters it provokes are caused by the custom of using transliteration (words with same sounds) rather than translation (words with same meaning). In this case, the Cantonese words that are close to the sounds of those in the sign mean Red Flower Building/Restaurant. Which is a far cry from the meaning of the words with those sounds in English. We Americans have much yet to learn, don't we?

NO SMOKING
WITHIN
305,286
FEET. PLZ

Above: So basically no smoking within a 58-mile radius of Portland's Vegan MiniMall. PLZ.

Pieces
of
Portland

Above: Given all the paper stickers and posters plastered and stapled all over utility poles across the city, you'd think a quilt would be welcome, too. But when we tied one to a pole on Hawthorne Boulevard, it was gone by sunset. We were not amused. We're planning our next move. Expect us.

Above: One has to admit that when posters are removed from poles, they can leave a rather distinctive and attractive detritus behind. We think it's reminiscent of some of the things we've seen in the unconventional materials challenge on *Project Runway*.

Above: Had we not embarked on this project, I would never have discovered the existence of sticker nerds. Yes, they are among us, apparently in large numbers considering the frequency of sticker sightings in our fair city. I imagine there is much to learn about stickers, and somebody could construct a story from the ones on the back of this stop sign. Unfortunately, I do not have the right decoder apparatus. A couple of years ago there was a Sticker World Conference and of course it was held in Portland.

Above: Official signs can be seen as opportunities for outsider art that contributes to our gross happiness index. Like the before and after signs where someone used a Sharpie to fill an otherwise boring bus with riders who look like they're on a roller coaster. On right: Please note there is no parking allowed from 7am-6pm Mon-Fri unless you are loading or unloading a truck inside a truck.

Above left: Portlanders love to support one another at all times. The homemade sign of encouragement above is near the top of a very long upward slope you don't realize is actually a hill until you bike it. Above right: Even the sheet metalists join in the signs-of-the-times fun.

On left: The connection between bikes and beer motivated a person who likes both to create their own stencil as a helpful street guide. On right: Somebody took Stop sign changing to a new level when they changed All Way to All War. But so far it doesn't seem to be working. Bottom right: We want to pay homage to the fact that the "I Like Turtles" meme started in Portland.

When the zombies come, Portland will be ready. Not only do we have local Zombie Apocalypse training for children, we do collective public reenactments. If we can talk that way about something that hasn't happened yet.

But it's true that Portland is very zombie friendly. I am talking hundreds, if not thousands, of people in stunningly convincing dress and makeup staggering through the city like, well, zombies. There are well-attended practices for the huge *Thrill the World* group synchronized dancing to Michael Jackson's "Thriller." Followed by the popular Run Like Hell run.

And then there's Haidee Vangen and her Unit 13 Biohazard Volkswagon she fondly calls her Bio Bug.

Joyce and I first spotted this impressive automobile while photographing in the vicinity of the St. Johns Bridge. We were setting up to take a picture of one of Portland's distinctive green water storage towers when we spotted the shiny black car with all the art.

It was early Sunday morning, not the time you want to be knocking on random doors in an unfamiliar neighborhood. We had the license number but no way to track down its owner (at least in a way that was both legal and free).

Again and again, Joyce returned to the site of the sighting, but the car was not to be found.

We put out queries on Facebook and Twitter, to no avail. We were beginning to believe we might have imagined it, despite photographic evidence. You know, like those unmistakable photos of Sasquatch that turn out to be something else or fake. But somehow I knew it would pop up again, and sure enough, on the morning I was headed out to meet up with Joyce for some photography on Sauvie Island, I pulled into a coffee shop drive through in northeast Portland, and there it was. In all its glory. Imagine my joy!

I went inside the coffee shop, which was pretty crowded, and asked each and every last customer if the car belonged to him or her. No luck. I waited a bit to see if someone might be in the bathroom. Nope.

At this point, I was about to be very late for my appointment with Joyce, and I have been unable to convince her to get a smartphone, so I wrote a note and left it on the car's windshield. And eagerly waited for a call. That never came. There had been a torrential downpour that morning after I wrote my note in non-waterproof ink, so I figured my words may have been washed into the storm drain. From then on, Joyce and I looked in that parking lot every time either of us passed by, but there were no further sightings.

Then, on another morning on our way to another photo/interview session for the book, we drove by the lot, and there it was. In the same spot as before! I turned on two wheels and flung my car into the lot.

This time I was bolder about exploring the car for clues. I looked through the front windshield and could read a little bit of a

business card lying on the dash. It had the name of the coffee shop's manager. Bingo!

So we went inside and asked for her. To make this long story a little shorter, it turned out the car didn't belong to her but to one of her employees. She relayed our message to the car's owner and gave us her work schedule so we could come by after her shift.

So that's what we did. It was still raining, but two parking spots opened up right next to Haidee's car right before her shift ended, exactly like it was controlled by a higher power with a Jones for quilting, kind of like the waters parting in that Bible story, so we laid the quilt down beside it and Joyce snapped away.

In the meantime, I got a bit of Haidee's story. Turns out her father makes graphics for cars in his business called AutoGraphs. Get it? He's the one who decorated her car, to fulfill her passion.

She told me she is a Resident Evil gamer and Zombie nerd. Translation: there is a horror fiction video game called Resident Evil, and she really likes to play it and has for many years. She grew up watching horror movies and has developed an abiding love of the living dead, aka undead. Which probably means we can't count on her to kill them after all. She confesses her car's graphics make people look at her weird. Even in Portland. Imagine that, they must have been tourists.

The reason we had so much trouble tracking her down is that Haidee is a very hardworking young woman. She's a recent graduate of Roosevelt High School who begins her day with a 4:30 a.m. shift as a barista, then heads off to classes at a culinary institute in mid morning. She loves art and also spends time painting and sculpting.

But back to zombies, did you know that Cornell University actually did a study to determine how long it would take a zombie invasion to spread across the nation? The study assumed a 0.8 bite-to-kill ratio would be realistic (i.e., zombies are 25% more likely to bite a human than a human to kill a zombie). How long it would take to reach Portland depends on where Patient Zero (or Zombie Zero in this case) appears. Dense metropolitan areas are the worst possible places to be because transmission will be so fast.

Pro tip: No matter where in America the first zombie appears, researchers say rural areas of the Northern Rockies are likely to be the last infected. So our best advice is to head for the hills.

Just make sure they're the right hills. Like not Portland's West Hills. I'll be heading where Peter Bauer goes.

> Haidee Vangen and her Bio Bug are the closest things we found in Portland to Ghostbusters. But she loves zombies, so we might not be able to count on her. She uses Unit 13 in her biohazard work. In a strange coincidence, we had a quilt named Germania that seemed perfect for the occasion.
> ■ Quilt information on page 214.

Pieces
of
Portland

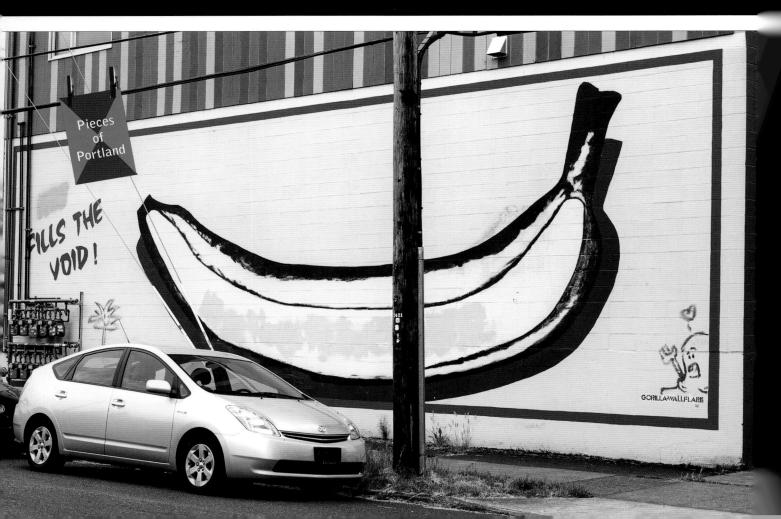

I can't tell you how I arranged it, but I managed to track down the spokesperson for Gorilla Wallflare, who agreed to talk to me as long as I promised not to reveal the identity of anyone involved with the operation. Matters are still that sensitive. Here's what I'm permitted to tell you about Portland's first guerrilla wall art. I was asked to redact the names when I published my manuscript. –MD

When ▮▮▮▮▮ lived in an apartment near the Clinton Street Theatre, he passed by an ugly blank wall at southeast 12th and Division every day on his way to work. "Oh man, I sure would like to paint something on that wall," he thought daily.

He even went so far as sketching out a mural on his drafting board. He was a painter and had worked at a sign shop painting wall graphics, but the drawing languished on his board until he met ▮▮▮▮▮. She saw it and said, "That's cool! Let's do it!"

So one Sunday, when the business in the wall's building was closed, the two of them set up scaffolding and ladders, put on painter's pants and painted a giant banana on the wall. "I wanted it to be fun. It was 1982, there was a lot of unrest in Central America," he recalls. "So it was a political and artistic statement. In fact, I planned to put '*Viva mi banano*' but in the end it became 'Art fills the void.'"

He punched holes in paper to outline the letters, and had a stencil for the Gorilla Wallflare logo, but the rest of it was freehand.

It was a great adrenalin rush, he remembers. "We didn't know if someone was going to stop us or report us. The wall was on a building that housed an office supply business. It had to be clandestine, we didn't ask permission because I figured they would want me to paint scissors and paper clips, and I wasn't into that. In the middle of the day, one of the business's salesmen came by to pick something up and saw us, and didn't say a word. He must have figured the owners had ordered the sign. Police cars came by, just sat there for a while, then moved on."

While they were painting, people walked by, watched and talked with them about what they were doing. A small old man put down the two heavy bags of groceries he was carrying and watched for a while, then said, "That's enough banana to feed a family for a whole month."

"We finished it and sent anonymous letters to the business and the *Oregonian* and *Willamette Week*. We opened up the Living Section and there it was. And sure enough, when the *Oregonian* called Pioneer Building Specialties Co. office supply company for a response, the secretary-treasurer said she thought it was fun but added, "Too bad it wasn't a bottle of glue or a hinge or something pertaining to our business." The company

subsequently incorporated the banana in some of its sales promotions.

Today, the only parts of the mural that are still original are the stem and words. Even the word "Art" has been painted over. That particular void invited us to add a quilt to the message.

The 1982 letter to the *Oregonian* included a warning: "GORILLA WALLFLARE has set out to fill the dull gray void of Portland's blank walls. THIS IS ONLY OUR FIRST ATTACK! Paint and brushes in hand, WE WILL STRIKE AGAIN!"

Gorilla Wallflare painted two additional walls, but neither still stand. "We painted a thumbprint on the side of Genoa. I don't think they were too happy about it," ▮▮▮▮▮ says. "And we painted an explosion in 1984, as a statement about 1984 being the end of the world, on a building now gone where the Burger King is at the east end of the Hawthorne Bridge. That was a challenging mural, we had to get help because we had to paint on a third story, and I'm not good with heights and ▮▮▮▮▮ was pregnant at the time."

He has offered to repaint the Art Fills the Void mural to restore it to its original glory, but the building owner declined. He was disappointed they chose the mural as the location for the gas meters that now mar its appearance, along with a utility pole that makes it hard to photograph.

▮▮▮▮▮ came to Portland in 1976 from a little town in Pennsylvania, ▮▮▮▮▮ arrived from New York about the same time. "In 1982 keeping Portland weird never occurred to me," ▮▮▮▮▮ says. "It was just something we did."

Even after all these years, ▮▮▮▮▮ prefers to remain anonymous. "It's just better that way," he says.

Just as we were preparing to print this book, we heard a rumor that the mural might be repainted. So keep your eyes open. *Viva mi banano*, after all??

Gorilla Wallflare would not be able to pull off such antics nowadays. In all likelihood, Homeland Security would get involved and ruin it for everybody.

After a Clear Channel lawsuit, Portland adopted rules and regulations about wall murals and you have to apply for a permit to put one up. This doesn't sound very Portland to us, and we worry that weirdness is going to be regulated out of us all. Which would take all the fun away. Trust me, nobody wants that. The good thing is that at least there's a nonprofit arts organization, Regional Arts and Culture Council (RACC), making decisions about the art.

In any case, by now Portland has one heck of a lot of wall murals. There are murals of Portland neighborhoods, musicians, cultures, civil rights, leaders, birds, departed people, and a whole lot that defy categorization. We've included a few examples in the following pages.

There are a whole lot more than we have room for, but fortunately there are other sources that have cataloged them. RACC has a gallery of murals on its website, Portland Street Art Alliance has a website, and A. Tarantino has published two books. You could spend the rest of your life touring them.

Opposite page: Before and after of the iconic "Art Fills the Void" mural in southeast Portland that was the birth of guerrilla street art in Portland. The top photo was taken when the artists were watching the paint dry, the bottom one in 2014 after considerable desecration/alteration. Many would like to see it repainted. But wait, what? Is that a quilt filling the void for now?

Pieces
of
Portland

Above: Portlanders are generally a pretty trusting lot when it comes to sharing their art, evidenced by the pottery display and store above, where people can purchase items and leave payment in the little hole. **Below:** It's also pleasing and inspiring to watch street art grow and transform over time. Like when neighbor collects keys and other metal items and glues them into a sidewalk sculpture, then populates it with plastic people. By now I expect many neighbors have added their own contributions.

Above: Portland's earliest known street art was paintings done by Greek immigrant Athanasios Stefopoulos from 1948 to 1952. Unable to earn a living as an artist, he was a watchman for the SP&S Railroad. When the yards were quiet, he painted nearby concrete columns that held up Lovejoy Street at the west end of the Broadway Bridge. Paintings included "whimsical images of doves, owls, lions, anthropomorphic trees, Greek mythical gods, biblical figures, and Americana." Tragically, many of the painting were destroyed when the area was redeveloped in the early years of the 21st century. Two are featured in a courtyard at NW 10th Avenue and Flanders Street. A documentary film chronicles the story of the columns, and several more are said to be stored away, awaiting someone with passion and funds to give them their rightful home. That is, of course, always the risk with street art, as it's forever exposed to the elements and vandalism.

■ Quilt information on page 214.

Pieces
of
Portland

At left and below: Sometimes street art is designed to be ephemeral, like the "Invasion of Place" installation that appeared in an empty lot at SE 20th Avenue and Taylor Street in 2010. Created by artist Graham Klag, the sculpture was made of vines of "Traveler's Joy," a plant native to Eurasia that covers trees and eventually smothers them, in much the same manner as English ivy. These vines were removed from Crystal Springs Rhododendron Gardens and constructed to show how the plant invaded the Pacific Northwest. Viewers were encouraged to "Watch the revegolution grow." **Bottom of page:** The Burnside Skatepark is another place to watch for changing art, as artists keep adding to the walls. This strip is from a mural at the park.

■ Quilt information on page 214.

Pieces
of
Portland

Above: After the Taylor Electric building in the southeast industrial area burned, the bare walls served up canvases and verily invited graffiti artists to fill the space. It was like a post-apocalyptic art museum—what's left after the people are gone. The Last Dance was held before its rumored demise, to make way for a multi-story, mixed-use building like a number of others that have appeared nearby. It's probably gone now. Hey, is that a quilt or another part of the mural?

■ Quilt information on page 214.

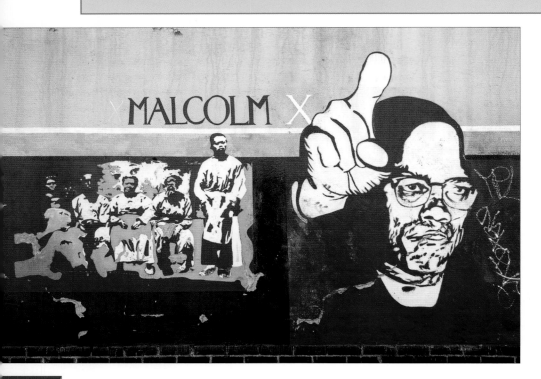

On left: This Malcolm X mural in northeast Portland was painted by artist Lewis Harris in 1984. The paint in this mural is fading, reminiscent of the demographic changes that have been taking place in the Alberta Street neighborhood, with young white people replacing "a fragile and calm neighborhood of working class African American families—many of whom have lived along Alberta for decades. To those on their way out, Malcolm X is a signal call, a single human being who stood up and refused to back down."

Above: The mural on the east wall of the Apambichao Building on northeast Glisan Street is called Pambiche and is "a cultural depiction of Cuba, inspired by its history, people and traditions. It blends Cuba's unique music, dance, architecture, historical figures and natural beauty." The mural "gives visibility to the historically misconstrued people and culture of Cuba, and provides an educational opportunity for the community at large." This might well be the most colorful building in the city, designed after architecture in central Havana. This part of town is frequented by Cuban refugees and the mural "seeks to aid the tough transition they undertake when relocating." It was painted by artists Emily Beeks and Rachel Oleson in 2011.

■ Quilt information on page 214.

On right: This mural on the north wall of Music Millennium was painted by artists The Lost Cause and Jon Stommel. They worked with Terry Currier to create a design that would be reminiscent of the record store's psychedelic roots. They decided on a "colorful Beatles-inspired array of happy characters and swirling patterns." With more than a bit of weirdness thrown in the mix.

Above: This mural at Wilshire Park in northeast Portland by Anna Girabay is of a mother and child in a natural environment, representing the children and families that use the park. The mural skyline is a familiar one, with Mt. Hood and downtown Portland clearly recognizable. The painting also emphasizes the importance of fish-friendly water in the local landscape. **On left:** A lot of street art in Portland is unsanctioned, unexpected and somewhat inexplicable. Like painted shoes climbing up a utility pole. I'd love to know the back-story for those.

Opposite page: You'll also find art at your feet, like drawings people make before newly poured concrete sidewalks dry. For example, on the facing page is a drawing of Bart Simpson by Matt Groening, creator of *The Simpsons*. Matt grew up in Portland and graduated from Lincoln High School, where this particular sidewalk is located. A lot of names of Simpson characters are familiar to Portland residents. See, for example, the street sign on the opposite page. An extra "d" will suddenly and mysteriously appear on NE Flanders street signs so they read NEd Flanders. It's a Portland thing. Some "Ds" are more noticeable than others. Near Bart Simpson's sidewalk portrait is an ode to the raccoon, a permanent resident in most Portland neighborhoods.

By this time in our project, we were running low on quilts, so we loosened the rule that every photo required a quilt.

Pro Tip: The best advice I can give to help one find the art in Portland is to keep your eyes wide open at all times, because there will be magical unexpected things to discover nearly everywhere. Look up, look down, look all around. Pretty much everybody has something inside them that wants to be expressed, and you never know what form and place it will take. It really never ends. Any one of us can and do add to the city's public art collection at any time and any place.

Pieces
of
Portland

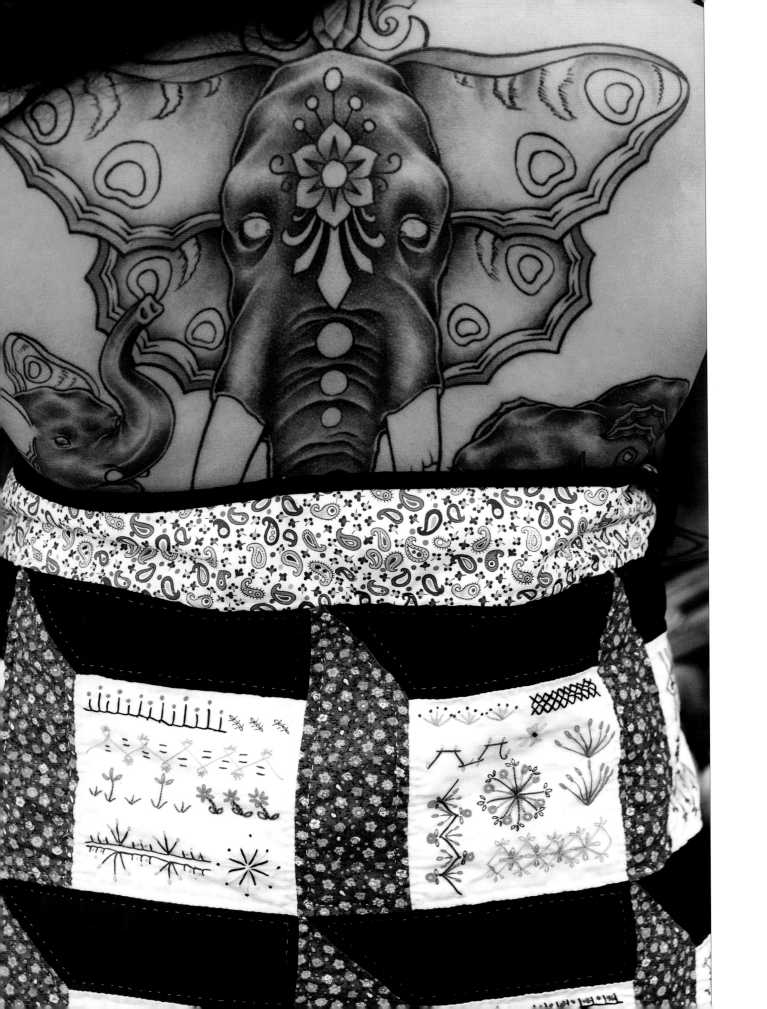

More Than Skin Deep

A tattoo is a painting using the skin as the canvas. One sees many tattoos in our city. In fact, one tattoo artist was quoted saying there are more tattooed people in Portland per capita than in any other U.S. city. How do people figure out these things? When and where is the counting done and by whom?

To my quilter's eyes, they are akin to embroidery.

Being a port city, with sailors and everything, Portland was a natural skin place, and its early artists were known for traditional style, with bold outlines and lots of dark shading. As Portland grew and attracted more and more artists who were looking for an affordable, open-minded place to live, their influence meant tattoos became more like fine art. In fact, the Portland Art Museum held a summer long "experience" called *Marking Portland: The Art of Tattoo* in 2009.

I'm not totally sure how many tattoo parlors there are in Portland, but 154 are listed in the Yellow Pages. People still use the Yellow Pages? I did not know that.

To learn more, I turned to my most-tattooed friend, Karissa Lowe. She says she always wanted tattoos and had been drawing them on herself for as long as she can remember. One day when she was 14, she told her dad she wanted a tattoo. It turned out he'd always wanted one too, so they went together. "Mom wasn't wild about the idea," Karissa remembers, "but she came along to show support and keep an eye on us. To this day she remains inkless, yet supportive of my dad and me getting tattoos."

Her first was by an artist named Bones, a little dragon on her ankle she named Sparky. Her second was on her 18th birthday, by artist Mary Throp, an armband featuring two dragonflies and "art nouveau-ish neotribal black swirly things." Karissa explains that dragonflies are important to her, partly because they have a symbolic meaning in her Cowlitz Tribe's culture.

Her third tattoo is on her lower back, another art nouveau style with dragonfly, by artist Jennifer Bilig. "I figured getting some work done on my lower back would give me a vague idea of the pain and time a full back piece would take. I also thought it would look rad when I belly danced. It still does." (Explanatory note: Karissa runs Offbeat Bellydance performances every third Friday evening at Analog.)

Her next tattoo was a half sleeve from her right elbow to her wrist and includes the name of Egyptian goddess Hathor in hieroglyphics and a petroglyph called She Who Watches. Karissa recounts the story: A long time ago Coyote approached a woman who was a great leader and told her that changes were coming. He asked her if she wanted to live out the rest of her days and then go on to the next world, or be put onto a rock overlooking her people's land where she could watch over them forever. She chose to go onto the rock because she wanted to protect her people through the ages."

"I'm on my tenth year serving as a Tribal Council member," Karissa says. "We serve three-year terms, and we're elected by a vote of the general membership of the Tribe. Having She Who Watches tattooed on me helps me remember that one is elected to serve the interests of the people, not the interests of the self.

Her next tattoo, also by Jennifer Billig, is called "Hold Fast" because it commemorates the purchase of Karissa's first home. "The house was a foreclosure owned by HUD, and the transaction to buy it was an absolute dragged-out nightmare that took months. The family slogan became 'Hold Fast,' which to us meant 'hang in there, don't give up.'" Her dogs Lulu and Nelly inspired the next two tattoos—paw prints on both shoulders by artist Igor Mortis.

Karissa's most recent tattoo is a work in progress, pictured here. "I see the big elephant as the matriarch and the two babies as the next generation, and to me this tattoo symbolizes intergenerational connection, cultural transmission, and the duality of the environment in that it's incredibly fragile and vulnerable to human carelessness but ultimately it's also far more powerful than any one species."

Why are there so many tattoos in Portland?

"I think we have a lot of amazing artists in town, so it's easier to get high-quality, awesome-looking work done here than in other communities. Seeing fabulous tattoos all over town probably helps inspire people to get some of their own. I also think that the young folks who move here in search of Portlandia probably get tattooed as a way to rebel against their old life back in Connecticut or wherever they're all coming from. And since their parents are on the other side of the country, they're unfettered by supervision."

"I love having tattoos," she says. "I hate getting tattoos. It hurts and it sucks. I've lived a very fortunate, relatively painless life—I've never been hospitalized for a traumatic injury, set on fire or given birth so I realize I haven't truly pushed my pain receptors to see what they can do. That said, if there are things that hurt worse than getting tattooed on your ribs and near your armpits, I don't want to meet them."

"I cover my tattoos at work," Karissa continues. "My mother has embraced the fact that dad and I love tattoos, but she always reminds us of the importance of keeping them covered in the workplace. Plus, I have blue streaks and sparkles in my hair, I wear blood-red lipstick, and I have a hard time not saying 'Yarrrr' in the workplace, so I feel like people who don't know me already have a lot of eccentricity to wade through."

No wonder she seems so normal.

Opposite page: Karissa Lowe bares her back to show her most recent tattoo that is a work in progress. She works with selected artists to come up with a design that has special meaning for her life. The subjects are inspired by many things, from her Native American heritage to buying her first home to her dogs. Before she got her first tattoo at age 14, she drew them on her skin herself. **This page:** Karissa's face.

■ Quilt information on page 214.

Pieces of Portland

A Story with a Lot of Holes

The most fascinating piece of Portland earth might be found in a place that lacks it, shaped like a very large hole and a labyrinth of caves beneath a yard in southeast Portland.

There are more questions than answers about the origin of the hole, homeowner Barron explained. "I had a feeling there was a hole in this one spot in my yard. But it was hidden by dirt when I moved into my house in 1985. I checked it out empirically with a shovel and found out I was right. And the more I dug, the more hole I found."

As he dug ever deeper, he discovered "a Gaping Tunnel™ with a Giant Double Arch™ (Barron trademarks most things) perfectly aligned with the North Star, at a slight angle." There are chambers in the hole, with artifacts and "cryptic rock inscriptions appearing to be laser-blasted in a strange, stone-like material indistinguishable from our modern day concrete."

Barron (yes, that's his whole legal name...and his hole name) wonders if he might be archeologically psychic. "I have a feeling there could be more hole to find. But I was already in way over my head."

He's never measured the hole using modern scientific methods, but he knows one thing for sure: "It goes all the way to the bottom." There's a ladder into the hole, and Barron conducted public tours until a well-known architect visited the hole and said, "It's not safe."

"Since it's not safe, protection is needed," Barron said. "For this purpose, liability waivers are available for signatures before descending into the depths."

So it's become a word of mouth thing, spreading through the underground grassroots of the people. With a website and Facebook page, of course.

Next to the hole is the Fun Regenerator,™ which broadcasts a massive Spiral O' Fun™ into the cosmos. And magically regenerates it. Or something like that. It's topped by a rowboat. When you peer inside the Fun Regenerator,™ what you see is mostly invisible. Through both holes. But one kind of invisibility looks closer than the other. I can't remember the explanation for the boat, but I'm pretty sure it made sense at the time.

"They say when you're having Fun, time flies. Since I had to do so many unFun things, I had to keep digging because nothing is as Fun as digging. Time ceases to have any meaning." (He always capitalizes Fun because it's his religion.)"

Barron recycled all the sand and gravel and rocks he removed from the hole elsewhere in his yard, although I detected no unusual tallness anywhere. Another mystery, perhaps explained

by the nearby Stupefying Double-wide Stairway to Upthere.™ I bet the History Mole™ of the Mystery Hole™ knows where it went.

Barron ticks off the main theories about the origin of the hole: "It could be a bomb shelter from the 1950s, an ancient Indian kiva or an outpost of aliens from outer space. Or maybe somebody just dug a hole. Recreational tunnelers are an underground group, so little is known about their work."

The Deluxe Mystery Hole™ is moving into a new phase now. "I'm inviting people to bring lidded containers of sand and gravel and rocks and pour them into the hole," Barron said. "When they reseal the container, they'll be taking some of the hole with them." He imagines the hole could spread across the world.

That prospect pleases Barron. He imagines future generations rediscovering the renewly hidden hole. "Maybe they'll find my body inside." I hope he lives long enough to see that happen.

We made our way through the Funnel of Love 'n Rebirth™ and emerged into his backyard. Which looked oddly normal. Pastoral even. With an inviting hammock and a pond! Croquet wickets were set up all over the lush lawn, and Barron invited us to join in a game of zombie croquet with friends who would be arriving soon. Then we learned it was skyclad, and we would have to put the camera away unless we could come up with enough quilts to cover all the private bits. We only had the one quilt and wisely confessed that we are rather square pegs, murmured our regrets and withdrew from the place with the round hole.

Barron wished us a swell weekend, if that concept still applies to our schedule.

You must be this tall — to peek into Fun Regenerator

Pieces
of
Portland

Music to Our Ears

If you love music, you love Portland. The hardest part is figuring out what to choose on any given night. This city is full of incredible musicians, venues galore, admirable producers, state-of-the-art recording studios and everything I'm leaving out. But with a very laid back vibe.

Every other person you meet likely has recording equipment in their bedroom or basement. Basically, you have to go out of your way on purpose not to hear music.

My musical experience in Portland began at Music Millennium, "a place where music and people still matter." The store opened in 1969, in 800 square feet at the corner of east Burnside Street and 32nd Avenue, offering alternative music not sold in department stores and the few mainstream record stores that existed then.

It was one of the first places I found that let me know I had arrived in a special city. It wasn't because of all the black light posters or the smell of patchouli incense. Going to Music Millennium was where people went not so much to find a popular record, although you might find it there. It was where you could go to discover music. Staff members were not just fans, but often connoisseurs of music. Many were musicians themselves, and you could have long and interesting conversations that introduced you to something or someone new. It was kind of a Wikipedia experience, because other shoppers would join in the conversation and offer up their own knowledge, and a kind of collective expanding and updating of wisdom happened.

Lots of us have at least one amazing MM story. Here's mine: One day as I was driving to a meeting at my son's school, I heard a rendition of a song that made all the hairs on my body stand at attention. I was completely mesmerized. As soon as the meeting was over, I got back in my car and drove straight to Music Millennium. I stepped up to the clerk behind the counter and told him I had heard the most amazing song, I thought the name might be Mountain Greenery and it sounded like it was just a woman's amazing voice and an upright bass. He started flipping through the ginormous music catalog on the counter, but after a few moments he stepped away and said, "Follow me." We entered the bowels of the store, descending at least two levels, and he walked up to a woman older than me who was organizing stacks of used cassette tapes on a shelf. He asked her if she had done Mountain Greenery. She said, "Sure, it's on *Impending Bloom*."

All at once I got it. She was the woman's voice on the song. So I was now standing next to and talking with Nancy King, who was working in the store. I almost fainted and that's no lie.

She autographed the CD I bought and invited me to a performance at the Portland Brewery that weekend. I went, and Nancy King and bass player Glenn Moore played in a little loft above the bar. As expected, it was mind-blowing. How could something as cool as this actually happen in real life?!

Terry Currier, previously introduced to you as father of *Keep Portland Weird*, played clarinet and saxophone in school and

started working at DJ's Sound City at Janzten Beach after high school. But he spent most of his wages buying albums at Music Millennium because of the wider range of music it offered.

He hired on as MM's manager in 1984, and eventually bought the business, increasing his ownership share over time. MM pioneered record stores as a place for live music in 1989, and that has contributed to its national reputation. In its 20th year, it had 20 straight days of live music in the store. "At one time, we were up to 300 per year, we still have about 150 per year," Terry says.

In 1993, country singer Garth Brooks led a music industry effort to ban used record, tape and CD sales. Even though he didn't have much used inventory at that point, Terry didn't take kindly to the industry dictating what consumers and retailers could do with items they owned, so he led the fight against it. He launched his campaign by burning Garth Brooks records on the barbecue, then took to the road to rally support. Before long, the music industry caved.

So thank Terry Currier next time you buy or sell previously-owned music.

Opposite page: Music Millennium, Portland's church of music sales, features live informal performances and is still holding its own in the digital age. **Above:** Blues fans in the thousands come by land and by water to take in the sounds of the 2014 Portland Blues Festival at the natural amphitheater in the bowl in Tom McCall Waterfront Park.

■ Quilt information on page 214.

Terry's importance to Oregon's music scene and beyond was recognized by his induction into the Oregon Music Hall of Fame in 2008. He's now president of its board of directors and very much involved in Portland's music scene.

But it hasn't been a bed of roses for Terry and MM in the Rose City for the last 15 years. You could say that Y2K disaster did indeed fall on the record-selling business. MM's northwest Portland store closed in 2007, and Classical Millennium shut its doors in 2012.

Now Music Millennium is the oldest record store in the Pacific Northwest. It has struggled over the years as music formats changed. Is there any other industry that has gone through more formatting changes than the music biz? In my lifetime, it went from 78s, to 33-1/3 vinyl LPs, 45s, reel-to-reel tape, 8-track cassettes, DAT, compact disc, mini disc, DCC, CD-ROM and digital downloading.

At my age, there are albums I bought as vinyl, then on cassette tapes, then as CDs, and later as mp3s. It's been *deja vu* all over again and again and again.

"Digital format is something we can't stock," Terry says. But he finds hope ahead.

"We still have loyal customers," he says as he waves to one he sees getting into his car, with a purchase in his hand. "About 20% of the population thinks in that direction (buying local). The other 80% shop based on other factors like price, convenience. But 20% will go out of their way and pay extra to support local. Local stores have more expertise to offer the customer, are more

Pieces
of
Portland

passionate about their product. I feel optimistic about the future of record stores now," he says. "When Napster happened, we lost the youth. Our older customers are dying, downsizing, our regular customer base is shrinking," he says. "But the resurgence in vinyl is starting to bring youth back into the store."

"Vinyl is the best format for music ever invented," he continues. "It's the most interactive experience. CDs are 60-70 minutes, that's too long for a listener's attention span. They go off and do other things while the music is playing, they're not as engaged with music. With vinyl, you have 17-20 minutes before you have to flip it. You pay attention to the music, take good care of the record, read the liner notes, study the art on the album cover, you like it more and more over time. That doesn't happen with CDs or mp3s. Especially with shuffle, you lose the concept of an album, which is a work of art. A lot of time and effort go into making an album, it's meant to be heard at one sitting. In our day, we treated music like art."

All of us in my generation are nodding our collective heads right now. He's talking our music. I think back on all the conversations and listening get-togethers about what the lyrics meant when the Beatles' Sgt. Pepper album came out.

Terry's faith in the future is demonstrated by the recent successful Kickstarter campaign to replace MM's leaking roof. "I promised I would sleep on the roof if we didn't raise enough to fix it," he says. "Luckily I didn't have to."

He's also adding a bar space inside the store. "People want their beverage when they're listening to music, especially for live performances. There used to be a mini-mart across the street where they could go, but it's gone."

Never too much service for the Music Millennium customer.

§

For such a green city, Portland sure has a lot of blues. You can hear them every Fourth of July on the waterfront south of the Hawthorne Bridge.

The festival started in 1987, with a lineup that included John Lee Hooker, Curtis Salgado, Paul deLay and Norman Sylvester (the last three being home-grown performers).

As with so many large public events in our city, the festival is tied to a worthy cause—in this case the Oregon Food Bank. In the first year, it raised $7,500 and 650 pounds of food. By 2013, those numbers had grown to $1.3 million and more than 78,000 pounds. Not bad for a free festival, with free admission, but audience members are asked to make a donation and bring non-perishable food. The exception is the last day, when major headliners perform and tickets go for $50.

Music is now scheduled over four days, and 120 acts perform on four stages. Besides great sounds, it's a great venue for people-watching—if nothing else to see the variety of size and shape and purpose of things people bring with them. Which in turn provokes rule making about what's permissible to bring. Like size of cooler (soft sided only), size of blanket. And designating special sections based on height of lawn chairs over 12 inches off the ground. And so on.

It's impossible not to notice the blues are turning gray, with three-fourths of the blues festival audience older than 50. That doesn't bode well for the future. We better figure out how we're gonna give young people the blues. I hope the Cascade Blues Association is all over this in its efforts to preserve and promote

blues and roots music. Maybe they can convince millennials to turn out for the many blues performances in local venues all year long.

§

Jazz is another thing that's put Portland on the map. Do the names Esperanza Spalding, Thara Memory, Leroy Vinegar and Nancy King mean anything?

Jazz came to Portland with African Americans who moved here during World War II to help build ships for the Navy. At one time, Williams Avenue was lined with clubs, and Portland's Jumptown was a regular stop for many on the jazz circuit, until the area was wiped out by construction of Memorial Coliseum, and Emanuel Hospital.

There are two annual jazz festivals in Portland, one in February (what used to be the Mt. Hood Jazz Festival) and the Cathedral Park Jazz Festival in July (described as "the oldest continuous free jazz festival west of the Mississippi River.")

§

We have a symphony orchestra and an all classical radio station, and I've heard they too struggle to expand their audiences into younger demographics. But they're trying!

It's not that young people aren't into music. By no means. Lots of music thrives in Portland because of young enthusiastic audiences. I'm no longer sure what to call music genres because there are so many blurred lines between rock and roll and indie rock and alternative and contemporary and pop and punk and electronic and hip hop and rhythm and blues and so on. I just know what I like, and there's a lot to like in the local scene, from then to now.

§

Do you have any idea how many bands there are in Portland? Go ahead, guess. Now take that number and multiply it by 10. I'm pretty sure you're still close without going over.

You probably haven't heard of most of them. But your mind would be uberblown by how good they are, if you had. Here's the story of one of Portland's bands you may not know yet.

Colin, Haven, Tyler, Sam and Figley grew up in Homer, Alaska. That's a town of about 5,000 people that calls itself the Halibut Capital of the World. It's right on the Pacific Ocean, near the southern tip of the Kenai Peninsula. It's ridiculously scenic, I mean, you can't even imagine.

In high school, Colin was in a band with Haven, Tyler and Sam were in another band, and Figley, who lived in Talkeetna, was writing a lot of songs.

Colin came to Portland to attend Portland State University. Then Sam and Tyler independently came. They knew Figley and convinced him to join them. Then Haven arrived. Their first band house was two doors down from me. We knew they had arrived when we heard the bass reverberating through the 'hood, but they proved to be the most polite and considerate people ever, and the neighbors all loved them. They've since moved to another band house with a basement.

So how did all five of them choose Portland? "I don't know, everything just seemed to point to Portland," Colin says. "We heard way more things about Portland than anywhere else." Even a bass player who had played with Miles Davis told Colin to check out the music scene in Portland when he was in Homer.

Wait til you hear this. I've uncovered something really really

weird that might well explain this "coincidence" and I'd like to run it by you. When I looked at Homer's official city website, I couldn't help but notice that it included a cost-of-living section that compared Homer's cost for all sorts of things to costs in Anchorage, which makes sense because it's Alaska's largest city. Homer selected one place to represent the lower 48 in the comparison. Guess which? Yeah, Portland.

For example, the cost of electricity in Portland is listed at $109.78 for 1000 kWh, compared with $211.58 for Homer. No wonder everything pointed to Portland! It's like the city's officially designated "other place." Is it a stealth campaign by Portland to seduce Homer's most creative residents? Or maybe because Homer knows both places have a lot of "fugitives and refugees"? Colin reports that the band members' parents are cut from that cloth.

Maybe it's just about the music. "We really liked the music we heard coming out of Portland. We were just out of high school when we heard Menomena. It was a sound we'd never heard

before, it was really new and exciting. We didn't know music could sound like that, heavy and light at the same time." They opened for Menomena at Project Pabst in September 2014, which was really awesome for them. (Personally, I think Animal Eyes is better, don't hate me, Menomena.)

When the band first started in Portland, it was called Monkey Puzzle, but Haven thought it sounded too much like *Curious George.* One day he used his "animal eyes" to communicate with his dog, and everybody thought it expressed their feelings of being part of the natural world so they adopted Animal Eyes and it stuck.

They love making music in Portland. "Portland ended up being the perfect place for us," Colin says. "We're able to do our own thing, there's not a huge emphasis on 'making it.' There's a community of musicians and music lovers here who get excited about what you do. Musicians support one another, we go to other bands' shows, they come to ours."

Their favorite places to play in Portland are Doug Fir and Mississippi Studios because they feel they have the best sound. When they started, they worried only 10 people would come to their shows, but now they generally draw more than 100. "We don't have groupies," Colin laughs. "We just have a lot of good friends and we're lucky to be part of an awesome group of people." Every summer Animal Eyes returns to Alaska to play for the home crowds, and to join their friend, Seattle-based musician Andrew Vait, in teaching a music camp for kids age 9

Above: members of Animal Eyes gather with the bears near Pioneer Courthouse that remind them of their native Alaska. From left are Tyler Figley (songwriting, guitar, vocals), Colin McArthur (bass, vocals), Tyler Langham (songwriting, guitar, vocals), Haven Multz-Matthews (drums and video star) and Sam Tenhoff (songwriting,accordion, keys, octapad).
■ Quilt information on page 214.

Pieces
of
Portland

though 15. Band members still work other jobs to earn enough to live, but thankfully they've moved beyond the selling plasma stage. "We're still young enough to sleep on floors and do crazy things," Colin says, although he had to leave PSU because it was too expensive. "Our goal is to earn enough from our music to pay for our lives without sacrificing creative control, making a living doing what we love."

Tyler, Figley and Sam are the main songwriters, with the whole band contributing to fleshing out the sound. "Often we'll start with a drum beat from Haven or Tyler, Sam, or Figley will have a song already done, and we just fill it out, or sometimes we'll just jam on a riff or part of a song, and see where it takes us," Colin says.

Colin thinks "psychedelic rock" best describes Animal Eyes' music. It has a "general rock energy and uses wild effects, noises, experimental sounds that are out there." *Willamette Week* called the sound "spacious, syncopated progressive rock."

If you don't know their music yet, Colin recommends you check out their EP *Ursus*. They're working on a new album now, including doing their own recording and engineering.

"Basically," Colin says, "we make music we want to hear."

§

You don't have to try very hard to find music on the street in Portland. It's pretty much everywhere I go, anyway. Busking is a common occupation here.

And in summer, you'll find pianos out and about where anyone can strike up a tune. It's the work of an organization called Piano! Push! Play!, whose mission is to "rescue pianos, put them on the street for everyone to enjoy, and then give them to schools and others who will love them as much as we do." Funds from Awesome Portland helped pay the costs of the program during 2014. Leslie Rogers, Dean of Awesome Portland, noted that "Nobody vandalized them, homeless people played them, young people played them, older people played them. It brought joy, which is the definition of what we want: Wow! That's awesome!"

We found Luke Sensei playing the piano next to the bike pyle one sunny summer afternoon.

Portland is also known for being a good place for recording music, for those who aren't doing it themselves in their basements and bedrooms. There are way more studios here than we have any right to expect, along with very skilled producers, mix scientists, sound engineers, and so on. And many musicians you've heard of have recorded here, from the Decemberists to Sleater-Kinney to the Shins to Spoon to Eddie Vedder to the Go Betweens to OMG, the list is too long. Please go look for yourselves.

There is a bit of tarnish on Portland's music reputation, though, summarized in a *Buzzfeed* article, "Fighting for Hip-Hop in the Whitest City in America." Arianna Rebolini wrote,

"Portland, Ore., is known as a haven for progressive culture. So why does it seem like police consider rappers and their fans a threat to the city's specific brand of weird?"

Rap artists feel their performances are targeted by police and fire marshals, while police cite shootings at prior similar events as reason for their scrutiny. Immaculate tweeted after a show interrupted by police that "I will not perform in this city as long as the blatant targeting of black culture and minorities congregating is acceptable common practice."

Even when hip hop shows go forward, artists can feel awkward rapping about their experiences being black in America to largely white audiences, as is often the case in Portland. Is that a sign of successful integration or continuing intimidation of black audiences here? Because it's not the first time African America music has experienced problems in Portland. Remember Jumptown, mentioned a couple of pages back, and its thriving jazz scene? Ironically, the best known of the Jumptown clubs—the Dude Ranch (author Bob Dietsche called it "the Cotton Club, the Apollo Theatre, Las Vegas and the wild west rolled into one"—was closed by city officials decades ago after a shooting.

It's been hard to find a central place for African American music in Portland since. Its most visible presence now might just be the mural on the side of the Musicians Union building on northeast 20th Avenue. Jazz clubs that remain are dispersed.

§

To end things on a more harmonic note, Portland has also distinguished itself as a place of fine instrument making. Is it because we are in the middle of so much great wood? Or because we are a city of musicians and artisans?

Well, actually, it's probably not the wood. Gilmer Wood Company in Portland's northwest industrial area supplies wood for musical instruments, and most of the species listed on its supply page are from other continents, ranging from Pink Ivory from South Africa for tunery and inlays to African Blackwood Bagpipe Set to Quilted Mahogany from Central and South America used for acoustic guitar backs and sides. Did you just say Quilted Mahogany?? I swear, quilting is everything now.

The annual Handmade Musical Instrument Exhibit is held here, featuring local handmade classical, flamenco, steel string, archtop, resonator and electric guitars, violins, bows, ukes, dulcimers, banjos, mandolins, cellos, basses (acoustic and electric), flutes, harps, lutes, replicas of medieval instruments, and more. There's even a special section for "unusual, interesting and sometimes bizarre instruments."

There's also a community of musicians who wouldn't dream of making instruments from virgin materials, preferring instead to work entirely with discarded goods. Like an electric guitar made from an old shovel, an upright bass from a washtub, a sitar from a tomato can.

No one is surprised.

Opposite page: Luke Sensei plays the Push! Play! Piano! piano near the bike pyle on an August afternoon with a guitar player. Above: A section of the mural by Isaka Shamsud-Din, Joe Cotter, Hector Hernandez and Baba Wagué Kiakité on the side of the Musician's Union Building in northeast Portland pays homage to the many kinds of music that contribute to a rich musical tapestry here. Or at least once did.
■ Quilt information on page 212.

197

Pieces
of
Portland

Using Our Words

Soon after I arrived in Portland in 1974, I stumbled into a bookstore in a funky below-street-level space in the center of downtown Portland. After seven straight years in academia where I had read little outside assigned books and texts in the fields I studied, I asked the tie-dye-wearing guy behind the counter at Looking Glass Books to suggest something fun to read. He introduced me to Hunter Thompson and *Fear and Loathing in Las Vegas*. Whoa! Not at the university anymore!!

In the days and weeks that followed, I discovered that Portland was a city of bookstores. They were everywhere!

Looking Glass moved to a more spacious downtown space during transit mall construction, and then out of downtown in 2007 because of rising rents, construction chaos and shifts in downtown office locations. A large chain bookstore had gone in a couple of blocks away. Looking Glass hung on at its Sellwood location until it closed in 2011, actually outlasting its large chain neighbor bookstore downtown. Many, in fact most, independent bookstores in Portland have met a similar fate.

But one independent bookstore in downtown Portland has not only survived, but thrived, putting Portland on the national—even global—map. I'm talking, of course, about Powell's Books.

Joyce and I have a weird connection with Powell's. The original bookshop is in the Hyde Park neighborhood of Chicago. We both were undergraduates at the University of Chicago when graduate student Michael Powell opened the first Powell's on 57th Street in 1970. I remember browsing the dark and musty stacks of used books, although I don't remember buying anything. But that's certainly not the case with the Portland Powell's, where we both have left ridiculously large sums of cash.

The Portland Powell's was started in 1971 by Michael's father, Walter, after he had helped out in the Chicago store that first summer. He started buying all the used books he could get his hands on. I remember an early Friends of the Library of Multnomah County used book sale in the parking garage beneath the Galleria building in the late-1970s or early 1980s, where a few guys were just sweeping books into boxes and filling one after another. When I asked them what they were doing, they said they were buying books for Powell's. I saw the future and it started with a P.

Michael returned to Portland and joined his father at Powell's, which added new books to its inventory and moved to the much larger space (a former automobile dealership) where it is today. It takes up an entire block now, a veritable "city of books." There are also stores on Hawthorne Boulevard, at PDX airport and Cedar Hills Crossing in Beaverton; Powell's Books for Home and Garden is near the Hawthorne shop. And of course, Powells.com.

Now Powell's is owned by Michael's daughter Emily. Powell's is a bona fide Portland institution and holds a special place for those of us who have known it practically our whole adult lives.

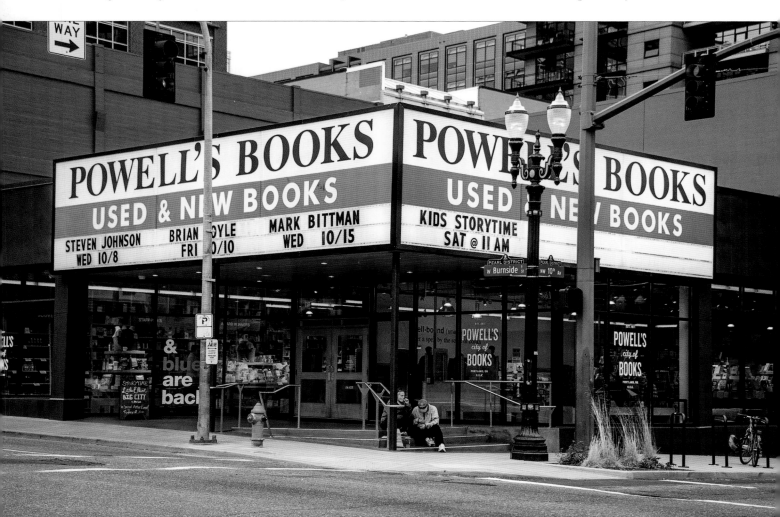

There's a lot of Oregon history there as well. One of my favorite scores is a copy of *Tristam Shandy* that had come from the library at Rajneesh Puram after it shut down. That's a whole other weird story, with little to do directly with Portland, except for all the people I used to see in my neighborhood dressed in the colors of the sunset.

A fascinating conversation with Powell's CEO Miriam Sontz helped make clear why and how Powell's became a pillar of Portland. Sole CEO since 2013, and co-CEO and chief operating officer before that, Miriam knows the book business from the title page to the back cover. She came to Portland to attend Reed College, and when she graduated in 1973, she wanted to stay, so started working as a book buyer for JK Gill, a downtown Portland institution since 1870 that sold books and stationery.

In 1984, Miriam started working at Powell's books, which occupied 25,000 square feet at the time. She was manager of the Beaverton store, then managed the expansion at the mothership, from one story to two stories in 1990, and from two to three stories in 2000.

In the beginning, prices were written in pencil just inside the book. She was there when the inventory was 100% unlabeled and helped it reach its present 100%-labeled state. When she described the process, it sounded like an outdoor adventure: they were dealing with a river (the flow of books coming in) and a lake (the existing inventory). Powell's first developed a system to label and manage the river. Once that was in place, they dove into the lake, labeling a section at a time.

Now Powell's has an inventory of around two million fully-labeled and inventoried books, half of which are at the downtown store and the rest in its other locations. Downtown Powell's is so big, it color codes its rooms and provides maps for its customers. And, of course, nowadays there's a free app that guides shoppers to the location of a book they want, giving GPS-like directions.

Why is Powell's so successful when most of the other independent bookstores and some large chains have disappeared?

"The community owns Powell's in a way that other businesses can't imagine," Miriam explains. "They built Powell's up with their books. A lot of Portlanders' books have been and are our inventory. A classics professor who sold his book collection to us used to come in and visit his books. He was kind of sad when the last one was sold. That's really a unique thing in a retail business. People in our city have relationships with what's on our shelves."

Powell's is accustomed to being on Best Bookstore lists that are frequently published by national and international pundits. "We're proud to be on the lists," she acknowledges.

"But we're unique among the others there. A lot of the bookstores are selected because they have great architecture or some historical significance."

"For example, there's one in a church outside Amsterdam. Another is in a beautiful structure in Argentina. But I want to know what their inventory is like. How many books do they

have? And are the books arranged to make for a convivial spirit? Here, it's all about the BOOKS. ALL about the books."

"We call ourselves the biggest independent bookstore in the world," she says, "and if somebody disagrees, we'll invite them to prove we're not."

Powell's has become a major tourist destination in Portland. "We love our tourists," she smiles. "They give us a second holiday season in June, July and August." Powell's is open every single day of the year, and an average of 8,000 customers come in each day.

Visitors from other cities much larger than Portland ask Miriam why they don't have a Powell's. "I think there are several reasons," she says. "One is real estate, bookstores can't afford the rent. Selling books is a high-volume, low-price-point business. We are very fortunate to own this block at a central downtown location. And in the past 15 years, this neighborhood has really taken off. It's transitioned from industrial to residential and retail, and the people who have moved in read and buy books."

She continues, "To be a successful bookstore, you need both a noon crowd and an evening crowd. In many cities, downtown becomes a ghost town at night. You can't make it without an

Opposite page: One of the best known and most visited corners in our fair city is West Burnside and Northwest 10th Avenue, the downtown home of Powell's Books. **This page:** Powell's Books CEO Miriam Sontz visits one of her favorite sections of the store, books for children and youth.
■ Quilt information on page 214.

aisle and something catches your eye. Customers take books into our coffee shop and look them over or read. Conversations happen. Powell's is a social environment."

Miriam recalls that "ten years ago, Bill Gates predicted that print books would not exist in five years." But she begs to differ.

What really excites her is the fact that the Children and Youth section is the most popular and vibrant in the store. "The young adult audience, especially the 16-25 year olds, are reading more than any prior generation. I'm very bullish on the next generation. They are the future of books."

As we strolled through the newly-remodeled main floor area, Miriam pointed out the massive wood beams they discovered when they uncovered the ceiling, and the signs of the original automobile store were revealed. "That's Portland history," she points out.

Behind the cashiers, a plain wall is emblazoned with an inscription: "smellbound: held as if under a spell by the scent of books."

"We gave a lot of thought about what to put on the wall," she says. "We wanted something really special, we considered a lot of quotes from famous authors. But in the end, we made up our own word that represents the value added provided by a brick and mortar store."

"You can't find the scent of books online."

§

Portland has also gained book fame through its exceptional library system, which Miriam views as a complementary institution that nurtures the same readers as Powell's.

A group of Portland citizens organized a subscription library and reading room in 1864, the first step in establishing the oldest public library west of the Mississippi River. It became a tax-supported free public library in 1902, and over the years grew to an 18-library system, with a large central library downtown and 17 branches in neighborhoods. It's Oregon's largest public library, serving about one-fifth of the state's population. In 2014 it was one of only five large libraries in the country that the *Library Journal* awarded five stars, as it has each year since the rating system began.

I nearly cried with joy the first time I entered the beautiful downtown Central Library in 1974. It's where I prepared for my PhD exams. I was astonished at the breadth and depth of the collection in my somewhat obscure subject area. I found the grand old reading rooms to be wonderfully inspirational places for researching, thinking and writing.

By one measure, Multnomah County Library is the hardest working library in the country, circulating 24.8 million items in 2013, more than any other system except the New York City library that serves way more people. For the 11th year in a row, our per capita use rate is highest in the country—33.4 items per man, woman and child—among large libraries. Each item in the library is checked out at four times the national rate.

evening crowd. We have so many readings and other events in the evenings that bring in quite a crowd."

"We also have several universities within a small radius, and that helps."

Before talking with Miriam, I had assumed that e-books represent the biggest threat to brick and mortar stores like Powell's, but that turns out not to be true. "The biggest challenge we face," she explains, "is meeting customer expectations, which are so much higher than they were before the web. Customers expect us to have what they are looking for, and if we don't, they expect us to get it and deliver it within two days. They expect us to have resources to be able to identify a book from two words they think might be in the title."

And, yes, Miriam concedes, Powell's nearly always can meet those expectations because of the stellar people it hires and the technology it has invested in.

"Another challenge is that customers have come to think that books are overpriced. They willingly pay $10 or more for a movie that entertains them for an hour and a half. When you look at it that way, books are a great bargain."

She boils it down to its essence: "To succeed now, brick and mortar operations have to provide value added that you can't get online. There's a human touch we provide, a serendipity that comes when you walk down an

smell·bound ('smel-ˌbau̇nd) *adj* : held as if under a spell by the scent of books

Multnomah County Library's success is partly due to its relatively enthusiastic embrace of changing technology and diversifying demographics. Its website is available in English, Spanish, Russian, Vietnamese and Chinese languages. Patrons can download audiobooks and e-books and stream music and video. It won a Digital Government Achievement Award in 2013. Today more patrons visit the library online than in person.

The library is also known for its amazing reference services, due to its insanely great librarians, who may well be the most underrated folks in Portland. Another popular feature is its Title Wave used book store in northeast Portland, where it sells items removed from circulation. The library consistently enjoys popular support, with voters approving all its tax levies so far.

A lot of community events are held at the downtown library. I had so much fun helping staff the Free Geek table at the first "Keep Portland Weird" festival held there in 2007, for example.

Friends of the Library (FOTL) of Multnomah County was established in 1972, growing out of a strong public response when a county budget cut threatened to close 12 beloved neighborhood libraries in Portland. FOTL has provided funds to the library system through used book sales since 1974, and operates the retail space inside the lobby of the downtown Central Library. It sells items of higher value through amazon.com.

§

There's another library service in Portland that must be mentioned and that's Street Books, established in 2011 by Portland writer, artist and adjunct professor at Marylhurst University Laura Moulton. Street Books is "a bicycle-powered mobile library serving people who live outside." You won't find the librarian shushing anybody, and there aren't any fines for overdue books. That's

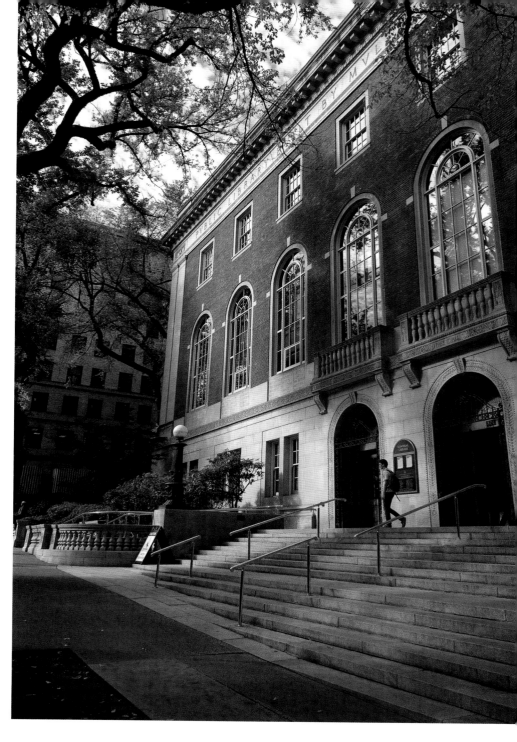

because patrons are just asked to return books they check out when they're able.

"Early on, naysayers said that the books wouldn't be returned," writes Laura on the Street Books website. "To be honest, we didn't know whether or not this was true. We decided to operate the library on the assumption that people living outside have more pressing concerns than returning a library book, and that every time a return came in, it would be cause for celebration. Four years into the project, patrons have returned with their books, or sought us out to tell us they'd be unable to do so."

Laura is happy that Street Books has "fostered engagement between our patrons and the housed community, and good books and conversations form the bridge."

Opposite page: When Powell's Books remodeled its building in 2014, the overhead beams were exposed and left as is to reflect the history of the building as an automobile dealership. When they wanted a memorable phrase for the wall behind the cashiers, Powell's staff invented the word "smellbound" to convey the magic of real books. As CEO Miriam Sontz says, "You can't fine the scent of books online." **This page:** The entrance of the grand Multnomah County Central Library downtown practically lures visitors in the front door.

People in Portland love libraries so much they often create their own out on the streets where they live. Like the blue one below, made from used doors, set in the parking strip along a typical southeast Portland street. I'm always surprised that I keep finding more and more of them. Portland may well be on a mission to end booklessness.

And this is why you must keep alert at all times in Portland. Because you never know what you're going to find.

Random treasures abound.

Photo by Jan Darby

Opposite page: The St. Johns Library is one of the lovely neighborhood libraries in Portland built in the Carnegie era. It is part of the Multnomah County Library system that is the busiest in the country. **This page:** Above, Librarian Laura Moulton introduces Street Books to a man visiting Right2DreamToo. On the left is one of the many impromptu little libraries that pop up pretty much everywhere in Portland neighborhoods. Below, these are the books available now. Yes, science fiction nearly always has its own shelf in this town. ■ Quilt information on page 214.

When Words Flow Like Water

Portland is also a poetic place. You will find poetry boxes in every neighborhood. Oregon has some very famous poets. Like William Stafford, who is no longer with us, but his poems will be here forever.

My favorite famous poet living in Portland is Elizabeth Woody. She won the American Book Award in 1990 (at age 30!) and, from 1994-96, was Professor of Creative Writing at the Institute of American Indian Arts. And that's just the beginning of what she's accomplished. And is still at it. Even her Facebook posts are poetic. I just don't think I've ever met anyone anywhere who is better at words or more brilliant.

We photographed Liz at Portland's new Poet Beach, a stretch of sand and rocks on the Willamette underneath the west end of the Marquam Bridge that carries Interstate 5 over the river. Let's just say I hope the traffic noise does not cause poet's block. It's, uh, kinda way loud.

Liz's early years were spent in and near the Confederated Tribes of Warm Springs Reservation of Warm Springs, Wasco and Paiute tribes. She started making art at a very early age. "According to my aunty, who has this drawing, I started with

drawing a saltine cracker with pencil on paper," Liz remembers. "As soon as I could hold a pencil or crayon, I drew everywhere: the multi textured walls in the dining area, sequential images of a story on pages of notebook papers in a binder, and scrolls from a butcher roll of paper. I recall pulling a piece of my saltine drawing off and sucking out the salt," Liz laughs. "My favorite instrument was my grandfather's ink pen. He allowed me to draw with it. I made the tiniest pictures with it. I loved the ink's qualities with different pressure and strokes."

Liz says she was never interested in poetry. "It was lyrical language and stories of my family and community I loved. People say I wrote poetry in high school, which I don't recall." In her senior year, the chair of the high school English department asked her to submit some work to the Oregon High School Writers program. "I sat on the back porch and summoned up some feelings and wrote two poems the night before deadline. The only reason I tried was James Welch, a Gros Ventre novelist, was one of the persons teaching. The other was Sandra McPherson, actually a living poet. I was interested in meeting them. We were in writing workshops with them for a week while staying on Lewis and Clark campus. Sandra said I had an ear, and unusual word choices for sound."

The high school principal proudly posted in the hallway the letter from the writers program congratulating the school for producing such a fine writer. That same week, the vice principal expelled Liz for truancy, even though she had all her credits. She got her GED in 1978 and, ironically, the vice principal then asked her to teach art in the school's summer program.

"My high school art teacher worked many years later to lead the charge where the state gave me an honorary diploma in 1994," Liz says. "But since I only had a GED, instead of applying to art school with my black and white photography, I had to go for a general education. I took all the writing classes at PSU and then applied with writing samples to the Institute of American Indian Arts, majoring first in Creative Writing with Phil Foss, but eventually going for a double major in 2D arts." Liz has published three books: *Luminaries of the Humble, Seven Hands Seven Hearts, Hand Into Stone,* and her poetry, essays and fiction have been widely anthologized. Liz is a visual artist, has coordinated a science and technology program for K-12 students, was a studio manager for artist Lillian Pitt and served as Director of Indigenous Leadership for Ecotrust, a Portland nonprofit that is "working to build a new economy that restores nature and invests in people." Now she is a program officer at Meyer Memorial Trust

Her strength and resilience are breathtaking.

"I grew up in the house my grandfather paid for in cash," she says. "We spent our time on the reservation where he worked. They moved to town so their children would not have to commute the hour to two hours a day to school and back. In 1973 our house burned down, my grandfather died in the house fire. I saved my grandmother and sister. We moved to HUD housing in Warm Springs."

In 1983, Liz moved to Portland. "Because I did not have a car or job, I lived in a subsidized Single Room Occupancy room and ate out of soup kitchens, and on food stamps while I wrote the first drafts of my book *Hand into Stone*." That's her book of poetry that won the American Book Award, given for "outstanding literary achievement."

Liz has very powerful role models. "My aunty and mom are geniuses, and have done great work to make Portland a better place for Native Americans."

Liz describes how her mom helped start "the first free clinic in skid row, the first free, pay-as-you-can cafe, and became the first woman to be an alcohol and drug counselor at Native American Rehabilitation Association of the Northwest and served on the founding board of one of the first urban Indian centers in the country. She also ran the American Indian Movement house in Portland. The one where the FBI was parked 24/7 in front."

Her mother was also instrumental in establishing the use of American Indian Spiritual practices in treatment. "American Indian religion and practices were outlawed at the time in the U.S." Liz remembers. "She was part of the movement that was strong in Oregon that used American Indian spiritual practices for treatment."

"She opted to do these things, and turned down acceptance into Harvard and a full scholarship," Liz says.

I would say that brilliance runs in the family.

Liz is an enrolled member of the Warm Springs Confederated Tribes of Oregon and is descended from the Yakima Nation, as well. "My tribal affiliations are land based and listed as: Wasco/Wishram/Watlala (Hood River to Cascade Locks, OR people), Tygh (Tygh Valley people), Tenino, Milleethlama (People of the Kah-Nee-Ta Hot Springs), Wyampum (People of Celilo Falls), Ty-tilpum (People of the Willamette Falls). This is how deeply connected I am to the land and waters of Oregon."

From her father's side she is of the Bitter Water clan of the Navajo Nation.

Liz says she "loves the emotive quality of language, especially how it can connect people and share multiple perspectives. Persuasive language is used in many contexts, but most times does not include research into multiple perspectives like creative works on the story telling level."

Storytelling is her passion. She speaks of her life as a story unfolding:

"I am earth and part of all life. I come from the earth, am nurtured by the earth and will return to the earth. All of its life is my energy source, and all that I do gives back. It is a cultural legacy of my ancestors to know this."

Opposite page: One of the hundreds of poetry boxes planted along Portland streets. **This page:** Poet Elizabeth Woody feels at home along the banks of the Willamette River, near where her ancestors lived and told stories that became her way of being in the world.

■ Quilt information on page 214.

Pieces
of
Portland

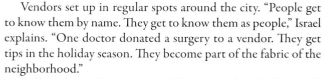

It's no secret that newspapers are literally shrinking. Portland used to have two daily papers. Then one. And today our city of 600,000 plus does not have a daily printed newspaper. *The Oregonian* is printed four days a week and its page size, thickness and number of staff seem to be dwindling, along with advertising and paid subscribers.

The free weeklies are still standing, but it seems to me their focus is increasingly going online, which is mostly the only place I read them. From every corner, I hear people whispering, "The media is dying." It's hard to avoid feeling depressed, especially for someone who came of age in the Watergate era when it was the press that uncovered a scandal that eventually brought down a president.

But all is not doom and gloom. There is a print newspaper in Portland that is actually expanding, increasing its publishing frequency. Beginning in January 2015, it moved to a weekly edition, from a biweekly publication since 2003, when it grew from a monthly.

I'm just going to say it. *Street Roots* is the Portland paper I most enjoy reading today. I'm not saying that to be nice. And I'm not the only one who thinks so. After publishing for only seven years, the Society for News Design called *Street Roots* "one of the best, if not the best, street papers in the country." Since then the paper and the nonprofit organization's leaders have won a boatload of awards.

Street Roots began publishing monthly in 1999 to address issues of poverty and homelessness in Portland, topics the organization didn't feel other publications were covering.

Beyond producing journalism, the paper is designed to give people who are living in poverty and/or are houseless a means to earn income by becoming vendors. They buy a copy of the paper for 25 cents, and sell it for $1. Over time, income from selling *Street Roots*, along with support from the nonprofit's hard-working and amazing staff, has helped prevent several hundred people from becoming houseless, and enabled hundreds more to find homes. More than 70 people sell *Street Roots* at any given time, with sales topping 40,000 papers a month.

"Ninety-five percent of our vendors now have health insurance," Executive Director Israel Bayer says, "and more than 60% have a primary care doctor. That's the kind of thing that changes the course of lives."

Vendors set up in regular spots around the city. "People get to know them by name. They get to know them as people," Israel explains. "One doctor donated a surgery to a vendor. They get tips in the holiday season. They become part of the fabric of the neighborhood."

"When the vendors get treated like people, light bulbs go off. They gain self-confidence and begin to rebuild their lives. They start saving for first and last month's rent."

Being a vendor is hardest on people who grew up in Portland, he reports. "They are horrified that they'll run into their sweetheart from high school. There's such a shame factor for these people. We also have a bunch of Ukrainian men who are vendors. They show up in suits and carry the newspapers in suitcases. Selling *Street Roots* is their profession."

Street Roots staff helps many vendors work through issues, which might include mental illness and other health problems like addiction. Vendors include ex-prisoners.

In addition to its newspaper designed to be "a catalyst for individual and social change," Street Roots publishes a comprehensive list of resources and services for people living in poverty and/or without homes. It also advocates for the population it serves at local, state and federal levels. "*Street Roots* started out as a charity buy—people loved to buy it to help out, but nobody read it," says Israel. "Now we're taken seriously for our journalism. We've broken stories, we've done in-depth investigative reporting on serious issues that have had an impact."

For example, the Northwest Housing Authority cut 300 Section 8 housing vouchers (that subsidize rents for people without financial resources) in Astoria and gave people 60 days to move out. "None of the local press picked up on it, so we did a series of stories about it. Nancy Pelosi, who was chair of the U.S. House of Representatives at the time, quoted from our story on the House floor to get more Section 8 funding," Israel says.

Another story brought to light the abundance of houseless people with traumatic brain injury, who were misdiagnosed and not receiving proper medical treatment. Its reporting fueled a change in social service agency intake forms, now being adopted across the country. *SR* reported on how people with Asperger's syndrome were affected by changing their diagnosis to autism.

Many stories are the work of Managing Editor Joanne Zuhl, who has received several awards for her in-depth investigative reporting from the Society of Professional Journalists.

Street Roots doesn't report directly on homelessness as much now. "We monitor other media in our area," Israel explains. "A lot of them have taken on the homeless issue now. We stop covering things when we would be the fourth iteration of a story that comes out two weeks late. Rather than follow press releases

Opposite page: Lori Lematta sells the latest edition of *Street Roots* on her regular corner in downtown Portland. She is one of the 70 vendors earning an income by selling the weekly paper. **This page:** Street Roots Executive Director Israel Bayer talks about how the paper has helped hundreds of people who don't have a permanent home earn a living and get off the streets.

■ Quilt information on page 214.

Pieces
of
Portland

or the newest scandal, we want fresh content, we want to cover what other media doesn't."

To do that, *Street Roots* relies on people in the community. "We are a staff of eight, we can't do it all. So every 4-6 weeks, we bring our Brain Trust together. It's a group of very smart, diverse, unique people from different arenas. We ask them what's going on, what's not being covered. That's how we plan our coverage."

In some ways, Israel's early life wasn't all that different from the people Street Roots serves. He calls himself a trailer park kid from around St. Louis without much formal education who dropped out of school in the 10th grade. He bounced around the mid-South, Deep South and Midwest for a while, eventually making his way to Denver. "That was my first urban experience," he said. "I lived in a Latino neighborhood, worked the graveyard shift in a convenience store, and I saw a little of everything."

On a whim, he took a road trip to the Pacific Northwest with a friend. "We were driving through the Columbia Gorge, and I was blown away. Everything was so green. I'd never seen anything like it. It just felt like home."

Israel first lived in Seattle where, during the World Trade Organization protests in 1999, he was at the wrong place at the wrong time, got arrested and spent seven days in the King County jail. His cell mates included longshoremen, Greenpeace members, anarchists and a rabbi.

"Everybody had to give half hour classes in whatever they knew something about, from how to hop a freight train to how to fix a car to how to do civil disobedience and on and on. At night, the rabbi told the history of the Jewish people." Those seven days changed his life and introduced him to a new way of thinking.

So when he worked the graveyard shift at a convenience store at SW 4th and Washington in Portland, he read and read and read. He worked graveyard and on-call shifts at social service agencies and began volunteering at Street Roots, and was hired as executive director in 2007. "And I've been married to Street Roots ever since," he smiles.

In 2010, Israel received the Skidmore Prize, awarded to community leaders no older than 35 who make less than $35,000 a year.

For the first five years, Street Roots was strictly a volunteer operation with no paid staff. Now there are eight who are paid a living wage, with benefits. When Israel started as executive director, he admits he had no idea how to run a nonprofit. "It's been trial by fire," he smiles. "We did everything through pure grit, sweat, blood and tears." Grants from McKenzie River Gathering supported the organization through the first several years.

"Then a devout Buddhist who is a life coach became interested in Street Roots, and he coached us in strategic planning," Israel remembers. "He helped us change the board and work more on

development, and off we went. It took us three years to start to see a real turnaround. We all dug deeper and figured out how to engage the community more, how to boil down complex issues to make a difference. It made us a lot more confident and gave us a sense of maturity. Four or five years ago, things started popping. The movers and shakers started paying attention to us," he continues. "Foundations like Meyer Memorial Trust began to fund us."

From its office in Old Town, Street Roots has a front row seat on the poverty ecosystem of Portland and sees how complex and nuanced it is. "A lot of people don't understand this, but we openly work with opiate addicts," Israel says. "About 10 percent of our vendors are active users. Selling papers is what keeps them from stealing to support their habit, and out of the criminal justice system, and we think that's better than the alternative. The police know who and where the active users are, and there's kind of an understanding that if they squeeze Old Town too hard, the users will go into downtown and the businesses don't want that. So they pretty much let them be as long as they stay out of trouble. It's a very complex issue."

§

I would be remiss if I didn't at least mention some of the many other ways we use our words in Portland.

For the past 30 years, Literary Arts has an Arts and Lecture series that brings "celebrated writers, artists and thinkers" to Portland's biggest downtown venue, usually attracting audiences as big as music concerts. Sometimes bigger. Literary Arts is taking over Wordstock, the book festival that began in 2005, with the next event planned for November 2015 at the Portland Art Museum. Literary Arts also brings authors to high schools to inspire student writing and awards prizes and fellowships to Oregon writers.

And oh do we love to read. It is an undisputed fact that every person in Portland is in a book group. Well, let me rephrase that. Every woman I know in Portland is in at least one book group. Some are in several. I guess it's really true that reading is fundamental!

Joyce and I are in a book group together. We call it the World's Smallest Book Group because there are only four of us. We started out with more but some dropped out for unknown reasons. We have our meetings at a restaurant for Sunday breakfast. Right now we meet at Bread and Ink. A most appropriate venue, wouldn't you agree? We started in September 1990. Three of us are charter members, and one joined a couple

Opposite page: Overlooking the printing area of the Independent Publishing Resource Center in southeast Portland is an impressive sight. **This page:** An IPRC staff member demonstrates the use of a letterpress.

of years later. We still consider her status probationary. We aren't accepting applications because the noise at Bread and Ink gets too loud for more than four people. And the place before that had booths that only seated four. So there's that. And one more thing. I'm not naming any names but some of us might be on the curmudgeonly side and don't like change.

Live storytelling is incredibly popular here. In some ways, storytelling is the new poetry, as in there are now twice a month story slams. And of course there is a Portland Storyteller's Guild. BackFence is where the storytelling started in Portland, and now it's so big it fills the Hollywood Theatre or Disjecta and has several series of events, including a storytelling roulette contest where you spin the wheel to get a story idea then have five minutes to make up a true five minute story. Cray-cray!

If you have an embarrassing story, head to Mortified. If you have more serious material, you might want to take workshops from Portland Story Theater and become an Urban Teller. The most unusual storytelling event I've heard of is Testify, "a musical storytelling revival" that describes itself as an "irreverent experiment of queer storytelling and music" that is "a radical sendup of tent revival meetings." In a coffee shop. And of course The Moth radio show makes appearances in Portland.

Another great wordy Portlandy place is Reading Frenzy, a "small, specialty bookshop/gallery/event space devoted to supporting independent/alternative media and culture." It has many zines, anthologies, comic books and graphic novels. Microcosm Publishing is another thoroughly Portland wordy place that "emphasizes skill-building, showing hidden histories, and fostering creativity through challenging conventional publishing wisdom with books and bookettes about DIY skills, food, zines, and art."

In 1998, Chloe Eudaly and Rebecca Gilbert founded the Independent Publishing Resource Center (IPRC), where thousands of people create and publish their own artwork, writing, zines, books, websites, comics and graphic novels. It's so very DIY and there are so very many classes and workshops in how to do lots of stuff. One can do all the verbs: Make. Mail. Print. Compute. Archive. Exchange. Research. Publish. Browse. Create. Learn. Talk. Bind. Read. Many people think IPRC is one of the most awesome things found in Portland. And they are correct.

Which brings us to writing. You can learn a lot about writing in Portland. And you can expect to be invited to join a writing group at some point.

The best known writing program in Portland is Write Around Portland (WAP). WAP is about writing, of course, but it's also about respect and community. It offers 10-week writing courses that change lives and build community. Participants go on to complete their GEDs, attend college, stick with treatment programs, transition back into the community after incarceration and break cycles of abuse.

The writing is shared through readings and published anthologies. It's pretty darned phenomenal. Between 1999 and 2014, WAP held more than 600 workshops for more than 4,400 people and published 45 anthologies. It's now serving as a model for programs in other states.

Because everybody has a story.

April 1,
2015

Perfectly Portland Post

$1
FREE
if you
promise to
share your
copy

Documenting Portland's Unique Essence One Page at a Time Since the First Weird Thing Happened

City Expands Cat Urine Recycling Program

Volunteers Sought to Implement Collection Among Feral Cats

After a successful trial among domestic cats and their human companions, the City of Portland is expanding its program to collect and recycle feline urine to the many feral cats roaming the Portland area.

"We realize feral cats present more of a collection challenge than house cats," Portland's Mayor said. "But we're certain our city's entrepreneurial spirit will come forward once again to provide innovative solutions."

Several local makers invented tools to collect urine from domestic cats. The best known is EpicSponge—a liner with extraordinary absorption qualities when laid on the bottom of cat litter boxes—that was developed at a local open design space in inner southeast Portland and is now sold at all retailers in the city.

The Neighborhood Office of Reuse Every Single Thing (NO-REST) reported that a record 1.8 billion ounces of feline pee was captured in 2014. The liquid is sold to local craft breweries as flavor enhancers and alternative health care providers who create a variety of wellness potions in their artisan formularies. Portland has more artisan formularies than any other city in the world and has the only ones that process cat urine.

"The city gets a tidy sum of revenue from our feline recycling program," the mayor said. "Without it, we would have to shut down the City's Recycled Chewing Gum DodgeWad leagues. If this expansion goes as we expect it to, we could make Portland the home of the DodgeWad Olympics, another untapped source of tourism."

FERAL CAT COLONIES—City expects vacant areas where untamed cats gather to be among first visited by entrepreneurs who see a promising future in feline urine.

Portland will provide protective gear to volunteers who collect from feral cats. "We don't want the public to take unreasonable risks going after wild cats," he said, "but you don't become the weirdest city in the country without putting a few lives and limbs on the line now and again."

The City will work with SCAT (Stray Cat Alliance Theater)—a local nonprofit that stages street theater events to bring awareness to the plight of stray cats—to design collection protocols. It reports it may offer financial incentives for the first few months until the program catches on.

NEW
For 2015
Portland Marathon—
Divisions For Vegans,
Nude Senior Runners,
DIY Footwear Designers & Makers

Inside This Issue:

- **Exposing Portland Celebrities Who Don't Recycle**
- **Anarchist Group Adopts Strict Governance Rules**
- **Aggressive Behavior Training for Portland Natives**
- **NoPants Max Ride Day Expands to Month of July**
- **Council To Consider Ban on Auto Use During Daylight Hours**

I Read the News Today, Oh Boy...

Nothing shakes Portlanders out of our comfort zones more than a forecast of snow or ice. And it's a good thing because most of us have no idea how to drive in those kinds of inclement conditions, so we are all in a world of hurt unless we just stay home. You know those crazy winter driving videos that go viral, the ones where an SUV loses control at the top of a very long hill, then slo-mo slides down a long icy street, slo-mo bouncing back and forth off parked cars, all the way to the bottom, like a billiard ball caught in a perpetual slo-mo ricochet? Well, 98% of those videos were filmed on Portland streets.

In the first place, we don't get a lot of snow most years. Some winters Portland proper doesn't even get a flake. Its rarity means it's pretty easy to whip up excitement and drama among the populace. We go into a kind of anticipatory trance, where we imagine horse-drawn sleighs dashing through the snow, transporting us across town where our friends are roasting chestnuts on an open fire. So imagine our disappointment when all our hopes and dreams come pouring down around us as regular old rain.

But since snow does happen sometimes, and once in a while we experience a snowpocalypse, we have to be ready. For something. Schools are often closed upon the perceived threat of snow or ice, but it can be a moving target because sometimes at around 5 a.m. the schools announce they'll be open as usual, then at 6:30 a.m. comes a new message that they'll be closed after all.

Just as well, because otherwise we might miss local TV stations covering the storm. With the first flake, you can pretty much count on them canceling all regular programming and going with 24/7 storm team coverage. Reporters will be shivering on the Sylvan Hill overpass, monitoring traffic and reporting on the cars crawling uphill, slip sliding off the highway or into one another or just flat out stopping, with cars being abandoned and drivers walking little short-short stutter steps across a six-lane freeway.

Other reporters will be dispatched to Troutdale, where they will try to remain upright while standing on solid ice in the face of 60-mile-per-hour winds slamming down through the Columbia Gorge, at the edge of an frozen freeway where truckers are still trying to make it home by midnight. This is, of course, pretty much worst case scenario weather news. What makes it amazing, though, is that intense coverage begins before an actual weather nightmare commences. Which leaves us pretty much watching live coverage of pretty much nothing yet.

And of course it all plays out on social media. That's where some of the best on-the-scene reporting occurs. Fortunately, there's a hashtag: #pdxtst

Because we happen to be close to the edge of so many things that affect weather, it's very challenging to predict here. More snow and ice predictions are made than actually materialize. But television people have to be ready...it's kind of a thankless job because people pretty much hold them personally responsible for what does or does not happen.

Oddly, it seems to me that our worst snow comes when it's not predicted. Like a few years ago, after all the television weather people told us we would be snow free, a snowstorm began midday and kept on going, and no one in the entire city could get home that night. You do not want to be a television weather person in Portland when that happens. I believe we have actually adopted a special false witness protection program for such cases.

Another thing about local television news in Portland is they always need to find a local connection. Earthquake in Turkey? Surely we can find someone whose son or daughter is in Turkey right this very moment to interview. No? Well, can we find someone who moved here from Turkey? No? Has anybody in Portland ever been to Turkey? Oh, your neighbor's sister-in-law's uncle's cousin by marriage has a neighbor who was in the Peace Corps and traveled through Turkey after leaving her assignment in Lesotho 26 years ago? Get her on the phone now, and send a camera crew stat!

If you doubt that Portland is no longer a small city, just watch local news. A friend from a real city, Chicago, was astonished to discover that when the Trailblazers played the Bulls in the NBA finals a number of years back, local news anchors traveled to Chicago and broadcast the news show from there. In Chicago, it was hardly even a sports story because the Blackhawks were playing for the Stanley Cup! Bulls playing for another championship? Ho hum, been there, done that.

I feel especially sorry for reporters on slow news days. I swear there are days when the race to fill 90 minutes of local news goes to places no one ever thought they would go. Pretty much anything becomes newsworthy when that happens. Like the time we got 20 minutes of coverage of a cat that had gone rouge and attacked its owners. The saga went on for days. I think they're still doing updates. And there was the time I actually saw a story about a car accidentally running into wet concrete. Film at 11.

We get a lot of "person-on-the-street" interviews, and most of those interviewed end every sentence with the words "and stuff." How does this happen? Is it a tic?

It's not just television news that goes to desperate places. Last year, *The Oregonian* tweeted that actor Al Pacino had been spotted dining in a downtown restaurant the previous night. It wasn't in a gossip column, it was a news story! Geez, news people, act like we've been here before. I rant responded.

 The Oregonian @Oregonian   329d
Al Pacino makes surprise visit to
Portland restaurant:
ORne.ws/1i1IQL4

 Marie Deatherage @mariad...   329d
@Oregonian omg are you seriously
reporting that al Pacino ate dinner
in pdx as a news item??

 The Oregonian @Oregonian   329d
@mariadeathstar We are tweeting it
as info ppl may be interested it.
It's our 2nd most RTed story today
after 22-pound attack cat.

Please direct me to the express lane for resigning from the world.

Just how long has a Portland theater been showing *Rocky Horror Picture Show*? Every Saturday at midnight since 1978. And yes, it's the longest continuous running of *RHPS* in the world. Sometimes there are virgin games before the show, which still involves much audience participation, and yes you can throw rice and toilet paper and snap your rubber gloves. There's also BIY but I'm going to let you discover what that means on your own. Costumes encouraged.

The movie still draws crowds here. I wonder if it's the same people every week or if people take turns.

Clinton Street Theater shows lots of other movies, often things nobody has heard of. I think it's probably the indiest of the indie arthouses in Portland, which has more arthouse screens than in other city per capita.

The Hollywood Theatre is an official tax-exempt nonprofit organization, and also hosts independent films and community events. The pre-screening of the first episode of *Portlandia* played to a full house there, for example. Yes, of course we went.

Many of the smaller independent theaters haven't been able to finance upgrades to a digital projection system, so are good places to see low-budget and older movies.

To have this many indie theaters, Portland has to have a lot of cinephiles. And we do. That likely explains why film festivals

are so popular here. Although I have not witnessed this myself, I've heard that people fight over PIFF tickets. PIFF (Portland International Film Festival) is the biggest and best known, and gives us a chance to see many many foreign films that we might not otherwise discover.

We also have the Portland Film Festival, NW Film and Video Festival, Northwest Filmmakers Festival, Oregon Independent Film Festival, Power of Women Film Fest, Portland Queer Film Festival, Portland Queer Documentary Festival, TopDown Rooftop Festival, H.P. Lovecraft Film Festival, REEL Music Festival, Experimental Film Festival, Portland Underground Film Festival, African Film Festival, Latino Film Festival, German Film Festival, Filmed by Bike Festival, Motorcycle Film Festival, BikeSmut, Flicks on the Bricks and even a Faux Film Festival. And yes, I'm sure I missed some, don't hate me.

Say, I wonder if this veritable fount of festivals is related to our prolific rain?

There are multiple ways you can learn to make your very own movies in Portland and meet with other people making theirs. You can take classes and workshops at the Northwest Film Center and NW Documentary. There's a Stumptown Movie Makers Meetup Group and so on and so forth.

Portland and Oregon are beginning to see more movies and television projects shot here too. We have a great variety of natural and built environments, along with an unlimited supply of mood lighting, aka degrees of cloudiness. There is a Film and Television Office in the Governor's Office whose job is to work with producers to help them choose our places as a location for their projects. Oregon offers financial incentives: a 20% rebate on movie-production expenses and a 16.2% rebate on production payrolls costs for movies with budgets of at least $750,000. These are cash rebates rather than tax credits, so the movie makers recover money faster than in other places. And, of course, we always remind everybody that Oregon has no sales tax. The State office reports that $10 comes in for every $1 rebate that gets returned.

The Film and Television office says that more than 400 feature films and television projects have been made here, with several blockbusters like *Twilight*, *Goonies*, *Animal House*, *Stand by Me*, *Free Willy* and so forth. Portland is the location for television series *Leverage* and *Grimm*, in addition to *Portlandia*.

Sometimes movies provide a historical record of places in the city that disappear. For example, present and future generations might never know Corno's but for *Breaking In*. Corno's nostalgia trigger warning!

But more than big commercial ventures, Portland is best known for independent films, like the ones Gus Van Sant makes. He lives here, and I used to see him walking his dog through the parking garage of the building where I worked. Several of his films (e.g., *Drugstore Cowboy*) capture something of the essence of part of Portland's gritty eccentricity.

Some think independent is too mild a word for a lot of the movies made here, coining terms like "superindependent" with "low-fi misfit values." Many come from personal passion, with

the knowledge that commercial success is unlikely at best. And here's the thing: a whole lot of people in Portland are not out to make a bunch of money. Ostentatious displays of wealth are not widely admired here. We do admire large gifts to charitable institutions, however, like the one Phil and Penny Knight made to help Oregon Health Science University cure cancer.

I have the fondest memory of attending my first movie in Portland. It was at the old Movie House on southwest Taylor, since closed. I don't remember what movie was playing, it was what happened before the movie that I'll never forget. First, a woman came out and welcomed us to the movie, talking a bit about it. That was new to me and it was a lovely touch. Then she told us about the short we would see before the feature. It was the first thing made by a local artist, Will Vinton and his Claymation studio. The little film was called *Closed Mondays*. I had never seen anything like it

and I just fell head over heels in love. Yes! I wanted to live in a city with people doing things as brilliant and creative as that! Since then, Phil Knight bought Claymation, now known as LAIKA. Phil's son Travis is president and CEO it's continuing to make a name in animated, stop-motion and computer-generated films.

Recently, an even more alternative film group has come to my attention. The Church of Film is a completely free, volunteer-run gathering of people interested in obscure films. The more obscure the better.

You may be wondering why there is a picture of a quilt next to a bike rack in this section. Here's the deal: near the end of the 1990s decade, the Hawthorne Bridge was shut down for nearly two years as it was repaired and upgraded. Businesses on Hawthorne Boulevard and commuters who used the bridge were in a world of hurt for a long long time. Then, what seemed like minutes or hours after that project ended, the bridge was closed to film a movie, *The Hunted*. Seriously? Hadn't we suffered enough?

To soften the blow, the movie company paid for a "bike oasis" on Hawthorne. BFD. But I wanted you to see it.

Which brings us to the subject of *Portlandia*. Yes, we love it! And we recognize our friends, neighbors, acquaintances, coworkers, compatriots, and so forth in each episode.

Not ourselves though. We're nothing like those people.

Opposite page: The bike shelter built on SE Hawthorne Blvd. to thank commuters who had to use another bridge for weeks while scenes from a movie were filmed on it. This page: The Clinton Street Theater is one of the many independent movie houses in Portland and is best known for showing Rocky Horror Picture show every week since 1974.
◾ Quilt information on page 214.

Pieces
of
Portland

Index to Quilts

Pieces of Portland

YES, BUT...!

HAVE WE CREATED
WHAT WE WANT?
CAN WE DO BETTER?

Is Everything Perfect in Portland?

Based on all these wonderful and wacky things I've described so far, one might assume that Portland is Utopia and everyone wants to move here and that no one ever leaves. And there is never any criticism and everyone loves us. Well, one would be wrong.

Portland has its haters. And they are very outspoken, sometimes posting mean manifestos as they leave. Often with a sense of bitter betrayal flowing through their words. Like we promised we would be perfect and they would find nirvana here. Only they didn't.

So let's go through the top eight points in their critiques:

1. Portlanders are passive aggressive.

I think what people who complain about this mean is that Portlanders are loathe to tell you to your face all the innermost thoughts they have about you. And they think Portlanders talk about them behind their backs. I think there is an element of truth to that. But I think we come by it honestly.

Here's the thing. Native Oregonians are a pretty naive bunch. We grew up in a wonderful setting. On a daily basis, we encounter moments of beauty that take our breath away if we are paying attention. We don't like to be unhappy, so we lean toward bliss. We are the flannel version of west coast chill. Go with the flow. Hang loose. We don't really want to go aggro on anybody.

Now I want to be clear that it's not all a bed of roses. Portland has a high suicide rate. A lot of people are depressed. Hard drugs are a big problem. There's a very gritty side of the city.

There is a wide gap between the haves and have nots. Maybe not as wide as bigger cities, but we have places nicknamed Snob Hill, Trendy Third and Felony Flats.

But most people you encounter on a daily basis are from the lemon into lemonade bunch. You find that most people are pretty dang friendly. We're not big on putting on airs; most of us don't have ambitions to rule the world. We genuinely like most people. Our lives are pretty hassle free, when you compare them with big cities where senses are assaulted daily, the air might not be healthy to breathe and people have to scramble and scratch their way to get a tiny sliver of pie.

It is actually true that if someone cuts you off in traffic, they will likely pull over at the next opportunity and apologize.

So, unless we are raised with abuse and violence at home, we don't develop a defensive hostility that lies just beneath the surface, ready to blast someone without warning at a perceived slight. Others call that being honest, but to us it kinda just feels like being mean.

My own experience might help clarify it. Here's how it works for me: I start out loving everybody I meet. When I see behavior that is hard or impossible for me to love, I will tell you if that's the only way I can set things straight. Since that's really uncomfortable for me to do, I will pretty much just try everything to avoid engaging with you, including constantly changing the subject or staying quiet. And that's after I toughened up in Chicago for four years. But four years wasn't long enough to learn to do flat out confrontation very well.

I lived in inner city Chicago long enough to alter my perception, however. I remember the first time I went grocery shopping when I moved to Eugene in the fall of 1971. The checkout clerk noted my items and asked me if I was going to a picnic and within the first 20 seconds, began interviewing me to ascertain my biography. I was stunned and appalled. I was almost all like "WTF!? What's with the third degree? Just operate the bleeping cash register." Then I realized that I had just experienced years of grocery shopping where the clerk didn't even make eye contact, let alone speak to me. And remembered how I learned about "oversharing in public" when I arrived in Hyde Park. By the time I left Chicago, I no longer expected politeness and had learned to be suspicious of it.

I dated a guy from New York City once. One of his hobbies was pointing out and ridiculing the backward ways of Oregonians. Nothing filled him with greater glee than catching me or some other Oregonian mispronouncing a word. To my Oregon heart, it felt like he was wound so tight he was gonna explode and splatter.

We just don't get why anybody wants to live that close to the edge of anger. I'm not sure we have the right conditions for producing that in Portland. We can't help it. It's the culture of our place. And to tell us to change, to start confronting you with our opinions at every turn, that makes as much sense as going to the *Real Housewives of New Jersey* and telling them to modulate their volume, dress more age-appropriately and stop with the overdone makeup. I'm not sure one should expect to move to a place with a different culture and expect it to change so it's just like the one you came from.

Yes, I too remain astonished that every performance of any kind almost always results in a standing ovation in Portland. We like people to feel appreciated, we want them to be happy, we want to show our respect for their efforts, if nothing else. And really, where's the harm? If our culture bothers you, and you don't want to adapt, you will probably never be happy here. Unless complaining and making fun of people is your hobby.

I suppose if enough people from other cultures come here and bring their culture with them, the persona of Portland might change. As people move here from aggressive aggressive environments, I wonder if natives of Portland and Oregon will become more like them or if they will become more like us. Time will tell, but here's a question that might help guide us: Which approach is more authentically of this place, more like that established by its First People?

And we should probably tell you that nobody is talking about you behind your back nearly as much as you think they are. That's not our happy place; we don't even think about you that much.

Oh dear, was that passive aggressive?

2. Portlanders are annoyingly sanctimonious.

I have it on good authority that there is now a bumper sticker that reads, "Keep Portland Sanctimonious." There is painful truth in this statement. Sometimes I am so afraid I'll make a mistake and someone will notice and point it out. In public.

Like being at Laughing Planet and someone sees you put a plastic fork in the landfill bin when everybody knows perfectly well that it goes in recycling because they use biodegradable plastic. Of course. Nothing ever goes in the effing landfill bin. We don't believe in landfills, that bin is there to remind you of all the bad that happens when you don't live in Portland.

Or when a friend looks at your household cleaning products and sniffs, "You use something with chlorine?!? Don't you know what that does?!" And you just know she's going to out you among all your mutual friends. And you are desperately hoping she didn't spot your secret stash of oven cleaner or tarnish remover. The shame can be overpowering. No wonder our suicide rate is so high. But people really do feel they are failing when they let anything go that might harm the environment.

3. Portland has become too self-satisfied.

Another thing that's kinda true. I think it can be partly traced back to the underdog status we had for so long, when people either didn't know we existed or could not even manage to correctly pronounce the name of our state. Rather than roll ones eyes at our over-enthusiasms, perhaps one could take a more charitable approach and forgive us for being amazed and then proud we are being noticed, let alone that others are envious of our qualities.

We're on another "best of" list? Of course we are, we smile. But secretly, in the back of our minds, we are worrying somebody made a mistake and they will redo the math and the revised list will come out tomorrow and we will lose our newly admired status.

I don't know how long it will take for us to truly feel as cool as we hope to be. I think that might be partly why we laugh just a little too loud, and clap just a little too long at public performances. To some extent, we are reassuring ourselves and others that we get it, that we are the cool kids at school now.

Some find this off-putting. I understand where they're coming from. I find myself feeling a little embarrassed by it at times. But if you stop to look at things from our perspective, from a position way under the dog, it can look a little endearing. Like a child who discovers for the first time she can keep her balance with the training wheels off and immediately heads to the next county.

4. There's nothing to do in Portland.

Oh geez, just stop! Are you even conscious? There is everything to do in Portland. Maybe because we're all so amped up on caffeine, we need endless activities to use up our energy. We attend things in record numbers. Every activity has a waiting list before it opens. Even waiting lists have waiting lists. Younger folks do serial events in an evening. There's kind of a laid back approach—everybody knows you committed to more things than a human can possibly do in a given time period, so they understand why you are three hours late to everything.

It's true that Portland is not a very fertile ground for growing outsized egos. If amassing a huge fortune and wallowing in the conspicuous consumption that affords is your thang, you may well find more plentiful pastures elsewhere. Because we probably aren't gonna sit around and be adoring fans, and we don't want to be in your posse. Maybe people who think there's nothing to do here just want to do the wrong things or have extremely limited imaginations that prevent them from starting something that hasn't been done yet. And I feel really sorry for them.

5. People aren't friendly, it's hard to make friends.

I will admit this one has me puzzled, because I've never found this to be the case. I think I've made friends as easily in Portland as anywhere. It usually happens when you and other people are brought together through a shared interest or experience, rather than going out "looking for friends." And believe me, there are plenty of opportunities for that in Portland. Starting with good ole Meetup. Has anyone started a Meetup for people who are looking for friends? Maybe it could be called Friendless in Portland. But then people would either have to quit or change the name if they became friends, wouldn't they? Maybe there should be levels, like from Friendless to Overfriended.

Now there's one scenario I have observed. If there are a group of women or bros who formed their group of friends in high school and/or college sorority or fraternity, then returned or moved here as a group, it's probably not easy to join the group. They might think they are complete as is. If I were you, I wouldn't bother trying, but that's just me.

Another issue might be that we're already overextended. Like we can barely keep up with our life as it is because we've joined too many groups or have too many things going on. A lot of us are like that, if only we had time to consider it and figure out what to do about it. In the meantime, start small, go where the beer is and talk to people. (No extra charge for the life coaching/relationship building advice.)

6. It's impossible to get a job here.

Some people believe that Portland really is a place young people go to retire. Because there are no jobs. Fiddlesticks! There are a lot of job openings. Despite anecdotes, as economist Joe Cortright recently pointed out, Portland's unemployment rate of 4.8% for people with college degrees ages 24-35 is actually lower than in other cities like New York, Chicago, Atlanta, Los Angeles, etc.

But, here's the thing. There are a lot of people applying for every job, and I'm just gonna guess that employers are often overwhelmed with huge stacks of applications so you might need to do something that makes you stand out from the masses. Many of Portland's good paying job openings these days require mad skillz and experience. If you know Ruby or Python, you're prolly good.

7. Portland is changing, losing its weirdness.

Yes, I see changes and some of them really bother me. I believe this is something we need to worry about. As Rick Turoczy asks, "Are we making the bold decisions people in Portland made 40 years ago that have made what we have today possible?"

I don't really have complete confidence that the best people to make these decisions are in the positions of those who will make them. In the scramble to fund city services, it feels like decisions are skewed to increase the city's revenue, often at the expense of the city's more quirky places and people.

We must require a transparent, accountable government and decision-making process. And we the people are the only ones who can make that happen. More power to the people!

8. Portland lacks diversity and is too white.

Well, this one's gonna take a while. Please turn the page.

Pieces of Portland

Know Better to Do Better

Caucasian Americans of Portland, we need to talk. By the way, I'm one of you. I've been thinking long and hard about this all the while I've been working on this book, trying to figure out how to say what I'm about to write. Some things will make many of us uncomfortable. Some of them make me uncomfortable. And I feel pretty vulnerable thinking that I, an educated professional grownass granny of six, is sticking her neck out to tell it like she sees it about this topic. But I must.

It would be so much easier if we could pretend we were starting with a clean slate and just go from this day forward. But our slate is not clean, and we can't go forward in good conscience and trust one another if we don't examine the dirt and wash it.

Portland is said to be the whitest of the largest cities in the U.S., with a non-Hispanic Caucasian population of 72.2% in the 2010 census. That's not as white as it was in 2000 (78%), or 1990 (84.6%), or 1980 (87.5%). The city's demographics have changed considerably since 1940 when Portland was more than 98% white. It's just that other metropolises have seen more growth in diversity than Portland, which was the 29th largest city in America in 2013. Only eight cities grew faster than Portland from 2000 to 2010 in the nation's top 50 cities. Portland's metropolitan area has about 2.3 million people, the 19th largest in the country.

Here's the deal. A lot of the things that make Portland different—that make it weird, that make it so attractive to the creative types who move here—are not all that meaningful to people in Portland whose life path has not put them in a place to drink nano-brewed beer, eat artisan ice cream or commute by bike from the distant neighborhoods where they now reside. Rather, they are trying to figure out how to feed their children, pay the rent and keep the car running or how many bus transfers it will take to get to their minimum wage job.

Somebody once explained Portland's quirkiness by saying this is what happens when white people go wild. They have a point. A lot of what happens in Portland requires a kind of "what, me worry?" vibe. At all moments, we want to raise the level of fun and merriment in our lives. We love feeling free to get out the paint and create art. People like it when we make stuff. Our instincts and aesthetics are constantly validated. Portland feels just like home, where we belong.

When I try to imagine what it must be like to watch those antics from the have-not side, the words from that Gil Scott-Heron song keep running through my mind, the one he did in 1970, soon after the moon landing.

A rat done bit my sister Nell
with Whitey on the moon
Her face and arms began to swell
and Whitey's on the moon...
Was all that money I made las' year
for Whitey on the moon?
How come there ain't no money here?
Hm! Whitey's on the moon
Y'know I jus' 'bout had my fill
of Whitey on the moon
I think I'll sen' these doctor bills
Airmail special
to Whitey on the moon

Kind of hard to get all amped up for a naked bike ride when it feels like life keeps biting you in the ass.

It wouldn't hurt for white Portlanders to show some sensitivity and humility along the way. I'll try to help by providing some reasons to do so.

We have to begin with the fact that other people already lived on this land when the white folks showed up. They were doing just fine, living fulfilling lives, in harmony with the land, water, flora and fauna. Their culture was astonishingly rich. There is not one single thing anyone can say to justify the fact that whites introduced diseases, took their land and lives and more or less rounded up the few who remained and contained them in places we didn't want. The treaties that had been agreed to and signed by the U.S. government were widely ignored and broken. It's downright shameful.

When a place and a culture experience that, both the perpetrated and, yes, the perpetrator suffer until there is restorative justice. I believe the trauma from that history affects all of us today, because none of us is as good as we can been if we keep the past hidden and deny what got us to this point.

Other injustices followed. We still use the railroads that Chinese men built for us, in conditions that were inhumane, arduous and horrifically dangerous. Then we forbid them from owning property in our state and sent them packing when whites felt economically threatened.

When Oregon became a state, it agreed to ban slavery. But our forefathers (yes, all men; women couldn't even vote) just outright forbid the presence of African Americans. But when Uncle Sam needed the sweat of their brow to help build ships for World War II, African Americans were allowed to move to Portland in large numbers for the first time. And they were nearly all housed in a temporary community developed near the Columbia River. When it flooded in 1948 and they looked for new places to live, they were restricted to a small area in northeast Portland, where they built a community. But then, when Portland wanted land for Memorial Coliseum, it seized sections of that neighborhood and destroyed many homes and businesses, and the people who lived there had to move again. (We'll get more deeply into this issue in the next section.)

And, of course, Japanese Americans were rounded up and sent to prison camps away from the coasts during the war, losing their homes, businesses and possessions in the bargain. In Portland, 3,676 people of Japanese descent were confined to the Portland Assembly Center for five months in hastily converted animal corrals at the Portland International Livestock Exposition while waiting for transfer to permanent camps in other states. The Portland Expo Center is located there now.

Ever wonder why the same wasn't done to German Americans?

Opposite page: *The Dream* statue at the Oregon Convention Center Max station features Dr. Martin Luther King as a heroic figure determined to deliver a message of universal equality, freedom and justice to the world, with other figures behind him representing those who have joined the struggle to make the dream a reality.
■ Quilt information on page 228.

Pieces of Portland

I'm not enumerating these things to just make Caucasian American Portlanders feel guilty. I'm saying we must acknowledge what has been done before us, perhaps with the perpetrators justifying their actions because they would make a better world for their children and grandchildren and on and on. Their heirs are many of the Caucasian American people in Portland now. Part of the Portland we enjoy and love today was created through treating people very badly.

When we live on this land now, we bear the weight of the past. And must do it justice. Hear this:

There's a relatively new field of study called epigenetics. *Matter* recently reported that scientists at McGill and Columbia Universities and University of Zurich are finding that when young children are subjected to extreme stress, it alters the amount of a receptor protein that helps "control the hormones that cause stress: the more of the receptor we have, the better we're able to respond to stressful situations. The reverse is also true: low receptor levels are associated with disorganized, chaotic responses to stress."

And in animal studies, the chemical imprints of stress are inherited by the offspring, making them less able to deal with stress even if they hadn't been exposed to trauma themselves. And preliminary studies suggest that they in turn pass the chemical imprint on to their offspring.

When we consider the trauma experienced by whole cultures and peoples in our country's history—those whose land and culture was invaded, those who endured slavery, those whose labor was harshly exploited, those who were rounded up and imprisoned—I wonder if that level of cultural, ethnic and racial trauma sets generations up for continuous trouble and hurt. Especially when daily racially-related stressors continue, as my friends of color experience.

Let's bring that up the next time we hear someone say, "That was years ago, why don't you people just get over it?" Living while being Caucasian American in Portland is easier and safer and healthier than living while being some other color—on the streets, in homes and neighborhoods, shops and supermarkets, schools and workplaces, hospitals and financial institutions, and pretty much every place you can name. I don't have room here to cite all the evidence, but it's easy to find if you want to see it.

When we grow up white in Oregon, we likely haven't had the range of experiences as those who grow up where there are a lot more people, and the people aren't all pretty much alike. If you haven't experienced a time and place where you are the only white person, you can't entirely know what it feels like to be a member of a minority group. Many Oregonians have what I like to call the luxury of cluelessness. While Oregon is becoming more diverse,

the cluelessness hasn't been entirely overcome. But in today's world, it's a luxury.

I'm astonished by some of the things I hear come out of the mouths of perfectly kind and generous people who grew up here. What's even worse, I'm shamed beyond belief when I remember some of the things I used to think and say when my only experience of place was rural or small town Oregon, even when I intended to be sensitive and helpful.

I'll never forget something that happened at the first event I attended during orientation week in college. It was a university in what then was the second largest city in the U.S., which had a tense relationship with the African American neighborhood just across the midway, because that was the direction the university was expanding. The event was a Black Power Panel. This was in September 1967, right after a summer when black neighborhoods had burned. A young man on the panel announced that he hated all white people. I was stunned. "How could you possibly hate me," I asked. "You don't even know me."

That's when I started learning that we can't go through life assuming that all our relationships are based on in-person experiences. There is a context, a history that surrounds all our interactions. It is our responsibility to learn as much as we can about that history so we better understand one another. It would be arrogant of us to do otherwise. You might be talking to the grandchild of someone whose business and home were demolished by the Memorial Coliseum project. You know, the building Portland can't figure out what to do with now, that sits mostly unused, and might be torn down?

It's not enough for one's heart to be in the right place. Once we realize there were wrongs in the past, we assume the responsibility of getting clued in, despite the fact that we weren't the ones who did the evil deeds. We also need to understand and admit the ways we Caucasian Americans may have directly or indirectly benefited from them. Often that means spending time in other places and with people unlike ourselves. Or by reading and other forms of self-education. For those of us who grew up without diversity, we can acquire it. And I believe we must, for both others' sake and for our own.

As Maya Angelou said, "I did then what I knew how to do. Now that I know better, I do better."

This page: Clara Peoples was honored in the Oregon Wall of Women for introducing Juneteenth to Portland. She came among those moving here during World War II and found that many of Portland's African Americans didn't know that June 19th is set aside to remember the day the slaves got the news that they were free at last.

◾ Quilt information on page 228.

That job belongs to all of us. And to all the Caucasian Americans who now feel victimized by immigration and affirmative action and diversity education, the ones who say they are being discriminated against now, I want to remind you about that dirty slate. Which is not yet clean.

One of my closest and best friends, a professional, middle-class, well-educated woman my age—who told me I understood her better than anyone she knew and I shared more of myself with than most anyone else I've known—is dead because she was an overweight black woman. In her final days, she reported a sudden horrible pain and numbness in her jaw that went down her left arm. She went to the emergency room and also to her own primary care physician, several times, and came away with a diagnosis of TMJ (basically, a pain in the jaw joint). She tried so hard to get a diagnosis and medical help. To live. Her children found her lifeless on her bedroom floor the morning after her 53rd birthday. She sent me an email just before she went to sleep that night, likely her last living communication. Her doctor said an autopsy was not necessary and wrote coronary disease as her cause of death. She came in with classic symptoms of a heart attack and you didn't do an EKG or check to see if she had any blockage in her arteries? You didn't treat her? Really? How dare you?

What if she had been a white man? My Caucasian American husband had chest pain a couple of years before she did, and when he went to the ER, he got an immediate angioplasty and stent, and it saved his life. My friend had great health insurance. She was educated, and very articulate. She advocated for herself. She followed up. So how do we explain the difference to her children? Knowing what I know now, I regret to inform you that she died of racism. My heart breaks missing her and I'm still angry that she wasn't treated as well as my husband. And that I didn't just drive to her town and demand that she get treatment. The presence of a white friend might have helped. #thatreallysucks

The whole idea of race, of course, was invented by people; we are all from the same first humans. And now genetic research is revealing our decidedly mixed DNA. Our physical differences are the result of isolation due to human migration and settlement patterns. As global connection and exchange increases, that isolation is diminishing and our made-up races are becoming less distinct. Someday future cultures will wonder what all the fuss was about and why our era was so unenlightened.

In summer of 2014, a small group of Caucasian Americans went to the Immigrant and Refugee Center of Oregon to hold up their large banner that read "Diversity = White Genocide" across the building's entrance. Why you gotta be so rude?! And ignorant? Do you not know that many immigrants to the Portland area are from former Soviet republics and European nations? And they're white, just like you. Or can only Caucasian Americans born here be white? Besides, this ain't "best in breed" at a damn dog show.

I think most people have good hearts and want to be kind. But a lot of how we live now was developed when racism was built into many of the systems and institutions we still live with today. As Caucasian Americans, we don't have to be racist ourselves to benefit from systems built on past legal racism.

Wealth accumulates in families when passed down through generations. The most common form of wealth in families is home ownership. But think how few generations it has been since African Americans, Chinese Americans and others were legally permitted to own property in Portland, and how very limited their options were. And how recently they have been subject to overt legislated discrimination that totally disenfranchised them both politically and economically. No wonder a Pew Research Center study found the wealth of an average white family is 13 times more than an African American one, 10 times more than a Hispanic family.

As children in Portland families grow up and go out to make their way in the world, higher education is much more readily available to young adults from high-income families than those from middle- and lower-income groups. I am stunned sometimes to observe the power of networks among professional white Portlanders. These connections pave the way and ease the passage for internships, experiences and employment opportunities for their children and others they choose to help. Families who are not part of these networks don't even realize how far behind the starting line they already are before the race begins. You understand there is no such thing as equal opportunity when you see what happens behind the scenes. Hence, the need for and development of affirmative action.

Of course, there are a lot of white families who don't get the benefits of those professional networks either. I certainly didn't and neither did most of the people I grew up with in rural and small town Oregon. My grandparents and their children (including my father) eked out a living picking cotton in Oklahoma, before fleeing west out of the Dust Bowl during the Great Depression. My mother grew up in an actual log cabin and her father killed himself because that was the only escape he saw from debt because of the Depression. Kinda left his family in a world of hurt, though. And that was just the beginning of the family's trauma. So a lot of us white folks struggled along our paths through life, too. We didn't benefit from the privileged networks I described above. But when any of us acquired means, we weren't limited or treated differently because of the color of our skin. We didn't have that extra layer to get through before we could progress.

Please let me live to see the day when our entire community comes together and tells the truth, hears one another out, acknowledges the wrongs, and figures out how to deal justly with what has been done so we can go forward with understanding and pride? When that day comes, as I believe it must, a great burden will lift from the city and we will all be better for it.

I have seen so many promising signs lately, I think the tipping point is here. In 2014, Oregon Humanities sponsored conversations led by PSU Professor Walidah Imarisha titled "Why Aren't There More Black People in Oregon? A Hidden History." She met more than 1,000 Oregonians and introduced them to a timeline and program she developed to take the past out of hiding. Several of our state's biggest foundation's are working to figure out ways to make equity a reality in Oregon. Know Your City is helping. Civic groups and city officials are learning about how racism has been part of what created the city we love.

In 2000, the U. S. Census added multiple races as an option in its racial composition section. The percent of people who identify that way increased by 32% by 2010. I think there will come a time when most people in the United States will check that box. Many of us are far from "pure bred." And I'll wager that includes the folks holding the White Genocide banner.

We need to listen. Talk. Learn. Then do. But first, a related topic.

In the last half of the 20th century, home ownership was the American Dream wagon that most families hitched a ride on to begin to accumulate wealth that carries over to the next generation. Those who didn't have full access to home ownership were denied the American Dream.

The biggest consideration I had when buying my first home—the one I still live in 37 years later—was that it be close to public transportation and be within walking distance to services like a grocery store, etc. I had been greatly shaken by the gas shortages in the early-1970s, when people waited in line for hours just to get gasoline in their cars. I thought it was a glimpse into the future, and the best defense was to live where one didn't need a car. In fact, for several years of my first decade in Portland, I didn't own a car.

My house is in what is now known as the Hawthorne part of inner southeast Portland, in the Buckman neighborhood. In PSU Professor Carl Abbott's comprehensive study of Portland in *Portland: Planning, Politics and Growth in a Twentieth-Century City*, he classified Buckman as a "stopover" neighborhood that was close enough to downtown and affordable enough for people in low-wage jobs. It was seen by planners in the 1960s and early 1970s as beyond salvage and would inevitably be demolished and replaced. Old houses were being razed, replaced by cheap ugly apartment buildings so investors could make money until the neighborhood was replaced. Commercial streets were lined with dive bars, second-hand stores, porn shops and other low-rent businesses.

Almost 40 years later, it's a neighborhood that's undergone what's called "gentrification." But it happened organically. As the old-time residents of both homes and apartments aged and became frail, many moved to assisted living centers. Others died. The turnover in ownership happened fairly quickly, as long-time residents were pretty much all in the same age bracket. Most of us who moved in didn't have a lot of money and were not part of the gentry class, so it stayed a very affordable neighborhood for another 10-15 years. Now it's a mix of single family homes and an assortment of apartment buildings. Those of us who lived here through the 1970s and 1980s, and even into the 1990s, endured some pretty discouraging public drug use and dealing, out of control parties and crime. But in the last 10-15 or so years,

the neighborhood has been transformed and housing prices have jumped. Today it's a highly-sought-after part of town.

About five years after moving in, one day I took an informal inventory. We had, within a three block area, a woman who had been a child in Hiroshima the day we dropped the bomb; another woman from Japan who knew almost no English but we managed to communicate well enough to figure out we shared a birthday exactly 50 years apart; an African American family whose eldest daughter became a backup singer for Norman Sylvester; a lesbian couple; hippies turning into yuppies; hippies staying hippies; a self-described redneck with a bumper sticker on his pickup that read "Fight Organized Crime: Abolish the IRS" (who later lost his house because he didn't pay any taxes); a white woman nearing 100 whose house had been built by her husband as a wedding gift in 1908 and had lived in it for the rest of her life; an apartment building next door owned by a Korean family; an Odd Fellows Hall that served as the neighborhood polling place; a house of Sikhs; a Hare Krishna house (and the Moonies lived just a couple blocks further down); artists; college students; a Japanese church; and a NBA player. Yes, a Trailblazer on our modest little street, Darnell Valentine. (He's an awesome person!) And oh yeah, with the birth of my son, the disability box got checked off, too.

So when people said Portland was not diverse, I always kinda smiled inside. It wasn't just census category diversity on our street, but a more subtle kind, where you didn't fully realize it until you got to know your neighbors and their backstories. Which means you actually know them, and form a little community.

As I learned more about Portland, I discovered that Italian Americans had tended to settle in one part of southeast Portland, Chinese and Japanese immigrants in part of what is now Old Town, early Polish immigrants had settled in another part, and Vietnamese refugees were landing in another. There weren't the ethnic enclaves like I had seen in Chicago, as there had already been a lot of dispersal among early- to mid-20th-century immigrants.

Except for the African American community. Because of "ethics." Seriously. In 1924, the National Association of Real Estate Boards published its first code of ethics. Article 34 read:

The photo on the left shows Vanport, the largest housing project for wartime workers in the nation. During a flood in 1948, it took only minutes to sweep the temporary buildings away and create the scene in the photo on the right. Fifteen people died and 18,500 were displaced. In many ways, Vanport was Portland's Katrina.

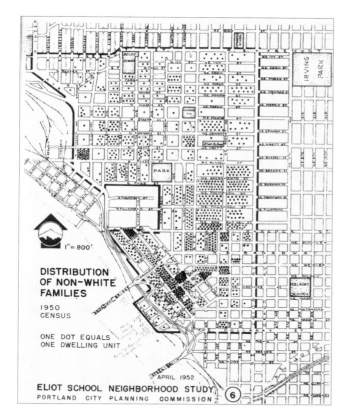

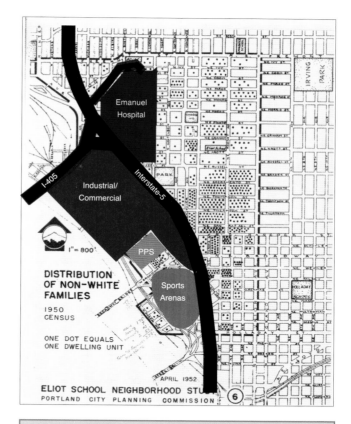

"A Realtor should never be instrumental in introducing into a neighborhood a character of property or occupancy, members of any race or nationality, or any individuals whose presence will clearly be detrimental to property values in that neighborhood." Yes, they put that in writing.

A U.S. Supreme Court ruling in 1948 made those kinds of restrictions unenforceable, and the real estate board removed the reference to race in the code, replacing it with "A Realtor should not be instrumental in introducing into a neighborhood a character of property or use which will clearly be detrimental to property values in that neighborhood." Most acknowledge that race was still implicit, because it was "detrimental."

Portland and Vancouver became a center of shipbuilding in World War II, and some 72,000 people moved here to join the labor force. Many came from southern states and about one-third were African Americans. There wasn't enough housing for this population bubble, so a housing project was built on land next to Columbia Slough between the Northern Pacific rail line on the west and Denver Avenue outside the city limits. Called Vanport, it was the largest wartime housing development in the nation and the second largest city in Oregon. It was built in 110 days, with apartments and homes made of fiberboard walls resting on wooden blocks. Vanport's population was 42,000 in December 1944, and its housing was racially segregated, although its schools, community center and businesses were integrated.

After WWII ended, about half of the 20,000-25,000 African Americans who had moved to Portland stayed here. Many continued to live in Vanport. On Memorial Day weekend in 1948, the Columbia River flooded (its flood season is in late spring from snowmelt in the Rocky Mountains). A railroad embankment not designed to be a dike was breached and water flowed into Vanport. The 18,500 residents had only 35 minutes

WHAT HAPPENED TO RESIDENTIAL PROPERTY IN ALBINA? The map on the left shows the location of each non-white household in Albina in 1952. Compare it with the map on the right, which has been altered to show what happened to the land where homes of African Americans were destroyed, beginning in the 1950s and continuing for decades.

to escape and 15 died. The rest of them lost everything they had.

I think it's fair to say that Vanport was Portland's Katrina. Thousands and thousands of those displaced were sent to temporary trailers and barracks on Swan Island and drained wetlands in northwest Portland. Conditions were deplorable. Some lived there for as long as four years. During the 1950s, many African Americans looked for housing in and around Portland's metropolitan area. Despite the recent Supreme Court ruling, realtors and owners found ways to make sure homes in other parts of town weren't sold to African Americans, who also couldn't get favorable mortgage loans that were available to white buyers.

Most African Americans who stayed in Portland were limited to an area between Oregon Street on the south, Russell Street to the north, the Willamette River on the west and what is now Martin Luther King Blvd. on the east. Its proximity to the rail yards and station made it a convenient place for the earliest African Americans to settle in Portland, because they were allowed to be employed as railroad porters. The area was known as Albina.

But when a location for a sports arena was needed in the 1950s, the city declared the area where African Americans had been confined blighted and replaced it with Memorial Coliseum (yes, that same one that the city can't figure out to do with now and might be torn down). Interstate 5 took out another large part of Albina during the 1960s. Twenty-two blocks of the neighborhood were

Pieces
of
Portland

demolished for expansion of Emanuel Hospital. Then in 1973, the hospital put on hold the third phase of the expansion after federal funds were cut back. A block at the very heart of the Albina neighborhood—at Williams Avenue and Russell Street—is still empty more than 40 years later.

So the neighborhood where African Americans had been sent, the only place available to them, was systematically erased through actions funded by government. African Americans who had lived in lower Albina were steadily forced out—more than once in many cases—moving north to the Boise, Humboldt, Vernon, Sabin and King neighborhoods.

In the 1970s, *The Oregonian* investigated the mortgage business in Portland and found damning statistics, like loans being made in predominantly African American neighborhoods only one-sixth as often as in other parts of the city. This drove down property values, reduced home ownership and left residents vulnerable to unscrupulous lenders.

By the 1980s, these further north neighborhoods of Portland were predominantly African American. The median home value was 58% lower than the city's average. Rental housing was neglected by absentee landlords, and when gangs arrived in the 1980s, the area became rife with violence and drug dealing. Homes were foreclosed, sometimes by the county when property taxes went unpaid, and houses and businesses became vacant and were boarded up. By 1990, two neighborhoods in northeast Portland—Boise and King—had 26% of the city's abandoned homes. City commissioner Gretchen Kafoury led a charge to bring a halt to predatory lending and get local entities to direct community reinvestment funds to the neighborhoods. Houses that had gone into foreclosure because of tax liens were transferred to community development organizations, who improved and sold them. But there was no provision to ensure that people from the neighborhood purchased them.

During the 1990s, demographics began to change, but in the 2000 census, there were still 10 tracts in northeast Portland that were majority African American. Between 2000 and 2010, a huge shift took place. Commercial streets saw a big influx of businesses, especially the artisan small businesses we've seen examples of earlier in this book. The percent of white residents grew markedly, accompanied by a corresponding decline in African Americans.

By 2010, not one single census tract in northeast Portland was majority African American. Not only had Caucasian Americans moved in, but African Americans moved out. In the King neighborhood for example, there was an almost complete switch in racial composition of the neighborhood: in 1990, it was 64% African American and 30% white. By 2010, it was 26% African American and 60% white. The neighborhood lost 1,123

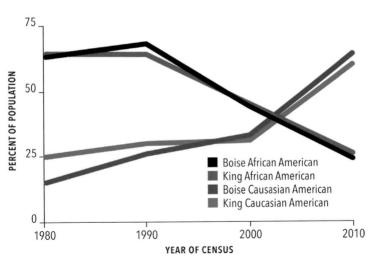

Racial Transition in NE Portland 1990-2010

Boise African American
King African American
Boise Causasian American
King Caucasian American

African Americans between 2000 and 2010. Census data for the Boise neighborhood transition shows how it escalated after 2000 as well.

A study reported in *Governing Magazine* found that Portland was the city with the most gentrification in the 21st century. Census tracts that reported median household income and median home value in the bottom 40th percentile of all census tracts in the metro area were considered eligible for gentrification, which occurred when their stats moved up into the top third percentile of all tracts. It found that 58% of eligible tracts in Portland in 2000 had moved to the top third by 2013.

Why did this happen? Why, after African Americans had been displaced again and again, even from the only places in the city they were allowed to buy homes, why are they losing their homes again in the 21st century?

First, a bit more history. When Portland developed a plan to address segregation in its schools, for a time it adopted forced busing, but only in one direction. Black students were sent out of their neighborhoods, but white students didn't have to go into their empty seats. This had a demoralizing and devastating effect on schools and neighborhoods that were traditionally African American. The high school sports teams were the pride of the community. It was a big blow to neighborhood identity, and those who were affected still speak of it with pain and bitterness.

Schools in African American neighborhoods were behind white schools in test scores and family income. People who worked inside the district have privately told me that at one time, the least experienced teachers were assigned there. Students counted on fewer resources to supplement and encourage their education. Over the decades, Portland Public Schools developed plan after plan to address the inequity. But there is still a significant gap in test scores and graduation rates between students of color and white. African American students are more likely to get expelled from school. Portland Public Schools was sanctioned three times between 2009 and 2014 for expelling African American special education students at a much higher rate than white students. Nonprofit organizations and government programs have been developed to provide some of the missing resources, and their efforts have made a huge difference in the way individual lives have gone and are going. But the number of students they serve is limited by the donations they can raise.

When white people started buying homes there, housing market values and prices went up in short order. Property taxes rose. Because of unfair policies and practices already described, African Americans are less likely to inherit wealth, get a good education and/or training that leads to a high-paying job, be offered a conventional mortgage or have well connected networks to tap into that provide entré into valuable careers and social circles of power that drive upward mobility. African Americans are more likely to get pulled over by police, be asked for identification, get arrested, go to jail/prison and be killed by police.

So it's no wonder they are not able to keep up with rapidly rising rents, house prices and property taxes in their neighborhoods. And since all people with lower incomes are more likely to be victims of predatory lenders, their financial status is more fragile. In many of Portland's inner city neighborhoods, we homeowners get near constant offers in the mail from developers to buy our homes. With so many foreclosures during the Great Recession, investment firms began purchasing residential real estate to cash in when property values rise again. Portland is one of the cities where that is happening; its property values have been among the most rapidly rising in the country in this decade.

The story has a pretty predictable ending. Renters leave for more affordable places, homeowners sell or lose their homes to foreclosure. Since young creative artisans who move to Portland wouldn't dream of living in the suburbs now, the only place the displaced African Americans can afford are places far from the center of the city. Often, these are areas with limited services and underdeveloped infrastructure, few parks and greenways, and more likely to be close to industrial areas and further from jobs and everything they are used to.

The turnover in my neighborhood was a more organic process that began when homes naturally emptied. Later, midway through the first decade of the 21st century, there were instances in our neighborhood when people were evicted from apartments as they were converted to condominiums. Many homes across the metro area have been demolished, replaced by huge houses, row houses or apartment complexes. New apartment buildings are sprouting like weeds once did in inner southeast Portland where I live, and people are worried that the culture of the neighborhood is changing, with aging hippies being replaced by hipsters of the urban artisan persuasion.

Several times a week, I get offers in the mail to buy or sell my house. One realtor enclosed a $1 bill as a down payment. Some days it feels like there is a target on our home. There would be more profit to be made, jobs created and property taxes paid to local governments, if the old homes on our block were replaced by new row houses, condominiums or fancy apartments. The city coffers will be enriched were that to happen, and I imagine the City rather likes it when there is more money in their budget. I'll probably be that last batty old lady whose house is surrounded and dwarfed by the multi-story buildings that will rise around me, yelling "Get offa my lawn!" to the developers circling like sharks. Oh, that's right. I don't have a lawn. And assuming I can afford the property taxes.

There is a lot of talk about trust funds fueling many of the housing purchases by young people in our neighborhood and others. I have no idea if that's true, but it certainly could explain the presence of funds for a down payment, and I see resentment building. But inner southeast has weak grounds for resentment compared with northeast Portland neighborhoods. We got to choose where we live, limited only by what we could afford. I've never been turned away from housing because of the color of my skin. But I saw that happen with my own eyes to an African American man. Yes, in Portland. Ask me about it sometime.

But there is no doubt that the racial makeup of some northeast Portland neighborhoods has seen a seismic shift. I have no doubt that data from the 2020 census will show that the northeast Portland neighborhoods have become more white, while outlying areas to the east of I-205 see increasing diversity, with low income folks of all identities locating there.

And that shows why this move by African Americans is different than in the past. In the past, their forced moves were to adjacent or nearby neighborhoods. So the city's African Americans remained within range of their churches, services that met their unique needs (for example, many hair salons and barber shops in other parts of Portland have nobody trained in African American hair), community groups, advocacy organizations and other institutions. The things that make people feel they belong in a place.

When I hear Caucasian American Portlanders say it's racist for Portland's African Americans to lay claim to a neighborhood, I am embarrassed. How many times must their survival skills be tested? Can you imagine what it must feel like to be treated so callously that your very homes and streets are bulldozed, by the government that collects taxes from you. I'm told by long time residents of northeast Portland neighborhoods that they used to live in thriving neighborhoods, a testament to their strength and perseverance in the face of blatantly unfair real estate practices. They came together in spite of discrimination and formed a community, one that withstood sequential government-sponsored assaults on its existence and resiliency.

What moral obligation is there for the Caucasian Americans who moved in—especially those who used inherited money to help make the purchase, thus benefiting from the chain of unfairness that eventually drove African Americans out—to hear their grievances and work together to restore justice to those who were wronged?

When I was finishing this text, I came across a Restorative Listening Project in Portland. The name may have changed to a Restorative Action Project and it appears that it meets monthly. I tried to gather some information about it but it was too late to stop the presses.

I have been looking for ways to end this look at Portland with reasons for hope. Hearing that a restorative listening and/or action project exists is heartening. I will continue to explore it after this book is printed and add it to our website.

I found some specific people and projects that give me enormous reasons for hope and you will see them soon.

Just yesterday I heard about a very interesting and innovative art installation by Pamela Chipman called "Jumptown Video Wall." She put four video touch screens among the bricks of a building facade in a new housing development in northeast Portland. The small screens show continuous video loops of historic photos and recent footage shot in the neighborhood. Kind of a then and now view of the neighborhood that was once home to a thriving jazz scene, commercial district and homes.

When I heard about this art, I thought, "That's an interesting and novel thing for a building to have, I think I'll check it out."

But there was a nagging feeling of discomfit I couldn't shake. I remembered I had the same feeling when I looked at the mural just off Alberta Street in the photo on the next page. The plaque next to it explained it was a gift to the Alberta Arts District from Art on Alberta in 2010 to "honor African

American leaders and Alberta Street history."

Then it hit me. These are museum things. When the real thing is gone, we design exhibits that depict what once was, in order to show something that has been lost. To have these things memorialized like this made me sad because it feels like an official admission that a real African American presence in northeast Portland is over. It makes me feel like we've given up and moved on, now it's just history.

Is Portland really ready for this? Or am I misreading things?

§

Like many urban areas, when cars came into widespread use after WWII, the effective commuting limit expanded considerably, so suburbs like Gresham saw housing booms as commuters sought less crowded spaces than were available in the inner city. As a result, many urban areas had donut rings of skipped over land during the rapid growth of the 1950s and 1960s.

That happened in Portland, resulting in a ring of unincorporated land on the east side between Portland and Gresham. Before it was developed, much of the land had been small farms. Neighborhoods in this ring look different: while there were some planned developments, many streets are unpaved and lack sidewalks, much of the development was haphazard because county infrastructure standards were less demanding than those of Portland, and more than 65,000 homes had cesspools because there was no sewer system. Property taxes were comparatively low and some of the services in the area (e.g., police, infrastructure) were subsidized by the higher property taxes paid by city residents.

In the early 1980s, the City of Portland needed more industrial land that had urban services (like water and sewers) and wanted to reduce the amount its residents were subsidizing services to those outside the city. Multnomah County wanted to focus on its priorities (e.g. assessment/taxation, elections, correction, courts, human services, etc.) and hand over police, parks and land use planning to the City. To accomplish this transition, Portland annexed much of the unincorporated area up to the Gresham city limits by 1994. Because the cesspools and septic tanks were leaking into the groundwater, connecting to city sewers was mandated, property taxes went up and sewage hookup fees charged (although once again the cost of the new sewers was partly subsidized by the rest of the city's residents).

The land area of what is now being called East Portland (or outer east) is about 20% of the whole city in land area, and in 2010, it had about 26% of the city's population, an increase of 18% since 2000. There were fewer locally-based services and amenities like those that had been developed in neighborhoods designed for pedestrians and streetcars. In 1996, a comprehensive plan was adopted for the area that encouraged high density apartments and infill development, with rents more affordable than

in much of the rest of the city. That's one reason why so many immigrants and refugees settle there. Since the early 1970s, Portland's investments in development that contribute to livability have been in downtown and inner city neighborhoods, resulting in rising property values and greatly increased property taxes, which then drive long-term residents from those neighborhoods in search of something they can afford. Usually they move to outer east Portland. The area is more racially and ethnically diverse, although it is still approximately 67% white.

East Portland still lags behind in nearby services and amenities. It has only 13% of the city's park acreage, while 40% of the city's kids live there. Without sidewalks and paved streets, there are more fatal auto collisions and pedestrian deaths than older parts of Portland. People who live in East Portland report feeling worse about city services than residents in other parts of the city in each of the 16 years surveys have been conducted.

All city council seats are at large, elected by whole city, and there's never been a single one from east of 82nd Ave. For several decades the unincorporated area tried to create its own city, but failed after the most valuable industrial land near PDX was annexed by Portland. There is still talk of and another active campaign to secede from Portland, but it's hard to see a path that would make that financially viable.

A city or metropolis is never finished, it is forever a work in progress. City planning is based on whatever paradigm is considered conventional wisdom at the time. Sometimes the conventional wisdom turns out to be wrong because the people who live in cities make unpredictable choices. Then a new paradigm is developed and applied, until once again it becomes outdated. There is a tension between the desire to plan and map everything ahead of time so development is orderly and a wish to just sit back and let market forces rule, allowing spontaneity and serendipity. Both approaches have their costs.

Policies and practices that make sense on paper (i.e., promoting development that increases city revenues so more and better services can be delivered) can force people who've lived in a neighborhood their whole lives to move to a place where no one knows their name. In the past, people with the power to make decisions that affect lives and neighborhoods were sometimes awfully cozy with people who stood to make

This page: The mural was a gift to the Alberta Arts District from Art on Alberta in 2010. It honors African American leaders and Alberta Street history. This cultural identity has mostly gone missing from the neighborhood. Opposite page: East Portland, where prospects can seem as bleak as the streetscape. Not an artisan boutique in sight.

money from those decisions. The average person watches the rich get richer and the poor get poorer. Children without hope sometimes live as if their lives don't matter, and no good can come from that. If we don't figure out a way to bring the people of all parts of Portland together and offer all an equitable chance at a life that the best of Portland offers, I am very worried for our collective future.

Oregon economist Joe Cortright thinks focusing on gentrification distracts us from the most important pressing issue for U.S. metropolitan areas: concentrated poverty. "In the past 40 years," he reports, "the number of high-poverty urban neighborhoods has tripled and their population has doubled, to 4 million. Growing up poor is difficult; growing up in

neighborhoods where a large fraction of your neighbors are also poor is worse, exposing kids to higher crime and lower quality schools, resulting in increased mental health issues, fewer job and educational opportunities, and...permanently lowers life prospects relative to otherwise similar kids who grow up in mixed income neighborhoods." No matter where in our city these conditions exist, they will not be tolerated forever.

And that's where the hard way comes in. Doing nothing will be unacceptably hard on everybody. If we can't muster the will to face and fix the causes of deep poverty for the sake of people who are poor, maybe we will do it to save society. I believe that's what's at stake. Whatever the reason, we have to do this.

People get ready.

Index to Quilts

Some of the quilts in this book are available for purchase from quiltlandia.com

This page: Once you make a certain number of quilts, storing them can be an issue. You don't really want to put them away in a closet where you can't see them. But what to do? After visiting a fine rug store and noticing the racks that held the rugs, I asked my dear hubby to build something like that for quilts. And he did! I love seeing all this color lining one of the bedroom walls..

HOPE

**Before
1992-2011**

This page: Before and after photos of what is now the June Key Delta Center, a living building project the Portland Delta Sigma Theta Sorority chapter created from an old gas station. The property was a brownfield and had been a boarded-up eyesore for years. Its transformation is a powerful story of redemption and an example of how social and environmental justice can be achieved simultaneously in Portland.
Opposite page: Chapter President Jean Loomis is quick to deflect credit for the group's accomplishments to others who came before.

What a Wonderful World

The corner of Albina and Ainsworth in north Portland is where we choose to begin the story of our hope for redemption and reconciliation in our city.

In 1992, there was a derelict boarded up gas station there. Because gasoline had leaked into the ground, the soil was toxic. If there was ever a case for demolishing a building, it was here. That same building is now a thriving community center that is a "living building," which is the most advanced measure of sustainability in the built environment possible today.

And it was the women of the Portland chapter of Delta Sigma Theta Sorority who pulled it off, along with many local people and businesses who contributed time, services and materials.

Delta Sigma Theta Sorority was established in 1913 by 22 women students at Howard University to "use their collective strength to promote academic excellence and to assist people in need." Its first activity was participating in a Women's Suffrage March in Washington, D.C. Today the sorority has around 200,000 members around the world and is a "sisterhood of predominantly Black, college-educated women."

We met with the organization's current president Jean Loomis, who was quick to give most of the credit for the Living Building project to Chris Poole Jones, a Delta member who passed away in April 2014. "We're so happy she got to see the Center open and operating," Jean says. "If it weren't for her, we wouldn't be here today."

The June Key Delta Community Center was named after one of the 10 charter members who pulled together the $2,000 to purchase the abandoned property in 1992. The group began raising funds to renovate the property, and Chris Poole Jones encouraged the group to explore green building.

The Deltas decided that rather than pursue a customary LEED certification, it would go for the Living Building Challenge, which first launched in 2006 to encourage buildings to simultaneously achieve both very high environmental and social equity goals.

"We wanted to show that you could take an ugly site and make it attractive using sustainable resources and recycling resources from the area," Chris was quoted saying in an interview for *Trim Tab* magazine in 2011.

The project nearly doubled the building size to provide meeting space for the sorority's 250 members so it could also be used for a variety of neighborhood activities, especially for youth. Chris worked tirelessly to get all the materials donated.

Here's a short list of some of the building's features:

- a geothermal heating and cooling system has loops as deep as 100 feet into the earth to exchange heat
- solar panels on the roof have reduced the center's monthly electric bills from about $400 to $100 per month, and before long they will earn money from the grid
- used cargo containers were added to the original building and made into the kitchen and bathrooms
- all materials came from within 200 miles of Portland
- the general contractor was a Haitiian-American family business, and 60% of the subcontractors were minority- and/or women- owned businesses

- the parking area is made of permeable pavers so water seeps into the soil below rather than running off into the sewers
- a water reclamation system captures rainwater and uses it as greywater for toilets and irrigation.
- Oregon Tradeswomen Inc., a nonprofit that trains women for the construction industry, donated 633 hours of labor
- the back part of the lot is used for a community garden that provides fresh healthy food for the Humboldt neighborhood.

The Center hosts a number of programs for students, including tutoring, STEM (Science, Technology, Engineering and Mathematics) classes, gardening and cooking classes, and a host of other opportunities for both girls and boys. It plans to add a computer center in the future.

The evening we visited, a Portland Delta member was working with teen girls to get everything ready to deliver and serve food they had prepared to a shelter for houseless families in southwest Portland.

The very day we met with Jean, the Center got word it had won the 2014 Green Power Purchaser of the Year Award from the U.S. Environmental Protection Agency.

During her presidency, Jean has focused on finishing the work Chris started, and it's nearly done, despite the fact that Jean was deployed to Afghanistan twice during her term. Her current project is raising money to commission and place a sculpture of Chris Poole Jones in the front garden to honor her memory. I can't imagine a higher calling.

This is the resilience that shows the strength, courage and capacity of what's left of Albina. After everything that has happened to the neighborhood, and all the injustice done to its residents, these women are the ones showing us it's a wonderful world.

See what we can be, Portland?

Pieces of Portland

Where Kids Range Free

I t was the GPS tracking device strapped to the arm of the few-weeks-old infant who was still buckled into a car seat as she napped at a baby shower that sent me over the edge.

I was already appalled at the reports of parents calling college professors to intervene on their adult children's behalf about grades. In all the years and all the colleges where I taught three decades ago, not once did a parent call me about anything. Even grades. Athletic coaches yes. Parents no.

Not to mention hearing about parents in attendance at their 20-something offsprings' job interviews. Trust me, parents, no one will hire your spawn if you go to their job interview. Never ever.

So the day I heard about infant GPS tracking, I suddenly realized that we have come to a point where our chickens are more free range than our kids.

To be fair, we must concede that society has pretty much made helicopter parenting the standard, and parents who actually let their kids run free are at risk of being accused of neglect or abuse. For example, a Maryland couple who had given their 10 year old and six year old permission to walk home from a park without adult supervision found their children delivered home in a police squad car after someone called to report them. The children were questioned by police and social service representatives, and the parents were warned they could lose their children to protective services. In other places, parents have even been arrested for letting their children walk or play without adult supervision.

We have moved beyond helicopter parenting to velcro parenting. Or maybe handcuff parenting is a more apt term.

If like me, you grew up when during summer kids left the house first thing in the morning, ran through for lunch, then didn't come back til dinnertime—playing with other kids who were doing the same, at the park, in one another's yards or roaming the countryside—this new paradigm just seems unbalanced. Free play allowed us to organize ourselves and negotiate and resolve disputes and who knows what else without our parents interfering and messing up things.

I refuse to get into an argument about whether our places are more dangerous now, or whether we just hear about the dangers over and over again until we are afraid that every single person is a potential child snatcher, but I suspect there is more truth in the latter than we allow ourselves to admit. I certainly hovered over my young child, but I couldn't tell how much of it was related to his paralysis or to ambient contagious fear.

But I'm pretty sure we need to figure out how to let our kids go more free on the range. Fortunately, some have already thought about all this and have created programs that give kids freedom to become confident and caring people who know how to contribute to a family and community.

> **Opposite page: Above,** Terra Fleischer peeks out from the debris shelter he has built so he can survive any kind of weather at Trackers Earth camp. **Below,** an apprentice uses an elk jaw bone to cut grass for a primitive thatched shelter. **This page:** Trackers cofounder Tony Deis teaches his four-year-old son Robin how to safely use a knife to whittle wood.
> ■ Quilt information on page 228.

One such program is Trackers Earth. As its cofounder Tony Deis puts it, Trackers does not believe in tepid ways of doing things. On the day we visited, dozens of extremely well-behaved kids from about age four to 13 were in small groups led by young adults, practicing skills like stealth tracking, evil secret agent spying, debris hut building, axe and star throwing, archery, wilderness survival, animal tracking, folk craft, etc. Unfortunately, we were too late for zombie apocalypse preparation training.

I honestly cannot remember the last time I saw this many kids this engaged. Nobody was slacking, nobody was left out, every child was eager and attentive.

Trackers has summer camps, year-round and after-school programs, classes for preschool through adults and pretty much everything else too long to list. Long term-apprenticeship classes are organized in guilds. Rangers Guild mentors youth in stealth, archery and wilderness survival; Wilders Guild offers wild plant, folk craft and restoration gardening; Mariners guild includes kayaking, fishing and water ecology; and Artisans teaches fine crafts, storytelling and leadership.

When Tony and Molly Deis started Trackers Earth in 2004, 40 kids turned out. Now attendance is in the thousands, at several locations. Trackers was voted Best Summer Camp in *NW Kids Magazine* in 2014 and was Totally Awesome Red Tricycle winner in 2013.

Trackers runs many programs at Roslyn Lake not far from Sandy, a small town on the road between Portland and Mt. Hood.

The Trackers homestead, where the Deis family lives, was previously owned by Joe and Amy Miller, whose lawsuit against the U.S. Forest Service eventually got logging halted in the Bull Run watershed, which is visible from the homestead.

Being there feels something like joining the ends of an unbroken circle to me, as I think the Millers would approve of Trackers Earth.

How does Trackers manage teaching kids risky skills? "I am obsessed with safety," Tony admits. "Our curriculum makes safety a priority, and we make safety a big focus when we train our instructors." Trackers also has a high staff-to-child ratio.

"We are not day care," he explains. "Don't send your kids if they don't want to come. We help kids feel good about being outside and feel accomplished there. We don't grade them. We show them it's about their relationship with the woods and animals, we help them to get to know them like family."

Trackers lives by what it calls the Code of Common Sense, teaching kids four basic things:

1. Pay attention to everything and everyone around you.
2. Be truly helpful. Do what gets results, not just what you want to do.
3. Respect the flow and way of things, the way nature does.
4. You're doing it wrong. You can do it better.

He rushes to explain the last point. "Perfection is boring. Show me perfection and I'll show you someone covering up mistakes. We find beauty in imperfection, because it allows us to learn and improve."

Tony applies the same principles to himself, rattling off a number of times and ways he's been imperfect and learned to improve. In fact, it feels like he is doing it during our interview, as he constantly checks his own words and critiques what he's just said as he explains how Trackers works.

"We're also very much driven by data," he says. "To improve what we do, we try to overcome our cognitive biases with data."

Molly administers the organization, working as many as 80 hours a week. But there's no time for counting, as there are new camps to plan and organize all year long.

"Basically, free play in nature opens kids to a world they wouldn't otherwise get," Tony says. "Once kids have that, they will insist on that kind of freedom the rest of their lives. We give them a scaffolding to apply to the rest of their lives. And that gives them huge responsibility. We want them to be sharp observers, to always be tracking their surroundings. We teach kids to always be looking through their whiskers when they move through space."

Kind of like animal eyes!

Tony left high school after freshman year. "I needed a more functional way to go," he says. He spent a lot of time in his family's three-acre garden and nearby woods. His parents drove him to the Pacific Crest Trail, where he would spend two weeks hiking. "My parents didn't pander to me, but realized they need to flow with me. They would do anything possible for the family. That's what I try to emulate in my own families, both my related family and Trackers."

He explains that pandering would be letting someone be creatively indulgent. Something is creatively relevant when you do something that no one expected that is truly helpful to the family, the community, the village.

"If self-realization is your goal, you'll end up alone and bored. We look for deeper value and connection. We are terminators of stuff that doesn't add value. We call people out when we catch them going through the motions. We don't let people coast on charisma. I don't care what interests you if it isn't good for the village."

Four years ago, Tony became a parent himself and is now the father of a four year old and a two year old. His son Robin is with him during our visit, and Tony has him learning and practicing the same skills Trackers teaches.

"Becoming a parent makes me more paranoid," he admits. "I was always obsessed with safety but it made me understand it in a more visceral, physical way. People have given me their trust. I cannot fail that."

"I had a lot of gray hair by time I was 30," he laughs.

What about Trackers brings him the most joy? "Things go on here that I have no control over and don't understand."

What brings the most angst? "Things go on here that I have no control over and don't understand."

This page: When we visited the Da Tung and Xi'an Bao Bao (Universal Peace and Baby Elephant) in the North Park Blocks—a place we knew to be popular with kids in Portland—we experienced one of those precious moments that show us what it means to be part of a village, where everybody is connected. A man whose mobility was quite limited got off a nearby bench and came over to loan me his grabber and help me put the quilt on the large elephant's back. After Joyce photographed him and while we were taking more of the elephant, he vanished. We've returned several times to try and find him without success. We were so very touched by his gesture and have been looking for him to give him copies of the photos ever since. If you know who this wonderful man is, will you please put us in touch with him? Reach us at www.piecesofportland.com.

■ Quilt information on page 228.

235

They Did Come Home Again

We hear a whole lot about people who move to Portland and what a profound effect they're having on the city. But what about our homegrown talent who are members of the so-called creative class. What's their perspective on the whole Portlandia thing?

I asked two very creative and talented people who grew up in a small town within the Portland metro area, lived in Portland for several years after college, moved to London, then New York, and are now back in Portland. They just bought a home, so it looks like they plan to stay a while.

Amy Sample Ward is CEO of NTEN, a national nonprofit organization with headquarters in Portland that helps nonprofit organizations make the best use of technology to help them meet their missions. She got her bachelor's degree from Valparaiso University in Indiana, where she majored in new media and English. I met her one summer when she worked for a project that shared office space with the foundation where I worked. She spent several months in Spain, then we worked together before they moved to London, so I got to see her brilliance and passion up close. She is truly a force for good.

Max Ward's theater graduate education and career were the reasons for the move to both London and New York, after his undergraduate degree from Lewis & Clark College. Now he works in set design and construction for local theater productions. Recent projects include *Parade* produced by Staged! and the full 2014-2015 season at Defunkt.

Amy credits a lot of her confidence and success to her parents, Tim and Barbara Sample. "My parents are very clear, consistent, and strong so I grew up seeing that as the model," says Amy. They encouraged her to not settle for anything less than her best. Again and again, I've heard Amy say proudly when explaining her go-for-it approach to life with, "I'm a Sample!" Growing up on a farm outside Dilley in rural Washington County directly west of Portland, she did a bit of everything in her childhood, from feeding chickens to playing the cello to surfing a secret place of big waves on the Oregon coast (whose location cannot be revealed).

I don't think there's anything she can't do. Well, I take that back. She hasn't taken up quilting, so she commissioned me to create one as a gift for her parents, shown in a photo on the next page.

Summer acting camp was key in building Max's identity. "I was pretty shy as a kid, and when I was in elementary school, my mother enrolled me in a summer acting camp in the hopes of getting me to open up," he remembers. "I ended up really enjoying my time in the program and it quickly became the highlight of my summers growing up. From there it was a pretty easy transition to joining the high school drama club and 'schmacting' it up on stage.

It wasn't until college that I gradually became more interested in the academic and technical side of theater, which eventually led me down a somewhat circuitous route towards set design."

While in London, after getting his master's degree from the Royal Central School of Speech and Drama, Max worked as a freelance scenic designer, collaborating with the English Touring Opera and other small companies.

It remains to be seen whether he can make a fulfilling theater career Portland. "The theater scene in Portland is incredibly active right now," he says. "That being said, for many people, theater is more of a passion than a career and that transfers to the work that's being produced. There is so much talent and enthusiasm in this city, but the infrastructure needed to cultivate, fund and train all of that energy is lacking."

Max and Amy were living in New York City when Portland became the "it" city.

"It was pretty bewildering for me to be in NYC while the love affair was going on," Max remembers. "I'd read articles talking about all the reasons why Portland is a great place to live and I'd just be like, 'Well, yeah.'"

Amy wishes that *Portlandia* was not so focused on Portland. "I've been surprised that people don't take it as a stage for commentary about any urban center with a good dose of privilege and easy living," she explains. "It could have been set in Brooklyn or Austin or so many other places. It is interesting to me that people from elsewhere seem to want it to be only about Portland."

Are Max and Amy surprised to be back in Portland?

"I really love where I grew up, and recognize that it very much made me who I am," Amy says. "When I was getting ready to go to college, I knew I wanted to find somewhere out of Oregon and out of the Pacific Northwest. Because I loved it so much here, I knew I would come back and I wanted to have at least those few years out exploring and understanding the world from another angle. What I didn't anticipate was that I would then live in Spain and England and have the opportunity to travel all over the world. No place is quite like home, though."

For Max, absence made the heart grow fonder. "If anything, moving away from Portland has given me a greater appreciation of my quality of life," he explains. "New York is an amazing city and a tremendous place to work, however it's an absolutely horrible place to live. Yes, there's a million things I miss about living there but the humanity living on top of humanity is not something I'll ever regret leaving behind."

Max says he has "always appreciated Portland's dueling identity as either a very large town or a very small city. It varies greatly from neighborhood to neighborhood and yet somehow manages to maintain close knit pockets of community all throughout. The people who make up Portland are passionate about their home and are invested in making it a great place to live."

"I love that Portland is a place where you can be who you are," Amy chimes in. "You can find ways to do what you are passionate about, you can create—whether it is creating yourself, your business, or art, music, etc. I think that we have to be explicit in our work to be sure we don't set ourselves up for failure by

Opposite page: Amy Sample Ward and Max Ward, who both grew up just outside Portland, have returned to the city to commit to a Portland and global agenda of equity and environmental responsibility. And they're not afraid of helping keep things weird in their home town.

■ Quilt information on page 228.

Pieces
of
Portland

thinking Portland is Oregon or that only those in Portland are part of the conversation."

"When we lived in the U.K.," she continues, "we were often asked to compare it with the U.S. and when we lived in NYC we were asked to compare it to Portland. Like I said, nothing compares to home. Ultimately, growing up in Oregon shaped us in ways we hadn't noticed until we lived elsewhere. We really value being part of a community and living in a place where people are proud to put down roots. London and NYC both felt like exciting, important cities. But they also felt really transitory. Everyone was there for a certain time in their life but wasn't from there and wasn't planning to stay."

"I want to do what I can do make our city and state and region and world a more engaged, safe, and inclusive one," she adds. "I want to continue exploring. I want to be happy."

Now do you get what I'm saying about home grown talent? This is who we are making here, people! Intelligent, passionate, articulate and kind people, with a love for this place they call home. Even when they leave, Portland is in their hearts. And they do come back.

No wonder I'm so hopeful and optimistic about Portland's future.

I think you can be, too.

Amy's parents—Barbara and Tim Sample—hold the quilt made just for them from their respective sides of the bed. Amy asked for a quilt that would reflect the grounded colors of the earth on the left side to represent her mom, while the right side would represent her dad with colors of water. The sides would meet in the middle and blend. Barb and Tim agreed to pose with the quilt for the photo out in the summer sun, and I feel really bad that it was the hottest day of the year. This is the most still I've ever seen them, as they are both full of energy and enthusiasm and a joy to be around. Of course, Amy and Max's dog wanted in on the action. What dog can resist a quilt?
■ Quilt information on page 228.

DEAREST PORTLAND,

A Love Letter...And a Whole Lot More

Dearest Portland,

So I guess you've heard that I've been writing about you for several months now. I hope you're okay with it, I mean I'm sure there were a few awkward moments. I've been trying to figure out how to wrap this up. There's so much I want to say, but I hate doing the predictable thing so I'm not into some kind of left brain summary.

There's an old and fundamental rule of writing: Don't tell, show. That's what I've attempted to do in this book. Rather than create a master list of what makes Portland like it is, I hoped a reader would gradually build her or his own picture as the story unfolded, a person at a time, an event at a time, a thing at a time. By now I hope readers feel they understand Portland better and know more of it.

So I to wrap things up, I decided to just write a letter to you, and share some of what I've felt, observed and learned. You know, like friends do, just chatting over coffee.

I guess you know I've loved you since I first met you. I was young then, I knew nothing about Portland really, I was just out of graduate school. My husband and I found an affordable little bungalow near 59th and Fremont in northeast Portland to rent and set about exploring our new home.

Within a few months I was teaching Geography at Portland State University, then Lewis & Clark College and Willamette University, cobbling together a means for a living, as so many of us here do. Professor James Ashbaugh had developed a class at PSU called *The Environment of Portland*, and when he took ill, I taught it again and again, among other classes. It was my all-time favorite class to teach. I learned a lot. We covered so many fun topics, students really enjoyed it, too. In fact, I was teaching it years later, until just a few days before my son was born.

Blaine's birth, and the fact that he had spina bifida and hydrocephalus and a few other related things, changed the course of my life. I started desktop publishing a newsletter that was actually more like a zine, but zines hadn't been invented yet—that was a shame—writing about medical, educational and social issues kids like Blaine encountered in terms that were accessible to parents like me. Then I was hired to establish and publish a disability rights advocacy newspaper for Oregon. But those activities did not provide a living wage, nor benefits, and I

was a single parent by then, so I had to find a different job—but one that would allow me to work at home and care for my son during his multiple hospitalizations. There were a lot of surgeries in those days.

That's when I began working for Meyer Memorial Trust. Charles Rooks put his trust and faith in me, for which I will be forever grateful. I had a variety of roles over the 20 or so years I worked there. My work life circled all the way back to the beginning after Blaine had a series of medical issues that landed him in the hospital in 2013, prompting me to retire in January 2014 so I could be more present with him at home.

That's when I started this book in earnest. It turned out I had a lot to say (big surprise, huh?) and what I thought maybe we could stretch to 100 pages swelled to more than 250. You should see what I left out!

So what is this Portland we speak of today? In a lot of ways I think of you and us as pieces of patchwork.

We're still a city with logging trucks on the freeways. At the same time, we're exploring the leading edge of technology, making prosthetic hands with 3D printers.

We are artisans, we are makers. We are crafters, we are skaters. We roast coffee, we craft beer. We're not jaded, we're still dreamers. We tend our gardens with a passion, we are generous, we are silly. We've got hippies, we have hipsters. We are stardust, we are golden, we are billion-year-old carbon. (Okay, those last three came from Joni Mitchell.)

This page: On left, Sage Wolffeather displays the exact reduced-size replica of his vintage VW Van, which pulls the smaller one. Above, we pass a logging truck on I-205 near the Washington Street exit. Opposite page: People dispense free hugs at the attempt to set the Guinness Book record for tree hugging at the Hoyt Arboretum in Summer 2014. At the bottom of the page, a skater takes a break at Burnside Skate Park.

■ Quilt information on page 248.

Pieces of Portland

We take risks, we play it safe. We are a place of contradictions. We are simple, we are complicated, we are right and we are wrong. Bikers ride our streets in fear of being hit by arrogant drivers of cars way bigger than they need, car drivers go in fear of hitting a biker who suddenly appears from nowhere without lights in the dark and ignores traffic signals.

We don't have all the answers, we haven't even discovered all the questions. To a great extent, we are making things up as we go along, and we're okay with that.

Are you with me so far? Did I leave anything out?

Well, of course I did. I confess that I began with a list of about one-third of the things now in the book, but I kept adding to the list of positively-absolutely-had-to-be-included items. There was a point that I feared Joyce was going to throttle me unless I stopped. (Just kidding, she was a great sport even when she pointed out that every time we crossed a photo off our list after she took it, I added two more new ones. True dat.)

Left to my own devices, I would probably still be writing. Well, actually, I am still writing, but I'm about to stop. It feels like I should try to say something important. But as usual, I just started writing to see where it goes.

I thought I loved you, Portland, before this project began, but once I started, I realized I've been taking you far too much for granted. Now I love you infinitely more. Because to know you is to love you and I know you better now. You are the real deal. Again and again, when I approached people to see if they would be willing to participate in this project, nearly every single person or group said yes—even the ones who didn't know me from Adam's off ox (oh, wow, I've been waiting to use that phrase in a sentence forevermore!!)

And the people! Not an arrogant jerk among them. We managed to find passionate, kind, idealistic, generous, skilled, brilliant people at every turn, without even looking for those specific qualities. And here's the thing: I don't think a single one of them has any idea how awesome they are, because they are so focused on their mission.

They don't spend a lot of time looking in the mirror, if you know what I mean. There's something pretty amazing about that. Portland, you attract people like that and bring out the best in them. I hope you believe in yourself now, or at least soon.

Do you ever feel like you are filling a national need among the creative class to have a city on the hill, a place that actually works like we want it to, where artists and designers and makers are admired and supported? Well, there might be a few chinks in the supporting armor, I'll get to that in a bit.

Portland, you have a strong sense of place. And it is such a wonderful place, we are right smack dab in the middle of breathtaking natural beauty.

We live a pretty hassle-free existence compared with a lot of other places. Of course, like on the animal farm, some of us are more equal than others, so the hassle factor is unequal too.

Some of the reasons we appear weird come down to the fact that we are ahead of the game; certain trends that suggest where we are headed either began here or were adopted here earlier and taken further than most other places. If that's weird, I guess we proudly plead guilty, am I right? From people power in lawmaking to more artisan everything to more craft beer to more Project Runway winners to book selling and library circulation numbers to food carts and all the many things we've covered, we are inventing new and better ways of doing things.

There are some weird things I couldn't bring myself to include. Like Cuddle Up To Me, the business that opened here in 2014 to provide people with "safe and secure" human touch, followed by the first international cuddle convention on 2015 Valentine's Day weekend. Now don't get me wrong. I am 110% in favor of cuddling and I don't for a minute doubt that this is a legitimate business, and I'm certain the people behind this are very caring and well-intentioned. It just makes me too sad to hear we have come to a place where we have to pay someone $60 an hour to cuddle us. What does it mean about our culture? What happened to the free hugs, people? Can we all just promise to give out like 20 free hugs wherever we go every day. That would unbreak my heart a

little. More people getting a dog might help with cuddle deficit, too.

We also found the world didn't stop turning because I had written the first draft. So I need to squeeze in some updates.

For example, believe it or not, the airport carpet cult bar has been raised even higher. A roll of it has been fixed with googly eyes and it will be the grand marshal at the 2015 Rose Festival Starlight Parade (the younger sibling of the Grand Floral Parade). Many people found this to be a perfectly Portland thing to do.

But here's the thing: It seems just a bit too safe to me for 2015. Surely you understand, my dear Portland, we have reached the point that the carpet should be grand marshaling the Grand Floral Parade. That's the 2015 Portland thing to do. Weird is no longer relegated, it flows in the mainstream now. You should have asked.

I LOLed when I spotted the airport carpet T-shirt on a Los Angeles-based television reality show, worn by a person who is exceptionally careful about his fashion, so it is significant that he chose to wear it on the show. I would tell you what the show is but you would lose all respect for me and I would not ever be able to show my face in this town again. To out my comrades who share my shame, his name is Tom Sandoval, and that name won't mean anything to the non-watchers, which I assume is pretty much all of you because it is the anti-Portland. It's like watching an exotic but seriously troubled tribe with extremely odd and superficial rituals. Hmm, now that I think of it, maybe that's how we Portlanders look to everybody outside our city when they watch *Portlandia*?

Then the day after I started this letter, we got word that Teamaker Steve Smith had passed away. We were shocked, as he made no mention of being ill when we interviewed him in December. He was gracious and accommodating and we were really impressed with his knowledge and humility. We are sad and really feel for his wife and children. We're happy his company will keep moving forward as he had planned, with his wife and right hand man carrying the tea-tasting baton.

§

As Rick Turoczy pointed out, there are a lot of things going right because of decisions made by people 40 and more years ago. Those people are no longer with us. I heard a lot of people of my generation in Portland say they long to see another Tom McCall come forward. They want leaders—people with the courage of their convictions, not driven by focus groups and campaign donors. I met a lot of young leaders in the course of this project, so I am filled with hope on that score. But unless the political process becomes more sane and less toxic, who could blame them for not wanting to enter politics?

But before we get too big for our britches, (yikes, did I really just type that?), let's keep our "aggressively humble" perspective and understand that this is our moment to shine and it will pass. Again, I think Rick Turoczy (whose phrase I just used) said it best:

"I am concerned that we get too enamored of our temporary moment in the sun. Portland is popular right now. It won't always be. We're currently Seattle Grunge in the 1990s. And it's just as fleeting as that was. We have to remember that and be conscious of creating something sustainable."

Is Rick worried about Portland losing the culture he values so much? "I always say that Portland has been the same town for the 20 years I've lived here, even though it has grown exponentially. The only thing that has changed is that Portland's flavor of crazy is cool now."

It is both relatively and absolutely true that we Portlanders are willing to go against the grain or the norm in our personal expression of style. We feel pretty confident about being led more by our gut and the feeling of doing the right thing than what we are told to believe. We don't mind a little chaos, and some of us think a dose of anarchy here and there is necessary to keep things interesting.

One thing that surprised me is that a fair number of people doing great things in Portland dropped out of high school. Considering how intelligent and educated they are, it worries me that the public education system was not able to serve them, and even alienated them. The fact that they are some of the smartest and most creative people I know is something of an indictment against our education system. Many people we met don't expect much from an education system they say was first designed to produce compliant factory workers in the early part of the last century. I hope the people working on education reform understand that we don't need little fixes around the edges, but there might just be a need to start completely over in designing public schools.

> ## The only thing that has changed is Portland's flavor of crazy is cool now.

On the other hand, I learned that a lot of the things and people I admire most in Portland were brought to life by people who came here to attend Reed College and decided to stay. There are so many pieces in our patchwork, it's nice to take the time to notice them and see how they work together.

It's good to know that many people in Oregon are working on building a better education system. But I worry because progress on closing what we call the "achievement gap" is very slow, and likely won't be fixed until we have community conversations about racism and seek restorative justice for those whose paths had boulders placed deliberately and directly in the trail, time and again.

I would love to believe that everybody in Portland judges people on the content of their character, not on the color of their skin or where they were born or what their sexual preference is or what part of their body or brain is different. I actually believe that most of us are really pretty decent at the core. I also think some of us are held back to some degree by the luxury of cluelessness. Because our city and state haven't been as diverse as many others, we don't have the broad range of experiences that help us figure out what to say or how to act and how not to be all self-conscious and awkward and clumsy. All of which make us more likely to say or do something offensive and embarrassing. So if we don't have those skills now, we better get right on acquiring them. It shouldn't be the job of people in minority groups to hold our Caucasian American hands and gently coach us what not to say or do whenever we feel uncomfortable. I'm pretty sure you'd appreciate that, am I right, Portland?

There are quite a few ways you aren't so weird on the national scale. Not every backyard has chickens. Or goats. It is actually possible to find strip malls and other spaces completely dominated by auto culture here. But to be fair, our public transit system seems much more visible and present.

As I look back over the pages I wrote, we covered a whole lot of things we do well. But we also covered how we aren't perfect,

and of course attaining perfection sounds pretty irresistible, but impossible. But we can do better. There are things I believe we need to improve. Here's three for starters:

❶ **The cheapskate factor**

First, I feel criticism is in order for those of us who proudly point out great things about our city but don't support them with money. This place attracts and keeps amazing people who have remarkable ideas and are able to make them happen to a formidable degree. But, Portland, you do realize this isn't the only place they could choose to live and work, right? They are the people who have created and built the things that have brought fame and recognition to our city from far and wide. But guess what? Many of the most notable work gets no funding from we tax payers. Since we don't get to direct our money when we pay our taxes, we need to communicate our wishes to those who decide how our money is spent. Like government officials at the City of Portland, Portland Development Commission, Multnomah County, Metro and so forth. I don't think we should take credit for the work if we haven't put any money on the table. I feel pretty awful about that. Can we figure out who decides what and let them know how we feel?

How much more could Mike Houck accomplish if he didn't have to spend so doggone much of his time raising funds for his work. Fundraising is not his expertise, and frankly, he's just not that good at it. Give the guy some ongoing funding to support the work he does that saves what is left of the wild in the city. It wouldn't take that much money, he lives a frugal life, and a lot of tax payers would support this, I bet.

Another example: ADX—the maker space that brings throngs of people to the city, where city officials send people to see cutting edge things that are happening here—has needed to make ginormous investments to get enough equipment and skilled people on board to open. Guess how much money any public agency has contributed? Zilch. Nada. Zero. Most maker spaces in other cities are getting city funding and other government support. Shouldn't we put our money where our mouth is? As a taxpayer, I feel guilty.

It's not just you, Portland. The fact that Oregon hasn't put any funding toward the Citizen Initiative Review, which won the International Project of the Year from an international democracy group, actually embarrasses me.

To tell the truth, just between you and me, sometimes it feels like we're running some kind of sweatshop of innovators and thinkers and inventors and makers who work pretty much every moment they're not sleeping. Do we really not want to help them at all with expenses? Maybe it's time we were visited by three ghosts. Well, it got Scrooge to open his wallet. And heart. Theater people, I challenge you to show us what this would look like...

And yes, I know there are many competing priorities, but maybe budget discussions should include conversations about what we stand to lose if these folks are priced out or just plain burn out? Where will we send visitors to admire us then?

At the very least, can all the public bodies we taxpayers fund come up with something to put in the pot to hire somebody to help raise funds for these geniuses and heroes so they spend their precious time on what they do best?

It's not just tax dollars. I'd like to see Oregon's foundations step up to the plate as well. How about establishing a shared fund to provide support to organizations that excel at place-making. People and groups and things that make our city and state special. Experiments on the cutting edge. Reward the risk takers, the reachers, help them gain traction and focus on their dream.

Remember, we love dreamers. So let's show them some love.

❷ You're harshing our mellow.

Okay, this will seem like I'm picking on your government again. Well, I guess I am, but I think I'll be done when I finish this one.

Portland, I'm starting to worry that your officials and bureaucracies are becoming increasingly up tight; some days it almost feels like the pole-up-the-butt-uptight-threshold is rearing its ugly head once again. Trust me, nobody wants that—it doesn't become you. Like when City Council ordered the "Welcome to America's Bicycle Capital" covered with paint on the side of that downtown building. Come on now, don't you have better things to do with your paint? Do you know how long we had to wait for the tourists taking photos of that sign to clear out so we could get a shot with our quilt? People loved that sign in Portland. And I don't know anyone who noticed there was a bike shop nearby until you told us. Don't deprive us of *all* our anarchy.

And now you want people to pay $100 to use a photo of the Portland, Oregon sign at the west end of the Burnside Bridge? Have you noticed there's no photo of that sign in this book? There should be, but when people totally self-fund a project they are passionate about, like we are, they don't have $100 to throw hither

and yon. Raymond Kaskey responded within a day to give us permission to use our photo of Portlandia, no charge. Same with Travel Portland and its Cuckoo Clock. This will not look good on your resume.

Not only are you not funding the things that give us cachet, you are nickel and dime-ing and hundred dollar-ing those of us doing creative things that might help Portland be even better.

People still wear flannel shirts to the symphony. We're still pretty far out on the chill scale. So simmer down now. Ask yourselves, "WWTCD?" (I'll explain that in a moment.)

❸ Inequity exists, and it will not be tolerated forever.

Like the old saying goes, "We can do this the easy way, or we can do it the hard way." The way I see it, the easy way (which sounds hard until you grasp what the hard way really means) is to take this on as a city-wide top-of-the-agenda issue. I'm not talking about a city council meeting agendas, I'm talking about the entire citizenry agenda. People avoid awkward subjects. But we actually have a chance to make something happen here, Portland, that many might think impossible. But I know it's possible, I see signs of it everywhere.

We have to acknowledge the wrongs that have been done to those who aren't white since the first Euro American set foot on the northwest corner of this continent. No minority group went unscathed. And many people in Portland have not heard that history.

But the word is getting out. Groups like Oregon Humanities and Know Your City are showing and telling the sordid story of some of our past. What if we really did have in person conversations with one another about hard but important subjects? What if we really heard the challenges people face from their mouths to our ears and ours to theirs? Bud Clark was elected mayor in the face of overwhelming odds by just meeting with people all across the city and listening. So why not all of us?

How about we hear from African Americans

displaced from the very neighborhoods they were restricted to when Caucasian Americans figured out those neighborhood locations were conducive to their lifestyles. Can we reach a deeper understanding of what and why things happened as they did? Can we figure out how to stop the erosion? And make amends for mistakes? Bring about some restorative justice and healing?

I don't have answers to all these questions. After my son was born, I worked so hard to help create a world that included him in his wheelchair. I didn't want us to be relegated to a "disabled section" that was separate but never quite equal. So all my instincts have aimed laser-like in the direction of greater integration. But I see that neighborhood identity and sense of community can mean different things in different places. And only some neighborhoods serve specific needs of specific people.

One of the most interesting ideas we came across in researching this book came from two women who established Portland Meet Portland, a kind of matchmaking service to connect refugees with long time residents who can mentor them. The name was carefully chosen, because the part of Portland where Susi Steinmann and Kay Reid work is never shown on *Portlandia*. And the people who live beyond the outer ring road don't always feel part of Portland, they are often invisible to those of us inside that line.

Susi and Kay are doing this in their so-called spare time, but the results from their first few matches are changing the way they think about delivering social services. When I started writing this letter I was searching for something meta to offer up from what I had observed and learned about Portland. But here's the thing: As Susi and Kay, who have been working with invisible people for years have learned, real change happens when one person truly connects with another. It happens one moment at a time, one conversation at a time, one exchange at a time. A conversation leads to understanding to trust to relationship to love.

And in real life, many of the people who are spoofed on Portlandia are actually creating and making and doing a whole

lot of good. Like the earnest young man Sam Smith we met at Alberta Guild Hall, very near the Caravan: The Tiny House Hotel. Growing out of the Occupy movement, he and his partner started an ambitiously named organization Community Supported Everything.

They work with folks who want to accomplish things for the community. One of the completed projects is the "free store" out front next to the sidewalk. As Sam told us, "People want to help, they just don't know how. The hard part is connecting people who need help with people who want help."

There's an organization in Portland called the Coalition for a Livable Future, with about 65 member groups, working together to create a more equitable and sustainable Portland metropolitan region. They use data to make maps that illustrate inequities in order to identify opportunities to correct them and make all parts of our region more livable. The Regional Equity Atlas aims to lead to better planning, policy and investment decisions as government bodies decide where to put new housing, transit, parks, services, infrastructure and other amenities.

It would be a wonderful thing if Community Supported Everything consulted the Atlas to figure out where its projects are needed. Perhaps their next step will be to create a free store and/or other projects out past I-205.

This is not where young people come to retire, or if it is, we couldn't find them, maybe they don't get out much. Where else are people working this hard? These Portlanders are fueled by passion for their work, they're not in it for the money.

In *Portlandia*, a lot of the people of Portland are invisible. Even though we're the whitest major city, about a quarter of our residents are not Caucasian Americans. That's one of four. Portland has become home to many immigrants and refugees from other continents. How often do people west of I-205 see them?

When I look at the issue of police brutality, I wonder if police officers and profiled groups ever sit down and talk, sharing their experiences. Like the police might say, "Wow, this is a really stressful job, we know that our lives are always on the line and at any moment, we have to make a split second decision, for us it feels like a kill or be killed world. And sometimes we get it wrong and we need to apologize. We need figure out how to stay alive without killing you." And they could talk about their families and hobbies.

And the profiled group, let's say African American men since so many have been dying at the hands of police lately, might say, "Hey, you need to come to our neighborhoods and get to know us, we have children too. Even when we're doing nothing wrong, we're seen as the enemy, we have to learn 'just survive the encounter' from the time we're old enough to go outside. We see no future for ourselves, nobody's hiring us, we have to find a place where we feel we belong and feed our kids. What would you do in our place?"

Well, of course, I am not qualified to speak for either group but that's how I imagine things might begin.

I have this fantasy that I ask all the people featured or named in this book to get together in a room, they figure out who else needs to be there but keep it at a manageable size, and put them on the inequity case and tell them we will keep feeding them but otherwise they will be like a sequestered jury. They will have to come up with a plan about how to make these in person conversations begin before they leave. These are some of the best and brightest among us. Ward Cunningham could get things started, by asking "What's the simplest thing that could possibly work?"

I made a list of a few ideas of things all of us could think and talk about once our community conversation begins, but maybe you have better ones, if so, please show us:

1. Change the names of major land and water features to honor the names they already had before whites changed them. I mean, seriously, do we want our favorite mountain in the whole wide world to be named after some British military dude who fought for the British in the Revolutionary War and never laid eyes on it? Hell to the no. That's wackadoodle. No, seriously, it was named Mount Hood in 1792 to honor Lord Samuel Hood, a British Admiral at the Battle of the Chesapeake. Do I even need to point out how stupid that is?

2. Local governments, agencies, commissions, etc. step up and acknowledge the damage done by the urban renewal/development policies and practices, even when they accomplished their intended goals designed to increase city revenue, provide public spaces, add venues for entertainment and cultural activities, etc. Listen to what the people who were displaced have to say about it, and effing apologize.

3. Pledge to include people to be affected in all future planning and projects from the beginning. People are not superfluous, treat them as integral. If people have to be displaced, the new place they go should be better than the old one.

4. Neighborhood identity and sense of community can mean different things in different places. Learn how the neighborhood views and defines itself and just listen before even thinking about any initiative there.

5. Cities, including Portland, don't so much solve issues of houselessness, drugs and gangs wars, etc. as just move the problems to a place where people won't complain as much. Either out of sight or close to others who are also invisible and disenfranchised. Does this mean we are conceding that nothing can be done about the root causes of these issues? I don't remember being asked if that was okay with me.

We have two or more Portlands only if you accept the idea that we see people in categories or places as their labels. If we go one by one, one person to one person, there is but a single city, a single place. When growth happens but there is an urban growth boundary (one reason we have such ready access to farmers markets and farm to table food), increasing density is inevitable. But what form does it take and what does the new form erase? What and who does it replace?

Sometimes it seems that people want to keep things just as they are when they move in, but what made it attractive for one makes it attractive to many more, who also want to live there.

Before long it's not the same neighborhood and we can't find a place to park. The parking wars are coming, in fact they're here. To continue to permit new apartment complex construction in dense neighborhoods without requiring them to provide off street parking is like shouting fire in a crowded theater. Don't be naive about the consequences.

A while back I began to summarize some of the things I learned over the course of writing this book about the people of this place:

1. There is great care taken to behave in a way that supports a sustainable existence.
2. People are not prone to aggressive confrontation but prefer to settle conflicts in more indirect ways.
3. Most people look to collaborate and work with others, because it strengthens the village/neighborhood/community.
4. Sharing is a big part of the way of life.
5. People put a premium on making things fun and living happy lives.
6. People are seen as quite intelligent by others.
7. People have created a special place here that others envy.
8. Wanting the special qualities of this place causes hordes of people to move here.
9. There are a lot of very creative designers and makers here who have developed sophisticated tools and practices.
10. People love to be in the out of doors and lead pretty active lifestyles.
11. People pay attention to what they eat and make good use of local fish, meat, fowl, greens, fruit, etc.
12. There are equity issues that are quite visible and people have significantly fewer resources, including inferior housing.
13. Lots of people have tattoos and wear body-piercing jewelry.
14. People here are more inclined toward nudity than most other places.
15. People here more often reject rigid religious rules because they don't make sense to them in their own circumstances, but they are quite spiritual in ways that resonate with them.

Okay, let's just go with 15, knowing there are plenty more things we could add to our list. It paints a fairly complete picture of you, does it not, Portland? Except I wasn't listing things Portlandia. I was listing characteristics of the Chinooks who were the first to live on this land and water. Are you surprised?

The extent to which we have surely inadvertently adopted some of the ways the first humans lived, even at a limited level, feels so right somehow. The original people who came to this place had pretty well figured out how to live within their means, harvesting natural resources while protecting nature, getting along with their neighbors but not conforming to others expectations, developing their own style and identity, making playful fun part of their everyday lives. They also had slaves. They let them live in their longhouses, but in the least desirable part.

I didn't realize these "coincidences" until I was trying to sum things up. There has to be a lesson for us here. Remember a page back, I wrote that we should ask ourselves WWTCD? And you didn't know what I was talking about. It means "What would the Chinook Do?" Maybe that should be our first question.

Maybe knowing that will lead us to consider how we can honor and make amends for the harm that was done to the first people. We live on the land that supported them and have created many obstacles that have kept them from their way of life.

It feels like we are doing a lot of things right, Portland, and that we have a number of wrongs to right. I think there may well be more good ideas and good will per acre here than anywhere else. So maybe we should try to be that city on the hill and set a real example that is good to the core? Somebody has to go first. Why not us?

And seriously, we got on all these lists and garnered all this attention, not because we were trying to, but just by being ourselves. So when our 15 minutes or years are over, we can just keep on being ourselves and we'll still be weird. As Bill Murray (or someone pretending to be him) has tweeted, "Weird is just a side effect of being awesome."

§

Just as I was finishing the first draft of this book, I experienced the most devastating loss I believe any human can have. My beloved son, Blaine Deatherage-Newsom, the one in the picture holding one corner of the quilt at Free Geek and on this page, very suddenly and unexpectedly died. Although his death is related to the condition he was born with, and he had experienced medical complications at an increasing rate in recent years, there was no warning that the end was near. I believed he would be with me until the end of my days.

We had just enjoyed several holiday celebrations and he was his happy, smiling self. Then he was gone.

After celebrating his wonderful life in a packed Wonder Ballroom, I fell apart. A big part of me had up and gone missing. We had been side by side for all 35-1/2 of his years. Every evening that he returned from volunteering at Free Geek, the five of us (Blaine, Ric, dogs Poppi and Drifty, and me) would gather and relax like you do when the whole pack is back together. He had been reading the drafts of the book as I wrote them, cheerily discussing them, suggesting ways to make it flow better.

He was so excited and happy at the prospect of its publication. In many ways, Blaine was my collaborator in life, always participating

In Loving Memory of
Blaine Michael Deatherage-Newsom
July 21, 1979 – December 31, 2014
One of my very favorite photos of Blaine, he was so happy the day
Ric Seaberg and I were married at Lan Su Chinese Garden in 2001.

in everything I did, in either a small or large way. We had something like mindmeld. We were meant to be mother and son, this I know for sure.

For some time, I didn't know if I would ever write another word or layout another page. The only thing that mattered was that my son was gone. And I was shattered.

As days went by, then weeks, a resolve grew in me. Blaine had believed so strongly in this book, was so convinced it was good and worthy and even important, I decided to throw myself back into it with as much might as I could muster, considering part of me was gone. And maybe by doing it for Blaine, part of me would be restored so I might even begin to feel whole again.

In so many ways, I am me because of Blaine. His disability affected nearly every system and part of his body. He was paralyzed from about the armpits down, so had no voluntary control of anything in nearly all his body systems. He was absolutely brilliant, but some parts of his brain worked differently than most.

Despite all the work it took for him to just get through the day, and all the places in the world he still couldn't access, and all the times he got left out or fell behind his peers as they moved so quickly through school and community, he never once complained about anything. There were times he spent days, weeks and even months in the hospital. No matter, his heart was full of love. He viewed everybody as somebody to love and reach out to in kindness.

Given the hand he was dealt in life, everybody would have forgiven Blaine if he was bitter and resentful. But he was as far from that as anyone I've ever known. He found a way to make an important contribution to the world at Free Geek. And Free Geek gave him a place to belong, something that many people like Blaine never get to have.

The way I see it, if Blaine can view the world with love and do whatever he could to help others, despite all the reasons he had not to, then we all can. The amazing example of love from Blaine that I witnessed is strong enough for me to live the rest of my life without him. And that will be the hardest thing I've ever done.

In so very many ways, Blaine epitomized the best of Portland. He had no pretensions and really and truly never thought or said a bad word about anybody. He was very much his own man, and yes, a little weird. That's why he loved Free Geek and it loved him back. I think it would be fair to say that he made everybody who got to know him a better person, that's what so many people have been telling us since his death. And if we all pay that forward, it will make Portland a better place. If Blaine could, in all his 35-1/2 years, view everyone and everything with love and joy, then I know for sure we can all do that.

And if we do, Portland will finally be as good as it can be, we will deserve this incredible corner of the world

§

When selecting the pieces of fabric for a quilt top, Joyce and I go for enough variety to make it interesting and engaging, usually selecting colors from across the spectrum that work together. Quilters try out different arrangements to see what works best, what creates harmony. Pieces are laid out so they make us feel something. Sometimes we go free form and just start sewing things together and watch what happens. After all the pieces are sewn together in the top of a quilt, we get batting and backing fabric and we use stitches or tying to join the layers together. It's that joining that makes it a quilt. When the quilting is done well, when the pattern of the stitches is wisely chosen, all the pieces join in a kind of harmony, you can hear a song that turns the craft into art.

That's what we tried to do in this book. We chose the fabric and put the pieces together, but it isn't finished until the reader does the quilting. Your participation is what makes it a quilt, the act of reading, talking about it with others, trying out some of the ideas, checking out people and projects that interest you, begin noticing things about Portland you might have overlooked or under thought, decide to take action to help fix things that need repaired.

Then, and only then, will all the pieces of Portland come together in a beautiful quilt. As it is meant to be.

So let's seal it with a rose, and take ourselves to the next level, Portland.

Love from your BFF,
Marie

P.S. Write back soon!
P.P.S. OMG, Denise just told me about the clown room at the Fun House Lounge on SE 11th, near Division. It also features "douchtastic" Kamikaze Karaoke on Wednesdays. Last year she saw an improv Star trek musical. Portland, you need to stop with more "all the things" so I can get this thing to the printer.

What? You can't stop? Oh, okay, never mind. What was I thinking??

Index to Quilts

But I feel I must explain my expression in this photo. We were taking pictures at a Portland Loo in the early morning, and had waited quite some time to ensure nobody was using it, as we didn't want to disturb an occupant. No feet were visible, so we were confident we were alone. I was holding the quilt up so I was hidden, when suddenly we heard what sounded like a fire hose gushing into Walden Pond. The Loo was occupied after all! Joyce caught my startled expression despite being startled herself. That's how it came to be known as Skip to My Loo. Sending thanks to Phoebe O'Leary for this one. She knows why.

Portland Calls It Quilts!

While working on this book, I've had the nagging thought that I need to make a quilt that represents Portland, as a way to end the book. But the truth is that I haven't made a quilt in the past year or so, because I've been spending all my creative energy and time on getting this book finished.

But, oh have I missed quilting. Kind of ironic, huh? A quilter takes on a project that prevents her from quilting. Not the first time that's happened, I'm sure.

I started making an iQuilt, taking little bits of photos from the book and putting them together in a pleasing design. But it just wasn't the same. Quilting is a very tactile experience. Sometimes I just need to make stuff with my hands, you know? And somehow I accidentally deleted the file. The Universe was talking to me, I guess.

Then, in a completely serendipitous thing, Rev Phil came to town to help me get through my grief, but found me so immersed in finishing this project that he had to find ways to amuse himself. As if that's hard. He visited his friend Skye Blue and discovered that lately she is heavy into quilting. And had, in fact, been the person who created the quilt on display at City Hall on January 20, 2015, proclaimed Decemberists Day by Mayor Charlie Hales, honoring our home town heroes upon the release of their latest album. The mayor noted that the Decemberists "embody the Portland values of passion, engagement, and communitarianism with the Portland aesthetic of homegrown, forthright, slightly hippie, and often bespectacled glory."

Which was reflected in the quilt to the nth power. So I had a summary quilt, after all. And its creator agreed to share it here.

Skye Blue of Skye Blue Can Sew learned to sew from her grandmother when she was very young. She got a BFA from Savannah College of Art and Design, and started her sewing business in 2007. Skye has been active in Portland fashion and design movements, teaching mending classes (her motto is "mending is better than ending.") She's big into bicycle commuting and urban farming, and hosts weekly events on her front porch for Food With Dignity, a community project that gleans produce to give to people who need food.

The quilt was a community project organized by artist Carson Ellis, art director for the Decemberists and its record label, Capital Records. Carson selected 48 local artists and small businesses to each contribute a 12-inch-square block for the quilt, in the design and medium of their choice. Wow! That's a challenge for a quilter to piece together. But since Skye Blue can sew, she collaborated with Portland native Veronica Medici of Veronica Booking, a boutique national booking agent for independent musicians, to put the pieces together into a very large quilt.

This makes a far better statement to sum up Portland than I could have done by myself. That's why there is so much collaboration and partnering in Portland, because we know that many heads and many hands are better than one. Portland may call it quilts, but we will never call it quits.

And that's a wrap. Actually, let's call it a quilt.

Photo by Caroline Smith

The Decemberists

Individual blocks were designed and created by 48 local artists and small businesses (listed below), then pieced together into a quilt designed and constructed by Skye Blue of Sky Blue Can Sew. The quilt was revealed to the public on Decemberists Day at Portland City Hall, in a ceremony honoring one of Portland's favorite bands. It's mounted on a canvas background and is supported by steel rods when on display. Its final home is yet to be determined.

Businesses and artists contributing blocks include Music Millennium, Showdeer/Chris Bigalke, Kinfolk Magazine, Pip's Original Doughnuts, Collage, Kerns Kitchen, Marshall's Haute Sauce, Eyes + Edge Blog, Bridge & Burn, Bombshell Vintage, MapleXO, Hair of the Dog, Marmoset Music, Poler Outdoor, See See Moto & Coffee, Girls Rock Camp PDX, Salt & Straw Ice Cream, SE Wine Collective, Penner Ash Winery, ADX Collaborative Makerspace, Cassandra Frances, Nicole Georges, Kaysie Condron, Carson Ellis, Claire Harrison, Sara Starr Medici, Neil Perry and Susannah Kelly of Antler Gallery, Morgaine Faye, Jennifer Parks, Matt Linares, Laura Jean Graham, Jason Sturgill, Seann McKeel, Nancy Prior, Kate Bingaman-Burt, Chad Crouch, Melody Owen, Brad Adkins, Sherry Pendarvis, Mike King, Amy Ruppel, Brooke Weeber, Souther Salazar, Ashod Simonian, Khris Soden.

Pieces of Portland

About the Makers

This is Marie writing this, so that means I get to tell you about Joyce and say whatever I want. She had her chance to write her own part, I begged her even, but she declined.

If you read this far, you pretty much already know me. My bio summary is that I grew up in very very rural southern Oregon, my dad was a logger and we moved around to where the next trees to cut were. For most of my childhood, we grew and raised pretty much all our own food. We kids (one sister, two brothers) were also free to run about the countryside, as long as we promised to keep an eye out for rattlesnakes.

I think it's also significant that I grew up where it got all the way dark at night, so seeing the Milky Way galaxy and meteor showers was a regular thing. I got the concept of feeling very small in a vast universe. I was fascinated by the lay of the land and from a young age, I drew maps of our little world on the South Umpqua River and invented my own place names.

I graduated from Cottage Grove High School. When I was 15, I had been hired on at the town newspaper, the *Cottage Grove Sentinel*, where I learned everything from typesetting to photo processing to reporting to designing pages. Much to my surprise, I actually even won an award for feature writing at the ripe old age of 16. So I decided I would be a journalist and break earthshaking stories! I also learned to sew in 4H and my granny and mother both sewed and quilted.

When I got a scholarship to the University of Chicago, I felt I had won the lottery, and excitedly said yes, of course I'll come!! Not until I got there did I discover it didn't offer Journalism. Looking back, I can't quite believe I made it through four years and got my degree, as I was utterly unprepared for that rigorous an academic setting, let alone living in a major metropolis when my parents had never let travel to Eugene by myself. In the end, I grew to love Chicago and the University, it was an exciting time to be in college in the late 1960s and early 1970s, and it changed the way I see the world, because I got to see that the part I had grown up in was only a slice of something way bigger with way more people who had way different ways of looking at things.

I came back to Oregon for graduate school at the University of Oregon (#goducks) and then taught Geography at Portland State University, Lewis and Clark College and Willamette University. Then I became a disability rights advocate and learned desktop publishing, ultimately working at Meyer Memorial Trust.

The very best part about college was that in the dorm first year, Joyce Brekke was in the room next door. She was from Peoria, Illinois, with very solid Midwest roots. Her father was a chemist and she grew up in a neighborhood like the ones I saw in storybooks. Her mother was a master sewer, and Joyce wishes now she had paid more attention to what she was doing, but in those days, homemade clothing was not something a fashionable teen saw herself wearing. During summers in college she worked at the post office in Peoria, an era so long ago that she was commonly labeled the "fe-mailman." Despite our different backgrounds, we really hit it off and became fast friends, going on adventures together. Even among the group of the smartest people I could possibly imagine at U of C, she still stands out as one of the smartest people on one hand I've ever met.

After graduation, I came back to Oregon for graduate school at the University of Oregon, studying geography, which was what my undergraduate degree was in. Joyce went to law school, first at the University of Washington, then transferred to UCLA.

Despite any number of other legal careers she could have had, she spent her entire career practicing law at Legal Aid, including directing offices in Longview, Spokane and Vancouver. After retirement she tried her hand as a seasonal employee at a garden center and a book store.

I was so happy that she ended up settling in the Pacific Northwest. She also became a world traveler, with several trips through Europe and much of Asia, northern Africa, Middle East, South and Central America. After retiring as an attorney, she did several extensive stays in China, teaching English to university students in Beijing. It was while traveling that she started photography, she has a wonderful talent for taking pictures.

I'm so grateful she tolerates me and we have grown to share many common hobbies, especially reading, gardening and quilting. We've taken some quilting classes together and no matter how much time we spend together, we never ever run out of things to talk about. We enable and encourage one another's plant and fabric purchasing habits, which is a whole lot of fun at the time but can be sobering at the final tally. (8>D

She has seen me through some outrageously tough times, it seems I've had more than my share. I have to live with the fact that I will never be able to help her as many times as she has supported me, she is that far ahead.

I hope Joyce does not regret the day she said "Sure!" when I asked if she'd like to work on this project with me. Neither of us had any idea how massive it would grow by the end, but she's been there every step of the way, and in some cases at least, I'm quite certain we went beyond her comfort zone, remember, she is from Peoria.

And you know, that's actually the best part of this whole undertaking. We got to spend a lot of time together, figure out how and why we are different, and use those differences to complement one another. She is so modest and so underestimates her own talent, she doesn't know how good she is, so sometimes I just had to overrule her when she objected that her photo didn't live up to all her expectations.

We took my left-coast kinda-laid-back-chill lets-just-go-with-the-flow, everything-will-work-out vibe, and combined it with her midwestern values of being very responsible, let's put all this on the calendar, did you bring the release forms? you are keeping these in a file somewhere, right? how many lists and tablets do you have and what are all these scraps of paper anyway? genius IQ, and laughed together about our different ways.

At least I was laughing. (Joyce says she was, too.)

Oh, now all of a sudden Joyce wants to say something after all:

Since Marie wrote the text and wouldn't let me get a word in edgewise, this is the only place I can use to thank her—for roping me into this project, for putting up with all the ways we are quite different from each other, and most of all for being such a good friend for such a long time. A person would have to look far and wide to find a more generous-hearted, energetic, resilient, talented and creative person than Marie.

And then there's her sense of humor...Marie and Portland are made for each other.

■ Quilt information on page 248.